General George B. McClellan
Shield of the Union

McClellan—"The Young Napoleon of the West"

GENERAL GEORGE B. McCLELLAN

Shield of the Union

By WARREN W. HASSLER, JR.

111905

GREENWOOD PRESS, PUBLISHERS
WESTPORT, CONNECTICUT

Library of Congress Cataloging in Publication Data

Hassler, Warren W
   General George B. McClellan, shield of the Union.

    Reprint of the 1st ed. published by Louisiana State
University Press, Baton Rouge.
    Bibliography: p.
    1. McClellan, George Brinton, 1826-1885.
[E467.1.M2H4 1974]   973.7'41'0924   74-9619
ISBN 0-8371-7606-9

*The quotation which appears facing Chapter One
is from* JOHN BROWN'S BODY, *by Stephen Vincent Benét,
Copyright 1927, 1928, by Stephen Vincent Benét.
Copyright renewed, 1955, 1956, by Rosemary Carr Benét.*

Originally published in 1957 by Louisiana State University
Press, Baton Rouge

Reprinted with the permission of Louisiana State University
Press

Reprinted in 1974 by Greenwood Press,
a division of Williamhouse-Regency Inc.

Library of Congress Catalog Card Number 74-9619

ISBN 0-8371-7606-9

Printed in the United States of America

TO MY FATHER AND MOTHER

Preface

"THE Civil War," writes historian Francis F. Wilshin, "was perhaps the most dramatic and significant event in the history of the United States as an independent nation. It was the climax of a half century of social, political, and economic rivalries growing out of an economy half slave, half free. In the race for territorial expansion in the West, in the evolution of the theories of centralized government, and in the conception of the rights of the individual, these rivalries became so intense as to find a solution only in the grim realities of civil strife."

With war upon the land, the soldiers in blue and gray took over where the statesmen and politicians had failed to reach a decision. The performance of our citizen-soldiers in 1861-1865, the desperate character of the battles they waged, and the example of their supreme sacrifices have left an imperishable heritage for future generations which has not yet ceased to astound scholars and military men everywhere. Instructive today, too, are the problems of civil and military relations which confronted the Union and Confederate governments in the mid-nineteenth century.

Thousands of volumes have been written on the military and political aspects of the American Civil War. "The chronicles," declares Carl Sandburg, "are abstracted from a record so stupendous, so changing and tumultuous, that anyone dealing with the vast actual evidence cannot use the whole of it, nor tell all of the story. . . . Therefore the teller does the best he can and picks what is to him plain, moving, and important—though sometimes what is important may be tough reading, tangled, involved, sometimes gradually taking on interest, even mystery, because of the gaps and discrepancies. . . . What [the principals] say by act or deed is often beyond fathoming, because it happened in a time of great storm." The renowned captains of the Civil War have been reproved as frequent blunderers by many glib writers, both contemporary and modern. But it is one thing to seek information at the point of the bayonet and another to seek it in the peace and quiet of a library, with the latest maps and detailed information which were often lacking to the commanders in the field and the war directors in Washington during the conflict itself. " The conduct of a commander," writes William Swinton, " should be judged from the facts known to him."

In writing of a controversial general of the Civil War, the political ramifications of his actions are clearly interwoven with the strictly military. If it seems that in these pages Abraham Lincoln comes in for more than his fair share of censure, it is only because this study is focused primarily on the problems confronting a general in the field, and not on the myriad of issues facing the great wartime Union President. But, as John G. Nicolay and John Hay declare, " War and politics, campaign and statecraft, are Siamese twins, inseparable and interdependent." Consequently, it is necessary to refrain from making broad generalizations and assessments too quickly. Dispatches to and from commanders in the field and their civilian superiors in Washington must be carefully considered in the actual words written at the time, for it is oftentimes difficult to paraphrase with absolute fidelity. Although this may not make for so smooth and readable a narrative at all times, it seems highly desirable at many points.

The author's sincere debt of gratitude is extended to many kind and helpful persons, foremost among whom are George T. Ness and C. Vann Woodward. Others are Charles A. Barker, Charles S. Campbell, Jr., Bruce Catton, Charles Coolidge, E. T. Crowson, Wallace E. Davies, Ralph Happel, Ludwell Johnson, Robert W. Kramer, Roy F. Nichols, Sidney Painter, Lawson Pendleton, C. Percy Powell, Robert P. Sharkey, James E.

Russell, J. P. Smyth, Wallace T. Stephens, Benjamin P. Thomas, Frederick Tilberg, Bell Irvin Wiley, T. Harry Williams, Francis F. Wilshin, Franklin Wright, and Clifton K. Yearley, Jr. I would also like to thank Harcourt, Brace and Company for authority to use passages by Carl Sandburg, and Superintendents Francis F. Wilshin and Oscar W. Northington of the National Park Service for permission to quote statements by Mr. Wilshin.

WARREN W. HASSLER, JR.

The Pennsylvania State University
University Park, Pa.
1956

Table of Contents

Illustrations and Maps

Introduction

"McClellan is to me one of the mysteries of the war." So said U. S. Grant while seated on the deck of a steamer in the Indian Ocean many years after the close of the Civil War. This pronouncement by the Hero of Appomattox might well serve as a true indication of the almost unique position which "Little Mac" has occupied since the guns fell silent in April of 1865.

One of the most controversial and least understood major figures of the Civil War, George B. McClellan is thought by some writers to have been unfit to command even a regiment; while to others he was a genius of the art and science of war, who was sacrificed for political reasons. Truly, there is no leading general of the Civil War about whom there is such a wide difference of opinion.

Born in Philadelphia of well-to-do, upper-middle-class parents, young George McClellan graduated from the University of Pennsylvania Preparatory School at the age of fifteen. By special action, he was permitted to enter West Point two years before attaining the regulation minimum age. He established a brilliant record at the Military Academy, finishing second in his class. His active service in the Mexican War won for him two brevets for distinguished conduct under fire. He then served with high merit as a member of the American military mission observing the Crimean War, and his reports on military institutions and practices in several European countries won for him a splendid reputation in the army. Resigning his commission to become president of a railroad in Ohio, McClellan promptly volunteered his services to the Union when Fort Sumter was bombarded. After being relieved of his command in November of 1862, he again resigned his commission, and later became the Democratic candidate for President in 1864. In the years after Appomattox, he performed valuable service in several large engineering enterprises, and became one of the most popular and able governors the state of New Jersey has ever had.

How then was it possible for this man to be accused of gross incompetence, sheer stupidity, and even disloyalty in his military activities during the war? A close examination of the evidence tends to indicate that, contrary to the views of most writers on the period, McClellan was not only a most able organizer, drillmaster, and disciplinarian, but was also a soldier of superior strategic and tactical ability as compared with many of the other prominent generals on both sides. Political enmity toward him was largely his undoing. The fact that McClellan was a Democrat, favoring gradual emancipation with compensation to the slave-owners, caused the Radical Republicans in Congress to see red. Personality clashes went far also toward alienating the members of Lincoln's cabinet from the General and causing heavy pressure to be placed upon the President to remove McClellan from high command.

This study attempts to describe and analyze McClellan's military activities in the Civil War, and to remove the stereotype into which he has often been cast. Since military policy and actions seldom function in a vacuum, attention must be given in some degree to political pressures which influenced the military events. The work is based chiefly upon primary source material. The sketch maps—drawn by Robert W. Kramer—are included wherever they might aid the reader, and are intended to show clearly and simply the important areas of operations. Representative photographs of McClellan and other principals, and a selective critical bibliography round out the work.

General George B. McClellan
Shield of the Union

If you take a flat map
And move wooden blocks upon it strategically,
The thing looks well, the blocks behave as they should.
The science of war is moving live men like blocks
And getting the blocks into place at a fixed moment.
But it takes time to mold your men into blocks
And flat maps turn into country where creeks and gullies
Hamper your wooden squares. They stick in the brush,
They are tired and rest, they straggle after ripe blackberries,
And you cannot lift them up in your hand and move them.
—A string of blocks curling smoothly around the left
Of another string of blocks and crunching it up—
It is all so clear in the maps, so clear in the mind,
But the orders are slow, the men in the blocks are slow
To move, when they start they take too long on the way—
The General loses his stars and the block-men die
In unstrategic defiance of martial law
Because still used to just being men, not block-parts.

—Stephen Vincent Benét, John Brown's Body

Chapter One

"Secession is Killed in this Country"

> The General-in-Chief, and . . . the Cabinet, in-cluding the President, are charmed with your activity, valor, and . . . successes. We do not doubt that you will . . . sweep the rebels from Virginia, but we do not mean to precipitate you as you are fast enough.
>
> —*Winfield Scott to McClellan*

THE railway president was expected. With sectional rivalries having erupted into open hostilities, Governor William Dennison and an anxious group of citizens of the Buckeye State had been waiting impatiently in Columbus for the arrival of the chief executive of the Ohio and Mississippi Railroad. It was toward the end of April, 1861, and, in answer to President Abraham Lincoln's call for Federal Volunteers, the Governor was determined to place at the head of the Ohio contingent a man well versed in large-scale military and administrative affairs. One man in Ohio seemed best able to meet these demanding qualifications: George Brinton McClellan, then a railroad president at the annual salary of ten thousand dollars. Brilliant as a cadet at West Point, a twice-brevetted hero of the Mexican War, and a man of considerable experience in the art and science of war—notably as observer in the Crimean War—McClellan was in 1861 but thirty-four years of age. After considering a similar appeal from the governor of his native state

3

of Pennsylvania, McClellan, at the beck of the Ohio governor, had left his young wife, Ellen Mary Marcy, in Cincinnati, and had accepted the task of organizing the state troops.[1]

Arriving in Columbus on April 23, McClellan was met at the station by Brigadier General Jacob D. Cox, a high-ranking officer in the state militia. Cox scanned the new commander closely. Before him he saw a handsome blue-eyed man, five feet eight in height, broad-shouldered and muscular, with dark hair, mustache, and touch of a goatee. The impression which McClellan made at the station in Columbus was favorable. " His whole appearance," writes Cox, " was quiet and modest, but when drawn out he showed no lack of confidence in himself. He was dressed in a plain traveling dress and wore a narrow-rimmed soft felt hat. In short, he seemed what he was, a railway superintendent in his business clothes." [2]

On the day he arrived in Columbus, McClellan was appointed major general of volunteers by Governor Dennison, and assigned to the command of all Ohio troops, who were then being called to the colors for but three months' service. According to Cox, in an interview between the Governor, McClellan, and himself, " McClellan showed that he fully understood the difficulties there would be before him, and said no man could wholly master them at once, although he had confidence that if a few weeks' time for preparation were given, he would be able to put the Ohio division into reasonable form for taking the field." Going immediately to the state arsenal, McClellan was painfully shocked at the lack of proper military equipment on hand. Then, there was serious difficulty in obtaining uniforms, in housing the eager recruits, and in supplying competent officers. The first two regiments to be raised were sent off—partially equipped—to Washington for the defense of the

[1] George B. McClellan, *McClellan's Own Story* . . . (New York, 1887), 29, 43; cited hereinafter as *M.O.S.*

[2] Jacob D. Cox, " War Preparations in the North," Robert Underwood Johnson and Clarence Clough Buel (eds.), *Battles and Leaders of the Civil War* (New York, 1887), I, 89, cited hereinafter as *B. & L.*; Oliver Otis Howard, *Autobiography of Oliver Otis Howard* (New York, 1908), I, 167.

National capital. In a few weeks, however, order began to emerge from chaos as the commanding general succeeded in creating an efficient system of supply and training. He could now begin to look ahead to the manner in which his troops and those of the other Federal armies could be used to best advantage.[3]

On April 27, McClellan boldly dispatched to Washington a message to the Union General-in-Chief, Lieutenant General Winfield Scott, embracing his thoughts on the grand strategy which he felt should be adopted to bring the Confederacy to its knees. In those days, few soldiers (or civilians) hesitated to press their own views upon their superiors, whether the matter under discussion was strictly within their sphere of authority or not. McClellan's lengthy plan called for a movement of his own army up the valley of the Great Kanawha River in western Virginia. Simultaneously, other Federal troops were to wrest control of important points on the Mississippi River, and move into Tennessee. Kentucky and Missouri, too, were to be occupied should they show signs of casting their lot with the other Southern states. Cox reported, after McClellan had read this dispatch to him, " I have never doubted that [this] paper prepared the way for his appointment in the regular army." McClellan's real talent for devising sweeping strategic movements was to be demonstrated a number of times in the months ahead.[4]

Scott replied to McClellan on May 3 with a plan of his own for defeating the enemy. This design—expanded in a subsequent message to McClellan on May 21—comprised what

[3] George B. McClellan, *Report on the Organization and Campaigns of the Army of the Potomac* . . . (New York, 1864), 6, cited hereinafter as McClellan's *Report* (N.Y.); Jacob D. Cox, *Military Reminiscences of the Civil War* (New York, 1900), I, 8-10.

[4] McClellan to Scott, April 27, 1861, *The War of the Rebellion: A Compilation of the Official Records of the Union and Confederate Armies* (Washington, 1880-1901), Series I, Volume LI, Part I, 228–39; cited hereinafter as *O.R.* (see under Government Publications, in Bibliography, for table converting the cumbersome official designations of series, volumes, and parts of this source into simple arabic designations). Cox, *Military Reminiscences*, I, 10–11.

soon became known as Scott's "Anaconda" policy. While McClellan's was the first large detailed plan for subjugating the Confederacy, Scott's was in some ways a sounder and more complete one, for it called for a blockade of the entire Southern coastline, as well as for a decisive thrust by land and water down the Mississippi. But, the General-in-Chief warned, " the greatest obstacle in the way of this plan—the great danger now pressing us—[is] the impatience of our patriotic and loyal Union friends. They will urge instant and vigorous action, regardless, I fear, of consequences. . . . I fear this." " You are likely to bear an important if not the principal part in this great expedition [down the Mississippi]," he declared to McClellan. The old general affirmed that he had " great confidence in [McClellan's] intelligence, zeal, science, and energy." [5]

By now, McClellan himself was in line for rapid promotion. The General-in-Chief, on May 3, nominated him as full major general in the regular army, and named him commander of the Department of the Ohio—including the states of Ohio, Indiana, and Illinois—with headquarters in Cincinnati. The appointment was approved and took effect on May 14. Except for Scott, McClellan was now the ranking general in the whole Union Army. [6]

Meanwhile, on May 13, pro-Union delegates from twenty-five counties of western Virginia met at Wheeling to consider methods of seceding from secession. While eastern Virginia—the tideland slaveholding district—voted to ratify the ordinance of secession on May 23, the anti-slavery upland counties of the western portion of the state voted against it. [7] Brigadier General Robert E. Lee, in command of the Virginia armed forces, determined from his headquarters in Richmond to try to hold the western part of the state for the Confederacy. Consequently, he sent Colonel George A. Porterfield to western Virginia to

---

[5] Scott to McClellan, May 3 and 21, 1861, 107 *O.R.*, 369–70, 386–87.
[6] McClellan's *Report* (N. Y.), 8, 11; Francis B. Heitman, *Historical Register and Dictionary of the United States Army . . .* (Washington, 1903), I, 656.
[7] John G. Nicolay, *The Outbreak of Rebellion* (New York, 1881), 140, 142–43.

6

raise a local army. Lee probably did not intend at that time to have Porterfield conduct offensive operations. He most likely sought to have him coerce the pro-Union men of the mountains —who were even then beginning to organize against the Richmond government—back into the Southern fold. Collecting a small force of pro-Confederate soldiery, Porterfield established a camp at Beverly, menacing the rail hub of Grafton.[8]

McClellan, at Cincinnati, soon became aware of the threatening position of Porterfield's Confederates, and determined to watch them closely. His vigil was not long in bearing fruit. The grayclad troops soon began burning bridges on the Baltimore and Ohio Railroad west of Grafton. " The initiative taken by the Confederates in West Virginia," writes Cox, " had to be met by prompt action, and McClellan was forced to drop his own plans and meet the exigency. The organization and equipment of the regiments for the three-years service was still incomplete, and the brigades were broken up, to take across the Ohio the regiments best prepared to go." To delay might have cost the North dearly.[9]

Although he did not receive instructions from Washington as to what to do, McClellan did receive from Scott on May 24 a kind of official authorization to move into western Virginia against Porterfield's force, which had now just seized Grafton. The sanction was in the form of an inquiry as to whether such a movement were feasible; it did not directly instruct him to undertake such an enterprise. McClellan telegraphed back that if the administration desired such a movement, he could make it. He received no reply to this message.[10] McClellan's reaction was decisive. On the twenty-sixth, on his own initiative, he threw units of his command across the Ohio River into western Virginia. Warned of the Federal advance, Porterfield collected his scattered raiding parties and fell back from

---

[8] A. L. Long, *Memoirs of Robert E. Lee* . . . (New York, 1886), 114; William Swinton, *Campaigns of the Army of the Potomac* . . . (New York, 1866), 34.

[9] Jacob D. Cox, " McClellan in West Virginia," *B. & L.*, I, 126.

[10] Scott to McClellan, May 24, 1861, 2 *O.R.*, 648.

7

Grafton to Philippi. On June 1, McClellan's forces entered Grafton. The first goal of the Union expedition had been won.[11]

Accompanying the soldiers in blue was a rhetorical " Proclamation " composed by McClellan on May 26. It began, " VIRGINIANS: The general government has long enough endured the machinations of a few factious rebels in your midst. . . . I have ordered troops to cross the Ohio River. . . . All your rights shall be religiously respected. . . . Sever the connection that binds you to traitors; proclaim to the world that the faith and loyalty so long boasted by the Old Dominion, are still preserved in Western Virginia, and that you remain true to the stars and stripes." Along with his proclamation to the civilians, McClellan issued an " Address " to his own troops. It said, in part, " Soldiers! . . . Your mission is to restore peace and confidence, to protect the majesty of the law, and to rescue our brethren from the grasp of armed traitors. . . . Preserve the strictest discipline; remember that each one of you holds in his keeping, the honor of Ohio and the Union." [12]

These discourses reveal several of McClellan's personal characteristics. Basically a kind and just man, he was ever wary of the rights of the individual and of the integrity of the law. He was, however, a Democrat and a gradual emancipationist, favoring compensation to the slaveowners; but he had no particular love for the Negro. These bombastic addresses show also his skill in appealing to the better qualities of his soldiers.

On the day that Grafton was captured, McClellan informed his superiors in Washington of his actions and sent them copies of his manifestoes. He said that he hoped the sentiments expressed in them were in accordance with the policy of the Federal government. Again receiving no answer to his dispatches, the General assumed that he was acting in line with the views of the authorities in the National capital, and went

[11] McClellan's *Report* (N. Y.), 14–15; 2 *O.R.*, 66.
[12] McClellan's *Report* (N. Y.), 15–17.

8

ahead on his own.[13] Probably the Lincoln administration had not had time to evolve a policy for occupied areas of enemy territory. Later in the course of the war, McClellan was to find closer supervision of his military activities by his superiors not only frequently embarrassing but also often highly irritable.

The country into which McClellan had projected his forces was one of harshness and rugged beauty. The land was covered with dense forests. Villages were few and scattered. Communications were hazardous. The numerous mountain ranges and terrible roads limited the use of artillery and cavalry. It was a hard country in which to conduct offensive operations, especially with raw troops. It was much easier for new soldiers to wait and fight in position than for similar recruits to make long fatiguing marches over mountains, form lines of battle in the woods, and attack the enemy's works on the crests of the ridges.[14]

Learning of Porterfield's new defensive position at Philippi, McClellan determined to move against it immediately. Converging Union columns closed in on the graycoats. In a surprise attack on June 3—the first land battle of the war—McClellan's forces routed the enemy in a brief but sharp engagement, the Southerners fleeing southward so rapidly that the affair soon became known as the " Philippi races."[15] McClellan had advanced thus far with commendable vigor.[16] But after the Federal victory, McClellan states, " the absence of means of transportation and of cavalry rendered it impossible to follow up this success."[17] On the treacherous, water-logged mountain trails, animals and supply wagons could not keep up with the marching infantry. Besides, the Union commander was a circumspect man, never rash in his military movements—one who

[13] *Ibid.*, 17.

[14] See [Louis Philippe D'Orleans], Comte de Paris, *History of the Civil War in America* (Philadelphia, 1875) , I, 221; Swinton, *Army of the Potomac*, 36.

[15] 2 *O.R.*, 64 ff.; Cox, " McClellan in West Virginia," *loc. cit.*, 127–28.

[16] See Douglas Southall Freeman, *Lee's Lieutenants . . .* (New York, 1942) , I, 37.

[17] McClellan's *Report* (N.Y.) , 18.

endeavored to make sure that nearly everything was in order before advancing against the foe and committing his men to battle.

But McClellan's mountain campaign was really only beginning. The railroad bridge over the Cheat River east of Grafton, and the mountain tunnels in that vicinity, were extremely important to both sides, and were still liable to destruction by Southern raiders. Lee in Richmond wrote on July 1 to his chief officer in western Virginia, Brigadier General Robert Garnett, " The rupture of the railroad at Cheat River would be worth to us an army." The Federals, however, were not to be caught napping. Determining to occupy the whole region of western Virginia to prevent further raids, McClellan, as soon as each of his regiments was properly equipped, threw it across the Ohio to the Virginia side. As a diversion, Lee countered by dispatching Brigadier General Henry A. Wise to the Kanawha Valley, there to organize a Confederate force capable of retaining that area. McClellan was obliged to detach Cox and some troops from his main body in order to contain Wise.[18]

Reinforced by Lee, Garnett took up his main position on Laurel Hill, facing west—an entrenched post which commanded the vital east-west road running from Wheeling to Staunton. He then commenced a series of annoying raids, intended to destroy the B. & O. Railroad and to intimidate the pro-Union civilians. In order to defeat the enemy's intentions once and for all, McClellan decided to move in force against Garnett's main body at Laurel Hill. The Confederates' chief line of retreat was the turnpike running southward from Laurel Hill and Leadsville to Beverly and Huttonsville. If Garnett were cut off from this pike, he could only hope to escape to the northeast over treacherous mountain trails. But a road from the west from Buckhannon penetrates Rich Mountain at a pass and strikes the turnpike at Beverly. To guard this approach to

[18] 2 *O.R.*, 908; Swinton, *Army of the Potomac*, 35; Cox, *Military Reminiscences*, I, 47; McClellan's *Report* (N. Y.), 18.

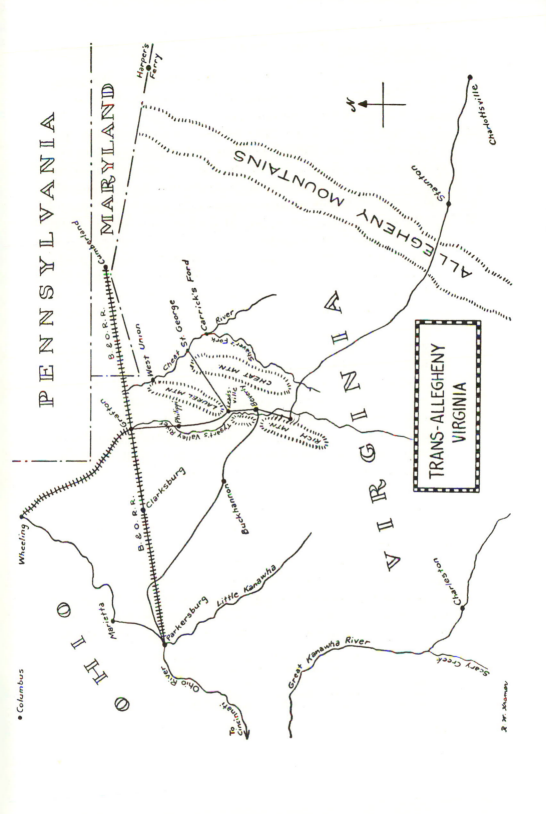

TRANS-ALLEGHENY
VIRGINIA

his rear, Garnett (himself at Laurel Hill with about 3,000 men) placed his second in command, Lieutenant Colonel John Pegram, at the Rich Mountain gap with six guns and approximately 1,300 men. Some light fieldworks were thrown up.[19] " I regard these two passes," Garnett said of the gaps at Laurel Hill and Rich Mountain, " as the gates to the northwestern country. . . ." [20] This seems to indicate that he was possibly thinking of eventual offensive operations above and beyond mere nuisance raids. However, McClellan, in superior force, was to beat him to the punch.

Just as he was moving into western Virginia against Garnett, unstable conditions in Tennessee and Missouri compelled McClellan to send all his Illinois regiments away for service in those areas. He still had a total force of nearly 20,000 men, of whom 5,000 were detailed to guard some 200 miles of railroad track.[21] En route to Parkersburg and Marietta, the General found time to write of his experiences to his wife Ellen: " We . . . had a continual ovation all along the [rail]road. At every station where we stopped crowds had assembled to see the ' young general '; gray-headed old men and women, mothers holding up their children to take my hand, girls, boys, all sorts, cheering and crying, God bless you! I never went through such a scene in my life. . . . The trouble will be to fulfill their expectations, they seem to be so high." [22]

Arriving at Grafton, McClellan wired General-in-Chief Scott his plan of operations designed to bring on a decisive combat with Garnett. He would move the bulk of his force from Clarksburg to Buckhannon on June 25, and advance from there upon the key Confederate road hub of Beverly and its covering strongpoints, Laurel Hill and Rich Mountain, where the enemy forces were waiting.[23] A few days later, McClellan issued another of his Napoleonic manifestoes, closing with this asser-

[19] 2 O.R., 236–38; Cox, " McClellan in West Virginia," loc. cit., 128–29.
[20] 2 O.R., 236–37; Nicolay, Outbreak of Rebellion, 147.
[21] McClellan's Report (N. Y.), 19; M.O.S., 57.
[22] McClellan to his wife, June 21, 1861, M.O.S., 57.
[23] 2 O.R., 195; Cox, Military Reminiscences, I, 50.

tion: "Soldiers! I have heard that there was danger here. I have come to place myself at your head and to share it with you. I fear now but one thing—that you will not find foeman worthy of your steel. I know that I can rely upon you."[24] Combination lecture, appeal, and sermon, this lengthy address was typical of the young general in the early months of the war. This pronunciamento and others like it were to win for him the sobriquet, " The Young. Napoleon of the West," an association that was enhanced by his somewhat short stature and by his attitude of posing for pictures in the classical style with one hand thrust inside his tunic.

After a brief delay at Grafton, in order to bring up necessary supplies, McClellan was able to put his army in motion. His main column, comprising two brigades, marched from Clarksburg toward Buckhannon, reaching the latter point by July 2. This placed the Union force twenty miles west of Garnett's positions at Laurel Hill and Rich Mountain. A third brigade of McClellan's was at Philippi. Including the unit at Philippi, the Federal commander had in all " about 10,000 " effectives. He was informed that Garnett had between 6,000 and 7,000 men.[25] Actually, as seen before, the Confederates near Beverly numbered about 4,300.

While on the march to Buckhannon from Clarksburg, McClellan penned an illuminating letter to his wife Ellen: " I would be glad to clear them [the Confederates] out of West Virginia and liberate the country without bloodshed, if possible. . . . I realize the dreadful responsibility on me—the lives of my men, the reputation of the country, and the success of our cause. . . . I shall feel my way and be very cautious, for I recognize the fact that everything requires success in first operations. You need not be at all alarmed as to the result; God is on our side."[26] These lines reveal at an early date certain of McClellan's dominant characteristics. One of these was his

[24] 2 *O.R.*, 196–97; McClellan's *Report* (N. Y.), 22–23.

[25] Swinton, *Army of the Potomac*, 37, 38; McClellan's *Report* (N. Y.), 26.

[26] McClellan to his wife, July 2 and 5, 1861, *M.O.S.*, 59–60.

13

sincere regard for the lives and welfare of his men; he preferred to win an objective, if possible, by skillful maneuvering rather than by the more spectacular head-on assault. Other traits shown in his intimate letters home were a certain humbleness blended with self-righteousness and a strong religious bearing—attributes which were ever a part of his make-up.

Although always the Christian gentleman in his personal relations with his officers, and though usually maintaining a gracious and polished mien and address, it should not be thought that McClellan was a " soft " general. A strict disciplinarian, he would tolerate no laxity or supineness among his subordinates. This is shown, in part, by his reply to a message from Brigadier General Thomas A. Morris at Philippi. In answer to Morris' call for more men to hold his easily defended position at a time when the Confederates in his front were retreating, McClellan said: " You have only to defend a strong position. . . . I propose taking the really difficult and dangerous part of this work on my own hands. I will not ask you to do anything that I would not be willing to do myself. . . . If you cannot undertake the defense of Philippi with the force now under your control, I must find someone who will. . . . Do not ask for further re-enforcements. If you do, I shall take it as a request to be relieved from your command and to return to Indiana. I have spoken plainly. I speak officially. The crisis is a grave one, and I must have generals under me who are willing to risk as much as I am, and to be content to risk their lives and reputations with such means as I can give them. Let this be the last of it. . . . I wish action now and determination." [27]

Morris was to show alacrity in responding to this call from McClellan, and, after several initial delays, was to carry out effectively his part in the final movement against Garnett.

Marching eastward from Buckhannon with the main Federal force, McClellan determined to dislodge Garnett at Laurel Hill

[27] McClellan to Morris, July 3, 1861, 2 O.R., 208–209.

14

and Pegram at Rich Mountain by striking their chief line of retreat and communications at a point on the road running from Beverly to Huttonsville. To capture or annihilate the whole Confederate force, the Union commander conceived the idea of moving another column under Morris from the north at Philippi to seize Garnett's remaining route of escape from Laurel Hill to the northeast. On July 5, McClellan telegraphed Scott in Washington that he hoped to " repeat the manoeuvre at Cerro Gordo " by which the celebrated old American soldier had defeated the Mexicans in an important battle during the campaign for Mexico City in 1847. He told Scott that he would maneuver rather than attack frontally with raw troops.[28]

On July 9, McClellan's main body reached Roaring Creek, two miles west of Pegram's position at Rich Mountain. His plan of battle was similar in several respects to that of his mentor, Winfield Scott, at Cerro Gordo. McClellan saw that if frontally attacked from the west, the entrenched Confederates on the crest of Rich Mountain, firing down the throats of any Federals who might come struggling directly up the steep mountainside, could easily repulse several times their own number. He determined, therefore, to hold one of his brigades in the enemy's front, while his other brigade, commanded by Colonel William S. Rosecrans, was to outflank Pegram's left-rear and seize the Southerners' line of retreat—the turnpike through Beverly to Huttonsville. Rosecrans was then to take the Confederate position in reverse, hammering it back upon the anvil of the other Union brigade in front. Morris was to amuse Garnett's own force at Laurel Hill in the meantime.[29]

In a downpour of rain, early on the morning of July 11, McClellan pushed Rosecrans off in the opening movement of the battle of Rich Mountain. After a steep and difficult climb, the Federals found themselves on the enemy's left flank and

---

[28] Swinton, *Army of the Potomac*, 37; McClellan's *Report* (N. Y.), 20, 28–29.

[29] Rosecrans' testimony, *Report of the Joint Committee on the Conduct of the War* (Washington, 1863–66), VI, 2, 3, cited hereinafter as *C.C.W.*; Cox, *Military Reminiscences*, I, 50–51; Paris, *The Civil War*, I, 222.

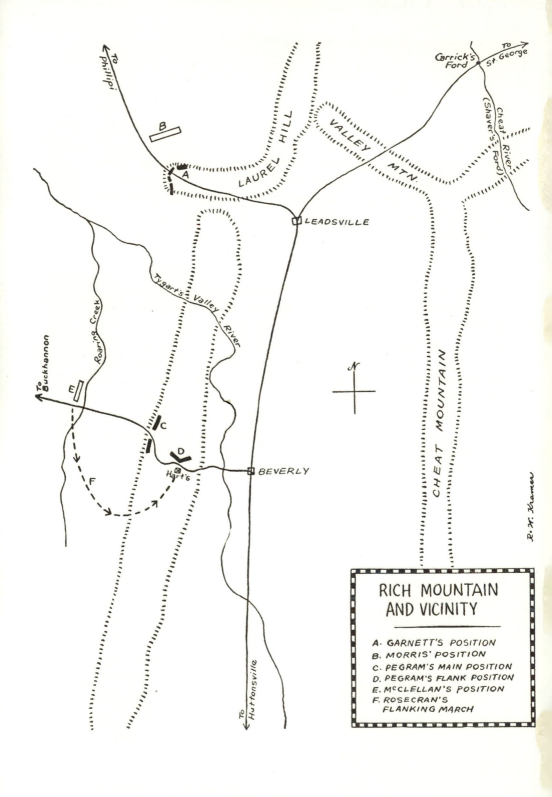

To Phillipi

Carrick's Ford

To St. George

LAUREL HILL

VALLEY MTN.

Cheat River (Shaver's Ford)

B

A

LEADSVILLE

Tygart's Valley River

Roaring Creek

To Buckhannon

E

CHEAT MOUNTAIN

C

D

Hart's

BEVERLY

F

N

R. H. Kramer

To Huttonsville

RICH MOUNTAIN
AND VICINITY

A. GARNETT'S POSITION
B. MORRIS' POSITION
C. PEGRAM'S MAIN POSITION
D. PEGRAM'S FLANK POSITION
E. McCLELLAN'S POSITION
F. ROSECRAN'S
   FLANKING MARCH

rear. Soon the stillness of the mountain vales was broken by the roar of cannon and the crash of musketry. Through a misunderstanding between himself and Rosecrans, McClellan did not push forward his brigade in front; but this was unnecessary, as Pegram was completedly routed by the Federal flanking operation. Over half of the Confederate force, along with their commander, surrendered themselves to McClellan on the thirteenth, the remainder of the grayclads being scattered about the forbidding forests. Seeing the danger of being trapped at Laurel Hill, Garnett, with the main Confederate force, attempted to flee over the mountains to the northeast on a narrow woods road toward St. George and West Union.[30]

The Federal forces now closed in for the kill. Closely pursued by McClellan's own command, Garnett was twice compelled to make a stand, in a running fight, and was worsted in both skirmishes. He was finally brought to bay, on July 13, at a bluff on the right bank of the Cheat River at Carrick's Ford. Aided now by Morris' column, McClellan defeated Garnett's efforts to fight his way out, the gallant Confederate general falling at the head of his read guard. Besides their heavy loss in prisoners, the Southerners suffered thirty other casualties. The attacking Union forces lost thirteen men killed and forty wounded. McClellan's successes at Rich Mountain and Carrick's Ford snuffed out organized Confederate resistance on any consequential scale in that immediate region of western Virginia.[31]

McClellan immediately reported the progress of his victorious campaign to Scott in Washington. His telegram elicited from " Old Fuss and Feathers " a most congratulatory reply: " The General-in-Chief, and what is more, the Cabinet, including the President, are charmed with your activity, valor, and consequent success of Rich Mountain the 11th and of

[30] Rosecrans' report, 2 *O.R.*, 215–16; J. H. Stine, *History of the Army of the Potomac* (Washington, 1893), 5; McClellan's *Report* (N.Y.), 29–32; William F. Fox, *Regimental Losses in the American Civil War . . .* (Albany, 1889), 543.
[31] Swinton, *Army of the Potomac*, 39; McClellan's *Report* (N.Y.), 32–34.

Beverly this morning. We do not doubt that you will in due time sweep the rebels from Virginia, but we do not mean to precipitate you as you are fast enough." [32] On July 16, the United States House of Representatives voted its thanks to McClellan for "the series of brilliant and decisive victories" which he had just gained. [33] His fame was rapidly spreading throughout the North—the war's first hero had been born.

McClellan's tribute to his raw soldiers in his official report to the Secretary of War was modestly worded: "I cannot close ... without bearing testimony to the good conduct, enthusiasm, and endurance of the young troops whom I then commanded. That they would be courageous was to be expected; but the patience and endurance they evinced under long marches, privations, and fatigue exceeded all my anticipations." But in contrast to this statement, McClellan issued on July 16 another of his exaggerated, verbose manifestoes to his soldiers, apparently designed for stage effect. In it, the General declared, "I am more than satisfied with you. You have annihilated two armies, commanded by educated and experienced soldiers, intrenched in mountain fastnesses fortified at their leisure. ... Soldiers! I have confidence in you, and I trust you have learned to confide in me." [34] Such written efforts, however, helped to win for McClellan the enviable reputation among the ranks of the Union soldiers as the best-liked general in the service.

Summarizing his successes, McClellan wrote, without understatement, to his superiors in Washington, "We have annihilated the enemy in Western Virginia, and have lost thirteen killed, and not more than forty wounded. We have in all killed at least two hundred of the enemy, and their prisoners will amount to at least one thousand. Have taken seven guns in all. ... Our success is complete, and secession is killed in this country." [35] The significance of McClellan's operations in

[32] Scott to McClellan, July 13, 1861, 2 *O.R.*, 204.

[33] James Ford Rhodes, *History of the United States* . . . (New York, 1896), III, 442.

[34] McClellan's *Report* (N. Y.), 36; 2 *O.R.*, 236.

[35] McClellan to the War Department, July 14, 1861, Nicolay, *Outbreak of*

western Virginia is succinctly summed up by William Swinton, war correspondent of the New York *Times*: " The result of this miniature campaign was most inspiriting to the people of the North, and had an effect far beyond its intrinsic importance. . . . It is the moral influence of small successes and small defeats, that in the first stages of a war makes their importance and forms the real measure of their value." [36]

Then, on July 21, the first great battle of the war was fought at a place called Bull Run, near Manassas, some thirty-five miles southwest of Washington. The result was a decisive defeat for the National Army, the raw Union soldiers abandoning the field to the Confederates and falling back in near rout upon the Federal capital. On the day after this catastrophe, Adjutant General Lorenzo Thomas, at the direction of Lincoln and Scott, urgently wired McClellan from Washington, " Circumstances make your presence here necessary. . . . Come hither without delay." [37] The Republican administration was turning to a conservative Democratic general to save the Federal government, and with it the Union.

At approximately the same time that fate beckoned McClellan to Washington, Congress passed a resolution on the objects of the war. It mentioned the preservation of the Union, but refrained from emphasizing the Radical Republican ideas on immediate abolition of Negro slavery. On the contrary, it pledged noninterference " with the rights or established institutions " of the Southern states.[38] Being in accordance himself with such mild and restrained views on slavery, McClellan had grounds for feeling confident of a sympathetic atmosphere prevailing in Washington, one in which he could work harmoniously and effectively with the political leaders of the North, both in the cabinet and in Congress.

Rebellion, 154. Lacking complete returns, McClellan's figures were not quite accurate.

[36] Swinton, *Army of the Potomac*, 39.

[37] Thomas to McClellan, July 22, 1861, 2 *O.R.*, 753.

[38] See *M.O.S.*, 149 n.

Chapter Two

The New General-in-Chief

An army is better directed by a single mind . . .
than by two superior ones at variance and cross-
purposes with each other.

—A. Lincoln

THE Young Napoleon stepped off the train at the Washington station on the afternoon of July 26, 1861.[1] Excitement bordering on panic was still evident in the streets, even though it was five days since the Federal disaster at Bull Run. As he was being driven from the depot, McClellan could not help but notice that the sprawling capital was a city of magnificent distances and sharp contrasts. Like the Union itself, the great Capitol was as yet unfinished. Much was sheer squalor, with shameful hovels and unpaved avenues apparent on all sides. It was to his own new headquarters, located on Pennsylvania Avenue at the eastern end of Lafayette Square, that McClellan was driven by the carriage. His private residence, to which he would bring in due time his wife Ellen and their infant child, was on H Street, diagonally across the Square from his headquarters.[2] On the day after his arrival in this distracted town, McClellan " assumed command of the division of the Potomac, comprising the troops in and around Washington, on both banks of the river." [3]

[1] John G. Nicolay and John Hay, *Abraham Lincoln: A History* (New York, 1890), IV, 440, 443.
[2] For an excellent description of the wartime Federal capital, see Margaret Leech, *Reveille in Washington, 1860–1865* (New York, 1941), *passim*.
[3] *Letter of the Secretary of War, Transmitting Report on the Organization of the Army of the Potomac, and of its Campaigns . . . under the Command of*

The General-in-Chief of the Union armies then was the most celebrated soldier in America, Winfield Scott. The aged " Giant of Three Wars " was in his seventy-fifth year, and was older than the capital itself. His services in the War of 1812 and in the Mexican War had been masterful. In 1861, however, Scott was almost incapacitated by gout, dropsy, and vertigo, and by two British bullets which he still carried in his ponderous body. Unable to mount or ride a horse, he was obliged to repose much of the time on an office sofa, while his active moments were spent ensconced in an enormous armchair at Army Headquarters. However, this splendid soldier possessed, in his massive person, a large degree of the professional knowledge and reputation then available to the militarily inexperienced National administration. Scott and the even older John E. Wool were the only Americans who, on the outbreak of the Civil War, had so much as commanded " the evolutions of a brigade " in battle. " He is, in fact, the Government," wrote Edwin M. Stanton of Scott in the early summer of 1861. But, after Bull Run, were not his many infirmities simply too much for him to bear and still effectively carry out the onerous duties of his high position? [4]

It was to Winfield Scott that McClellan immediately went upon his arrival in Washington. After reporting to the old hero, McClellan met the President, who invited him to return to the White House that afternoon to attend a cabinet meeting. Scott, furious at not being invited himself, detained McClellan all afternoon at headquarters. This delay prevented McClellan

Maj. Gen. George B. McClellan . . . (Washington, 1864), 2; cited hereinafter as McClellan's *Report*. This so-called Washington edition of McClellan's official report differs from the so-called New York edition—cited throughout Chapter I of this study as " McClellan's *Report* (N. Y.) "—in that it does not include the account of the campaign in western Virginia; therefore the page references differ in the two editions. Throughout the remainder of this study, all references to this source will be to the Washington edition, since it is the more authentic.

[4] See Charles W. Elliott, *Winfield Scott: The Soldier and the Man* (New York, 1937), *passim*; William H. Russell, *My Diary, North and South* (Boston, 1863), 148; Stanton to Buchanan, May 16, 1861, George Ticknor Curtis, *The Life of James Buchanan* (New York, 1883), II, 548.

from keeping the afternoon appointment with Lincoln and the Cabinet.[5] Writing after the war, the young general said of the old General-in-Chief: " It is a great mistake to suppose that I had the cordial support of Gen. Scott; the contrary was too much the case. . . . Gen. Scott was no longer himself when the war broke out. The weight of years and great bodily suffering pressed heavily upon him, and really rendered him incapable of performing the duties of his station. For some time before he retired he was simply an obstacle, and a very serious one, in the way of active work. He did not wish me to succeed him as general-in-chief, but desired that place for [Henry W.] Halleck, and long withheld his retirement that Halleck might arrive East and fall heir to his place." [6]

The republic had had, in the years before civil strife, a number of Presidents with military experience. Abraham Lincoln, however, was practically devoid of any real military training or background. In the Black Hawk War of 1832, he was elected captain of a company; but he found difficulty in maintaining discipline, and was ordered to wear a wooden sword for two days when some of his men went on a drinking spree. At another time, he was placed under arrest for firing a gun in camp. At no time did he see action.[7] Lincoln was, however, not a complete stranger to McClellan in 1861, nor was their acquaintanceship before Sumter an unfriendly one. Writes the General of his earlier association with the man from Springfield: " Long before the war, when vice-president of the Illinois Central . . . I knew Mr. Lincoln, for he was one of the counsel of the company. More than once I have been with him in out-of-the-way county-seats where some important case was being tried, and, in the lack of sleeping accommodations, have spent the night in front of a stove listening to the unceasing flow of anecdotes from his lips. He was never at a loss, and I could

[5] *M.O.S.*, 66.
[6] *Ibid.*, 136–37.
[7] See Benjamin P. Thomas, *Abraham Lincoln: A Biography* (New York, 1952), 31–33.

22

never quite make up my mind how many of them he had really heard before, and how many he invented on the spur of the moment. His stories were seldom refined, but were always to the point." [8] A friendly relationship was immediately established in the summer of 1861 between the President—whom McClellan often addressed as "Your Excellency"—and the young general, usually called "George" by Lincoln.[9]

When McClellan arrived in the capital, a few days after the Bull Run defeat, the Union military situation along the Potomac appeared desperate. In his official report, the General said of the picture confronting him, "I found no army to command; a mere collection of regiments cowering on the banks of the Potomac, some perfectly raw, others dispirited by the recent defeat." [10] New York *Times* correspondent Swinton states that it was "rather a mob than an army. Desertion had become alarmingly numerous, and the streets of Washington were crowded with straggling officers and men absent from their stations without authority, and indicating by their behavior an utter want of discipline and organization." [11]

Taking stock of affairs, McClellan found that he had under his command about 50,000 infantry, less than 1,000 cavalry, and 9 skeleton field artillery batteries of but 30 guns in all. As an essential beginning, the General set up an effective Provost Marshal department, which collected the stragglers and sent them back to their units, and which enforced a strict military discipline. Then, several hundred unfit officers were cashiered by reviewing boards which McClellan quickly established. Alcohol was immediately prohibited in the camps. But the bulk of building an army lay ahead.[12]

McClellan at first got along reasonably well with the Radical

[8] *M.O.S.*, 162.

[9] Russell's *Diary*, 480.

[10] Allan Nevins and Milton Halsey Thomas (eds.), *The Diary of George Templeton Strong . . .* (New York, 1952), III, 169; Adam Gurowski, *Diary, from March 4, 1861, to November 12, 1862* (Boston, 1862), 71; McClellan's *Report*, 44.

[11] Swinton, *Army of the Potomac*, 62–63.

[12] Alexander S. Webb, *The Peninsula: McClellan's Campaign of 1862* (New York, 1881), 2, 5; Paris, *The Civil War*, I, 271–72; McClellan's *Report*, 9–10.

Republicans in Congress. Senator Zachariah Chandler of Michigan—later one of his bitterest enemies—took pleasure in showing the General around Washington officialdom. However, the former Attorney General in the cabinet of James Buchanan voiced an early and accurate note of warning. Democrat Edwin Stanton, then a lawyer in Washington, wrote on July 26 that, even if McClellan possessed " the ability of Caesar, Alexander, or Napoleon, what can he accomplish? Will not Scott's jealousy, Cabinet intrigues, and Republican interference thwart him at every step? " Unfortunately for the North, Stanton, when he became Secretary of War in 1862, did not heed his own warning about " Cabinet intrigues " and " interference." McClellan's impressions of his new sphere of activity were given to his wife on July 27: " I find myself in a new and strange position here: President, cabinet, Gen. Scott, and all deferring to me. By some strange operation of magic I seem to have become the power of the land. . . . Refused invitations to dine today from Gen. Scott and four secretaries; had too many things to attend to." In the words of Lincoln's private secretaries, McClellan " was courted and caressed as few men in our history have been." [13]

The young general was fully impressed with the importance and the scope of the work before him. In a most revealing letter to Ellen, written shortly after his arrival in Washington, McClellan said:

> I went to the Senate to get [a bill] through, and was quite overwhelmed by the congratulations I received and the respect with which I was treated. . . . They give me my way in everything, full swing and unbounded confidence. All tell me that I am responsible for the fate of the nation, and that all its resources shall be placed at my disposal. It is an immense task that I have on my hands, but I believe that I can accomplish

---

[13] Chandler to his wife, July 16, 1861, and Chandler to McClellan, August 16, 1861, Zachariah Chandler Papers, Division of Manuscripts, Library of Congress; Stanton to Buchanan, July 26, 1861, Frank Abial Flower, *Edwin McMasters Stanton* . . . (Akron, 1905) , 109; McClellan to his wife, July 27, 1861, *M.O.S.,* 67 n, 82; Nicolay and Hay, *Abraham Lincoln,* IV, 444.

it. When I was in the Senate chamber today and found those old men flocking around me; when I afterwards stood in the library, looking over the Capitol of our great nation, and saw the crowd gathering around me to stare at me, I began to feel how great the task committed to me. Oh! how sincerely I pray to God that I may be endowed with the wisdom and courage necessary to accomplish the work. Who would have thought, when we were married, that I should so soon be called upon to save the country? [14]

The raw levies, constantly arriving in Washington from the North, as well as the green troops already there, were formed by McClellan first into provisional brigades, and kept on the north bank of the Potomac for instruction. Later, they would be molded into divisions. Although in favor of the eventual formation of army corps—each comprising three divisions— McClellan did not wish to hurry this step. He desired to wait until actual field operations gave some experience to division commanders and indicated those best qualified for the high responsibility of corps command. On August 4, McClellan assigned the following officers to head the brigades: Brigadier Generals David Hunter, Samuel P. Heintzelman, William T. Sherman, Philip Kearny, Joseph Hooker, William B. Franklin, and Charles Stone, and Colonels Erasmus D. Keyes, Louis Blenker, Israel Richardson, William F. Smith, and Darius N. Couch.[15]

Another task handled pretty much by McClellan—who had been an engineer in the old army—was that of erecting a series of powerful, permanent fortifications about the Federal capital. Interlocking forts, occupying commanding heights, were connected by infantry parapets. The ground over which an enemy could approach was swept by a cross-fire from several points. In all, thirty-three miles of works were laid out by McClellan and his Chief Engineer, Brigadier General John G. Barnard.

[14] McClellan to his wife, July 30, 1861, *M.O.S.*, 82–83.
[15] McClellan's *Report*, 10; Webb, *The Peninsula*, 7–8; Comte de Paris, " McClellan Organizing the Grand Army," *B. & L.*, II, 112-13.

So impressed was the famous London *Times* war correspondent, William H. " Bull Run " Russell, with McClellan's work in building the Union army, that he wrote back to his paper on September 2, " Never perhaps has a finer body of men in all respects of *physique* been assembled by any power in the world, and there is no reason why their *morale* should not be improved so as to equal that of the best troops in Europe." [16]

While McClellan was laboring to fashion an army, the Northern populace began to grow impatient again for action. It seemed, too, that no specific plan of campaign had been evolved by the administration or the General-in-Chief. On July 31, McClellan declared in a message to Scott, " I do not know your plan of operations." On August 2, he wrote to his wife, " I handed to the President tonight a carefully considered plan for conducting the war on a large scale. I shall carry this thing on *en grand* and crush the rebels in one campaign. . . . I was in the saddle nearly twelve hours yesterday." [17]

The paper which McClellan mentioned was a long memorandum for Lincoln's consideration, written at the President's request. It stated that the scope of the war was large, that a whole enemy nation would have to be conquered completely. To do this successfully, McClellan called for overwhelming numbers of Union soldiers to be hurled simultaneously upon the Confederacy from Virginia, from the Mississippi River, from Missouri, and from Kentucky and Tennessee. It was not altogether unlike Scott's Anaconda plan, and emphasized the value of the use by the Federals of internal waterways and railroads, as well as of amphibious operations by sea. Stating that 20,000 men would suffice for the garrison of Washington, the General urged that his main army in the East should number 273,000 men. " The force I have recommended," said McClellan, " is large; the expense is great. It is possible that a smaller

[16] Swinton, *Army of the Potomac*, 66 n; Russell to London *Times*, September 2, 1861, Rhodes, *History of the United States*, III, 493.

[17] McClellan to Scott, about July 31, 1861, George B. McClellan Papers, Division of Manuscripts, Library of Congress; McClellan to his wife, August 2, 1861, *M.O.S.*, 83–84.

26

force might accomplish the object in view, but I understand it to be the purpose of this great nation to reestablish the power of the Government and restore peace to its citizens in the shortest possible time." [18] This comprehensive scheme of McClellan's was the one actually used, in the main, to win the war. If the administration opposed these views given by McClellan in August of 1861, it refrained from saying so. Its silence seemed to indicate acquiescence. This silence was broken only in December, soon after Congress reconvened.

On August 8, McClellan drafted a message to Scott which was to have unhappy repercussions. The young general believed that the enemy had 100,000 men in front of the National capital, and that " the vital importance of rendering Washington perfectly secure " required that the defending Union force be augmented in numbers. McClellan urged Scott also to merge the departments of northeastern Virginia, Washington, the Shenandoah, Pennsylvania, and Baltimore into one, under the command of the general at the head of the main army of operations.[19]

While McClellan was over-alarmed about the safety of Washington then, he was probably correct in suggesting a more unified departmental structure. However, an angered Scott refused to reply to this message. In a statement of his own to Secretary of War Simon Cameron, the General-in-Chief was resentful in tone and word to his subordinate's views and to his alleged aloofness. " He has stood on his guard," wrote the old soldier, " and now places himself on record. Let him make the most of his unenvied advantages." He then asked the Secretary for the President's " earliest " approval of his application for retirement.[20]

Although it was perhaps natural for the seventy-five-year-old warrior to be a bit annoyed by the ability of the younger general

[18] McClellan's " Memorandum for the President," August 2, 1861, McClellan Papers.

[19] McClellan to Scott, August 8, 1861, McClellan Papers. A copy was sent also to Lincoln (*B. & L.*, II, 114 n) .

[20] Scott to Cameron, August 9, 1861, 14 *O.R.*, 4; *B. & L.*, II, 114 n–115 n.

to attend rapidly to so many duties in person, there was nothing in McClellan's letter to Scott which was unusual or disrespectful. But on August 10, Lincoln entered the growing rift between his two top generals by informing McClellan of Scott's letter to Cameron, and asking him for permission to withdraw his letter of August 8 to the General-in-Chief. McClellan replied to the President on the tenth: " It is . . . with great pain that I have learned from you this morning that my views do not meet with the approbation of the Lieutenant-General, and that my letter is unfavorably regarded by him. . . . Influenced by these considerations, I yield to your request and withdraw the letter referred to." Lincoln took this letter of McClellan's to Scott and asked him in turn to withdraw his reply to the earlier one from McClellan, given by the old general to Cameron on August 9. Scott replied—not to Lincoln but to Cameron—on August 12. He stated that he had been slighted and ignored by McClellan, and refused to withdraw his letter of the ninth as requested by the President. Again mentioning his own physical infirmities, Scott nevertheless emphasized the many high military qualifications of his young subordinate.[21] There the matter stood—for a time.

Meanwhile, the steady work of creating an army went on. A representative day for McClellan might be similar to the one he described to his wife Ellen on August 14:

> I was so occupied yesterday that I could not write. Profs. Mahan and Bache at breakfast. Then came the usual levee. Then Burnside turned up, and I had to listen to his explanation of some slanders against him; then some naval officers; then I don't know how many others before dinner. After dinner I rode out until about nine, when I found the President had been to see me and wanted me at the White House. After I got through there I went to see Montgomery Blair on business. Then, on my return, found some more of the cabinet, McDowell, etc., so that it was after midnight when I got to

---

[21] McClellan to Lincoln, August 10, 1861, 12 *O.R.*, 5; Scott to Cameron, August 12, 1861, 14 *O.R.*, 5–6.

my room, completely fatigued. So my days and nights pass, a steady course of conversations and orders all day. Except when I get out for a ride, no relief for mind or body.[22]

On August 18, McClellan's Department of the Potomac was extended to include the command of Major General Nathaniel P. Banks in the Shenandoah Valley and that of Major General John A. Dix at Baltimore—a request that McClellan had made previously. It did not, however, give him control of Fortress Monroe—the strongest fort in America—at Hampton Roads, where Brigadier General John E. Wool had superseded Major General Benjamin F. Butler on the seventeenth. On the twentieth, the order was issued which officially created McClellan's Army of the Potomac, destined to become one of the most famous bodies of soldiery in the world. McClellan followed this up by urging the Secretary of War to push recruiting in the North, and to employ conscription if necessary. By August, the General reported having 65,000 effectives, while his opponent, General Joseph E. Johnston, claims to have had, two months later, but 41,000 men " capable of going into battle." And on September 4, McClellan appointed as his chief of staff Colonel Randolph B. Marcy, a veteran soldier of wide experience, who was also his father-in-law.[23]

The young commander's relations with Secretary of War Cameron were quite amicable. On September 8, at the urging of the Secretary, McClellan presented to him a lengthy memorandum on the military situation, as he saw it. Stating that the total number of men in the vicinity of Washington was " nearly 85,000," he asserted that the Confederates had " at least 100,000 effective troops " in Virginia. In his paper of August 2, McClellan had called for 273,000 men for the Army of the Potomac. Now, in this message to Cameron, he felt that

[22] McClellan to his wife, August 14, 1861, *M.O.S.*, 87.
[23] *Ibid.*, 88, 89, 113; 4 *O.R.*, 601; 5 *O.R.*, 23; McClellan to Lincoln August 20, 1861, Edward McPherson, *The Political History of the United States* . . . (Washington, 1864) , 274; Joseph E. Johnston, *Narrative of Military Operations* . . . (New York, 1874) , 81; McClellan's *Report*, 23.

300,000 men were needed " in order to insure complete success and an early termination of the war." After all, were not the eager recruits then available in the North? [24]

Seeking relaxation from his arduous duties, McClellan found it in his custom of writing frequently to his wife, often in a light, breezy style. On the day he wrote to Cameron, he found time to pen her a few lines, saying, " What a shame that any one should spread such a wicked rumor in regard to my being killed! I beg to assure you that I have not been killed a single time since I reached Washington." Relating another incident of the day, the General continued, " I had another bouquet this morning, one from the ' Lady President.' Mr. Lincoln came this morning to ask me to pardon a man that I had ordered to be shot, suggesting that I could give as a reason in the order that it was by request of the ' lady President.' " [25]

On September 27, the increasing friction between Scott and McClellan became more evident at a meeting of the two generals with Lincoln and the cabinet. According to Secretary of the Navy Gideon Welles, Scott said to McClellan, as the younger general was about to leave the meeting, " You were called here by my advice. The times require vigilance and activity. I am not active and never shall be again. When I proposed that you should come here to aid, not supersede me, you had my friendship and confidence. You still have my confidence." McClellan kept his temper, bowed, and insisted on shaking the General-in-Chief's hand as he departed.[26]

A point of controversy was developing at this time over several artillery batteries which the Confederates had installed on the lower Potomac, at such places as Mathias Point and Cockpit Point. McClellan's Chief Engineer, Barnard, reconnoitered the enemy positions, and recommended against their being attacked at that time, in part because the navy was not

[24] Cameron to McClellan, September 7, 1861, McClellan to Cameron, September 8, 1861, McClellan Papers.

[25] McClellan to his wife, September 8, 1861, *M.O.S.*, 90–91.

[26] McClellan to his wife, September 27, 1861, *ibid.*, 91; John T. Morse, Jr. (ed.), *The Diary of Gideon Welles* . . . (Boston, 1911), I, 242.

able to spare enough vessels. Testifying under oath before the Committee on the Conduct of the War, McClellan stated, " I do not think that the army was in a condition to have occupied the Virginia bank of the river much before it actually moved from Washington. The question of attacking the rebel batteries on the Potomac was carefully examined, and the opinion ultimately formed was that it would require a general advance of the entire army," for the Southeners could keep changing the positions of the guns as rapidly as each site was threatened by the Federals from the water.[27] Still, public opinion in the North was uneasy.

On September 30, McClellan occupied the recently held Confederate advanced positions at Munson's Hill and Upton's Hill, which had marked Johnston's closest approach to Washington. On the same day, however, Attorney General Edward Bates was noting in his diary, " The public spirit is beginning to quail under the depressing influence of our prolonged inaction. . . . We absolutely need some dashing expeditions, great or small, to stimulate the zeal of the Country." In his official report, McClellan commented on the growing restlessness of the people of the North: " Time is a necessary element in the creation of armies, and I do not . . . think it necessary to more than mention the impatience with which many regarded the delay in the arrival of the new levies, though recruited and pressed forward with unexampled rapidity, the manufacture and supply of arms and equipments, or the vehemence with which an immediate advance upon the enemy's works directly in our front was urged by a patriotic but sanguine people. The President, too, was anxious for the speedy employment of our army." [28]

McClellan, however, was determined not to be hurried by public pressure into what he considered a premature advance

---

[27] 5 *O.R.*, 607–608; McClellan's testimony, February 28, 1863, *C.C.W.*, I, 420, 421–22.

[28] *M.O.S.*, 91, 92; Howard K. Beale (ed.), *The Diary of Edward Bates, 1859-1866* (Washington, 1933), 194; McClellan's *Report*, 6.

before his army was completely equipped and thoroughly drilled. Radical Senator Benjamin Wade of Ohio—once a supporter of McClellan—had, by October 3, lost all confidence in the General, and now disliked him intensely. He said in a letter to Chandler that neither McClellan nor Lincoln had any pride or backbone. He asserted that not even " a galvanic battery " could provide the spark needed by the administration. He claimed that McClellan would remain behind his intrenchments until his soldiers became grizzled veterans. Wade did not think the people would retain such an administration in power. By October 12, Chandler himself had begun to pull away from the General, and was now sneering at McClellan's grand reviews and occasional champagne-and-oyster banquets.[29]

If some of the civilians of the government were becoming disgruntled with the methodical organizational activities of McClellan, the General was unawed by his critics. He wrote to Ellen early in October, " I can't tell you how disgusted I am becoming with these wretched politicians. . . . I presume I shall have to go after [the Confederates] when I get ready; but this getting ready is slow work with such an administration. I wish I were well out of it." On October 2, he declared, " I am daily becoming more disgusted with this administration—perfectly sick of it. If I could with honor resign I would quit the whole concern tomorrow. . . . No one seems to be able to comprehend my feeling—that I have no ambitious feelings to gratify, and only wish to serve my country in its trouble, and, when this weary war is over, to return to my wife." [30]

With so many things to be done every day in building the Union Army, it was often impossible for McClellan to clear everything through the General-in-Chief. He often went ahead on his own with the various projects which had to be accomplished. This, however—perhaps understandably—nettled the old Lieutenant General. Scott had tried to resign before, but his

---

[29] Wade to Chandler, October 3, 1861, Chandler to his wife, October 12, 1861, Chandler Papers.
[30] McClellan to his wife, October 2, 1861, *M.O.S.*, 167, 168.

resignation had not been accepted. On October 4, therefore, in a sharp letter to Cameron, he charged that McClellan had often by-passed him and communicated directly with the President and cabinet. He claimed that, by so doing, the young general had disobeyed his orders. Mentioning again his many infirmities, Scott said, " I shall try to hold out 'till the arrival of Major Genl. Halleck." Then he would retire.[31]

McClellan had appointed the famous detective, Allan Pinkerton, to head his secret service. Pinkerton had collected a number of his operatives in Washington, and had sent them out as spies to gather information from the enemy. Unfortunately for the Federals, these agents were too prone to accept uncritically the exaggerated guesses of Confederate deserters and pro-Union civilians as to the number of grayclad soldiers facing McClellan. After the first of October, Pinkerton—now using the assumed name, " E. J. Allen "—in a whole series of reports to McClellan, insisted that there were over 118,000 Confederate troops in Virginia.[32] Thus, it was an imaginary enemy army, actually over twice the real strength of Johnston, that McClellan felt he was contending against. These intelligence reports from supposedly reliable agents served as a further note of caution to McClellan, warning him to be on his guard against any pressure aimed at forcing him into a premature offensive campaign before he was ready.

Lincoln's invitations to McClellan to attend cabinet sessions were often irritating to the General. Writing to Ellen on October 10 of one of these conclaves, he said, " When I returned yesterday, after a long ride, I was obliged to attend a meeting of the cabinet at eight P. M., and was bored and annoyed. There are some of the greatest geese in the Cabinet I have ever seen— enough to tax the patience of Job." Speaking of the impatience of the public and of government officials for an immediate

---

[31] Scott to Cameron, October 4, 1861, Edwin M. Stanton Papers, Division of Manuscripts, Library of Congress.

[32] " E. J. Allen " to McClellan, October 4 and 28, November 15 and 26, 1861, McClellan Papers.

33

advance, McClellan said to Lincoln after the meeting, " I intend to be careful, and do as well as possible. Don't let them hurry me, is all I ask." You shall have your own way in the matter, I assure you," replied the Chief Executive. The General's relations with the President still remained good, although he disliked Lincoln's frequent habit of dropping in unannounced at headquarters when he was overwhelmed with military details, even though this was the President's privilege. He wrote home on October 16, " I have just been interrupted here by the President . . . who had nothing very particular to say, except some stories to tell, which were, as usual, very pertinent, and some pretty good. I never in my life met any one so full of anecdotes as our friend. He is never at a loss for a story apropos of any known subject or incident." [33]

On October 15, McClellan reported having a total force— including noncombatants—of 133,201 men present for duty in and about Washington, along the Potomac from Chesapeake Bay to Cumberland, and in Baltimore. On the same day he organized his numerous brigades into divisions to be commanded by Banks, Brigadier General Irvin McDowell, Heintzelman, Brigadier General Fitz John Porter, Franklin, Stone, Brigadier Generals Don Carlos Buell and George A. McCall, Hooker, Blenker, Smith, and Dix. On October 24, he received a report from his Chief of Engineers and Chief of Artillery that " a little less than 34,000 men, including reserves," should be set aside for the defense of Washington once the main Federal army commenced its offensive operations. A few days later, McClellan reported that he had a grand total of 134,285 men present for duty in his whole department, of which 76,285 were then disposable for actual fighting. [34]

Meanwhile the popular chant " On to Richmond " was resumed by Horace Greeley's New York *Tribune* and by other

[33] McClellan to his wife, October 10 and 16, 1861, *M.O.S.*, 169, 170; Tyler Dennett (ed.), *Lincoln and the Civil War in the Diaries and Letters of John Hay* (New York, 1939), 27, 29, cited hereinafter as *Hay's Diary*.

[34] McClellan's *Report*, 10, 14–17; *M.O.S.*, 118, 163–64; Webb, *The Peninsula*, 6–7.

vocal elements in the North. But on October 21 occurred an event which should have demonstrated the folly of hasty advance before officers and men were adequately trained. This was the minor Federal debacle at Ball's Bluff, where a Union detachment was poorly led and suffered total casualties of 921 men, most of whom were captured. Among the killed, however, was Colonel Edward Baker, a political appointee who had served in the Senate, and who was a friend of Lincoln. Such a howl went up among the Radical Republicans that General Stone, nominally in command of the expedition, was thrown into prison for 189 days before being acquitted. Similar petty and vindictive treatment of political foes and innocent soldiers could be expected in the future from the new Joint Congressional Committee on the Conduct of the War, headed by Wade and Chandler.[35]

On the evening of the battle, as telegrams came into headquarters telling of the fiasco at Ball's Bluff, Lincoln was in tears over the loss of his dear friend, Baker. John Hay, Lincoln's private secretary, reported the scene in the General's quarters: " McClellan and the Prest talked sadly over it. McClellan said, ' There is many a good fellow that wears the shoulder-straps going under the sod before this thing is over. There is no loss too great to be repaired. If I should get knocked on the head, Mr. President, you will put another man immediately into my shoes.' ' I want you to take care of yourself,' said the President." [36] This minor military disaster at Ball's Bluff showed still a certain looseness in command and inexperience in handling men on the part of Federal officers. It probably led McClellan to delay until the following spring any intentions he might have had for an autumn advance in force.[37]

[35] New York *Tribune*, October 18, 1861; Swinton, *Army of the Potomac*, 76–77; Paris, *The Civil War*, I, 409–14; Richard B. Irwin, " Ball's Bluff and the Arrest of General Stone," *B. & L.*, II, 123–94; Fox, *Regimental Losses*, 543, 549; George A. Bruce, *The Twentieth Regiment of Massachusetts Volunteer Infantry . . .* (Boston, 1906), 24–59.

[36] *Hay's Diary*, 30.

[37] See Paris, *The Civil War*, I, 414–15; Paris, " McClellan Organizing the Grand Army," *B. & L.*, II, 114.

The impatient Radicals, however, could not see the need of the many months of labor required to mold a large, efficient fighting machine. On the evening of October 26, three Radical Senators—Wade, Chandler, and Lyman Trumbull—had a stormy interview with the President. They implored him to direct McClellan to attack the Confederate Army at Manassas and Centerville immediately. Chandler shouted that if an advance were not made soon, he was " in favor of sending for Jeff Davis at once " to concede defeat to him. Lincoln, however, would not be brow-beaten, and, in the words of Hay, " stood up for McClellan's deliberateness." Leaving the White House, the three angry Senators strode across Lafayette Square to McClellan's house. He received them in his usual courteous manner. For three hours they tried in vain to badger the Young Napoleon into attacking Johnston forthwith. On departing, they contended that defeat was preferable to further delay.[38]

A few moments after the three Senators left, McClellan received a visitation from Lincoln and Hay. The General, wrote Hay in his diary, talked with the Chief Executive about the Radicals. " McC. said that Wade preferred an unsuccessful battle to delay. . . . The President deprecated this new manifestation of senseless popular impatience but at the same time said that it was a reality and should be taken into account." Then, according to Hay, the President added, " ' at the same time, General, you must not fight till you are ready.' " [39]

On October 30, at Lincoln's request, McClellan drew up another lengthy memorandum for Secretary of War Cameron. Referring to his earlier papers, the General stated that the 273,000 or 300,000 men which he had asked for had not been provided him. He said that these large numbers were needed " to enable this army to advance with a reasonable certainty of success," while leaving Washington and the line of the Potomac

[38] Chandler to his wife, October 27, 1861, Chandler Papers; Benjamin F. Wade, *Facts for the People* (Cincinnati, 1864) , 1–2; *Hay's Diary*, 31; McClellan to his wife, October 26, 1861, *M.O.S.*, 171–72.
[39] *Hay's Diary*, 31.

entirely secure. Intelligence reports indicated, he continued, that the Confederates opposed to him numbered "not less than 150,000" effectives. McClellan now felt that he should have a total of 240,000 men, from which his active column of operations would number some 150,000 effectives, with 35,000 men for the defense of the National capital.[40] At no time in his career was the General backward in asking for what he wanted or in proffering advice.

The retirement of General-in-Chief Scott became effective on November 1, after a number of efforts on the old warrior's part to step down. Lincoln and the cabinet paid their respects to him in a dignified procession of honor to his office. McClellan's reaction to this news was contained in his usual letter home: " I saw yesterday Gen. Scott's letter asking to be placed on the retired list and saying nothing about Halleck. . . . They propose to make me at once [General]-in-Chief of the army. I cannot get up any especial feeling about it. I feel the vast responsibility it imposes upon me. I feel a sense of relief at the prospect of having my own way untrammeled, but I cannot discover in my own heart one symptom of gratified vanity or ambition." [41]

So ended the long and brilliant era of Winfield Scott in American military annals—one of the brightest pages in the history of the United States as an independent nation. That it was, in 1861, far beyond his waning physical resources to fill the arduous tasks of his great office was seen by most competent observers. It was simply an impossibility for the seventy-five-year-old soldier to labor steadily for twelve or sixteen hours a day. Lincoln's tribute to Scott was nicely stated in his First Annual Message to Congress: " During his long life the nation has not been unmindful of his merit; yet on calling to mind how faithfully, ably, and brilliantly he has served his country, from a time far back in our history, when few of the now living

---

[40] McClellan to Cameron, October 30, 1861, McClellan Papers.
[41] *Bates's Diary*, 200; McClellan to his wife, October 31, 1861, *M.O.S.*, 173.

had been born, and thenceforward continually, I can not but think we are still his debtors." [42]

Although he had at times treated the old general in a somewhat cavalier fashion and had felt occasionally that he was an " obstacle," McClellan found time, on the day of promotion to the chief command, to honor Scott in what was perhaps one of Little Mac's finest and most eloquent addresses:

> The army will unite with me in the feeling of regret that the weight of many years and the effect of increasing infirmities, contracted and intensified in his country's service, should just now remove from our head the great soldier of our nation — the hero who in his youth raised high the reputation of his country on the fields of Canada, which he hallowed with his blood; who in more mature years proved to the world that American skill and valor could repeat if not eclipse the exploits of Cortez in the land of the Montezumas; whose whole life has been devoted to the service of his country; whose whole efforts have been directed to uphold our honor at the smallest sacrifice of life — a warrior who scorned the selfish glories of the battlefield when his great qualities as a statesman could be employed more profitably for his country; a citizen who in his declining years has given to the world the most shining instance of loyalty, in disregarding all ties of birth and clinging still to the cause of truth and honor. Such has been the career, such the character, of Winfield Scott. [43]

One of the purposes in McClellan's writing this address was his hope that it would help to improve Scott's unfriendly feeling toward him now that the old general was departing, and in this he was successful. Writing to Ellen a few days later, McClellan said that his laudatory statement " changed Gen'l Scott's feelings entirely, and . . . he now says that I am the best man and the best general that ever existed! Such is human nature—the order *was* a little rhetorical—but I wrote it *at* him—

[42] James D. Richardson (ed.), *A Compilation of the Messages and Papers of the Presidents, 1789–1902* (Washington, 1904), VI, 56.
[43] General Orders No. 19, November 1, 1861, 122 *O.R.*, 613–14.

and for a particular market! It seems to have accomplished the object." [44]

The final scene occurred at 4:00 A. M. on November 3, when McClellan escorted Scott to the railroad depot. The young general was much moved by this experience, as he wrote humbly to his wife:

> It was pitch dark and a pouring rain; but with most of my staff and a squadron of cavalry I saw the old man off. He was very polite to me; sent various messages to you and the baby; so we parted. The old man said that his sensations were very peculiar in leaving Washington and active life. I can easily understand them; and it may be that some distant day I, too, shall totter away from Washington, a worn-out soldier, with naught to do but make my peace with God. The sight of this morning was a lesson to me which I hope not soon to forget. I saw there the end of a long, active, and ambitious life, the end of the career of the first soldier of his nation; and it was a feeble old man scarce able to walk; hardly any one there to see him off but his successor. Should I ever become vain-glorious and ambitious, remind me of that spectacle. [45]

When he took the reins as General-in-Chief, McClellan saw that all the armies of the Union—including those in the West—were stationary. However, among the politicians in Washington and the people of the North in general, whose eyes were perhaps naturally fixed upon the largest Federal army—the one about the National capital—the blame for inactivity fell chiefly upon McClellan and his own Army of the Potomac. It might be noted that the main Confederate army under Johnston at Centerville and Manassas was also inactive at this season, as were the other Southern armies. In fact, with but one disastrous exception, the Union army in the East was to remain largely stationary and quiet each winter throughout the war. The

[44] McClellan to his wife, about November 3, 1861, McClellan Papers.
[45] McClellan to his wife, November 3, 1861, *M.O.S.*, 173–74.

terrible condition of the roads rendered this course almost inescapable for both sides.[46]

In the days immediately after his promotion, McClellan diligently wrote long dispatches—discussing general policy and military operations—to Halleck in Missouri, to Buell in Kentucky, to Sherman on the coast of South Carolina, and to Butler, who was preparing an amphibious expedition to New Orleans. He sought to co-ordinate and synchronize the movement of his own Army of the Potomac with those of the other Federal armies. McClellan stated, significantly, in his official report that "the plan . . . comprehended in its scope the operations of all the armies of the Union, the army of the Potomac as well. It was my intention . . . that its various parts should be carried out simultaneously, or nearly so, and in cooperation along the whole line. If this plan was wise . . . then it is unnecessary to defend any delay which would have enabled the army of the Potomac to perform its share in the execution of the whole work." He said further that "even if the Army of the Potomac had been in condition to undertake a campaign in the autumn of 1861, the backward state of affairs in the West would have made it unwise to do so; for on no sound military principle could it be regarded as proper to operate on one line while all was quiescent on the others, as such a course would have enabled the enemy to concentrate everything on the one active army." [47]

Meanwhile, McClellan's personal relations with Lincoln were showing signs of a slight strain, although they still remained cordial and friendly. The President, on the evening of November 11, as was his custom, dropped into McClellan's busy headquarters for a visit. He was much interested in strategic matters, and talked at length with McClellan about them. Heintzelman, who happened to be present, noted in

[46] See Richard B. Irwin, "The Administration in the Peninsular Campaign," *B. & L.*, II, 436.

[47] McClellan's *Report*, 37–42; McClellan's testimony, February 28, 1863, *C.C.W.*, I, 422.

his diary, " The President continued to pore over a map . . . making remarks, not remarkably profound, but McClellan listened as if much edified." Later that night, Heintzelman recorded, " when Gen. McClellan had seen the President to the door . . . he came in & as he pushed the door to looking back said ' Isn't he a rare bird.' " [48]

" The friendly visits of the President to army headquarters," write Hay and Nicolay, " were continued almost every night until the 13th of November." On that evening, the President and Hay went, as usual, to McClellan's, but were told by a servant that the General was attending the wedding of an old army friend. They waited. Soon McClellan came in, Hay relates, and went directly upstairs to bed, leaving the President sitting in another room. Lincoln, however, did not seem at all upset over this incident. Although " there was no cessation of their friendly relations," Hay writes, " it was not unnatural for [the President] to infer that his frequent visits had become irksome to the general." Such an incident was so out of character for McClellan—who was always the model of courtesy and respect toward " His Excellency "—that it seems fair to assume that, if Hay's story was accurate, the General was not in a fit physical condition to confront the President at that moment. Perhaps he had had a bit too much to drink at the wedding party of his friend. The grizzled old veteran, Heintzelman, was present at this wedding and spoke briefly to McClellan there. He then noted in his diary of the ceremony that evening: " There was a nice supper & quite a pleasant party." [49]

Shortly after McClellan had arrived in Washington from the West, the former Attorney General in Buchanan's cabinet, Edwin M. Stanton, was recommended to him " as a safe adviser of legal points." Both men were Democrats. Stanton immediately " did his best to ingratiate himself " with the young com-

[48] " The Journal of Samuel P. Heintzelman, 1861-1865," entry of November 11, 1861, Division of Manuscripts, Library of Congress.

[49] Nicolay and Hay, *Abraham Lincoln*, IV, 468–69; Heintzelman's Journal, entry of November 13, 1861; *M.O.S.*, 160, 161–62.

mander. McClellan " had no reason to suspect his sincerity " or patriotism. " The most disagreebale thing about him," declares McClellan, " was the extreme virulence with which he abused the President, the administration, and the Republican party. He never spoke of the President in any other way than as the ' original gorilla.' " When Cameron made a speech to a newly arrived regiment, emphasizing certain Radical Republican views, Stanton beseeched McClellan " to arrest him for inciting to insubordination." The General stated that Stanton " often advocated the propriety of my seizing the government and taking affairs into my own hands." McClellan declared that Stanton actually was on intimate terms with a number of Radicals of the very party which he so viciously denounced, and that he was merely using him to win support in an effort to gain an important position in the Federal government.[50]

Along with consideration of the time element in his future offensive plans, McClellan was concerned also with the question of the best area in which to conduct his own major operations. Near the end of November, 1861, he was discussing with Chief Engineer Barnard several proposals for making a flanking movement down the Chesapeake Bay. Such a route would circumvent the need of frontally assailing Johnston's positions at Centerville and Manassas, and would give to the Federals the advantage of water lines of supply instead of the more tenuous land ones. McClellan reported that, in early December, he had present for duty—including noncombatant troops—a total of 169,452 soldiers. These were located in and about Washington, at Baltimore, at various points in Maryland and Delaware, and along the Potomac River. Of course, after leaving garrisons at Washington and elsewhere, his number of effectives for the active column of invasion would number little more than half of that figure.[51]

[50] M.O.S., 152.
[51] John G. Barnard, The Peninsular Campaign and its Antecedents . . . (New York, 1864), 52–55; Barnard to McClellan, December 6, 1861, 5 O.R., 676; McClellan's Report, 10.

An anxious Congress reconvened on December 1. In his First Annual Message to that assemblage, Lincoln made this incisive statement: " It has been said that one bad general is better than two good ones, and the saying is true if taken to mean no more than that an army is better directed by a single mind, though inferior, than by two superior ones at variance and cross-purposes with each other. . . . In a storm at sea no one on board *can* wish the ship to sink, and yet not infrequently all go down together because too many will direct and no single mind can be allowed to control." [52] Would the President, however, be able to adhere steadfastly to his own wise counsel on this point, or would he soon feel compelled by political pressure to turn his back upon it?

On the day that Congress met, Lincoln sent a questionnaire to the General-in-Chief in which the President's own strategic ideas were apparent. McClellan kept the paper nine days, and then replied to the questions as follows:

> Q. If it were determined to make a forward movement of the Army of the Potomac without awaiting further increase of numbers or better drill and discipline, how long would it require to actually get in motion?
>
> A. If bridge trains ready by December 15, probably 25.
>
> Q. After leaving all that would be necessary, how many troops could join in the movement from southwest of the [Potomac] river?
>
> A. Seventy-one thousand.
>
> Q. How many from northeast of it?
>
> A. Thirty-three thousand.

The President, in this questionnaire, then suggested moving 50,000 men from the southwest bank of the Potomac to threaten the Confederates at Centerville, while the remainder of the Union force southwest of the river would move by the Alexandria and Richmond road to its crossing of Occoquan Creek. They would be joined at that point by the Federal troops on

---

[52] Richardson (ed,), *Messages and Papers*, VI, 56.

the northeast bank of the Potomac, who would move by water to a point just below the mouth of the Occoquan, and then march by land along the southern bank of that river to its crossing with the road. The united National force would then proceed by the road " to Brentsville and beyond to the railroad just south of its crossing of Broad Run." These movements, the President implied, should, in his opinion, place the Federals between the main Confederate army—near Centerville—and Richmond. Lincoln did not say what would then be likely to occur, or what course the Federals should adopt after these preliminary movements.[53] Perhaps in this paper the President was only trying to hurry the General along in his preparations, or else was only trying to smoke him out as to his strategic views. If so, the President did not succeed very well. In a " confidential " letter to Lincoln on December 10—enclosed with his answers to the questionnaire—McClellan stated, " I have now my mind actively turned towards another plan of campaign that I do not think at all anticipated by the enemy nor by many of our own people." [54] This was undoubtedly one of the schemes for an amphibious movement down the bay which he had discussed with Barnard a few days before.

McClellan had probably already decided not to begin major operations until spring, due not only to the need to ready the Western armies for simultaneous advances with the Eastern army, but due also to the bad winter weather and execrable roads of Virginia in that season. By April or May of 1862, the Army of the Potomac would be better organized, disciplined, and equipped for the more difficult offensive campaign into the heart of the Old Dominion. It was easier for partly trained troops to await an attack behind prepared positions than it was for similar troops to move against such defenses. Of course, this delay would give the enemy time, also, to augment his force. McClellan felt, too, that he could not with safety tell anyone

[53] 14 *O.R.*, 6–7.
[54] McClellan to Lincoln, December 10, 1861, Robert Todd Lincoln Collection of the Papers of Abraham Lincoln, Division of Manuscripts, Library of Congress.

of this delayed general Union offensive, for fear that leaks of supposedly top-secret information would warn Johnston and permit him to transfer part of his army for operations elsewhere. The success of the peripheral Federal expeditions to New Bern and New Orleans would be better insured by keeping Johnston's army indivisible at Centerville. However, as was probably natural, an impatient public, Congress, and administration, largely ignorant of the real military conditions, could not readily appreciate McClellan's seemingly dilatory methods.

Shortly after Congress reconvened, Horace Greeley and Senator Chandler, both Radicals, urged the demotion of McClellan and the reinstatement of McDowell as commander of the Army of the Potomac. However, Lincoln still remained friendly with the General-in-Chief, and resumed his frequent visits to his headquarters. On December 19, the President received a visit from an old and close friend, Senator Orville H. Browning of Illinois. The Senator recorded in his diary that night: "[Lincoln] proposed that I should go with him to call on Genl McClelland [*sic*] which I did, being my first meeting with him. I was favourably impressed— like his plain, direct straight forward way of talking and acting. He has brains— looks as if he ought to have courage, and I think, is altogether more than an ordinary man." Other Republicans of a more radical stamp were, however, growing much less enthusiastic in their opinions of Little Mac.[55]

On the day after Browning's visit, McClellan was able to recoup what little prestige he personally had lost in the Ball's Bluff disaster two months earlier. On December 20, McCall's Pennsylvania Reserve Division was victorious in a small but sharp engagement at Dranesville. The casualties in this severe little action were, for the Federals, 7 killed, 61 wounded—a total loss of 68; for the Confederates, 43 killed, 143 wounded,

[55] New York *Tribune*, December 14, 1861; Robert B. Warden, *Account of the Private Life and Public Services of Salmon Portland Chase* (Cincinnati, 1874), 392; Theodore Calvin Pease and James G. Randall (eds.), *The Diary of Orville Hickman Browning, 1850–1864* (Springfield, 1925), I, 515–16. (See T. Harry Williams, *Lincoln and the Radicals* (Madison, 1941), 118, 131.)

8 missing—a total loss of 194. This success went far toward raising Northern morale to a higher level than had existed for some weeks during this generally inactive period. The Dranesville combat turned out to be the last one of any proportions in 1861, and marked the last important event before a serious mishap befell the Union General-in-Chief.[56]

---

[56] J. R. Šypher, *History of the Pennsylvania Reserve Corps* . . . (Lancaster, 1865) , 129–41; Fox, *Regimental Losses*, 543, 549; Paris, *The Civil War*, I, 418–19.

Chapter Three

"The Stride of a Giant"

> Much has recently been said of military combinations and organizing victory. I hear such phrases with apprehension. They . . . resulted in Waterloo.
>
> —*Edwin M. Stanton*

ON December 20, 1861, official Washington heard suddenly that McClellan had been struck down by a grave malady. Weakened by overwork, exposure, and exhaustion, the General-in-Chief was confined to his bed with a serious case of the dread typhoid fever. There was doubt even as to the thirty-five-year-old commander's recovery.[1]

Although at times so ill as to be unable to receive visitors—including the President—McClellan was, at other times, able to study reports and to conduct some of the necessary administrative functions of the army. About January 1, 1862, he received a memorandum from the Corps of Engineers which contained a detailed description of "The Peninsula between the Potomac and Rappahannock"—an area known locally as the "Northern Neck." This survey included a report on the terrain lying directly between Washington and Richmond, and emphasized the many east-west rivers which would offer the Confederates numerous defensive positions should the Union Army advance overland from its own capital toward that of the enemy.[2] Even while sick, McClellan was giving considerable

[1] Paris, "McClellan Organizing the Grand Army," *loc. cit.*, 120; Heintzelman's Journal, entry of December 24, 1861.

[2] *M.O.S.*, 155; "Memorandum of Civil Engineers for General McClellan," about January 1, 1862, McClellan Papers.

thought to the problem of the best line of advance. However, reports from his secret service operatives, reaching the General on January 6 and 7, were far from encouraging. They placed the total number of Southern soldiers in Virginia at anywhere from 160,000 to 450,000. As against this supposedly massive host, McClellan could muster but 191,480 men present for duty in the entire Department of the Potomac.[3]

The sudden illness of his ranking general naturally caused concern to the anxious Lincoln. While being obliged to make sure the Federal capital was at all times safe, the President was nonetheless in sympathy with public opinion which called for an early advance of the Army of the Potomac. Noting Lincoln's concern, Attorney General Edward Bates suggested to Lincoln on December 31 that there was, in his opinion, no need for a General-in-Chief at all, and " that, being ' Commander in chief ' by law, he *must* command." Unable to converse with McClellan, and not knowing when he would recover from his illness, it was quite plausible for the President to seek the advice of some competent military minds as to the possibilities of an early advance by the Union Army, as well as to discuss the best route upon which it should move. Upon the urging of the Quartermaster General, Brigadier General Montgomery C. Meigs, Lincoln called McDowell and Franklin to the Executive Mansion for consultation on these subjects.[4]

Several councils of war were held at the White House on January 10 and 11. The President, McDowell, and Franklin were joined by a number of cabinet members. Lincoln gave a gloomy interpretation of affairs, and then said that he " would like to *borrow* the army " for a few weeks while McClellan was ill. When asked by the President what route the Army of the Potomac should adopt in its movement on Richmond, Mc-

---

[3] " E. J. Allen " to McClellan, December 16 and 31, 1861, January 6 and 7, 1862, McClellan Papers; *C.C.W.*, I, 139, 173, 180, 195; McClellan's *Report*, 10.

[4] *Bates's Diary*, 218–20, 223, 225; Montgomery C. Meigs's Diary, entry of January 10, 1862, Division of Manuscripts, Library of Congress; Montgomery C. Meigs, " The Relations of President Lincoln and Secretary Stanton to the Military Commanders in the Civil War," *American Historical Review*, XXVI, 292.

Dowell recommended the overland one through Manassas and Fredericksburg. Franklin at first favored an amphibious operation which would move the army down the bay and then up one of the rivers emptying into the lower Chesapeake. When informed that vessels were not then available for such an enterprise, Franklin reluctantly acquiesced in McDowell's proposed line, although he felt the army not yet ready to begin an offensive. Salmon P. Chase and William H. Seward, although unversed in military strategy, called strongly for an immediate movement by the overland route. Montgomery Blair, a West Point graduate, favored the water route. Lincoln voiced no opinion at this time.[5]

Meanwhile, as these meetings were in progress, Cameron suddenly resigned as Secretary of War on January 11. His place in the cabinet was taken by the former Democrat, Stanton, who was recognized as a forceful advocate of an immediate advance by the Federal Army. As indicative of the President's desire for early operations, an expedition under the command of Burnside—whose troops had been originally earmarked for McClellan's use against Richmond—was detached by the administration from the Army of the Potomac, and, on January 11, embarked from Hampton Roads for a sortie against New Bern on the coast of North Carolina.[6]

Learning from Stanton that councils of war were being held without his knowledge, McClellan, in his own words, " mustered strength enough on . . . Jan. 12 . . . to be driven to the White House, where my unexpected appearance caused very much the effect of a shell in a powder-magazine." He told Lincoln " in a general and casual way " what his campaign plans were, and was invited by the President to appear the following day at a larger meeting with the cabinet and with Franklin and

[5] William B. Franklin, " The First Great Crime of the War," A. K. McClure (ed.) , *The Annals of the War* . . . (Philadelphia, 1879) , 76–77; Notes of Irvin McDowell on these meetings, Swinton, *Army of the Potomac*, 79–82.

[6] Erastus Corning to Stanton, January 13, 1862, Stanton Papers (see also Williams, *Lincoln and the Radicals*, 15, 93) ; Testimony of Flag Officer Louis Goldsborough, April 1, 1863, *C.C.W.*, I, 631; 4 *O.R.*, 566.

McDowell. Although still somewhat ill with a disease which has long-lingering after-effects, McClellan consequently appeared at the afternoon conclave at the White House on the thirteenth. At Lincoln's request, McDowell and Franklin explained again their views as to the advisability of using the overland route if it were determined to commence operations immediately with the Army of the Potomac. Then followed an awkward silence, with all eyes fastened expectantly upon McClellan. The Young Napoleon remained silent. While Lincoln made a few unimportant general remarks, Meigs moved to McClellan's side, and, pointing out that everyone expected him to speak out on his strategic plans, urged him to do so. McClellan, however, told Meigs in a low voice that the President could not keep a secret for a day, and maintained his silence. Finally, in a somewhat obnoxious manner, Chase demanded that McClellan tell them his campaign plans. After a pause, McClellan replied in general terms, mentioning a movement in Kentucky of one of the Western armies. When pressed by the Secretary of the Treasury for further details, the General replied that it was unwise to divulge plans to such a large gathering, and said that he would not do so unless the President gave him a direct order in writing to that effect. Lincoln asked him if he had at least a definite plan and date in mind for an offensive in the East, and when McClellan replied in the affirmative the President said that he was satisfied and adjourned the meeting.[7]

McClellan was much criticized for his deliberate silence at this council. But he was right in believing that leaks had frequently—although unwittingly—occurred in official circles in Washington, and that the Confederates in Richmond were being informed almost instantly of what was transpiring within the supposedly secret war councils of the Lincoln administra-

[7] *M.O.S.*, 156–58; Franklin, " The First Great Crime of the War," *loc. cit.*, 78–79; Meigs's Diary, entry of January 13, 1862; McDowell's notes, Swinton, *Army of the Potomac*, 83-85; Meigs, " The Relations of President Lincoln . . . ," *loc. cit.*, 293.

tion.[8] Although he must have known that such a tight-lipped policy on his part would cause considerable irritation and misunderstanding in civilian and political circles, McClellan nonetheless felt it to be essential to the welfare of the Union cause not to reveal his plans to so many persons. He never refused, of course, to give the President the details of his plans in private whenever they were requested. Lincoln still retained confidence in the General, despite any unfavorable impressions which might have arisen at the recent councils.[9]

A few days after these eventful meetings, Stanton assumed the duties of Secretary of War. Before his appointment, it will be remembered, the new Secretary had been a caustic and violent critic of Lincoln and his administration, as well as a friendly supporter and legal adviser of McClellan.[10] With his intimate comrade of six months now at the head of the War Department, McClellan felt that he would have a stanch supporter and ally in prosecuting the military campaigns against the enemy in the most efficacious manner. However, he found to his consternation that the recent friendly attitude of Stanton towards him had changed suddenly into a frigid one, and the General-in-Chief had difficulty now in even getting an interview with the new Secretary.[11] Although without military training of any kind, Stanton believed in an immediate advance of the Army of the Potomac, and began to apply pressure upon Lincoln, as well as upon McClellan, to set the army in motion at once.[12]

[8] Lafayette C. Baker, *Spies, Traitors and Conspirators of the Late Civil War* (Philadelphia, 1894), 108; L. E. Chittenden, *Recollections of President Lincoln and his Administration* (New York, 1891), 386; *M.O.S.*, 158; David Homer Bates, *Lincoln in the Telegraph Office . . .* (New York, 1907), 95, 399–400.

[9] *Browning's Diary*, I, 525.

[10] *M.O.S.*, 152; Gideon Welles's Diary, Gideon Welles Papers, Box 2, Division of Manuscripts, Library of Congress.

[11] *M.O.S.*, 152, 154; Gideon Welles, *Lincoln and Seward* (New York, 1874), 190, 191, 193; Welles's Diary, *loc. cit.*

[12] Paris, "McClellan Organizing the Grand Army," *loc. cit.*, 120; George W. Julian, *Political Recollections, 1840–1872* (Chicago, 1882), 204; Nicolay and Hay, *Abraham Lincoln*, V, 159. Nicolay and Hay are untrustworthy as regards their presentation of affairs pertaining to McClellan, for they both personally

The divergence of Stanton's views from those of McClellan were soon revealed when the Secretary placed a message in Greeley's New York *Tribune*. This declaration was recognized as an unmistakable slap at McClellan and his policies, since it came from the man next to Lincoln in command of the Federal armies. The statement read: " Much has recently been said of military combinations and organizing victory. I hear such phrases with apprehension. They commenced in infidel France with the Italian campaign, and resulted in Waterloo. Who can organize victory? Who can combine the elements of success on the battlefield? We owe our recent victories to the Spirit of the Lord, that moved our soldiers to rush into battle, and filled the hearts of our enemies with dismay. The inspiration that conquered in battle was in the hearts of the soldiers from on high; and wherever there is the same inspiration there will be the same results." Immediately after taking office, Stanton requested and obtained an interview with the Radical-controlled Committee on the Conduct of the War, whose pressure for an instant advance of the National Army was well known.[18]

Two weeks having elapsed since the councils of war had met at the White House, and with no forward movement of the Army of the Potomac as yet evident, Lincoln unexpectedly issued on January 27 his celebrated President's General War Order No. 1. This directive—drawn up without consultation, even, of the General-in-Chief—called for a forward movement

disliked the General intensely. Hay said, in a private letter to Nicolay, August 10, 1885, while they were in the midst of writing their ten-volume work, " As to my tone towards Porter and McClellan—that is an important matter. I have toiled and labored through ten chapters over [McClellan]. I think I have left the impression of his mutinous imbecility, and I have done it in a perfectly courteous manner. . . . It is of the utmost moment that we should *seem* fair to him, while we are destroying him. . . . Destroy this letter." William Roscoe Thayer, *The Life and Letters of John Hay* (Boston, 1915), II, 31, 33; Tyler Dennett, *John Hay: From Poetry to Politics* (New York, 1933), 139.

[18] Stanton to Greeley, February 19, 1862, Stanton Papers; New York *Tribune*, February 20, 1862; Charles A. Dana, *Recollections of the Civil War . . .* (New York, 1898), 158; *C. C. W.*, I, 62–63. See Williams, *Lincoln and the Radicals*, 72 ff.

of all the armies of the Union on George Washington's birthday, February 22. This sentimental date was arbitrarily selected without apparent thought or consideration of necessary preparation or of weather conditions. The order was written in strictly nonmilitary language, and was obviously drawn up by a civilian. It was issued by the President under the unrelenting pressure of repeated demands for action by Stanton, the Committee on the Conduct of the War, and by Secretary of the Navy Gideon Welles, as well as under the general compulsion of impatient politicians and the public. The extreme insistence of Stanton, however, was the greatest single reason for the President's issuing the order. Lincoln yielded to this pressure, his personal secretaries aver, only when at the end of his patience with McClellan's alleged dilatoriness.[14]

The President's order for an army advance in February, if carried out, would, at the start, place McClellan's army in a difficult position. The roads at that season were almost bottomless due to rain and melting snow, and the ground too soft for effective use of artillery and cavalry.[15] Also, an army moving offensively into enemy territory—with its lines of communication lengthening while those of the enemy were growing shorter—required considerably more preparation, drill, and numbers than that of the defending force acting on interior lines and behind fieldworks, where one defender was equivalent to two or three attackers. Alexander S. Webb writes in regard to Lincoln and his directive, " Should he lean implicitly on the general actually in command of the armies, placed there by virtue of his presumed fitness for the position, or upon other advisers?. . . . It was doubt and hesitation upon this point, that occasioned many of the blunders of the campaign. Instead of one mind, there were many minds influencing the management

---

[14] Richardson (ed.), *Messages and Papers*, VI, 100–101; *Welles's Diary*, I, 95; George W. Julian, *Political Recollections* . . . (Chicago, 1884), 204; Albert Gallatin Riddle, *Recollections of War Times* . . . (New York, 1895), 181; James G. Blaine, *Twenty Years of Congress* . . . (Norwich, 1884), I, 355; Nicolay and Hay, *Abraham Lincoln*, V, 159.

[15] Heintzelman's Journal, entry of February 3, 1862.

of military affairs." Lincoln, keeping one eye on the political situation, undoubtedly felt that he was acting in the best possible way to further the Union cause.[16]

Not only did the President and Secretary of War determine the *date* upon which McClellan's army would move, but, by Lincoln's Special War Order No. 1, of January 31, they defined precisely what *route* the invading Federal Army had to adopt in moving against the enemy. This directive stated " that all the disposable force of the Army of the Potomac, after providing safely for the defense of Washington, be formed into an expedition for the immediate object of seizing and occupying a point upon the railroad southwestward of what is known as Manassas Junction, all details to be in the discretion of the [General]-in-Chief, and the expedition to move before or on the 22d day of February next." [17] This order reflected Lincoln's earlier views, which had been given in his questionnaire to McClellan of December 1, 1861. This new order revealed the sudden transformation of the President and Stanton from general, overall supervisors of military operations into direct strategists and tacticians.

McClellan immediately asked Lincoln if this last order was final, or whether he might be allowed to submit in writing to the President his objections to it, explaining the reasons for preferring his own plan of operations calling for an amphibious movement down the bay. Permission was granted, and the General set to work to compose a lengthy study of the relative merits and defects of the overland and coastal routes. While he was working on this memorandum, McClellan received the faulty intelligence that there were from 120,000 to 150,000 gray-clad soldiers in northern Virginia, with " 260 guns mounted in and around Centerville and about 60 at Manassas." A short time later, the enemy strength was placed at 385,000! [18] Appar-

[16] Webb, *The Peninsula*, 15.
[17] 5 *O.R.*, 41.
[18] " E. J. Allen " to McClellan, January 31, 1861, February 1, 2, 10, 22, 1862, McClellan Papers.

ently the General-in-Chief could see no logical reason for butting his head against the Confederates in a fortified position of their own choosing.

Before McClellan could submit his memorandum to Lincoln, the President sent him on the morning of February 3 the following note involving a problem of complicated military strategy:

> You and I have distinct and different plans for a movement of the Army of the Potomac . . .
>
> If you will give satisfactory answers to the following questions I shall gladly yield my plan to yours:
>
> 1st. Does not your plan involve a greatly larger expenditure of *time* and *money* than mine?
>
> 2nd. Wherein is a victory *more certain* by your plan than mine?
>
> 3rd. Wherein is a victory *more valuable* by your plan than mine?
>
> 4th. In fact, would it not be *less valuable* in this: that it would break no great line of the enemy's communications, while mine would?
>
> 5th. In case of disaster would not a retreat be more difficult by your plan than mine? [19]

The attitude of the administration toward McClellan in early 1862 might be contrasted with that toward General Grant in 1864. On April 30, 1864, Lincoln wrote to Grant, " The particulars of your plans I neither know or seek to know. . . . I wish not to obtrude any constraints or restraints upon you." Said Grant of the matter (although not quite accurately) , " I did not communicate my plans to the President, nor did I to the Secretary of War, or to General Halleck." In reply to a friend's question about his placing such a large degree of military control of operations in Grant's hands in 1864, Lincoln said, " Do you hire a man to do your work and then do it yourself? " [20]

---

[19] Lincoln to McClellan, February 3, 1862, Lincoln Papers.
[20] Lincoln to Grant, April 30, 1864, Roy P. Basler (ed.) , *The Collected Works*

Lincoln's five questions were answered by McClellan in a lengthy and important letter submitted to Stanton, who, in turn, passed it on to the President. In this memorandum, the General stated that the attacking side should have many more men than the defenders, but that the force which he had called for during the summer had not been given to him. He declared that he was not interested in a " barren victory, but looked to combined and *decisive* operations." To be " fully prepared " before moving, McClellan felt, was essential. He then went into an elaborate criticism of the administration's overland plan, pointing out the obstacle of the Confederate fieldworks at Manassas and Centerville. " The enemy," he said, " anticipates the movement in question, and is prepared to resist it." The early time of the year for an advance, the terrible condition of the roads then, the great length of the Federal lines of communication, and the necessarily slow pace of an advance by that route were particularized. McClellan declared that use of this overland course would compel the Federals to fight the Confederates on ground of the enemy's choosing. The numerous east-west rivers between Washington and Richmond would enable the graycoats, in withdrawing, to take up successive positions which were naturally strong and defensible.[21]

Turning to the coastal route, advocated by himself, McClellan stated in measured words that this line of advance afforded " the shortest possible land route to Richmond and [struck] directly at the heart of the enemy's power in the East." His movement down the bay would by necessity compel the Confederates to abandon their artillery positions on the lower Potomac, and would force the evacuation of their strong works at Manassas and Centerville. The General proposed to transport his army of 140,000 down the Chesapeake Bay, then up the Rappahannock River to Urbanna. From there, it would

of Abraham Lincoln (New Brunswick, 1953), VII, 324; U. S. Grant, *Personal Memoirs of U. S. Grant* (New York, 1885), II, 123; James R. Gilmore, *Personal Recollections of Abraham Lincoln and the Civil War* (Boston, 1898), 228.

[21] McClellan to Stanton, January 31, 1861, McClellan Papers. See also Basler (ed.), *Collected Works*, V, 120–24.

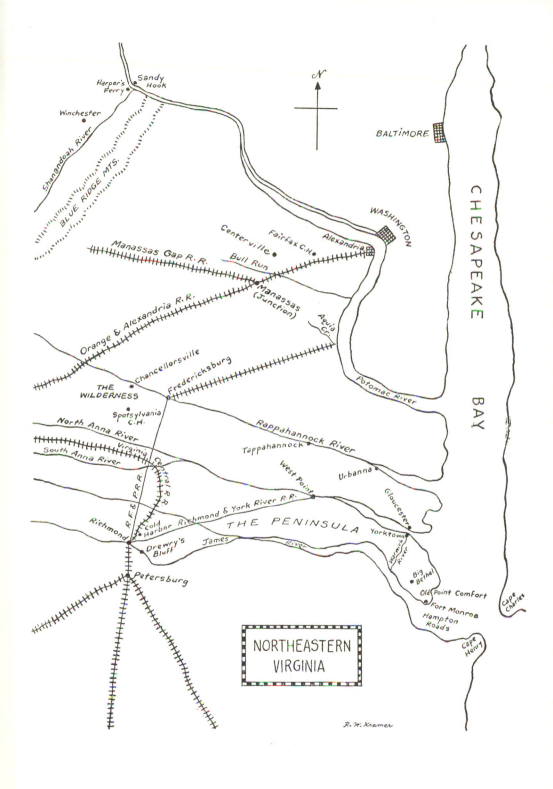

NORTHEASTERN
VIRGINIA

R. W. Kramer

be but a short one day's march to West Point on the York River, where a base would be set up. The railroad from West Point to Richmond would alleviate the supply problem. This movement, reasoned McClellan, would either cut off the Southern troops on the lower York-James Peninsula, or compel them to retreat rapidly into the environs of Richmond. It would also impel Johnston's main Confederate army to fall back hastily from Centerville and Manassas in order to make a desperate defense of Richmond. This operation, he asserted, would enable the superior Federal sea power to succor the army's advance. He mentioned here the possibility of crossing the James River and operating against Richmond from Petersburg and the south, thereby severing a number of important Confederate rail lines from the deeper South. In the event of defeat, the Army of the Potomac could retreat in safety upon Fortress Monroe, at Old Point Comfort on the tip of the Peninsula, which was then securely held by Wool's Union garrison. Should there be objections to the Urbanna route, McClellan recommended Mobjack Bay as an alternative point of disembarkation. As a third choice, Fortress Monroe itself could be used as a base for a necessarily slower and less brilliant advance up the Peninsula, with both flanks of the National Army being protected by Union gunboats on the York and James rivers. The General urged that if this coastal route were agreed upon, the government should begin at once to collect the transports to ship the army down the bay. Requiring less use of horses and mules for supplies than an advance on the overland line, McClellan felt that the movement down the Chesapeake would not cost the government much more in money than Lincoln's plan. Continuing, McClellan stated:

> If at the expense of 30 days delay we can gain a decisive victory which will probably end the war, it is far cheaper than to gain a battle tomorrow that produces no final results, & may require years of warfare and expenditure to follow up.
>
> Such I think is precisely the difference between the two plans discussed in this long letter. A battle gained at Manassas

will result merely in the possession of the field of combat—at best we can follow it up but slowly. . . .

In conclusion I would respectfully, but firmly, advise that I may be authorized to undertake at once the movement by Urbana.

I believe that it can be carried into execution so nearly simultaneously with the final advance of Buell & Halleck that the columns will support each other. . . .

He then added, significantly, " The movement [down the bay] if adopted, will not at all expose the city of Washington to danger." McClellan closed this most important dispatch by saying, " My judgment as a general is clearly in favor of this [coastal] project." [22]

When McClellan submitted his plan of operations, he expected the administration to either frankly approve it or reject it. The civilian authorities, however, remained silent. But they did not compel the General-in-Chief to carry out the movement on Manassas as ordered by the President's Special War Order No. 1. It just became assumed—possibly by conversation—that the Army of the Potomac would move via the coastal route.[23] Defending his decision before the Committee on the Conduct of the War, McClellan testified under oath, " I think no one regarded the line, by way of Manassas, as a practicable one, it being so long. The difficulty of guarding our communications was almost insuperable. . . . The other line gave us the advantage of water transportation, and rendered the largest possible amount of the force available for active operations, there being so few necessary to guard the depots and communications." [24]

A number of noted Confederate generals voiced the opinion that the water route was the best one the Federals could have adopted. McClellan's opponent in the early clashes on the Peninsula, Joe Johnston, said of the coastal line, " I did not

---

[22] McClellan to Stanton, January 31, 1861, McClellan Papers.
[23] Swinton, *Army of the Potomac*, 94; *M.O.S.*, 236–37; McClellan's *Report*, 49.
[24] Testimony of McClellan, February 28, 1863, *C.C.W.*, I, 427.

doubt that this route would be taken by General McClellan as it would be the most difficult to meet." The Southern commander on the lower Peninsula, Major General John B. Magruder, stated on February 1, 1862, that such an amphibian operation by McClellan, "landing in force on the Rappahannock," would "probably embarrass us greatly." [25]

After the tacit approval of McClellan's coastal project by the President and Secretary of War, the administration, for unknown reasons, delayed until February 27 in ordering the necessary steamers to transport the army down the bay.[26] Many of the authorities in Washington were criticizing the General-in-Chief for alleged tardiness in moving, while at the same time they themselves delayed, for almost one month, in even ordering the very means of transportation by which it had been agreed that McClellan's army would move against the enemy.

In the last week in February, a personal tragedy struck the occupant of the White House. Lincoln's little eleven-year-old son, Willie, died suddenly after a brief illness. To the distraught President and his wife, Mary Todd, there came but few messages of condolence. One of the finest was the one received from McClellan, who wrote Lincoln:

> I have not felt authorized to instrude upon you personally in the midst of the deep distress I know you feel in the sad calamity that has befallen you and your family. Yet I cannot refrain from expressing to you the sincere and deep sympathy I feel for you.
>
> You have been a kind true friend to me in the midst of the great cares and difficulties by which we have been surrounded during the past few months. Your confidence has upheld me when I should otherwise have felt weak. I wish now only to assure you and your family that I have felt the deepest sympathy in your affliction. I am pushing to prompt

---

[25] Johnston's *Narrative*, 101; Magruder to General Samuel Cooper, February 1, 1862, 9 *O.R.*, 41.

[26] Swinton, *Army of the Potomac*, 94; McClellan's *Report*, 49; 5 *O.R.*, 46; *M.O.S.*, 163, 237; Emory Upton, *The Military Policy of the United States* (Washington, 1916), 282.

completion the measures of which we have spoken, & I beg that you will not allow military affairs to give you a moments trouble. . . .[27]

But in a little over a week the amicable relations between Lincoln and McClellan took a turn for the worse. On March 8, the President summoned the General to the White House, and said that he had " a very ugly matter " to discuss with him. It was that the Chief Executive had heard, in such a way as to believe it, that the General-in-Chief had conceived the idea of transporting the bulk of the Army of the Potomac down the bay with the traitorous intent of deliberately exposing Washington to capture by the enemy. Lincoln ended his little speech, the General relates, " with the remark that it did look to him much like treason." McClellan leaped to his feet and hotly demanded an instant retraction and apology. The confused President quickly complied, saying that he had meant to say that there were such rumors afloat, but that he personally did not believe them. Stung by the relapse into hesitancy and the recurring doubts of the administration as to the wisdom of his approved coastal campaign plan, McClellan said that, in order to satisfy the President fully, he would perform the unusual military procedure of submitting his plan of operations to a vote of his twelve division commanders, then assembled at Fairfax Court House.[28]

Accordingly, McClellan explained his Urbanna plan in detail to his twelve subordinates. By a vote of eight to four, the plan was " approved " by the generals, the four opposing votes coming from McDowell, Heintzelman, Barnard, and Brigadier General Edwin V. Sumner—all Radical generals. McClellan was not in the room when the vote was taken. The twelve soldiers then repaired to the White House, where the eight who had voted in favor of McClellan's plan were closely questioned by Lincoln and Stanton. McClellan was not present.

[27] McClellan to Lincoln, Thomas, *Abraham Lincoln*, 304.
[28] George B. McClellan, " The Peninsular Campaign," *B. & L.*, II, 166; *M.O.S.*, 195–96; Paris, *The Civil War*, I, 612.

In answer to the question of when they thought the army could move down the bay, the reply was in about one month. Stanton then asked the eight generals if they were willing, as he phrased it, to make "this suffering country wait a month longer." The Secretary believed that the eight were actually afraid to fight. Lincoln closed the council then, Heintzelman writes, and "urged us all to go in heartily for this [coastal] plan." [29]

A little later on March 8, without consulting the General-in-Chief, Lincoln issued the President's General War Order No. 2, which directed McClellan to organize the Army of the Potomac into four corps, to be commanded by the senior division commanders—McDowell, Sumner, Heintzelman, and Keyes. Oddly enough, all were Radicals, and all but Keyes had voted against McClellan at the council of war held at Fairfax Court House. Of the twelve division commanders—all appointed by McClellan—a majority were "conservatives" and strong supporters of Little Mac. With all these soldiers now under the immediate command of four Radical corps commanders—none of whom could be termed a supporter of McClellan—the army commander and his favorites could now be more easily controlled by Stanton and his Radical friends in the cabinet and on the Committee on the Conduct of the War. Lincoln's order also placed the defenses of Washington and the troops in the works under the command of a political appointee—Brigadier General James S. Wadsworth. A fifth corps was to be created from the forces in the Harper's Ferry–Shenandoah Valley area, to be commanded by another political general, Banks, who had been former Speaker of the United States House of Representatives and Governor of Massachusetts. McClellan was opposed to the formation of army corps at this time, preferring to await active operations in the field which would reveal, under stress, the generals best fitted to command corps. In the Confederate Army, by contrast, army corps were not formed by Lee until after the Battle of Antietam, in September, 1862,

[29] Heintzelman's Journal, entry of March 8, 1862; *Hay's Diary*, 36; Thayer, *Letters of Hay*, I, 188–89; Franklin, "The First Great Crime," *loc. cit.*, 79–80.

when the Southern division commanders had seen eighteen months of service in that lower capacity.[30]

There was still another executive order forthcoming on March 8. Again without consulting the General-in-Chief, the administration issued the President's General War Order No. 3. This directive instructed McClellan to begin his movement down the bay not later than March 18. Moreover, the change of the base of operations could not be made until a force " in and about Washington " had been established so as to leave the capital " entirely secure." This force was to be determined by McClellan with the advice, again, of his corps commanders. The order further stipulated " that no more than two army corps (about 50,000 troops) of said army of the Potomac shall be moved en route for a new base of operations until the navigation of the Potomac from Washington to the Chesapeake Bay shall be freed from the enemy's batteries and other obstructions, or until the President shall hereafter give express permission." It also instructed the navy and army together to capture the Confederate batteries on the lower Potomac immediately.[31]

The effect of this well-intentioned war order was extraordinary in several respects. In the first place, it ordered an offensive for the middle of March without due regard to the weather conditions or state of preparations then existing. Secondly, although McClellan was held responsible for moving by the stated date, the ordering of water transportation had been taken out of his hands and placed in those of Assistant Secretary of War John Tucker. In the third place, the order to capture the Confederate batteries would require almost a major operation in itself, taking at best several weeks, and would thereby delay the approved and ordered main movement down the Chesapeake, as well as throw away the vital element

[30] McClellan's *Report*, 53; *M.O.S.*, 222; Richardson (ed.), *Messages and Papers*, VI, 110; Erasmus D. Keyes, *Fifty Years' Observation of Men and Events* (New York, 1884), 438; Swinton, *Army of the Potomac*, 64.

[31] McClellan's *Report*, 53; Stanton Papers, March 8, 1862; 14 *O.R.*, 57–58.

of surprise by forewarning the enemy at Centerville and Manassas of extensive operations against their right sea flank. In the fourth place, in allowing a movement of but two corps down the bay until the Confederate batteries on the lower Potomac were removed, the President's order failed to grasp the fact that these gun positions would automatically be evacuated as soon as the amphibious operation commenced. The restriction that the " express permission " of Lincoln would be needed before the remainder of McClellan's corps could go forward might well hamstring the General and place in jeopardy the two corps which would be landed from the lower Chesapeake, since the foe might rapidly concentrate a large force against these two unsupported corps. Also, it might seem odd that the wishes and views of the Union General-in-Chief were not consulted on such grave matters.[32]

On March 9, a new and complicating factor was thrust into the plans for the forward movement of McClellan's army. Word was received in Washington early that day of the destruction in Hampton Roads of two Union warships by the Confederate ironclad *Virginia* (ex-*Merrimac*). The news struck like a bombshell at the cabinet meeting which was then in progress at the War Department. According to Secretary of the Navy Welles, who was present, " the most frightened man on that gloomy day . . . was the Secretary of War. He was at times almost frantic. . . . The Merrimac, he said . . . could lay every city on the coast under contribution, could take Fortress Monroe; McClellan's mistaken purpose to advance by the lower Chesapeake must be abandoned, and Burnside [at New Bern, North Carolina] would inevitably be captured. Likely the first movement of the Merrimac would be to come up the Potomac and disperse Congress, destroy the Capitol and public buildings." Stanton was in a panic approaching imbecility when Welles calmly informed him of the arrival in Hampton Roads of the *Monitor*, and of the fact that the heavy draught of the

[32] See *M.O.S.*, 162–63; McClellan's *Report*, 54.

Virginia would prevent her passage of Kettle Bottom Shoals in the Potomac, thus keeping her below Washington. " The President himself was so excited," Welles wrote in his diary, " that he could not deliberate. . . . Stanton . . . ran from room to room, sat down and jumped up after writing a few words, swung his arms, scolded, and raved. . . . Both [Lincoln] and Stanton went repeatedly to the window—the view being interrupted for miles—to see if the Merrimac was not coming to Washington." Stanton thought the Confederates would " be in Washington before night." When news arrived of the *Monitor's* successful stand against the *Virginia,* a great feeling of relief came to the worried administration. Somehow or other, Stanton seemed to think that the Hampton Roads affair was, partially at least, McClellan's fault, and spoke to a friend " in terms which clearly indicated his want of confidence in " the General.[33]

The appearance of the ironclad monster and the threat to the Federal fleet in the lower Chesapeake led naturally to inquiries by McClellan and his chief subordinates as to whether the *Virginia* was now under sufficient control to permit the movement of the army down the bay, as planned and ordered. In answer to these queries, the able Assistant Secretary of the Navy, Gustavus V. Fox, assured the generals that the *Virginia* had been neutralized, and that the navy would be able to do its part in clearing the Confederates and their batteries from such rivers as the York and the James. Then, too, came some encouraging words from the Secretary of War to McClellan. " Nothing you can ask of me or of this Department will be spared to aid you in every particular," declared Stanton.[34] Thus assured, McClellan went ahead with his work to get the army ready to leave Washington.

The chance to make a movement came sooner than anyone expected. On March 8 and 9, Johnston suddenly withdrew the

[33] *Browning's Diary,* I, 532–33; *Welles's Diary,* I, 62–65; *Hay's Diary,* 36.
[34] 5 *O.R.,* 64; Fox to McClellan, March 9 and 14, 1862, Stanton to McClellan, March 13, 1862, McClellan Papers.

Confederate Army from its intrenched works at Centerville and Manassas. Perhaps he had gotten wind of the proposed Federal flanking operation down the bay and up the Rappahannock to Urbanna through unintentional leaks in Washington. On March 9, McClellan learned of the withdrawal of the Southern Army behind the Rappahannock. Since this development made the approach to Richmond by the Urbanna route impracticable, he determined to alter his plan of operations somewhat and disembark his army at Fortress Monroe, which offered a safe base for an advance up the Peninsula between the York and James rivers.[35]

McClellan decided to march the Army of the Potomac forward and occupy the abandoned Confederate works at Centerville and Manassas, and then to march it back to the environs of Washington before embarking for the lower Chesapeake. This march was severely criticized as useless and ridiculous. McClellan's reasons for ordering it, however, should be noted. "The retirement of the enemy," he stated, "presented an opportunity for the troops to gain some experience on the march and bivouac preparatory to the campaign, and to get rid of superfluous baggage and other impedimenta which accumulate so easily around an army encamped for a long time in one locality. A march to Manassas and back would produce no delay in embarking for the lower Chesapeake, as the transports could not be ready for some time, and it afforded a good intermediate step between the quiet and comparative comfort of the camps around Washington, and the rigors of active operations." [36]

Accordingly, the Army of the Potomac marched down to Centerville and Manassas. After examining the abandoned Confederate earthworks at these places, McClellan telegraphed Stanton on March 11, saying that he would occupy Manassas

[35] Johnston to Cooper, March 12, 1862, 5 *O.R.*, 526–27; *M.O.S.*, 222; Paris, " McClellan Organizing the Grand Army," *loc. cit.*, 121–22.
[36] McClellan's *Report*, 55; *M.O.S.*, 222–23.

" by a portion of Banks' command, and then at once . . . throw all the forces I can concentrate upon the lines agreed upon last week [*i. e.*, the lower Chesapeake]. The monitor [*sic*] justifies this course." Consequently, McClellan ordered Banks to entrench at Manassas, rebuild the Orange and Alexandria Railroad from that point to Washington, push forward cavalry vedettes, and reopen communications with the Shenandoah Valley. In the directive to Banks, McClellan emphasized this point: " The general object is to cover the line of the Potomac and Washington." In other words, Banks's command was an integral part of the defense network of the Federal capital.[37]

On this same day—March 11—Bates resumed his pressure upon Lincoln to remove McClellan as General-in-Chief, and to exercise direct command himself. " I . . . [urged] the Prest.," said Bates, " to take his constitutional position, and command the commanders—to have no General in Chief. . . . The upshot was that McC being in the field . . . is relieved from being Genl in Chief." It was true. Late that day, the administration issued the President's Special War Order No. 3, which relieved McClellan as Commanding General of the Union armies, and left him in command only of the Department of the Potomac. The order created also a new department situated amid the Appalachian Mountains, and known as the Mountain Department. It was to be commanded by the special friend of the Radicals, Major General John C. Frémont. Since no officer was named to succeed McClellan as General-in-Chief, the order instructed all department commanders to report directly to Stanton for their orders. Just before this directive had been issued, the Secretary, in an impromptu speech before a group including the President and cabinet, denounced " the imbecility which had characterized [McClellan's] operations." The administration did not promulgate the order until McClellan had left the capital for the field. Through a mix-up, McClellan and the

[37] McClellan to Stanton, March 14, 1862, McClellan to Banks, March 11, 1862, Lincoln Papers; *C.C.W.*, I, 311; McClellan's *Report*, 57; 5 *O.R.*, 742.

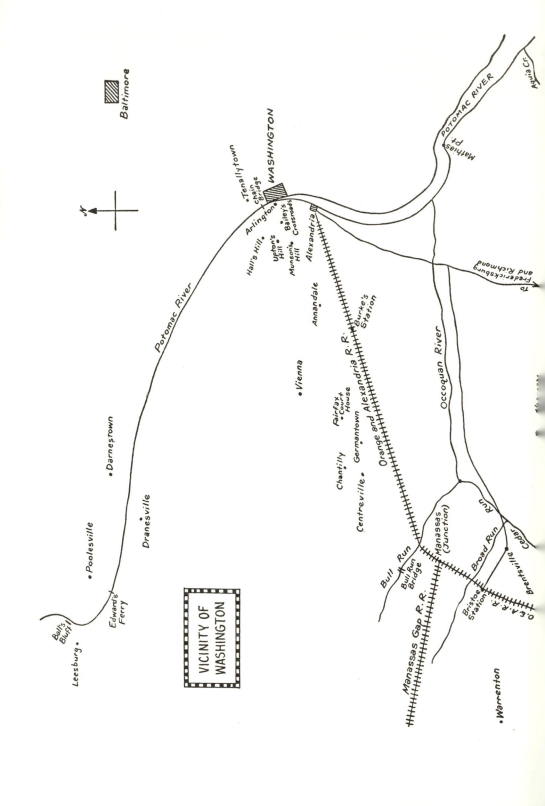

VICINITY OF WASHINGTON

army learned of his demotion the following day from the Washington *National Intelligencer.*[38]

Undoubtedly, in issuing this order, Lincoln felt that he was acting in the best interests of the Union cause. The political pressure on him was great. But the creation of yet another department—the Mountain—was unnecessary, and, as a sequel to this order, there was presented the spectacle of eight independent Federal armies in the East, with no General-in-Chief to command them.[39] Then, too, the demotion of McClellan was a humiliating vote of no-confidence by the administration in the general whose army was just beginning its maiden campaign against the enemy. No officer was named to succeed McClellan as General-in-Chief until July 23, 1862—four months later. Now, the strategic and even tactical command of the many and large armies of the Union rested with Lincoln and Stanton, " neither of whom professed any knowledge of the military art." [40]

McClellan took his unceremonious and sudden demotion in a manly and cordial way. He said in a note to Lincoln, " No feeling of self-interest or ambition should ever prevent me from devoting myself to your service. . . . I shall work just as cheerfully as before, and no consideration of self will in any manner interfere with the discharge of public duties." He thanked the President for " the official and personal kindnesses you have so often evinced towards me." In a letter to his wife that night, McClellan told her not to be worried about his demotion, and to " say nothing about it." He did, however, on March 13, protest to Stanton about the selection of the political general, Wadsworth, to command the intricate defenses of Washington, but to no avail.[41]

[38] *Bates's Diary,* 239; Richardson (ed.), *Messages and Papers,* VI, 111; Heintzelman's Journal, entry of March 12, 1862; Marcy to McClellan, March 12, 1862. McClellan Papers; Julian, *Political Recollections,* 205; McClellan's *Report,* 58.

[39] See Charles A. Whittier, " Comments on the Peninsular Campaign of General McClellan," Theodore F. Dwight (ed.), *Campaigns in Virginia, 1861-1862* (Boston, 1895), 293–94; Cox, *Military Reminiscences,* I, 195.

[40] See Upton, *Military Policy,* 284, 291–92.

[41] McClellan to Lincoln, March 12, 1862, Lincoln Papers; McClellan to his wife, March 12, 1862, McClellan Papers; *M.O.S.,* 224, 226.

Since the retirement of the Confederate Army behind the Rappahannock had forced McClellan to adopt a new line of advance, he had selected the Peninsula because Federal sea power would be able to be used to protect his flanks as the army moved on Richmond. Feeling the need for the backing of his corps commanders in the event of further opposition to his plans by the administration, McClellan submitted his revised Peninsula scheme to the vote of the four top generals at Fairfax Court House on March 13. Although McDowell, Sumner, Heintzelman, and Keyes were known as anti-McClellan Radicals, and although it was widely recognized that they were named to their commands by the administration against McClellan's wishes, they nonetheless approved his plan unanimously. Also, in accordance with the President's instructions, they spoke out on the question of the security of the National capital. They stated that a total of 40,000 men should be earmarked for the defense of Washington. They felt that the success of the great undertaking down the bay would necessitate the use of all four corps of the Army of the Potomac, plus the addition of 10,000 men from Fortress Monroe. McDowell's First Corps " was to be embarked last, as [it was] . . . intended to move it in mass to its point of disembarcation, and to land it on either bank of the York, as might be determined," in order to turn the Confederate strongholds of Yorktown and Gloucester. The corps commanders expected also effective assistance from naval gunboats in reducing these two Southern bastions on the York River. McClellan assented to these recommendations and informed the administration of the campaign details.[42]

In reply, Stanton declared that McClellan would have command over Wool's force stationed at Fortress Monroe, his base of operations at the tip of the Peninsula. " All the forces and means of the government," asserted the Secretary, " will be at your disposal." But in a later message that day to McClellan,

[42] 5 *O.R.,* 55–56; *C.C.W.,* I, 12; 14 *O.R.,* 58; McClellan's *Report,* 59–60; Barnard, *Peninsular Campaign,* 73; 15 *O.R.,* 223–24; Keyes to Stanton, March 14, 1862, Stanton Papers.

Stanton said that while Lincoln approved the new coastal plan, he gave three " directions as to it execution ":

> 1. Leave such force at Manassas Junction as shall make it entirely certain that the enemy shall not repossess himself of that position and line of communication.
>
> 2. Leave Washington entirely secure.
>
> 3. Move the remainder of the force down the Potomac, choosing a new base at Fortress Monroe, or anywhere between here and there, or, at all events, move such remainder of the army at once in pursuit of the enemy by some route.[43]

While Lincoln was justified in having emphasized the absolute need for safeguarding Washington from capture by the enemy, it was really unnecessary to insist upon holding Manassas in force. With McClellan's large army operating close to Richmond with secure water lines of communication, and with the bridges south of Manassas having been destroyed by the retreating Confederates, it was unfeasible for a large enemy force either to threaten Manassas or menace Washington by this overland route. A large-scale enemy movement east of the Blue Ridge Mountains toward Manassas and the Federal capital was not practicable because it would immediately expose the right flank, rear, and line of communication of the Confederate column to destruction by McClellan's main army in the vicinity of Richmond. A sudden dash by the graycoats upon Washington was unlikely, too, due to the garrisoned fortifications on both sides of the Potomac in front of the National capital. At the approach of any hostile force, the Federals could burn or blow up the three bridges over the wide, unfordable Potomac at Washington. To move in force and in safety upon Washington, the Southerners would have to march the round about way down the Shenandoah Valley, where their right flank would be protected by the Blue Ridge. And a Union force was stationed in the Valley to guard against such a movement in that quarter.

[43] Stanton to McClellan, March 13, 1862, McClellan Papers; Richardson (ed.), *Messages and Papers,* VI, 111.

Despite his protestations of support to McClellan, Stanton was seeking to remove him even from command of the Army of the Potomac. The Secretary had summoned to Washington Ethan Allen Hitchcock, sixty-four-year-old hero of the Mexican War, and religious mystic. Hitchcock was in such poor health that, en route from St. Louis, the excitement caused him to have "a serious and violent hemorrhage at Pittsburg." Upon his arrival in the Federal capital early in March, Stanton commissioned him a major general and placed him on special duty in the War Department as military adviser to himself and the President. Hitchcock also was named Chairman of the Army Board, made up of the bureau chiefs. Returning from the War Department to his hotel on the first day of his arrival, he was, as he describes it, "seized with a profuse bleeding at the nose—the sixth or seventh time in three weeks. Two physicians finally stopped the bleeding by mechanical means and I was sent to bed, very much exhausted." When he reported for duty the next day at the War Department, Stanton exploded a bombshell. Hitchcock reported it in this way: "On reporting to the Secretary, almost without a word of preface he asked me if I would take McClellan's place in command of the Army of the Potomac! I was amazed, and told him at once that I could not." [44]

The great invasion got underway on March 17 with the embarkation at Alexandria of Heintzelman's Third Corps.[45] This tremendous military operation has been called, by a foreign observer, "the stride of a giant," [46] and it fully justifies that encomium. It was one of the greatest amphibious operations of modern military history up to that time. Despite the dangerous restraining orders of the administration and the hostility of Stanton, McClellan and his splendid army were at

[44] William A. Croffut (ed.), *Fifty Years in Camp and Field: The Diary of Major-General Ethan Allen Hitchcock, U. S. A.* (New York, 1909), 437–39; Hitchcock to Mrs. Mary Mann, March 15, 1862, Ethan Allen Hitchcock Papers, Division of Manuscripts, Library of Congress.

[45] Webb, *The Peninsula*, 32–33.

[46] See Swinton, *Army of the Potomac*, 100.

last on the way to the arena of active operations against the main Confederate army. The blue chips were again in the center of the table. McClellan had high hopes for success, despite the restrictions of the government in Washington which had considerably limited the effectiveness of his plans. He still had four powerful army corps with which to cross swords with Joe Johnston, or so he thought!

Chapter Four

The Weapon Blunted

> If they will simply let me alone I feel sure
> of success.
> —*George B. McClellan*

WITH McClellan's vanguard sailing down the Chesapeake Bay to engage the enemy on the Peninsula southeast of Richmond, an examination of the relations between the General and the Secretary of War is of interest and significance. On March 19, in a telegram from Washington, Chief Engineer Barnard informed McClellan of a conversation he had just had with Stanton. The Secretary had stated to Barnard that " Gen. McClellan has no firmer friend than myself. . . . I think General McClellan ought not to move till he is fully ready." On the twenty-second, Stanton said to McClellan, " Please signify to me your wishes—I am rejoiced that you are getting along so well." However, just a few days later, in a conference with a group of legislators, "the Secretary arraigned [McClellan's] conduct in the severest terms, particularizing his blunders, and branding them." He felt that the President was in McClellan's power and that there were a number of traitors intimate with the General. The attitude then held by Stanton did not augur well for the future rapport between himself and McClellan. Certainly this was not the " confidence and cordial support " which Lincoln had said was essential to the young general's success.[1]

[1] Barnard to McClellan, March 19, 1862, Stanton to McClellan, March 22, 1862, McClellan Papers; Julian, *Political Recollections*, 210.

74

The War Department was interested in the probable development of the campaign on the Peninsula, and Stanton requested McClellan's views. " We shall fight a decisive battle," McClellan replied, " between West Point and Richmond, to give which battle the rebels will concentrate all their available forces." The Union commander felt the Federals should do likewise. He predicted that a siege of " many weeks " before Yorktown would result unless the Federal Navy were to cooperate with " it's most powerful vessels " in " a combined naval and land attack upon Yorktown." He went on to say that " a strong corps would be pushed up the York, under cover of the navy, directly upon West Point," where a base of operations would be established, just twenty-five miles from Richmond. In closing, McClellan spoke of Yorktown as " the most important point—there the knot to be cut." Especially concerned with the part the navy would play, he requested of the administration an immediate decision on this matter.[2]

The next day, however, brought word from Washington which was scarcely encouraging. After having spoken with Lincoln and Stanton, McDowell wired on March 20 that there was now doubt as to the navy people's ability " to do their part " in the operations around Yorktown, which, along with Gloucester Point across the river, was the key to the passage of the York River. Somewhat alarmed at the turn of events, McClellan immediately telegraphed Stanton, " Have you received my letter in regard to cooperation of the Navy? If so please see the President at once and telegraph the reply. On your reply much depends for as you will see from my letter I have now to choose between two methods of accomplishing an object." The answer came forthwith from the Secretary: " In order to determine the precise cooperation you want with the Navy the President will go immediately to Alexandria, and desires you to meet him at the wharf." [3]

[2] McClellan to Stanton, March 19, 1862, *C.C.W.*, I, 313–14; 5 *O.R.*, 57–58.
[3] McDowell to McClellan, March 20, 1862, McClellan Papers; McClellan to Stanton, March 20, 1862, Lincoln Papers; 14 *O.R.*, 18.

Meanwhile, when McClellan's advance divisions disembarked at Fortress Monroe, they were moved forward as rapidly as possible through "mud almost knee deep." Big Bethel fell to them on March 27, thus avenging a Union defeat there of the year before. The Federal maps of the Peninsula showed the Warwick River, on the lower Peninsula, to be a short stream running parallel to the York and James rivers, and thus forming no military obstacle. However, when advance elements of McClellan's army neared Yorktown on April 3, it was discovered that the Warwick was in reality a longer river running directly *across* the Peninsula and squarely in the path of the Union advance, thereby forming a serious natural obstacle. McClellan reported to Stanton that there were then about 15,000 Confederate troops defending Yorktown. He pushed his columns forward toward that point without even waiting for the usual number of supply wagons to accompany them. To handicap the Federal advance further, snow commenced falling on March 29.[4]

Political pressure back in Washington was also to have a serious effect on McClellan's operations northwest of Fortress Monroe. On March 30, the special military adviser to the administration, Hitchcock, urged the President to refrain from sending additional troops to Frémont in the Mountain Department, but rather, to augment McClellan's right flank on the York River.[5] Stanton then informed Lincoln that McClellan had just told the War Department that there were " to be left around Washington " the following Federal forces:

Banks Corps [in the Shenandoah Valley].... 30,000
Troops in Washington about.............. 20,000
                                          ─────
                                          50,000

There was no objection raised by the Secretary to the disposition

---

[4] Wool to McClellan, March 26, 1862, McClellan Papers; 14 *O.R.*, 41–42; *M.O.S.*, 256; Gideon Welles to Edgar T. Welles, March 30, 1862, Welles Papers; Heintzelman's Journal, entry of March 30, 1862; Webb, *The Peninsula*, 50–53; McClellan to Stanton, McClellan to his wife, April 3, 1862, McClellan Papers.
[5] Hitchcock to Lincoln, March 30, 1862, Hitchcock Papers.

of these troops. In fact, apparently feeling the capital to be protected more than adequately, Stanton made the following signal recommendation to the President which was directly contrary to that of Hitchcock:

> I would advise sending to General Fremont
>
> 1st Blenker's Division— 8,500
> 2 Hooker's Division— 9,000
> Total infantry—17,500 [6]

Just before McClellan himself sailed for Fortress Monroe, he met the President on a steamer at Alexandria. Here, obviously reflecting Stanton's influence, Lincoln told the General that he had been under pressure to remove Blenker's division from his command and to give it to Frémont. However, he then gave McClellan several reasons why he would not buckle under this pressure, and pledged that Blenker would remain with the Army of the Potomac. This was reassuring news to McClellan, whose army was then committed to a specific plan which was already underway, with calculations based upon the administration-authorized use of approximately 155,000 men. On March 31, however, on the eve of his own departure for the Peninsula, McClellan was " much surprised " to receive a sharp, stunning message from Lincoln: " This morning I felt constrained to order Blenker's division to Frémont, and I write this to assure you that I did so with great pain, understanding that you would have it otherwise. If you could know the full pressure of the case I am confident that you would justify it, even beyond a mere acknowledgement that the Commander in Chief may order what he pleases." This removal of Blenker, along with the earlier detachment of Burnside, was the real start of the splintering-off of sizable elements of McClellan's army which was to weaken very seriously the main expedition against Richmond.[7]

McClellan replied at once to this unfortunate order in a

[6] Stanton to Lincoln, March 30, 1862, Stanton Papers.
[7] 5 *O.R.*, 58; McClellan's *Report*, 63; *M.O.S.*, 164; Lincoln to McClellan, March 31, 1862, McClellan Papers.

" private " note to the President, declaring, " I need not say that I regret the loss of Blenker's division." The letter to Lincoln continued, " I fully appreciate, however, the circumstances of the case and hasten to assure you that I cheerfully acquiesce in your decision without any mental reservations. Recognizing implicitly as I can do the plenitude of your powers as Commander in Chief, I cannot but regard the tone of your note . . . as adding one more to the many of personal regard you have so honored me with. I shall do my best to use all the more activity to make up for the loss of this division, and beg to assure you that I will ever do my very best to carry out your views and support your interests in the same frank spirit you have always shown me." McClellan reported that, in a conversation with Lincoln a few hours later, the President promised " that no more troops beyond these 10,000 [of Blenker's division] should in any event be taken from me or in any way detached from my command." [8]

McClellan departed for Fortress Monroe on the afternoon of April 1 aboard the steamer *Commodore*. He wrote his wife Ellen, as he was leaving Washington, that he was " very glad to get away from that sink of iniquity." [9] As he was boarding the *Commodore*, McClellan dispatched to Adjutant General Thomas the following table of forces left behind by him for the protection of Washington, and directed him to place it before Stanton:

Wadsworth to have about.... 18,000 men for the Washington forts
At Warrenton.............. 7,780
At Manassas.............. 10,859
In the Shenandoah Valley... 35,467
On the lower Potomac...... 1,350
          In all.......... 73,456 men.[10]

---

[8] McClellan to Lincoln, March 31, 1862, Lincoln Papers; 5 *O.R.*, 59; McClellan's *Report*, 64; *M.O.S.*, 164–65.

[9] McClellan's *Report*, 53; McClellan to his wife, April 1, 1862, McClellan Papers.

[10] McClellan to Thomas, April 1, 1862, Lincoln Papers; 14 *O.R.*, 59–60.

There were some discrepancies in this table, but they did not materially reduce the total number earmarked for the defense of the Federal capital. He included in the force to be at Manassas a number of regiments to be brought down from Pennsylvania, as well as troops then acting as railroad guards in Maryland. He also inadvertently counted the force at Warrenton twice. McClellan included Blenker's division in the table, but he had been authorized to "detain [Blenker] at Strasburg [in the Valley] until matters assumed a definite form in that region before proceeding to his ultimate destination." This discretion had been given to McClellan on March 31 in a message from Stanton, which stated, "The order in respect to Blenker is not designed to hinder or delay the movement of Richardson or any other force. [Blenker] can remain wherever you desire him as long as required for your movement, and in any position you desire . . . and he may go to Harper's Ferry by such route and at such time as you shall direct." [11]

One of the greatest controversies of the Civil War rages around the question of whether McClellan, when he left for the Peninsula with his army, left Washington secure against any possible Confederate *coup de main.* Chief Engineer Barnard, on December 10, 1861, submitted a report on the state of the defenses of the capital, saying that "the number of guns . . . is about 480, requiring about 7,200 men to furnish three reliefs of gunners. The permanent garrison need consist only of these gunners, and even in case of attack it will seldom be necessary to keep full garrisons in all the works." He implied that about 20,000 men for "the total garrisons" would be needed. On March 13, 1862, it will be remembered, McClellan's four corps commanders had recommended a total of about 40,000 troops for the safeguarding of the capital. War correspondent Swinton states that "these [73,456] troops were not, it is true, all concentrated at Washington, but they were all available for its defense." Major General John Pope—McClel-

---

[11] See Colin R. Ballard, *The Military Genius of Abraham Lincoln: An Essay* (London, 1926), 74–75; McClellan's *Report,* 67.

lan's first successor—testifying under oath on July 8, 1862, before the Committee on the Conduct of the War, declared, " It is not necessary . . . in order to protect the capital, that I should interpose myself between the enemy and the place itself." He said that Union forces situated on the flanks of any northward-moving Confederate army, and in the Valley, would be in the best positions to defend Washington. Writing after the war, McClellan stated, " I left about 42,000 troops for the immediate defense of Washington, and more than 35,000 for the Shenandoah Valley—an abundance to insure the safety of Washington and to check any attempt to recover the lower Shenandoah and threaten Maryland." While McClellan's estimates were a bit too high, he was correct in saying that the capital was perfectly safe.[12]

Lincoln and Stanton, however, seemed to think that only troops in the immediate works of Washington should be counted in the total number of men disposed for the defense of the capital. McClellan subsequently testified under oath that " the force to be left in the Shenandoah Valley was counted in the number for the defense of Washington." And, as Emory Upton shows, " the Shenandoah Valley . . . was the only route by which the national capital could be safely approached " by the Confederates. In his official report to the Secretary of War, McClellan stated that, as the Southerners had withdrawn behind the Rappahannock, " they had destroyed all the railroad bridges behind them, thereby indicating that they did not intend to return over that route. Indeed, if they had attempted such a movement, their progress must have been slow and difficult, as it would have involved reconstruction of the bridges. . . . There would have been ample time to concentrate the entire force left for [Washington's] defense." The General said further " that the movement of the army to the Peninsula, would have

[12] Barnard's report, 12 *O.R.*, 107; 5 *O.R.*, 55–56; *C.C.W.*, I, 12; Barnard, *Peninsular Campaign*, 73; Keyes to Stanton, March 14, 1862, Stanton Papers; Pope's testimony, July 8, 1862, *C.C.W.*, I, 278; Swinton, *Army of the Potomac*, 92; McClellan, " The Peninsular Campaign," *loc. cit.*, 168.

the effect to draw off the rebel army from Manassas to the defense of their capital, and thus free Washington from menace. This opinion was confirmed the moment the movement commenced. . . ." [13]

Just before departing in person for Fortress Monroe, McClellan sent his Chief of Staff, Marcy, to Hitchcock with the list of troops to be left for the capital's security. Hitchcock refused to voice any opinion as to the adequacy of this arrangement, insisting that McClellan knew better than anyone else what force was sufficient for the safety of Washington since he had been for a long time in command of the building of the fortifications. Summing up under oath, McClellan testified, " Before I left Washington I was satisfied that it was not then in danger. . . . Of one thing I am confident, that with the facts fresh in my mind I thought that I left more than suggested by any corps commander." [14] McClellan should, however, have explained in person to Lincoln and Stanton the details of precisely what forces had been left, where they were, and what the defense strategy was for the capital's security, since the President and Secretary were themselves handling the duties which ordinarily would have been performed by the General-in-Chief, had there been one. Lincoln and Stanton were untrained in such technical military matters of strategy, and McClellan would have done better to have used more tact and to have treated his civilian superiors in a somewhat less cavalier fashion.

And what were the feelings then of Lincoln and Stanton toward their chief field commander in the East? On the evening of April 2, Senator Browning had an intimate conversation with the President at the White House. Browning was an old and close friend of Lincoln's, and the President spoke out freely to him, saying that " he still had confidence in McClellands [*sic*] fidelity . . . and that he had never had any reason to doubt it." Browning recorded in his diary Lincoln's description that,

[13] McClellan's testimony, December 11, 1862, 15 *O.R.*, 99–100; Upton, *Military Policy*, 288–89, 291, 292; McClellan's *Report*, 68; 5 *O.R.*, 62–63, 68.
[14] 5 *O.R.*, 63; McClellan's *Report*, 68; McClellan's testimony, December 11, 1862, 15 *O.R.*, 100.

when he had taken leave of McClellan at the wharf in Alexandria, the General had " shed tears when speaking of the cruel imputations upon his loyalty." However, the Chief Executive said that he still thought McClellan was too cautious and not quite up to meeting a crisis. Stanton then entered the room and declared aloud that he did not agree with the charges of some politicians that McClellan was a traitor. As Browning and Stanton " rode down the avenue," however, the Secretary, now beyond the President's earshot, " expressed the opinion that McClelland [sic] ought to have been removed long ago, and a fear that he was not in earnest, and said that he did not think that he could emancipate himself from the influence of Jeff Davis, and feared that he was not willing to do anything calculated greatly to damage the cause of secession, and that if I would propose to the President to appoint Col N B Buford of Illinois a Majr Genl. and give him Command of the army here he would second my application." Yet, just four days later, Stanton was writing to McClellan, pledging wholeheartedly all the confidence and support that the General could ask of himself and the War Department.[15]

On the rainy afternoon of April 2, McClellan himself arrived at Old Point Comfort to assume personal command of the Army of the Potomac in the field. Stanton's assistant, John Tucker, observing and helping to coordinate the mighty movement of 100,000-odd men, wired his superior on the second, " For economy and celerity of movement, this expedition is without a parallel on record." [16] At the same time that McClellan was stepping ashore at Fortress Monroe, Wadsworth, in command of the works at Washington, reported to Stanton that he had an aggregate of 20,477 men in the forts, with 19,022 present for duty. Wadsworth claimed that this force was " inadequate " for defending Washington, although he admitted that the

---

[15] *Browning's Diary*, I, 537–39; Stanton to McClellan, April 6, 1862, 12 *O.R.*, 14–15; McClellan's *Report*, 83; *M.O.S.*, 265; 14 *O.R.*, 73; Alexander K. McClure, *Abraham Lincoln and Men of War-Times* (Philadelphia, 1892), 167.

[16] Heintzelman's Journal, entry of April 2, 1862; *M.O.S.*, 265; *Swinton, Army of the Potomac*, 100.

enemy would not attempt an assault on the city. When asked how many troops in all were needed to guarantee the safety of the capital, he replied under oath that " not less than 25,000 first class troops " were necessary. He did not consider the Federal forces in the Shenandoah Valley or elsewhere in northern Virginia as comprising a part of the defending forces of Washington.[17]

The alarm spread. Hitchcock testified that " a good deal of concern was expressed and felt by the Secretary of War " concerning the number of troops left, and Lincoln " was manifestly under grave anxiety." Stanton sprang into action at once. He asked Hitchcock and Thomas to investigate whether the President's order to " leave Washington entirely secure " " had been complied with " by McClellan, as well as to inspect the military situation around Manassas. Although comparatively unfamiliar with these matters, Hitchcock and Thomas immediately set out on their mission. After a hurried ride along part of the thirty-three miles of forts and a quick survey at Manassas, they reported back to Stanton. They voiced the opinion that Lincoln's requirements for the security of the capital had not been fully satisfied by McClellan " if there was need of a military force for the safety of the city of Washington within its own limits." They stated that Manassas was not likely to be reoccupied by the Confederates, because the enemy had torn up the railroad south of that point; therefore, " no large force would be necessary to hold that position " by the Federals. They declined to express an opinion as to whether Banks's corps in the Valley " should be regarded as part of the force available for the protection of Washington." Later, under oath, Hitchcock testified that he personally did not consider the troops in the Shenandoah as properly constituting a part of the defense network of Washington.[18]

[17] Wadsworth to Stanton, April 2, 1862, Stanton Papers; *C.C.W.*, I, 14–15, 253; 14 *O.R.*, 60–61; Wadsworth's testimony, December 17, 1862, 15 *O.R.*, 113, 114, 224–25.

[18] Hitchcock's testimony, January 16, 1863, 15 *O.R.*, 219–20; *C.C.W.*, 15–17, 304–305; Stanton to Hitchcock and Thomas, April 2, 1862, Stanton Papers;

Lincoln immediately issued a directive to Stanton, instructing him to detain either the corps of McDowell or Sumner " in front of Washington," instead of permitting all of McClellan's army to continue embarking for the Peninsula. This detained corps, the order continued, was to operate only " in the direction of Manassas Junction." The President was, perhaps unconsciously, after everything had been supposedly settled, endeavoring to combine his own preferred overland route of advance with that of McClellan's coastal line. This well-intentioned order reduced by nearly 40,000 men—or by nearly one third—the authorized force with which McClellan had undertaken to conduct the campaign on the Peninsula.[19]

McDowell, who had spoken with Lincoln and Stanton at this time, testified, " I think that one division of Sumner's corps had gone [to the Peninsula], and that my corps was the only one intact; and the Secretary decided the matter himself, and ordered me to remain." McClellan had been counting on using McDowell's whole First Corps of about 40,000 men, augmented by 10,000 from Fortress Monroe, as a flying column up the York River to West Point, thereby outflanking and rendering untenable the enemy strongholds of Yorktown and Gloucester. His strategy had been seriously compromised. Although now once again having a *de facto* independent command, McDowell—although friendly with the anti-McClellan Radicals—opposed his detachment from the Army of the Potomac and voiced regret that it had taken place.[20] One of McDowell's division commanders, Franklin, reported to McClellan concerning the detention of the First Corps: " McDowell told me that it was intended as a blow at you. Stanton had said that you intended to work by strategy and not by fighting. That all of the opponents of the Administration centered

14 *O.R.*, 57; Hitchcock and Thomas to Stanton, April 2, 1862, Stanton Papers; 5 *O.R.*, 63.

[19] Hitchcock's testimony, January 21, 1863, *C.C.W.*, I, 305; Upton, *Military Policy*, 292; Lincoln to Stanton, April 3, 1862, Stanton Papers.

[20] McDowell's testimony, June 27, 1862, *C.C.W.*, I, 262; Franklin to McClellan, Fitz John Porter Papers, Vol. III, Division of Manuscripts, Library of Congress.

around you, in other words that you had political aspirations. There were no friends of yours present to contradict these statements, of course, but McDowell told Stanton . . . that he opposed the detachment of his corps from you. . . . He used all the arguments he knew of to convince Stanton that he was making a mistake." [21]

The order removing McDowell's corps from his command reached McClellan on April 4. In the absence of a General-in-Chief, the First Corps was now placed under the direct orders of Lincoln and Stanton. It will be recalled that McClellan had received written permission on March 20 from the Secretary to draw from Wool's garrison at Fortress Monroe a division of 10,000 men, as well as authority (on March 26) granting him control over the fort and its garrison. Then suddenly, on the evening of April 3, without warning or explanation, just as his troops were engaging the enemy at Yorktown and along the dammed-up Warwick River, McClellan received another staggering blow. This was an order from the administration stating that, although the President had placed the troops of the fort at his disposal, McClellan was not to reduce the number of men there below the figure Wool felt was needed at the fort. The directive went on to say that now Wool was to be in command of the fort and its garrison. The effect of this order was to reverse the earlier pledge to McClellan, to remove an additional 10,000 men from his active column of operations, and to withdraw from his control his main base of supply and communication. Thus, a total of 60,000 men had been removed from McClellan's invading army, so that now, instead of the 155,000 men he had counted on using, the General had but about 95,000. As events were to demonstrate, he would need the heavy numerical superiority for which he had earlier called.[22] As the New York *Times* war correspondent Swinton

[21] Franklin to McClellan, F. J. Porter Papers, Vol. III; Franklin, "The First Great Crime," *loc. cit.,* 80–81; Franklin to McClellan, April 7, 1862, McClellan Papers.

[22] Thomas to McClellan, April 3 and 4, 1862, Stanton to McClellan, March 20 and 26, 1862, McClellan Papers; Paris, *The Civil War,* II, 8; Webb, *The Peninsula,* 50.

85

writes, " In this [detaching of McDowell, Lincoln] acted from what may be called the common sense view of the matter. But in war, as in the domain of science, the truth often transcends, and even contradicts, common sense. It required more than common sense, it required the intuition of the true secret of war, to know that the men under General McDowell would really avail more for the defense of the capital, if added to the Army of the Potomac on the Peninsula, thus enabling that army to push vigorously its offensive intent, than if actually held in front of Washington." [23]

But this was not all. With large-scale battles and heavy casualties in the offing, Stanton issued on April 3 another misguided directive. This was General War Order No. 33, which " closed all the recruiting depots for the volunteers and [stopped] all recruiting." All recruiting officers were reassigned, and the government property sold at once to the highest bidder. Although these orders were intended to be in the best interests of the Union, it appeared to McClellan that the Secretary and the President were doing their best to keep men away from his army, then engaged in a life-and-death struggle with its adversary. Even that implacably hostile critic of McClellan, John Hay, was forced to concede to Nicolay that " Gen McC is in danger. Not in front, but in rear." Not until June 6, 1862, after heavy casualties had been suffered, did Stanton re-establish the system of recruiting abolished in April. But while Stanton was discouraging Union volunteering, the Confederate Congress was about to pass a conscription act to increase its armies. And to add to McClellan's discomfiture, when he stepped ashore at Fortress Monroe he was informed by Flag Officer Goldsborough that the navy was now unable " to take an active part in the reduction of the batteries at York[town] and Gloucester or to run by and gain their rear." [24]

[23] Swinton, *Army of the Potomac*, 104–105.
[24] 123 *O.R.*, 2–3, 109; McClellan, " The Peninsular Campaign," *loc. cit.*, 169, 170–71; Hay to Nicolay, April 3, 1862, *Letters of Hay*, 39; Confederate States of America, *Statutes at Large . . .* (Richmond, 1862–64), Vol. 2, 1st Cong.;

The decision of the Union government to withhold the First Corps from McClellan was a vital one for the Federal effort in 1862. In speaking of the original design of using McDowell's corps as an outflanking column up the York River, Franklin declares, " The result of carrying out this plan would have been that Yorktown would have been evacuated without a siege, the Williamsburg battle would not have taken place, and the whole army would have concentrated in front of Richmond in a few days after McDowell's corps would have joined—without serious loss." Thus, had McDowell not been detained, the Confederates would not have been given forty-five days in which to concentrate troops from all over Virginia and the South for a desperate defense of their capital. These six-odd weeks gave Lee and Davis time to assemble the largest Southern army ever marshaled during the war, and thus enable Lee, in the decisive battles in front of Richmond, for the only time in the war, to confront the Federals with approximately equal numbers. Although at first having far less men than the blundering Federal secret service estimated, Johnston admitted having " about fifty-three thousand men " in the Confederate " army on the Peninsula "—a force which was brought up to approximately 90,000 for the crucial clash near Richmond.[25]

On April 4—the same day on which he received word of the detention of the First Corps—McClellan received from Thomas a telegram stating that two new military departments had just been created. One was known as the Department of the Shenandoah, under Banks, and the other was the Department of the Rappahannock, under the command of McDowell. The latter, by April 22, was to arrive at Falmouth with his command. Thus, two more small, independent departments were established, and McDowell's First Corps was definitely taken away from McClellan's army. Not only that, but the boundaries

" Journal of Congress of the Confederate States," *Senate Documents*, 58th Cong., 2nd Sess., Vol. 2, 114 *et seq.*

[25] Franklin, " The First Great Crime," *loc. cit.*, 80; Thomas L. Livermore, *Numbers and Losses in the Civil War in America, 1861–1865* (Boston, 1901), 86, 135–36; Johnston's *Narrative*, 117

which the new directive set up for the various eastern departments removed from McClellan's control his bases of operation and supply at Fortress Monroe and Washington, and left him, as he says, with just his troops "and not even the ground they occupied until [he] passed White House" on the Pamunkey River.[26]

A few days after landing on the Peninsula, McClellan, with 42,000 effectives, confronted the Confederates' Yorktown-Warwick River line. The remainder of his army was either preparing to embark at Alexandria, sailing down the bay, or slogging up from Fortress Monroe in a period of heavy rainfall. The country in that season made offensive operations extremely difficult to conduct. Had he launched an immediate all-out attack with the forces then with him, it is probable that McClellan could have carried the enemy's position. But the Union commander was a circumspect man, with a tendency to magnify difficulties at times, and he hesitated to take what he considered to be an unnecessary risk of serious defeat. Although Magruder had put approximately 15,000 men at that moment along the Warwick line, the Southern army on the Peninsula under Johnston was soon to number at least 53,000 effectives.[27]

McClellan determined to test the strength of the enemy's Warwick line to see if there were any weak spots. Pressure was exerted on the grayclads as early as April 5, but their defensive works and artillery defeated the effort. Only a relatively few and narrow approaches could be made by the Federals through the water-inundated country to get at the enemy line, and at these points the Southerners had concentrated their guns. Another and larger probing attack was attempted on April 16 by William F. Smith's division at a point known as

[26] Thomas to McClellan, April 4, 1862, McClellan Papers; McDowell to the War Department, April 22, 1862, 15 *O.R.*, 279; McClellan, "The Peninsular Campaign," *loc. cit.*, 170; *M.O.S.*, 241–42.

[27] McClellan, "The Peninsular Campaign," *loc. cit.*, 170; Swinton, *Army of the Potomac*, 101. See Freeman, *Lee's Lieutenants*, I, 148–54; Johnston's *Narrative*, 117.

Garrow's Chimneys, about midway between Wynn's Mills and Lee's Mill. After making a slight dent in the Confederate position, this thrust came up against an alert and powerful defense, and sustained casualties of approximately two hundred without penetrating the rugged, water-protected line.[28]

Chief Engineer Barnard's official report contains details of the powerful enemy fortifications at Yorktown and along the Warwick. "The line," he stated, is certainly one of the most extensive known to modern times." The local Confederate commander on the lower Peninsula, Magruder, reported that, due to the five dams built by the graycoats and to the consequent backing up of the water, for " nearly three-fourth of [the Warwick River line's] distance its passage is impracticable for either artillery or infantry." The Union Fourth Corps commander, Keyes, stated that, as a result of the incessant rains, for " ten days, after reaching Warwick Court House, the ground was so soft and miry in places that the rations for the men at many points of the [Union] line had to be carried on the backs of the men." In his report, written during the siege, Keyes declared that " no part of [the Confederate] line, so far as discovered can be taken by assault without an enormous waste of life." McClellan wrote after the war that " no one *at that time* thought an assault practicable; moreover; that when we saw the works abandoned by the enemy it remained the conviction of all that, with the raw troops we had, an assault would have resulted in simply a useless butchery with no hope of success." [29]

On April 5, McClellan complained in a telegram to Washington that his force was now insufficient to achieve the goals originally set up for the campaign. He warned that his diminished force would require him to use caution. He implored

---

[28] McClellan to his wife, April 18, 1862, M.O.S., 311; Webb, *The Peninsula*, 46, 63–66; J. H. Stine, *History of the Army of the Potomac* (Washington, 1893), 44.

[29] Barnard's report, Keyes's report, April 16, 1862, McClellan's *Report*, 80, 84–86; Magruder's report, May 3, 1862, 12 *O.R.*, 405–406; Keyes, *Fifty Years' Observation*, 442; *M.O.S.*, 289, 317; McClellan, " The Peninsular Campaign," *loc. cit.*, 171.

Stanton to "reconsider the order detaching the 1st corps from my command." In my deliberate judgment," he continued in measured terms, "the success of our cause will be imperilled by so greatly reducing my force when it is actually under the fire of the enemy and active operations have commenced." He urged that at least Franklin's division of McDowell's corps be released to him on the Peninsula. In conclusion, the General said, "whatever your decision may be, I will leave nothing undone to obtain success." The only reply from Stanton was that "all in the power of the Government shall be done to sustain you as occasion may require." [30]

Then, on the evening of April 6, "before the arrival of the divisions of Hooker, Richardson, and Casey," Lincoln offered the Union commander some advice by telegram. "You now have over 100,000 troops with you," declared the President. "I think you better break the enemy's line from Yorktown to Warwick River at once." Of course, not all of McClellan's army had yet arrived, and he had considerably less than 100,000 effectives available. The day after receiving Lincoln's wire, McClellan wrote to Ellen his first reactions to it: "The President very coolly telegraphed me yesterday that he thought I had better break the enemy's lines at once! I was much tempted to reply that he had better come and do it himself." Writing of the siege of Yorktown after the war, the General said, "I never, at the time, heard of any contradictory opinion from any one, and, so far as I know, there was entire unanimity on the part of the general officers and chiefs of staff departments that the course pursued was the only one practicable under the circumstances." [31]

The Union siege operations against Yorktown were being slowed also by the miserable weather conditions. McClellan

[30] McClellan to Thomas, April 5, 1862, Lincoln Papers; McClellan to Stanton, April 5, 1862, M.O.S., 262, 265; Stanton to McClellan, April 6, 1862, McClellan Papers.

[31] Lincoln to McClellan, April 6, 1862, McClellan Papers; McClellan to Lincoln, April 7, 1862, Lincoln Papers; McClellan to his wife, April 8, 1862, M.O.S., 274, 308.

declared to Stanton that the " weather [was] terrible. Raining heavily last twenty-eight hours. Roads and camps in awful condition." He wrote his wife that they were experiencing " execrable weather; everything knee-deep in mud; roads infamous." One Federal officer reported that he saw a mule sink completely out of sight—except for the tips of its ears—in the middle of a main road. The Union commander wired Thomas that " it is with the utmost difficulty that I can supply the troops." Meanwhile, back in Washington, Hay wrote Nicolay that " the little Napoleon sits trembling before the handful of men at Yorktown afraid either to fight or run. Stanton feels devilish about it. He would like to remove him if he thought it would do." [32] And McClellan repeated his calls for more men to enable him to attack or turn Gloucester.[33]

This latest in a steady barrage of requests by McClellan for all or part of McDowell's corps finally bore fruit. On April 10, the administration, finally seeing that the Federal capital was not in peril, released Franklin's division for service with the Army of the Potomac. It was to begin arriving on the Peninsula on April 22. McClellan got the official word on the eleventh from Adjutant General Thomas, who stated that it was Lincoln, and not Stanton, who had made the decision and had ordered Franklin to the Peninsula by water. It was a courageous—even though a limited—action on the part of Lincoln, who really and honestly believed that McClellan had not left Washington secure when he left for Fortress Monroe.[34]

One can, of course, easily sympathize with the difficult position in which the harried President found himself in April of 1862. It was absolutely essential, politically and diplomati-

---

[32] Heintzelman's Journal, entries of April 8 and 9, 1862; *M.O.S.*, 308; McClellan to his wife, April 8 and 9, 1862, McClellan to Thomas, April 9, 1862, McClellan Papers; McClellan to Stanton, April 8, 1862, Lincoln Papers; Bruce Catton, *Mr. Lincoln's Army* (Garden City, 1951) , 109; Hay to Nicolay, *Letters of Hay*, 40–41; see Douglas Southall Freeman, *R. E. Lee, A Biography* (New York, 1934–35) , I, 601.

[33] McClellan to Stanton, April 10, 1862, McClellan Papers.

[34] Thomas to McClellan, April 11, 1862, McClellan Papers; Hitchcock's testimony, January 16, 1863, 15 *O.R.*, 220; McClellan's *Report*, 86–87.

cally, to make sure that the capital of the Union would not fall into Confederate hands. Washington was a great symbol, especially in a civil war, both at home and abroad. This was, correctly, a political decision which the Chief Executive could not dodge even if he had wanted to. The actual physical or military security of Washington, however, was strictly a military question, and should have been settled at the beginning on those grounds. The administration's superior and somewhat haughty attitude on this technical question, resulting in the useless detention of the First Corps, wrecked McClellan's strategy of striking a lightning and irresistible blow—especially by McDowell's 40,000 men up the York River—before the Confederates could adequately prepare for the defense of their own capital. When but one of McDowell's divisions—Franklin's—was finally released to the Peninsula, the golden chance had passed.

The President's personal impressions of McClellan at this time are of importance. On the evening of April 10, Browning conversed with Lincoln for more than an hour. " He told me," said the Senator, "[that] he was becoming impatient and dissatisfied with McClellan's sluggishness of action." But conditions on the Peninsula were so appalling that on this same day Stanton's assistant, Tucker, with the army, declared in a message to his chief that it took him five hours to travel five miles on horseback, so wretched were the roads. " The difficulties of transportation," said Tucker, " have been so great that some of the cavalry horses had to be sent back to keep them from starving. . . . I see an earnest determination to lose no time in attacking the enemy." And when Stanton sent Hitchcock down to the Peninsula to check up on McClellan's activity, the old soldier telegraphed back that McClellan's operations before Yorktown were " judicious," and that there was " no opening for any additional orders from the War Department." [35]

[35] *Browning's Diary*, I, 540; Tucker to Stanton, April 10, 1862, *M.O.S.*, 275;

At the beginning of May, while McClellan was still inching forward through the seas of mud toward Yorktown, the War Department issued the following returns of military departments, excluding those under McClellan and Wool:

Mountain Department............	26,783
Dept. of the Rappahannock........	44,445
Dept. of the Shenandoah..........	8,739
District of Washington............	12,812
Total........	92,812 [36]

And whether the Federal administration accepted it or not, all of these troops, except possibly those in the Mountain Department, as they were then located, in reality figured in the defensive pattern for the security of Washington. However, despite his claims that every effort was being made to succor McClellan, Stanton, in a letter to Halleck in Tennessee, calmly stated that, as regards augmenting the Federal Army, he merely wanted " to keep the force up to its present standard." [37] And Stanton's friend, Senator Wade of the Committee on the Conduct of the War, went so far as to state that McClellan was an out-and-out traitor.[38]

The relations, also, of McClellan and Lincoln were showing signs of strain. On May 1, in answer to the General's request for heavy Parrott guns from the capital, the anxious President sent to McClellan a terse, impatient blast: " Your call for Parrott guns from Washington alarms me, chiefly because it argues indefinite procrastination. Is anything to be done?" McClellan's reply demolished Lincoln's assumption that his request indicated delay: " I asked for the Parrott guns from Washington for the reason that some expected had been two weeks, nearly, on the way and could not be heard from. They arrived last night. My arrangements had been made for them,

Hitchcock to Stanton, April 15, 1862, Lincoln Papers; Hitchcock to Stanton, April 19, 1862, Stanton Papers.

[36] 18 *O.R.*, 308–13.

[37] Stanton to Halleck, April 27 and May 1, 1862, 123 *O.R.*, 29.

[38] *Bates's Diary*, 253.

and I thought time might be saved by getting others from Washington. My object was to hasten, not procrastinate. All is being done that human labor can accomplish." In a letter home, the General declared, " If they will simply let me alone I feel sure of success." And what did the opposing commander, Johnston, think of McClellan's unspectacular but steady engineering operations before Yorktown? On April 30, he asserted in a message to Davis' chief military adviser in Richmond, Lee, " We are engaged in a species of warfare at which we can never win. It is plain that General McClellan will adhere to the system adopted by him last summer, and depend for success upon artillery and engineering. We can compete with him in neither." [39]

Finally, on May 4, the impatient Federal public and administration received the news for which they had so eagerly been waiting. McClellan wired from the Peninsula: " Yorktown is in our possession." [40] It was so. The seemingly endless siege of one month had ended in success for McClellan and his Army of the Potomac; the Confederates were in full retreat toward Williamsburg. Johnston had seen that if he did not pull out of Yorktown, he would have been overwhelmed by McClellan's concentrated siege artillery. His decision to abandon the historic stronghold was indeed a wise one.

And in what light was the Young Napoleon now being considered by his government? Senator Charles Sumner of Massachusetts was quoted as saying that Lincoln and his cabinet were unanimous in determining to relieve McClellan from command; but upon hearing of the capture of Yorktown and the Warwick River line, they decided to " let the matter stand for the present." [41] It seems apparent that the civilian authorities in Washington did not quite appreciate the immense

[39] Lincoln to McClellan, McClellan to Lincoln, May 1, 1862, Lincoln Papers; Johnston to Lee, April 30, 1862, 14 *O.R.*, 477; McClellan to his wife, May 3, 1862, *M.O.S.*, 317.
[40] McClellan to Stanton, May 4, 1862, Lincoln Papers.
[41] See J. G. Randall, *Lincoln the President: Springfield to Gettysburg* (New York, 1945), II, 79.

physical and human obstacles which McClellan had to contend with on the Peninsula. Perhaps they expected too much of a man who was fighting with but two-thirds of the force which he was supposed to have had, and who was loath to gamble all to win all.

Now that the Army of the Potomac had flushed the foe from behind his works and was pursuing him in the open, could its commander now hope that he would be supported more cordially from Washington? He was soon to find out.

Chapter Five

The Weapon Tested

I . . . shall aid you all I can consistently with
my view of due regard to all points.

—*A. Lincoln*

THE old colonial capital of Williamsburg had witnessed
many history-making scenes in the days before the founding
of the republic, and in the early spring of 1862 the sleepy college
town was once again to find itself pulsating to stirring events.
Retreating from Yorktown, Joe Johnston's Confederate army
reached Williamsburg by noon on May 4. When McClellan's
forces entered the abandoned enemy works at Yorktown and
Gloucester, they found that the Southern withdrawal had been
so precipitate that seventy-seven heavy enemy guns had been
left behind—a loss which the Confederates could ill afford. The
Union commander immediately telegraphed Stanton of his
success, describing the strong nature of the works captured, as
well as giving details of the booty seized. He assured the Secretary that he was in pursuit of the foe, and that Franklin's
division was to be moved by transports up the York River to
West Point to try to cut off the enemy's retreat. He concluded
by saying, " No time shall be lost. . . . I shall push the enemy
to the wall." [1]

Although McClellan was a bit surprised and disappointed
by the sudden and peaceful Confederate evacuation of Yorktown, he nevertheless determined to advance as rapidly as con-

[1] Johnston's *Narrative*, 119; *M.O.S.*, 317; McClellan to Stanton, May 4, 1862,
C. P. Kingsbury to Marcy, May 5, 1862, McClellan Papers.

ditions would allow. However, the few roads were in "infamous" condition, and the rains continued. Some artillery batteries were "actually stuck fast in the mud." The frightful Virginia roads in the rainy season were enough of a handicap for the Confederates who moved over them first; but they were much worse for the pursuing Federals, since the enemy troops and vehicles moving ahead of them had already cut the muddy tracks to ribbons. The Union pursuit was slowed also by the land mines (called torpedoes at that time) left by the Southerners in strategic spots near Yorktown. However, their hasty retreat was not altogether orderly, the roads being littered "with broken wagons, abandoned ambulances, and all the debris of a retreating army." [2]

Although "there was an entire ignorance of the country at the Federal headquarters," McClellan asserted that he was aware that "there were strong defensive works at or near Williamsburg." A little before noon on May 4, the pursuing Union cavalry and infantry supports moved out of Yorktown to the west. Williamsburg—where the Peninsula narrows to an isthmus—is about thirteen miles from Yorktown. Johnston had left Brigadier General J. E. B. Stuart's cavalry to cover the two roads leading from the abandoned Confederate line to Williamsburg. The bulk of the grayclad infantry, which had reached Williamsburg, was ordered on toward Barhamsville. Major General James Longstreet was placed in command of the Southern rear guard. The rapid pursuit of McClellan, however, forced the Confederates to fight a sizeable battle at Williamsburg to protect their exposed, slow-moving wagon trains. [3]

Although a heavy downpour prevented food rations from keeping up with the advancing Union troops at the front,

[2] Webb, *The Peninsula*, 69; McClellan to Stanton, May 5, 1862, McClellan Papers; J. J. Marks, *The Peninsula Campaign in Virginia* . . . (Philadelphia, 1864) , 150–51; *M.O.S.*, 318.

[3] Paris, *The Civil War*, II, 16, 24; McClellan's report, 12 *O.R.*, 7; G. W. Smith, *Confederate War Papers* . . . (New York, 1884) , 41ff; James Longstreet, *From Manassas to Appomattox* . . . (Philadelphia, 1908) , 68, 72, 79; William Allan, *The Army of Northern Virginia in 1862* (Boston, 1892) , 16; Joseph E. Johnston, "Manassas to Seven Pines," *B. & L.*, II, 205.

Brigadier General George Stoneman's cavalry was nonetheless ordered by McClellan to try to cut off the enemy forces moving on Williamsburg by way of the longer Lee's Mill road. He directed the divisions of Hooker and Kearny of Heintzelman's Third Corps and those of W. F. Smith, Couch, and Brigadier General Silas Casey of Keyes's Fourth Corps to support the cavalry advance. Since McClellan was not anticipating any serious combats during the early pursuit, he decided to remain at Yorktown to superintend the important movement of Franklin's division by water to West Point in an endeavor to cut off, if possible, the retreat of the enemy. "The weather was so bad," writes McClellan, "and the wharf facilities at Yorktown so deficient that it was very difficult to bring order out of chaos." He intended to go himself to West Point with the amphibious force if no trouble occurred at Williamsburg.[4]

The Union forces moving by land were placed by McClellan under the command of his senior corps commander, Sumner, of the Second Corps. Stoneman's pursuing cavalry caught up with the enemy rear guard—comprising Stuart's mounted men —near the Halfway House, and skirmished with it in a running fight toward Williamsburg. At about 4:00 P. M. on May 4, his advance was brought up sharp by a line of some thirteen redoubts and numerous rifle pits stretching across the narrow Peninsula about two miles southeast of Williamsburg. The main Confederate work in the center was Fort Magruder, six hundred yards in width, and protected by a deep ditch. Marshes which extended inward from both flanks shortened to four miles the line which the enemy had to defend.[5]

---

[4] Heintzelman's Journal, entry of May 6, 1862; Regis DeTrobriand, *Four Years with the Army of the Potomac* (Boston, 1889), 191; Sumner's report, 12 *O.R.*, 451; Francis W. Palfrey, "The Period which Elapsed between the Fall of Yorktown and the Beginning of the Seven Days' Battles," Dwight (ed.), *Campaigns in Virginia*, 156; McClellan, "The Peninsular Campaign," *loc. cit.*, 172.

[5] Reports of Sumner, Heintzelman, Hooker, and Keyes, 12 *O.R.*, 450, 457, 465, 512; Swinton, *Army of the Potomac*, 112; Warren Lee Goss, "Yorktown and Williamsburg," *B. & L.*, II, 194; Prince de Joinville, *The Army of the Potomac* . . . (New York, 1862), 49.

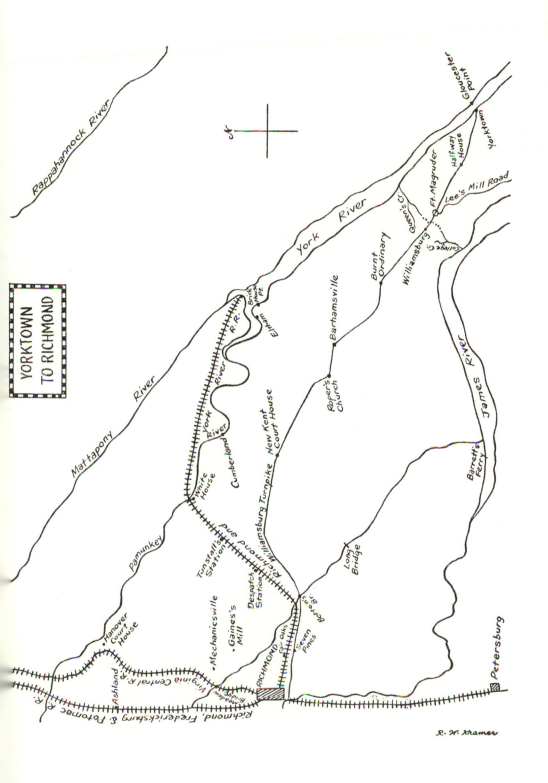

YORKTOWN TO RICHMOND

Rappahannock River

York River

Mattapony River

Gloucester Point

Yorktown

Halfway House

Ft. Magruder

Lee's Mill Road

Queen's Cr.

Williamsburg

College Cr.

Burnt Ordinary

Barhamsville

Brick House Pt.

Eltham

R.R.

York River

Cumberland

Roper's Church

New Kent Court House

James River

Barrett's Ferry

White House

Pamunkey

Tunstall's Station

York River R.R.

Despatch Station

Richmond & Williamsburg Turnpike

Long Bridge

Hanover Court House

Mechanicsville

Gaines's Mill

Meadow Bridge

Fair Oaks

Seven Pines

Savage's Sta.

RICHMOND

Ashland

Virginia Central R.R.

Richmond, Fredericksburg & Potomac R.R.

Petersburg

R. W. Kramer

While Stoneman was skirmishing indecisively with the enemy horse, grayclad infantrymen, who had marched past Williamsburg, were seen to be hurrying back into the redoubts. Just before dark, the vanguard of the supporting Federal infantry arrived. During the night, Hooker's division was deployed on the Union left opposite Fort Magruder, and W. F. Smith's division took position on the right. At first, the Federals had the advantage of numbers, the Confederates that of position. Sumner determined to attack at daybreak on the fifth, but failed to give Smith and Hooker specific orders.[6]

The battle of Williamsburg opened at 7:30 A. M. when Hooker launched a vigorous attack against Fort Magruder. After making initial progress, Hooker was halted and pushed back by the reinforced Confederates. After neglecting affairs on the Federal left, Sumner finally succored Hooker, and brought the enemy counterattack there to a halt. Then, on the extreme Union right flank, a conspicuous success was scored by Brigadier General Winfield S. Hancock. In a brilliant action, Hancock seized several redoubts on the Confederate left and repulsed with the bayonet a desperate enemy counterattack, one grayclad regiment being practically annihilated. This success, coming near 5:00 P. M., decided the fate of the whole field, for Hancock was placed squarely on the Confederate left flank. Their withdrawal from the entire line was insured.[7]

But what of McClellan himself during this day of battle? He was engaged at Yorktown in supervising the important and difficult task of embarking Franklin's division on steamers for West Point, in an effort to cut off the Confederate retreat. Shortly after noon on the fifth, however, he received word

---

[6] Stine, *Army of the Potomac*, 49–50; Webb, *The Peninsula*, 70–71, 73; E. P. Alexander, *Military Memoirs of a Confederate* . . . (New York, 1907), 67; Sumner's and Heintzelman's reports, 12 *O.R.*, 451, 454; Paris, *The Civil War*, II, 18.

[7] Goss, "Yorktown and Williamsburg," *loc. cit.*, 195–99; McClellan's *Report*, 89–91; Stine, *Army of the Potomac*, 50–56; Allan, *Army of Northern Virginia*, 17–18; reports of Johnston, Longstreet, Sumner, Heintzelman, Hooker, and Hancock, 12 *O.R.*, 275, 451, 455–59, 467, 565; Francis A. Walker, *History of the Second Army Corps* . . . (New York, 1886), 17; Freeman, *Lee's Lieutenants*, I, 185ff.

finally that a battle was in progress at Williamsburg, and that so far it wasn't going too well for the Federals. Returning swiftly to his headquarters, McClellan, realizing that the enemy might now wish to turn the engagement at Williamsburg into a full-scale battle, ordered Brigadier General John Sedgwick's division to march at once to that place. Those of Richardson and Fitz John Porter were instructed to stand by at Yorktown, prepared to follow Sedgwick if necessary. Franklin's division continued to embark on steamers for West Point.[8]

McClellan then left for the field. The ride took him thirteen miles through seas of mud, over roads encumbered with troops and wagons, and through dense and tangled forests. Despite the necessarily slow progress of the ride, McClellan—astride his famous jet-black horse, " Dan Webster "—easily outpaced his panting staff, and arrived before 5:00 P. M. on the battlefield of Williamsburg. He was wildly cheered by his troops, and his presence seems to have been a tonic to them, as they had been forced to fight all day without food; nor had the combat been going so well up to that time. McClellan had come up just as Hancock's fine effort was being carried through to success. He saw after a quick inspection that Sumner had fought the battle in two isolated actions, and that communications had not been opened with Hooker on the Federal left. " I found everything," McClellan declared, " in a state of chaos and depression. Even the private soldiers saw clearly that, with force enough in hand to gain a victory, we, the pursuers, were on the defensive and content with repulsing attacks, and that there was no plan of action, no directing hand." Many troops were " massed inactive in the clearings." McClellan opened up communications with the Union left, and reinforced Hancock and Hooker. His efforts were to provide for a more unified action, especially if the enemy would risk a continuance of the combat on the following morning.[9]

[8] Keyes to McClellan, May 5, 1862, *M.O.S.*, 301, 327.
[9] *M.O.S.*, 327–30; de Joinville, *Army of the Potomac*, 55; Paris, *The Civil War*, II, 23–24; McClellan's *Report*, 91; Webb, *The Peninsula*, 80–81; see John Codman Ropes, *The Story of the Civil War* (New York, 1899), II, 110.

During the night and early on May 6, the Confederates withdrew northwestward toward Barhamsville. Seeing that no additional troops were needed at Williamsburg, McClellan ordered the divisions of Sedgwick and Richardson, then coming up from Yorktown, to return to Yorktown preparatory to following Franklin and Porter up the York River to West Point. As to casualties, the attacking Federals, according to Livermore, lost 456 killed, 1,410 wounded, and 373 missing—a total loss of 2,239. The Confederates, fighting from behind fixed positions a large part of the time, lost 1,570 killed and wounded, and 133 missing—a total loss of 1,703. The field of battle, with its hundreds of killed and wounded of both sides, was in Union hands, the Federals being obliged to care for a host of wounded enemy soldiers, as well as to bury their dead.[10]

On May 6, the morning after the battle of Williamsburg, McClellan threw Colonel William W. Averell's cavalry in pursuit of the graycoats; but the hopeless condition of the execrable roads—already cut to shreds by the preceding Southern wagon trains—rendered it a physical impossibility for him to supply the men or animals. Nor could McClellan support them with infantry or artillery, for these branches were already short of food and ammunition, which were being slowly wrestled up from the rear along the boggy road. Consequently, Averell had to be brought back. An immediate land pursuit by the whole Army of the Potomac was out of the question. Although the James River was not yet open to the Federal gunboats, due to the presence of the ironclad *Virginia* and the retention of Norfolk by the enemy, McClellan was already contemplating the possible use of that river as an avenue of advance.[11]

The menacing proportions of the battle of Williamsburg had taken two of McClellan's divisions—those of Sedgwick and

[10] McClellan's *Report*, 91; Walker, *Second Corps*, 17; Marks, *Peninsula Campaign*, 159ff; Paris, *The Civil War*, II, 25; Livermore, *Numbers and Losses*, 80–81.

[11] McClellan to Stanton, May 6, 1862, McClellan Papers; McClellan's *Report*, 91–93; Paris, *The Civil War*, II, 26; Longstreet, *Manassas to Appomattox*, 79; W. F. Smith to McClellan, May 5, 1862, *M.O.S.*, 300–301.

Richardson—away from their intended embarkation at York-town, and thus delayed and weakened somewhat the movement by water to West Point. Meanwhile, the Confederate com-mander, Johnston, anticipating such a movement by the Fed-erals up the York, ordered the divisions of Magruder and Major General G. W. Smith to push steadily northwestward toward Barhamsville.[12] Had McDowell's First Corps been permitted to sail en masse up the York River at the start of the campaign, as planned by McClellan, the Confederates would have had to pull back swiftly from Yorktown and Williamsburg, or be taken in rear. Nor would the enemy have been given the valuable time to be reinforced by sizable forces from other parts of Virginia and the South.

The whole day of May 5 was spent by McClellan (until he left for the field at Williamsburg) and Franklin at Yorktown in overcoming, in a severe rainstorm, a series of large and un-fortunate engineering and transportation difficulties in getting Franklin's division, including his artillery and supplies, aboard the transports. When everything was ready, after dark on the fifth, the commander of the naval flotilla informed Franklin that it would be unwise to move up the river at night in such a storm, and the movement was put off until the next day. Fortunately, the sixth of May dawned clear and mild. Frank-lin's division, moving by ship at daybreak, arrived off West Point a little after noon, and began to disembark across from the point at a place known as Brick House Point. From there, the main body moved out a short distance toward Eltham's Landing on the south bank of the Pamunkey. On the morning of the seventh, on the Confederate side, Johnston's whole army was near Barhamsville, about eleven miles from West Point.[13]

Then, at about 10:00 A.M. on the seventh, Franklin was sharply attacked by Confederate troops of G. W. Smith's com-

---

[12] See Longstreet, *Manassas to Appomattox*, 79; Freeman, *Lee's Lieutenants*, I, 193.

[13] *M.O.S.*, 334–37; Warren Lee Goss, *Recollections of a Private . . .* (New York, 1890), 42; 12 *O.R.*, 276, 627; Johnston's *Narrative*, 126.

mand under the direction of Brigadier General W. H. C. Whiting. In a five-hour combat, Franklin, with the assistance of the fire from the Union gunboats, after an initial setback, repulsed Whiting's assaults which threatened to push him back into the river, and held firmly to his established beachhead. Union casualties in this battle of West Point (or Eltham's Landing) amounted to approximately 194 killed, wounded, and missing. The Southerners reported their losses as forty-eight men, but this figure is probably much too low. Later, Sedgwick's division arrived on the field, but too late to enable McClellan to move out in heavy enough force against the enemy rear, which passed safely through Barhamsville on the morning of May 8 on its way toward New Kent Court House. McClellan wisely instructed Franklin " simply to hold his position " until sufficient Union force arrived to support him.[14]

Although from the Confederate viewpoint the relatively small engagement at West Point was successful in saving their wagon trains again and allowing their troops from Williamsburg to pass safely on by the road to Richmond, the chief advantage of the movement and action rested nonetheless with McClellan. The Federal commander summed up his success in this way: " Franklin's movement had fully served its purpose in clearing our front to the banks of the Chickahominy." Even had the Confederates been more successful in the fight at Williamsburg, McClellan's stroke up the York River ensured their rapid withdrawal northwestward toward Richmond. Thus, the amphibious flying column to West Point, although decisively crippled and delayed at the start by the administration, nevertheless demonstrated even in its emasculated and impeded form the essential correctness of McClellan's design. Now the Union forces concentrating at Eltham's were to form the right wing of the Union Army as it closed in on Richmond from the east and north. However, McClellan was obliged to leave

[14] Stine, *Army of the Potomac*, 57–58; McClellan's *Report*, 92; reports of Franklin, McClellan, G. W. Smith, Whiting, J. B. Hood, W. Hampton, 12 *O.R.*, 24, 614–17, 627, 629–30, 631–32; Swinton, *Army of the Potomac*, 117; *B. & L.*, II, 222n.

behind garrisons at Yorktown, Williamsburg, West Point, and other places as he advanced, thus weakening somewhat his main striking force. At the same time, the Confederates, in falling back on interior lines, were concentrating their forces by picking up scattered garrisons on the retreat to Richmond.[15]

McClellan was finally able to begin moving out in force from Williamsburg toward New Kent Court House on May 8. Stoneman's cavalry led the advance guard, supported by W. F. Smith's division. The Union commander took advantage of official government permission to create two provisional corps, which soon became permanent. These were the Fifth Corps, commanded by Porter, and the Sixth Corps, commanded by Franklin. Then, upon the request of Stanton, McClellan gave his views on the military situation in Virginia. " The time has arrived," he declared, " to bring all the troops in Eastern Virginia into perfect cooperation." He would be fighting a concentrated Southern army in front of Richmond, he said, composed of " all the troops the Confederates can bring together." He called for all the reinforcements the Secretary could give him. " All the troops on the Rappahannock, and if possible those on the Shenandoah," asserted McClellan, " should take part in the approaching battle. . . . We ought immediately to concentrate everything. . . . All minor considerations should be thrown to one side and all our energies and means directed towards the defeat of Johnston's army in front of Richmond." [16]

For the previous two weeks, Lee had been communicating with Stonewall Jackson, exchanging ideas with that wily fox for a feint down the Shenandoah Valley designed to befuddle the Union authorities in Washington and lure them into preventing McDowell at Fredericksburg from marching southward to join McClellan's main advance on Richmond. Banks, stationed in the Valley, wired Stanton that " Jackson has announced to the people his intention to return to this valley. . . .

[15] Ropes, *Story of the Civil War*, II, 111; Joel Cook, *The Siege of Richmond . . .* (Philadelphia, 1862) , 86–87; Stine, *Army of the Potomac*, 58.
[16] McClellan's *Report*, 92, 93; Stanton to McClellan, McClellan to Stanton, May 8, 1862, McClellan Papers.

Object is doubtless to prevent junction of our forces." But the Secretary disagreed. "The probabilities at present," he argued, "point to a possible attempt upon Washington while the Shenandoah army is amused with demonstrations. Washington is the only object now worth a desperate throw." Like Lincoln, the Secretary seemed unable to see that with McClellan's powerful army moving on Richmond from the east, and with McDowell's 38,000 men at Fredericksburg, Davis and Lee would not dare to risk moving a large force directly on Washington, and that any enemy demonstrations in the Valley would be merely feints aimed at preventing the concentration of the widely scattered Union forces in northern Virginia and the decisive reinforcement of McClellan for the imminent battles near the Confederate capital. The administration received warnings precisely to this effect from Brigadier General James Shields, stationed at New Market in the Valley, from McDowell at Fredericksburg, and from Assistant Secretary of War Peter Watson.[17]

In the meantime, operations on the Peninsula were continuing. McClellan urged Stanton on May 10 to see to it that Federal gunboats were promptly sent up the James River, as soon as it was opened. The retreating Confederate forces on the Peninsula had been halted on the ninth for a brief rest, their right wing near Long Bridge over the Chickahominy, and their left, including the cavalry, "extending towards the Pamunkey through New Kent Court House." On the Federal side, McClellan's headquarters, on the tenth, had reached Roper's Church, nineteen miles beyond Williamsburg, as had the land-moving divisions. This force was now "in direct communication with the portion of the army which had gone by water," the whole army now being supplied from West Point. Preparations were being made in Richmond to remove the

---

[17] See Lee to Jackson, April 25, May 5, 1862, 18 *O.R.*, 859–60, 866, 871, 872, 875, 878; Banks to Stanton, May 7, 1862, 15 *O.R.*, 458; Stanton to Banks, Shields to Watson, McDowell to Stanton, May 9, 1862, 18 *O.R.*, 151–52; Watson to Stanton, May 9, 1862, Stanton Papers.

Davis government's papers if the city faced capture. Later on May 10, the weakly held enemy point of Norfolk fell to a small force under Wool, the Confederate ironclad *Virginia* being destroyed by the fleeing foe.[18]

McClellan now began contemplating the possible use of the James as an alternate line of advance. He declared to Stanton on May 10 that " should Norfolk be taken and the Merrimac destroyed I can change my line to the James River and dispense with the West Point Railroad." In a conference with the navy's Goldsborough on the nineteenth, McClellan and the flag officer discussed just such a transfer of the army to the James. Apparently, however, the General intended to use the line of the York and Pamunkey for a while yet, and move over to that of the James only when he got closer to Richmond, or if that of the York became too difficult to maintain.[19]

Another problem which caused McClellan anxiety was that of enemy numbers. On May 13, the Union generals were informed by their inept secret service agents that the Confederates had " concentrated 240,000 men " against them. Stanton's own assistant, John Tucker, at Fortress Monroe, telegraphed the Secretary this intelligence: " It is reported that 200,000 [grayclad] troops are in the immediate vicinity of Richmond and that Johnston has a strong force." McClellan reported having in the middle of May a total of 102,236 troops in blue.[20]

Meanwhile, the Confederate Army was ordered to cross the Chickahominy River to the southwestern side, Johnston apparently anticipating a possible Federal move by the James. The Confederate right wing under Longstreet had, by nightfall of

[18] Longstreet, *Manassas to Appomattox*, 81; McClellan's *Report*, 92; Paris, *The Civil War*, II, 28–30; 14 *O.R.*, 504.

[19] McClellan to Stanton, May 10, 1862, W. B. Franklin to McClellan, May 9, 1876, McClellan Papers; Paris, *The Civil War*, II, 32–33.

[20] William H. Powell, *The Fifth Army Corps . . .* (New York, 1896), 59; Heintzelman's Journal, entry of May 13, 1862; Tucker to Stanton, May 22, 1862, Stanton Papers; 14 *O.R.*, 184.

May 15, reached a position between the James and White Oak Swamp, while the left wing under G. W. Smith stretched from the swamp to the Mechanicsville turnpike. At the same time, the Union divisions of Casey and Couch were near New Kent Court House, and the divisions of Sedgwick and Richardson were at Eltham's Landing. By the following day, McClellan's headquarters reached White House on the Pamunkey River, which Stoneman's cavalry had captured after several successful jousts with the Southern horse. A few hours later, the divisions of Franklin, Porter, and W. F. Smith reached there also, despite the fact that " the roads [were] so bad that it took the wagon trains 36 hours to go the 5 miles from Cumberland to White House." A permanent supply depot was immediately established at the latter point. But a disappointing note was added when McClellan received word that Union gunboats, storming up the James River, had been repulsed by Confederate shore batteries at Drewry's Bluff, fifteen miles downstream from Richmond.[21]

White House was a fine, large plantation mansion, formerly the residence of Martha Dandridge Custis at the time she married George Washington. It was in 1862 still owned by the Lee family. Although establishing his headquarters in tents near the house, and using the landing area as his main base of supplies, McClellan would not permit his troops to enter the shrine, and placed guards around it. Although engrossed with the countless details of headquarters, he found time on May 16 to write Ellen a few lines: " I rode over a horrid road to [White House] this morning; spent some time at Washington's house, or at least his wife's, and afterwards rode to the front, visiting in the course of my ride the old church (St. Peter's) where he was married. . . . As I happened to be there alone for a few moments, I could not help kneeling

---

[21] Palfrey, ". . . Fall of Yorktown . . . ," *loc. cit.*, 165; Longstreet, *Manassas to Appomattox*, 81; McClellan's *Report*, 93; Heintzelman's Journal, entry of May 15, 1862; Cook, *Siege of Richmond*, 112–14; Paris, *The Civil War*, II, 31.

at the chancel and praying that I might serve my country as truly as he did." [22]

By the seventeenth of May, McClellan's advance reached New Bridge and Bottom's Bridge at the swollen Chickahominy River. This waterway, which was to play such a key role in the remainder of the operations around Richmond, was a great military obstacle at that season of the year. Rising in the region to the north of the Confederate capital, it flowed in a general northwest to southeast direction, finally emptying into the James River at Barrett's Ferry, near the old colonial settlement of Jamestown. Although the main channel of the Chickahominy was seldom more than sixty feet in width, the river had extremely low banks, and a slight rise in the level of the water would be sufficient to inundate both of the wooded shores to an extent of a mile on each side. The entire river basin, in the rainy season, became little better than a great swamp. With continuous rains falling ever since he had landed on the Peninsula, McClellan, in order to cross to the Richmond side of the Chickahominy, was obliged to throw up numerous bridges across the treacherous stream—bridges which, with their extensive corduroy approaches, could easily be swept away by a sudden rise in the current below. [23]

Back in Washington, the Federal administration was considering using McDowell's 38,000 men at Fredericksburg to better offensive advantage. Consequently, on May 17, Stanton issued the following directive to McDowell: "Upon being joined by Gen. Shields' division [from the Valley] you will move upon Richmond by the general route of the Richmond and Fredericksburg Railroad, cooperating with the forces under Gen. McClellan, now threatening Richmond from the line of the Pamunkey and York Rivers. While seeking to establish as soon as possible a communication between your left wing and the right wing of Gen. McClellan, you will hold yourself always in such a position as to cover the capital of the nation against

[22] McClellan to his wife, May 16, 1862, McClellan Papers.
[23] Barnard's report, 12 *O.R.*, 110–11.

a sudden dash of any large body of the rebels." But then a modification of the instructions to McDowell came from Lincoln, which tended to create a divided command. " You will retain," said the President to McDowell, " the separate command of the forces taken with you; but while co-operating with General McClellan you will obey his orders, except that you are to judge, and are not to allow your force to be disposed otherwise than so as to give the greatest protection to this capital which may be possible at that distance." The weakness of this order was that, when McDowell's army united with McClellan's, McDowell actually retained independent command to a degree which might well restrict McClellan's tactical plans and lead to endless debate between the two generals whenever McClellan might attempt to order part of McDowell's force to move some place.[24]

Following up the instructions to McDowell, Stanton dispatched an order to McClellan which was to be of momentous import in the ensuing days. Despite McClellan's call for reinforcements by water, the Secretary insisted that McDowell move by land. The directive to McClellan stated: " General McDowell has been ordered to march upon [Richmond] by the shortest route. He is ordered—keeping himself always in position to save the capital from all possible attack—so to operate as to place his left wing in communication with your right wing, and you are instructed to cooperate, so as to establish this communication as soon as possible, by extending your right wing to the north of Richmond. . . . You will give no order . . . which can put him out of position to cover the city [of Washington]. . . . The President desires that General McDowell retain the command of the Department of the Rappahannock and of the forces with which he moves forward." [25] The order started reinforcements moving toward the Army of the Potomac, but

---

[24] Stanton to McDowell, May 17, 1862, *C.C.W.*, I, 272; Lincoln to McDowell, May 17, 1862, 14 *O.R.*, 176–77. See Porter, " Account of Campaign in Northern Virginia 1862," F. J. Porter Papers, Vol. VII.

[25] Stanton to McClellan, May 17, 1862, McClellan Papers.

it actually played right into the hands of the enemy, for it unwittingly placed McClellan's army in one of the most dangerous military positions imaginable. It compelled McClellan to expose his right wing northeast of the hazardous Chickahominy River, while the government's impatience for an advance obliged him at the same time to throw his left across to the southwest side of that river in order to move against Richmond. It gave the alert Confederates a perfect opportunity to fall in overwhelming force upon a separated portion of the National Army and defeat it in detail before the rest of the Union divisions could come to its relief. McClellan had grasped the overall strategic picture, as shown by his message to Seward on May 18: " Indications that enemy intend fighting at Richmond. Policy seems to be to concentrate everything there. They hold central position, and will seek to meet us while divided. I think we are committing a great military error in having so many independent columns. The great battle should be fought by our troops in mass; then divide if necessary." Lee's hopes, as expressed to Jackson, were precisely along the lines of which McClellan warned.[26]

Elements of McClellan's army began moving out from the White House area on May 19. The railroad bridge over the Chickahominy had been partially burned by the retreating enemy, and needed major repairs. On the twentieth, the Union left reached Bottom's Bridge, which had to be rebuilt also. The flooded river was not fordable at any point at that season. The Confederates held with artillery and works the elevated bluffs commanding and enfilading the roads leading to Richmond at New Bridge and at the Mechanicsville Bridge on the Union right. McClellan therefore turned his attention to his left, which offered promise of an easier crossing of the river and subsequent advance toward Richmond. Following feverish

[26] See Thomas Goddard Frothingham, " The Peninsular Campaign of 1862," *Massachusetts Historical Society Proceedings, October, 1923–June, 1924* (Boston, 1924), LVIX, 106. McClellan to Seward, May 18, 1862, *C.C.W.,* I, 327; Upton, *Military Policy,* 299. See Lee to Jackson, 18 *O.R.,* 859–60, 865, 866, 871, 872, 875, 878.

work on the bridges, Casey's division crossed over and encamped at The Chimneys, one and a half miles beyond the Chicka-hominy. Stoneman's cavalry drove the gray vedettes out of Cold Harbor, and captured a baggage train. By sunset of the twenty-first, McClellan's movements had produced these dispo-sitions: Stoneman's cavalry was near New Bridge; Sumner's Second Corps was on the Richmond and York River Railroad, approximately three miles from the Chickahominy; excepting Casey's division, Keyes's Fourth Corps was near Bottom's Bridge on the road from New Kent Court House, with Heintzelman's Third Corps in supporting distance in the rear; Porter's Fifth Corps and Franklin's Sixth Corps were nearing New Bridge; army headquarters had arrived at Cold Harbor.[27]

The slow pace of McClellan's advance was due to the necessity of erecting eleven new bridges over the enlarged Chickahominy between Mechanicsville and Bottom's Bridge— spans which were " all long and difficult, with extensive log-way approaches." With the unusually heavy rains continuing day after day, the Chickahominy rose higher " than had ever been known for twenty years " by local inhabitants. Bridges were often swept away by the powerful current, and the soldiers working on the new trestles were frequently subjected to enemy sniper fire. A sizable force of the National Army, McClellan reported, had to be left on the northeast bank " to guard our communications or to protect our right and rear." [28] And on May 24, McClellan received support for his circumspect advance from the President, who also reversed an earlier administration directive as to who was to have ultimate control of McDowell's force. " I wish you to move cautiously and safely," declared Lincoln to McClellan. " You will have command of McDowell after he joins you, precisely as you intended." [29]

This good news to McClellan, however, was short-lived. On May 23, the day before Lincoln's message on McDowell, Wash-

[27] Cook, *Siege of Richmond*, 100, 117; McClellan's *Report*, 93–94; *M.O.S.*, 377.
[28] Palfrey, ". . . Fall of Yorktown . . . ," *loc. cit.*, 167; McClellan's *Report*, 93, 100; Cook, *Siege of Richmond*, 118–20, 121; Webb, *The Peninsula*, 97.
[29] Lincoln to McClellan, May 24, 1862, McClellan Papers.

ington received unfavorable word from the Shenandoah Valley. Banks, in a calm dispatch, announced that the Federal troops at Front Royal had been attacked and forced to retire northward. The Confederate troops actually numbered about 15,000, a figure which Banks had pretty accurately estimated.[30]

Then the Union administration unwittingly played directly into the hands of the enemy. Allowing himself to be diverted by Stonewall Jackson's relatively small force in the Valley, Lincoln sent an important order late on May 24 to McDowell at Fredericksburg: "You are instructed, laying aside for the present the movement on Richmond, to put 20,000 men in motion at once for the Shenandoah. . . . Your object will be to capture the forces of Jackson and Ewell." Shields, at Fredericksburg, at once protested to Stanton: "No help would reach [Banks] in time from here, and a panic there ought not to paralyze this movement just now prepared on the eve of execution." McDowell was staggered by the administration's order, declaring to the Secretary, "The President's order has been received and is in process of execution. This is a crushing blow to us." Speaking in blunter language to Wadsworth in Washington, McDowell declared emphatically, "It is idle to think of taking any force from this point to go after any force . . . in Banks' rear. . . . If they are really in his rear, nothing from here can get there in time to afford him any help. . . . Try and get over the flutter into which this [enemy] body seems to have thrown everyone. If the enemy can succeed so readily in disconcerting all our plans by alarming us first at one point, then at another, he will paralyze a large force with a very small one." Concerned with the absolute safety of Washington, Lincoln and Stanton were doing precisely what Davis, Lee, and Jackson wanted them to do. Lincoln broke the news to McClellan late on May 24: "In consequence of General Banks' position, I have been compelled to suspend McDowell's movements to join you."[31]

[30] Banks to Stanton, May 23 and 24, 1862, 15 *O.R.*, 525, 526.
[31] Lincoln to McDowell, May 24, 1862, *C.C.W.*, I, 274; Shields to Stanton,

McClellan's views on the McDowell detention were quite positive. "His withdrawal towards Front Royal," the General said, "was . . . a serious and fatal error; he could do no good in that direction, while had he been permitted to carry out the orders of May 17, the united forces would have driven the enemy within the immediate entrenchments of Richmond before Jackson could have returned to its succor, and probably would have gained possession promptly of that place." However, McClellan gave the President a soldierly reply upon learning the disheartening news that McDowell has been sidetracked for the moment: "Telegram of 4 P. M. received. I will make my calculations accordingly." The General noted, however, that he was still obliged to keep his army astraddle the swollen Chickahominy River even after McDowell's temporary diversion toward the Valley. "It will be remembered," he stated, "that the order for the cooperation of General McDowell was simply suspended, not revoked, and therefore I was not at liberty to abandon the northern approach." [32]

The authorities in Washington, however, were genuinely alarmed at the turn of events. On the afternoon of May 25, Lincoln dispatched an excited telegram to McClellan. "I think the movement [by Jackson] is a general and concerted one," he declared, "such as would not be if he was acting upon the purpose of a very desperate defense of Richmond. I think the time is near when you must either attack Richmond or give up the job and come to the defense of Washington. Let me hear from you instantly." McClellan replied immediately to Lincoln, saying, "The object of the [enemy] movement is probably to prevent reinforcements being sent me. . . . The mass of the rebel troops are still in the immediate vicinity of Richmond, ready to defend it." Writing to Ellen at the time, the General was provoked to wrath by the administration's action. "I have

McDowell to Stanton, McDowell to Wadsworth, May 24, 1862, 18 *O.R.*, 220–22; Lincoln to McClellan, May 24, 1862, McClellan Papers.

[32] *M.O.S.*, 375; McClellan to Lincoln, May 24, 1862, McClellan Papers; McClellan's *Report*, 100; see also Powell, *Fifth Corps*, 61.

this moment received a dispatch from the President," McClellan reported, " who is terribly scared about Washington, and talks about the necessity of my returning in order to save it. Heaven save a country governed by such counsels! " A few moments later, still seething with rage, the General continued his letter home: " Have just finished my reply to his Excellency! It is perfectly sickening to deal with such people. . . . I get more sick of them every day, for every day brings with it only additional proofs of their hypocrisy, knavery, and folly—well, well, I ought not to write in this way, for they may be right and I entirely wrong, so I will drop the subject." [33]

Stanton, too, was dreadfully fearful for the security of the Federal capital. He quickly sent a proclamation to the governors of the North: " Intelligence from various quarters leaves no doubt that the enemy in great force are marching on Washington." " The governors in turn," Senator James G. Blaine noted, " issued alarming proclamations, some of which were eminently calculated to spread the contagion of fear prevailing in Washington." [34] The Union administration was behaving very much like its pattern during the *Monitor–Virginia* affair.

While these events were transpiring along the Potomac, McClellan was steadily closing in on Richmond. On May 25, Brigadier General Henry Naglee's brigade of Casey's division was pushed one and a half miles west of Seven Pines, while the rest of the Fourth Corps under Keyes was instructed to occupy and fortify Seven Pines, at the junction of the Williamsburg pike and the Nine Mile road. With both the Third and Fourth Corps now across the Chickahominy on the right bank, Heintzelman was placed in command of both corps. Hooker's division of the Third Corps was watching the main bridge over White Oak Swamp, while Kearny's division of the same corps was placed a short distance in advance of Savage's Station on the

[33] Lincoln to McClellan, May 25, 1862, *C.C.W.*, I, 330; McClellan to Lincoln, May 25, 1862, Lincoln Papers; McClellan to his wife, May 25, 1862, McClellan Papers.
[34] Upton, *Military Policy*, 306; Blaine, *Twenty Years of Congress*, I, 365.

railroad. Sumner's Second Corps, forming McClellan's center, was on the left bank of the Chickahominy, just below New Bridge. Sumner began the construction of two bridges—the Grapevine Bridge and Sunderland Bridge—across the flooded river in his front, preparatory to crossing. The Union right wing, consisting of Porter's Fifth Corps and Franklin's Sixth Corps, extended the line six miles to Meadow Bridge, almost due north of Richmond. Stoneman's cavalry was patrolling the right flank and rear of the army and protecting the huge supply base at White House. The furthest Federal advance was Naglee's brigade, one and three-quarter miles west of Seven Pines and approximately four and three-quarter miles from the Confederate capital. McClellan's soldiers could see the spires of Richmond and hear the striking of clocks and the ringing of church bells.[35]

Meanwhile, there was activity in a new quarter. Lee had ordered the brigade of Brigadier General L. O. Branch from Gordonsville to Hanover Court House, nineteen miles north of Richmond. Brigadier General J. R. Anderson's brigade had been directed also to move from south of Fredericksburg to the court house. The forces of Branch and Anderson together numbered some 12,000 men. They now posed a threat to McClellan's right-rear and to his large supply base at White House, as well as forming a wedge between the Army of the Potomac and McDowell. McClellan therefore ordered Porter and his Fifth Corps to move on May 27 to eliminate this menace, to destroy the road and railroad bridges over the Pamunkey and South Anna rivers, and to cut the Virginia Central Railroad in several more places.[36]

Porter earmarked about 11,000 men for the venture. At about noon on May 27, encountering Branch's grayclad force near Hanover Court House, Porter immediately engaged it.

[35] Cook, *Siege of Richmond,* 122, 123–24; McClellan's *Report,* 93, 107; Webb, *The Peninsula,* 97.
[36] Allan, *Army of Northern Virginia,* 31; Porter's report, 12 *O.R.,* 680–81; Powell, *Fifth Corps,* 63; Fitz John Porter, "Hanover Court House and Gaines's Mill," *B. & L.,* II, 319.

In a short but sharp combat, the Southerners were driven headlong from the field, losing a gun and two supply trains. McClellan reached the battlefield at the end of the fight, well pleased with the result. The Federals at the battle of Hanover Court House lost 53 men killed and 344 wounded and missing. The Confederates were said to have lost approximately 200 killed, 200 wounded, and 730 prisoners. It was a handsome action on the Union side. During the day and on the twenty-eighth, McClellan's cavalry pursued the enemy, picking up additional Rebel prisoners. The bridges of the Richmond, Fredericksburg, and Potomac Railroad over the South Anna were burned by the Federal riders, and large quantities of Confederate quartermaster and commissary supplies were burned at Ashland by the free-wheeling blue horse. The Virginia Central was torn up in the direction of Ashland, and the enemy camp at Hanover Court House was seized and destroyed.[37]

The brief expedition had been eminently successful. Porter's victory cleared McClellan's right flank and rear for the time being. The Confederates now were unable to communicate with Stonewall Jackson by way of Gordonsville, but were obliged to use the round about route through Lynchburg. Nor did the enemy have ready contact with the area near Fredericksburg, or with northern Virginia in general, due to the severed rail lines. The Union front on its right wing was cleared now for McDowell's advance overland to join McClellan's right, so soon as the administration in Washington would allow him to resume his original movement. When it was learned, however, that McDowell was not coming at the present moment, McClellan, seeing that Porter's advanced position at Hanover Court House " was too much exposed to be permanently held," moved him back on May 28 to a position on the elevated ground at Gaines's Mill. Stoneman's cavalry returned to the vicinity

[37] Paris, *The Civil War*, II, 55–56; Porter, " Hanover Court House and Gaines's Mill," *loc. cit.*, 320–23; reports of Porter, J. H. Martindale, and George W. Morell, 12 *O.R.*, 682, 700–706; Allan, *Army of Northern Virginia*, 32-35; *M.O.S.*, 311, 371.

of Mechanicsville. The combat at Hanover Court House gave early indication that, among the Federal corps commanders, Porter was the ablest tactician and the most tenacious fighter.[38]

Tiring of the continual dickering with his civilian superiors over troop strengths, McClellan dispatched to Stanton on May 28 a strongly worded message. " It is the policy and duty of the Govt.," he asserted, " to send me by water all the well-drilled troops available. . . . I am confident that Washington is in no danger. Engines and cars in large numbers have been sent up to bring down Jackson's command. . . . The real issue is in the battle about to be fought in front of Richmond." As if to re-emphasize McClellan's views, McDowell declared to the Secretary, " I do not consider Washington City in any danger." But the President came back at McClellan with a prompt rejoinder. " That the whole of the enemy is concentrating on Richmond," said Lincoln, " I think cannot be certainly known to you or me. . . . I . . . shall aid you all I can consistently with my view of due regard to all points." War correspondent Swinton commented as follows on this statement of the President: " War is partial and imperious, and in place of having ' regard to all points,' it neglects many points to accumulate all on the *decisive* point." By pressing hard against Richmond with the principal Union army, McClellan was certain to bring to battle the main Confederate army in the East. On the thirtieth, he observed to Stanton, " From the tone of your telegrams and the President's I do not think that you at all appreciate the value and magnitude of Porter's victory." The issue between the commander on the Peninsula and his civilian superiors was sharpening. Then, on May 29, McClellan was forced to take to his bed with a recurrence of his old maladies, neuralgia and malaria, contracted in the Mexican War.[39]

[38] Webb, *The Peninsula*, 96; Paris, *The Civil War*, II, 56–57; McClellan, " The Peninsular Campaign," *loc. cit.*, 176; Longstreet, *Manassas to Appomattox*, 84.

[39] McClellan to Stanton, May 28 and 30, 1862, McClellan Papers; McDowell to Stanton, May 28, 1862, 18 *O.R.*, 268; Lincoln to McClellan, May 28, 1862, 12

But operations continued despite talk or illness. Naglee's brigade of Casey's division, leading the advance of McClellan's left wing, set up its picket line on the north side of the Williamsburg road about one and three-quarter miles west of Seven Pines and two miles south of Old Tavern. A Confederate reconnaissance by Major General D. H. Hill revealed that the bulk of Casey's division was a mile and a half west of Seven Pines, backing up Naglee. Noting the stiffening enemy opposition in front of Casey, Heintzelman ordered two brigades of Kearny's division to move a quarter of a mile in front of Savage's Station, in support of Casey. The Federal dispositions west of the Chickahominy on May 30 showed " Casey's division on the right of the Williamsburg Road, and perpendicular to it, the center at Fair Oaks; Couch's division at the Seven Pines; Kearny's division on the railroad, from near Savage's Station towards the bridge; Hooker's division on the borders of White Oak Swamp." Thus, McClellan's army was separated by the swollen Chickahominy—largely because of the administration order requiring him to throw out his right wing north of Richmond to meet McDowell. With two corps on the southwest side and three corps on the northeast side, the dispositions of the Union Army were such as to invite attack by the enterprising Confederates. The enemy did not keep the Federals waiting long.[40]

On the eventful day of May 31, McClellan was flat on his back in bed with a severe attack of neuralgia and malaria. Although his army was dangerously astride the Chickahominy, he was obliged to await two essential things before making the final movement against Richmond; namely, for the roads to harden a bit so that his superior siege artillery could move, and for the completion of the necessary bridges over the river to ensure his communications with his great base of supplies

O.R., 36; Swinton, *Army of the Potomac*, 105; McClellan to his wife, May 29, 1862, *M.O.S.*, 397.

[40] Cook, *Siege of Richmond*, 122; reports of Casey and D. H. Hill, 12 *O.R.*, 913, 943; Johnston's *Narrative*, 132; McClellan's *Report*, 107–108.

at White House. On the eve of battle near Richmond, the Confederate Army numbered at least 74,000 effectives, as opposed to McClellan's force of nearly 100,000 men.[41]

Joe Johnston, after having emerged triumphant at the First Battle of Bull Run, in July of 1861, had successively fallen back from Centerville and Manassas, and then again from Yorktown, Williamsburg, West Point, Norfolk, and Hanover Court House without fighting a general battle. Now he had recoiled within the environs of the Southern capital. He could retreat no further. As early as May 27, 1862, before "Jeb" Stuart had reported to him the withdrawal of McDowell's army from its intended march southward from Fredericksburg, Johnston had determined to attack McClellan before his army could be so enlarged as to render it hopelessly irresistable.[42]

Then, on the night of May 30, a furious rainstorm struck. It was the most savage storm that officers on both sides had ever seen. The terrible torrent and rising water endangered McClellan's bridges over the Chickahominy, threatening momentarily to sweep all of them away. If this happened, the two wings of his army would be isolated, thereby preventing him from reinforcing either wing if it were attacked in overwhelming numbers. Although the dreadful condition of the roads after the storm would slow the Confederate march and deployment, and limit the mobility of their field artillery, the physical conditions were, as Colonel William Allan of the Southern Army admits, much worse for the Federals, separated as they were and about to be attacked suddenly in heavy force at a place of the Confederates' choosing. In speaking of his critical condition at this time, McClellan stated that " Richmond could be attacked only by troops on the right bank. As the expectation of the advance of McDowell was still held out, and that only by the land route, I could not yet transfer the base to

[41] *M.O.S.*, 365; de Joinville, *Army of the Potomac*, 70; Frothingham, "The Peninsular Campaign of 1862," *loc. cit.*, 106; Alexander, *Military Memoirs*, 74; *C.C.W.*, I, 323.

[42] Johnston's *Narrative*, 131–32; Johnston, "Manassas to Seven Pines," *loc. cit.*, 211–12; G. W. Smith, "Two Days of Battle at Seven Pines," *B. & L.*, II, 224.

the James, but was obliged to retain it on the Pamunkey, and therefore to keep on the left bank a force sufficient to protect our communications and cover the junction with McDowell." [43]

With McClellan sick in bed at his headquarters at Gaines's Mill on May 31, the command of the Union left wing, comprising the Third and Fourth Corps on the right bank of the Chickahominy, fell to Heintzelman. The latter had, unfortunately for the Federals, not sufficiently concentrated his units within close enough supporting distance of each other, especially considering the execrable condition of the roads. There was, too, a serious gap between Fair Oaks and the Chickahominy, inviting a Confederate penetration. However, as the enemy plan evolved, the initial gray effort was to be at Seven Pines rather than at the more advantageous point of Fair Oaks. At these two points were two of the very few clearings in the whole region; " the rest of the country was one dense wood." [44]

Johnston's plan of battle was to attack the Union left wing southwest of the Chickahominy with twenty-three of his twenty-seven brigades. The Confederate plan of attack seemed sound: D. H. Hill's division, supported by that of Longstreet, was to move out the Williamsburg road and engage the Federals in front; Brigadier General Benjamin Huger was to fall upon the Union left flank; G. W. Smith was to advance toward Heintzelman's right flank by moving along the New Bridge road and the Nine Mile road (at which intersection Magruder had five grayclad brigades) , where he would be in position either to cover Longstreet's left or to fall upon Keyes's right flank. Longstreet was placed in command of the enemy right wing, while G. W. Smith commanded the left. The Southern divisions were to move at daylight on May 31. However, Johnston's excellent plan of battle was marred by the fact that he

---

[43] Keyes's report, 12 *O.R.*, 873; Casey's testimony, March 5, 1863, *C.C.W.*, I, 443; Allan, *Army of Northern Virginia*, 39; McClellan, " The Peninsular Campaign," *loc. cit.*, 176.

[44] Swinton, *Army of the Potomac*, 132–33; McClellan's *Report*, 108; de Joinville, *Army of the Potomac*, 72–73; a useful map of the battlefield is in *B. & L.*, II, 240.

issued his orders verbally, instead of putting them in writing, and some confusion resulted. In the initial clash, the thirteen Confederate brigades numbered, by Johnston's own figures, 32,500 men, while Keyes's Fourth Corps and two brigades of Kearny's division of the Third Corps together numbered some 16,200 effectives.[45]

On the Union side, Keyes had established three main defensive lines: the first line, held by Casey's division, was over three-quarters of a mile west of Seven Pines, and extending from a few hundred yards south of the Williamsburg pike to the railroad, the line crossing the road near Barker's house; the second line was held by Couch's division at Seven Pines (these first two defensive lines were not as yet completed) ; and the third line—the strongest—about one and a third miles east of Seven Pines, was unoccupied on the morning of the thirty-first.[46]

The Union Fourth Corps numbered about 10,000 men, including Casey's division of some 4,500 effectives. At approximately 1:00 P.M., Longstreet threw D. H. Hill forward against Casey, the attacking Confederates numbering about 9,000 men. The ground was so water-logged and inundated that a number of soldiers actually drowned in the swampy areas. The clash was sudden and vicious. After a stout resistance of several hours, Casey's division crumbled under the impetuous assault of the more numerous graycoats, despite the arrival of a few leg-weary Federal reinforcements. Seven guns were lost to the yelping enemy attackers. Casey lost approximately 1,750 of his 4,500 men in this murderous combat. His remnants first made a stand at Seven Pines, and then fell back at dark to Keyes's third defensive line, a little over a mile east of Seven Pines.[47]

[45] Johnston's *Narrative*, 132–34; 12 *O.R.*, 938; Johnston, " Manassas to Seven Pines," *loc. cit.*, 211–12; Smith, " Two Days of Battle at Seven Pines," *loc. cit.*, 225–29; Cook, *Siege of Richmond*, 186.

[46] Keyes's report, 12 *O.R.*, 872–73; Allan, *Army of Northern Virginia*, 38.

[47] Webb, *The Peninsula*, 100–106; testimony of Heintzelman, Casey, and Keyes, *C.C.W.*, I, 357, 443–44, 606–607; reports of Heintzelman, Couch, J. Peck, Naglee, Longstreet, and D. H. Hill, 12 *O.R.*, 812, 815, 816, 879, 888, 921, 940, 946, 971; McClellan's *Report*, 108–109; Swinton, *Army of the Potomac*, 133–35.

Keyes endeavored to assist Casey's retiring division by bringing up Couch's splendid division of less than 8,000 men, which took position in a line extending from Seven Pines toward Fair Oaks. Although Couch was slowly forced back, the Federal defense stiffened. Kearny's division was then put into line of battle near Seven Pines by Heintzelman, and this helped to stall the determined gray attack.[48]

There was delay on the Confederate left in bringing G. W. Smith's troops into action against the Union right. Not until about 4:00 P.M. did Smith throw forward Whiting's division against the right flank of Heintzelman's line, which was then contending with Longstreet in front. Johnston refrained also from committing to battle Magruder's division, his only reserve southwest of the Chickahominy. Smith's attack fell frontally and on the right flank of Couch's lone division in the vicinity of Fair Oaks Station. Couch was forced back slowly and grudgingly toward Dr. Trent's house in the direction of the Grapevine Bridge. Near Courtney's house, Couch formed a new line of battle, facing south now toward Fair Oaks. Thus, between 5:00 and 6:00 P.M., with Keyes in retreat toward White Oak Swamp and Bottom's Bridge, and with Smith bearing down in overwhelming force against Couch's depleted division, all seemed lost for Heintzelman's entire right wing of McClellan's army southwest of the Chickahominy.[49]

Across the Chickahominy on the left bank, at army headquarters near Gaines's Mill, the observation balloon of Professor T. S. C. Lowe had been grounded by high winds The first indication that the Union commander had of the fighting at Fair Oaks was the sound of the firing. When he heard the noise of battle, McClellan got up from his sick bed to try to meet the crisis. He immediately ordered Sumner to have his Second Corps in instant readiness to move at a moment's notice

---

[48] Stine, *Army of the Potomac*, 67–71; reports of Heintzelman and Kearny, 12 *O.R.*, 815–16, 840; Webb, *The Peninsula*, 107–108.

[49] Johnston's report, 12 *O.R.*, 934; Smith, " Two Days of Battle at Seven Pines," *loc. cit.*, 240–45; McClellan's *Report*, 109; Walker, *Second Corps*, 26–27; *M.O.S.*, 380.

to the aid of the hard-pressed Heintzelman. Anticipating the developing situation, and, from the sounds southwest of the river, divining the course of the battle, Sumner went one step further than McClellan's prompt orders, and at a little after 1:00 P.M. marched his corps out of camp and down to the bridges over the rampaging river. At 2:00 P.M., he received the order from McClellan—who had by then learned the course of the battle—to cross the Chickahominy and rush to Heintzelman's assistance. But could it be done in time? [50]

It would take too long for the Second Corps to reach the battlefield that day if Sumner used either Bottom's Bridge or the railroad bridge; therefore, his sole reliance had to be on the two temporary bridges which he had just completed in his front. It was to these spans that the old soldier moved his troops. After but one of Richardson's brigades had crossed by Sumner's Lower Bridge (also known as Sunderland Bridge), the structure was swept away by the raging current of the river. In a great feat, however, Sumner threw Sedgwick's division, followed by Richardson's other brigade, across the angry tide on the now-floating Grapevine Bridge (known also as Sumner's Upper Bridge). When the last troops had crossed in safety, this remaining trestle collapsed and was carried away. Men on foot could no longer cross. Only one artillery battery accompanied Sumner.[51]

Sedgwick's division (Richardson's did not arrive in time to take part in the combat on the first day) numbered about 8,000 men. Arriving at the crisis of the battle, just as the overwhelming forces of Longstreet and G. W. Smith were bearing down on the front and and flank of Couch's lone division, Sedgwick plugged the gap between Fair Oaks and the river. Had Sumner arrived a few minutes later, Smith's ten brigades would most likely have occupied the higher ground command-

---

[50] Paris, *The Civil War*, II, 63; *M.O.S.*, 365, 379–80, 397; Palfrey, ". . . Fall of Yorktown . . . ," *loc. cit.*, 181–82; Walker, *Second Corps*, 27; Webb, *The Peninsula*, 110.

[51] Goss, *Recollections*, 48; Walker, *Second Corps*, 28; Swinton, *Army of the Potomac*, 137; McClellan's *Report*, 110.

ing the southwestern *débouché* of the Grapevine Bridge. Needless to say, had Sumner been kept on the left bank of the Chickahominy with his two divisions, Heintzelman's twelve brigades would have been at the mercy of twenty-three enemy brigades.[52]

Johnston was caught by surprise by the sudden appearance of the Second Corps southwest of the river. Led by the gallant Sumner in person, Sedgwick's division repulsed G. W. Smith's heavy attack, and in turn counterattacked with the bayonet, driving the graycoats back with fearful losses. The firing ceased at darkness, just as Richardson's division was coming onto the field. McClellan himself arrived on the scene toward the close of the combat, and was satisfied with the course of the battle. Returning to his headquarters after affairs had been stabilized on the field, the Union commander narrowly averted death while recklessly riding across the booming Chickahominy.

Thus, it may be noted that McClellan, by his immediate appreciation of the tactical situation and by his prompt and correct orders, and Sumner, by his punctual and courageous action in bridging the treacherous river, along with their troops, had saved the day for the Army of the Potomac by succoring Heintzelman's struggling divisions, repelling the furious Southern attack, and hurling the foe back in retreat by a splendid counterattack.[53]

The fight on the thirty-first of May, 1862, had been a savage one. Of the nine general officers of Keyes's Fourth Corps, eight had been wounded or had had their horses shot out from under them. At the close of the day's action, Johnston had been severely wounded in the chest by a shell fragment, and borne from the field. The command of the Confederate Army—for one day—devolved upon G. W. Smith. Although the South-

[52] Cook, *Siege of Richmond*, 207; *C.C.W.*, I, 351; Walker, *Second Corps*, 26–27; Allan, *Army of Northern Virginia*, 48; Palfrey, ". . . Fall of Yorktown . . . ," *loc. cit.*, 198.

[53] Johnston's *Narrative*, 137–38; Walker, *Second Corps*, 29–37; Stine, *Army of the Potomac*, 64–65; Cook, *Siege of Richmond*, 202, 206, 213; Webb, *The Peninsula*, 111–13.

erners on their right had driven Keyes and Heintzelman back to a point a little over a mile east of Seven Pines, they had, on their more decisive left, after an initial advance, been repulsed and in turn thrown back. The main Confederate objective of crushing the entire Union left wing had not been realized. The casualties on the first day's battle were approximately 4,500 men on each side.[54]

The first of June broke misty and gray. With the guns silent in the leaden dawn, the Federal dispositions southwest of the Chickahominy were as follows: Heintzelman's troops were now strongly entrenched in a line perpendicular to the Williamsburg road, a little over a mile east of Seven Pines; Sedgwick's division was in position facing west, its left near Fair Oaks Station; Richardson's division was facing south, massed in a column of brigades, its right near the station. G. W. Smith's plan of battle for the Confederates was for his left wing under Whiting to hold steady on the defensive, while Longstreet's right wing resumed its attack of the previous day, pivoting in a counterclockwise wheel upon Whiting's right.[55]

At about 7:00 A. M. the fighting recommenced. The enemy heavily attacked Richardson's division—fighting its maiden battle—only to be sharply repelled and driven back with severe loss by a Federal countercharge, one of the grayclad brigades being routed in complete disorder. While the hesitant Smith continued to hold back the divisions of Whiting and Magruder, a Union offensive movement of Hooker's division was mounted by Heintzelman on the Federal left along the Williamsburg pike and the railroad, and succeeded in driving the Confederates back to a place near their starting point of May 31 at Seven Pines. The fighting on June 1 had lasted four hours.[56]

[54] DeTrobriand, *Army of the Potomac*, 231; Johnston's *Narrative*, 138; Heintzelman's report, 12 *O.R.*, 579–82; Palfrey, ". . . Fall of Yorktown . . . ," *loc. cit.*, 186.
[55] Palfrey, ". . . Fall of Yorktown . . . ," *loc. cit.*, 200–201; Cook, *Siege of Richmond*, 186; Webb, *The Peninsula*, 114; G. W. Smith's report, 12 *O.R.*, 992.
[56] Reports of Richardson, D. H. Hill, and G. E. Pickett, 12 *O.R.*, 765–66, 945, 983; Sumner's testimony, *C.C.W.*, I, 363; Walker, *Second Corps*, 47–50; Stine, *Army of the Potomac*, 62–65; McClellan's *Report*, 111.

Early on the morning of the second day's battle, McClellan himself appeared on the battlefield to the accompaniment of boisterous cheers from his soldiers. He had no tactical changes to make, being well satisfied with what Sumner and Heintzelman had done. The fact was that the whole Confederate Army was falling back in some disorder toward Richmond. The ineffective G. W. Smith had suffered a paralytic stroke after his failure on June 1, and Jefferson Davis had immediately named his chief military adviser, General Robert E. Lee, to assume command of the Southern Army. Seeing the defeat and hopeless position of the Confederate Army confronting the aroused Federals, Lee continued the withdrawal of the gray legions toward the environs of Richmond, thereby acknowledging McClellan's success.[57]

The National Army did not at once renew its offensive. In the early afternoon of June 1, Sumner received intelligence from the balloon—now aloft—of a very large enemy force moving upon him from the direction of Richmond. This information, however, proved to be erroneous. Nonetheless, the fighting was over. As a foreign observer wrote, "After such a struggle the two armies, composed of soldiers but little inured as yet to the hardships of war, were equally in need of rest." [58]

The battle of Fair Oaks, or Seven Pines, had been the greatest fought in the Eastern theater of war up to that time. The Confederates, according to Livermore, had had engaged on the two days of battle a total of approximately 41,816 men, while the Federals had had about 41,797 effectives engaged. The casualties were, for the Confederates, 980 killed, 4,749 wounded, 405 missing, a total of 6,134; for the Federals, 790 killed, 3,594 wounded, 647 missing, a total loss of 5,031.[59]

---

[57] George S. Hilliard, *The Life, Campaigns, and Public Services of General McClellan* . . . (Philadelphia, 1864), 168; Ropes, *Story of the Civil War*, II, 150; Alexander, *Military Memoirs*, 89.

[58] Palfrey, ". . . Fall of Yorktown . . . ," *loc. cit.*, 205; Paris, *The Civil War*, II, 72.

[59] Livermore, *Numbers and Losses*, 81; *B. & L.*, II, 219; 12 *O.R.*, 762, 942.

Johnston had made a herculean effort to destroy the entire left wing of McClellan's army. This wing comprised two-fifths of the Union Army. The able Confederate commander had maneuvered twenty-three of his twenty-seven brigades against this portion of the blue army southwest of the Chickahominy. The tremendous storm of May 30-31 had rendered it possible —although extremely difficult—for McClellan to reinforce Heintzelman's endangered force with but two divisions under Sumner. But, in his first large-scale battle, McClellan had met the challenge creditably. Not only had he succeeded in thwarting Johnston's excellent plans to annihilate two-fifths of his army, but he had managed to hurl the enemy back in some disorder upon the defenses of Richmond.[60]

The weapon molded by McClellan in long months of seeming idleness and procrastination had met the stern test of fire and had been tempered by it. The Army of the Potomac was to remain, throughout many discouraging days under inept commanders, a resolute, reliable, magnificent instrument and shield of the Union—a superb monument to its creator and to the citizens of the republic who spawned it.

[60] See Ropes, *Story of the Civil War*, II, 156.

Chapter Six

Change of Base

> Under ordinary circumstances the Federal army should have been destroyed.
>
> —*Robert E. Lee*

HE tall, lonely man in Washington had been waiting apprehensively near the telegraph office for word from the Peninsula. When the clicking instrument flashed the information from McClellan on May 31 that a great battle was in progress at Fair Oaks, Lincoln advised the General, " Stand well on your ground, hold all your ground, or yield any only inch by inch and in good order." Later, on June 1, after having received McClellan's messages describing in outline his success at Fair Oaks, the relieved President telegraphed, somewhat over-optimistically, " Thanks for what you could and did say in your dispatch. . . . If the enemy shall not have renewed the attack this afternoon, I think the hardest of your work is done." [1]

The battle of Fair Oaks ended about noon on June 1 with the withdrawal of the Confederates toward Richmond. It was again raining. The Chickahominy valley was so flooded that it was to take McClellan three weeks to rebuild the requisite number of bridges across the swollen river—bridges which not only had to cross the main channel itself, but which had to span the extensive swamps and marshes on either side. The nearest bridge still standing at the close of the battle was Bottom's Bridge. For McClellan to have thrown his whole army

---

[1] Lincoln to McClellan, June 1, 1862, McClellan Papers.

immediately across the Chickahominy against Richmond in pursuit of the enemy would have necessitated his marching it down the left bank to Bottom's Bridge and then up the right bank to Fair Oaks, a distance of twenty-three miles through seas of mud. This would have been a futile enterprise. So bad was the weather to continue until approximately the middle of June, that no major forward advance was made by McClellan, except to move all but the Fifth Corps across to the southwest bank of the Chickahominy.[2]

As if in reply to the President's statement that the hardest part of his task was over, McClellan declared in a telegram to Stanton, " I expect still more fighting before we reach Richmond." The heaviest rains known for twenty years were to persist until about June 20, causing artillery pieces to sink inextricably into the mud, and condemning the bulk of both armies to static warfare. Still, the blueclad host was within sight and sound of its objective. McClellan's outposts on June 2 were but five miles from Richmond. The entrenched Union corps southwest of the Chickahominy were disposed in the following manner: Keyes's Fourth Corps was at White Oak Swamp; Heintzelman's Third Corps was on Keyes's right, astride the Williamsburg pike; Sumner's Second Corps was to the right of the Third, on the Richmond and York River Railroad. Franklin's Sixth and Porter's Fifth Corps were still northeast of the river in the direction of Mechanicsville.[3]

One of Lee's first acts upon assuming command of the Confederate Army was to contact the Union commander concerning Lee's wife and daughter, who were then situated behind Federal lines near White House. McClellan informed Lee that they would be released at any time convenient to him. When a Southern staff officer appeared under a flag of truce at Union headquarters, he was received in a friendly fashion

[2] Heintzelman's Journal, entry of June 1, 1862; 12 O.R., 115; Webb, The Peninsular, 118; Ropes, Story of the Civil War, II, 158–59.

[3] McClellan to Stanton, June 2, 1862, 12 O.R., 44; McClellan's Report, 113, 116; Paris, The Civil War, II, 74; McClellan, "The Peninsular Campaign," loc. cit., 178

130

by McClellan, who trotted out his best liquors. When the ladies were ready to depart, McClellan bade them goodbye in his usual courteous manner, even offering to escort them personally as far as the picket lines. Such an incident was typical of McClellan's mild policy toward civilian noncombatants.[4]

Meanwhile, operations were still underway in the Shenandoah Valley. On June 2, McClellan received an encouraging communiqué from the Secretary of War. "The indications are," said Stanton glibly, "that Frémont or McDowell will fight Jackson today, and as soon as he is disposed of another large body of troops will be at your service. . . . All interest now centers in your operations, and full confidence is entertained of your brilliant and glorious success." A few days later, however, *Stonewall* "disposed of" two pursuing Federal forces at Cross Keys and Port Republic, thus ensuring his escape toward the southern end of the Valley. Lincoln sadly confessed to Browning that the administration's personally conducted campaign to capture the wily fox of the Valley had failed. Shields, on June 2, urged Lincoln and Stanton to allow McDowell to return now to the original project of moving to reinforce McClellan at Richmond. On June 8, the President directed the futile chase of Jackson to be broken off.[5]

McClellan took the opportunity while the armies on the Peninsula were bogged down in the mud to issue another of his bombastic proclamations to his army: "Soldiers of the Army of the Potomac! I have fulfilled at least a part of my promise to you. You are now face to face with the rebels, who are held at bay in front of their capital. The final and decisive battle is at hand. . . . The result cannot be for a moment doubtful. . . . Wherever you have met the enemy you have beaten him. Wherever you have used the bayonet he has given way in panic and disorder. I ask of you now one last crowning

---

[4] W. Roy Mason, "Origin of the Lee Tomatoes," *B. & L.*, II, 277.

[5] Stanton to McClellan, June 2, 1862, 12 *O.R.*, 44; Walter Geer, *Campaigns of the Civil War* (New York, 1926), 96; *Browning's Diary*, I, 548; Shields to Stanton, June 2, 1862, 18 *O.R.*, 322, 354; 15 *O.R.*, 653.

effort. Soldiers! I will be with you in this battle, and share its dangers with you. Our confidence in each other is now founded upon the past." [6] The Young Napoleon had lost little of his rhetorical skill in appealing to his troops. Nor was he apparently contented with his position astraddle the dangerous Chickahominy. He was, at this time, conferring with the navy's Goldsborough about the possibility of a future movement of the Army of the Potomac to the James River.[7] On June 3, he ordered a reconnaissance to the James to open communications with the Federal gunboats. The operation lasted from the third to the seventh.[8] McClellan realized, however, that until the promised arrival of McDowell, the administration's order to him to extend his right wing to the east and north of Richmond remained unrevoked. On the seventh, he reported to Stanton that the Chickahominy had risen from three to four feet in its wide bottoms, and that both banks were inundated. "The whole face of the country," declared the General, " is a perfect bog. The men are working night and day, up to their waists in water, to complete " the bridges.[9]

With affairs looking more secure in the lower Shenandoah Valley and at Washington, the Federal administration now sought to augment McClellan's army. On June 8, McDowell was instructed to move " as speedily as possible in the direction of Richmond, to cooperate with Major-General McClellan." McCall's division was already on the way to the Peninsula by water, and McDowell was to follow by land as soon as he returned to Fredericksburg from the Valley. But the authorities· in the Federal capital had once again pulled a switch: McDowell was now to retain independent command of his army when it joined up with McClellan. However, delays in the Valley were to prevent McDowell's army from ever reaching the Peninsula, except for McCall's detached division. So, in

---

[6] Cook, *Siege of Richmond*, 224; Hilliard, *Life and Campaigns of George B. McClellan*, 68–69.

[7] Goldsborough's testimony, April 1, 1863, *C.C.W.*, I, 633.

[8] 12 *O.R.*, 998–1000.

[9] McClellan to Stanton, June 7, 1862, Lincoln Papers.

effect, Jackson's masterly movements in the Shenandoah Valley had succeeded brilliantly in preventing reinforcements from reaching McClellan.[10]

McCall's division began arriving by ship at White House on June 11, just a little over five days after the order for it to move had been given. McCall brought with him approximately 9,000 men. This splendid division, known as the Pennsylvania Reserves, was designated temporarily as the Third Division of Porter's Fifth Corps. McCall's brigade commanders were Brigadier Generals John F. Reynolds, George G. Meade, and Truman Seymour. As the new division was disembarking, McClellan received a dispatch from Stanton in which the Secretary proclaimed, " Be assured, General, that there never was a moment when my desire has been otherwise than to aid you with my whole heart, mind and strength since the hour we first met and . . . you have never had and never can have any one more truly your friend or more anxious to support you." [11]

McClellan was overjoyed at hearing of McDowell's ordered march to join him. But he told the Secretary of the bad roads existing and of the destruction by high water and by the enemy of the railroad bridges south of Fredericksburg. He said that this would greatly delay McDowell's progress overland, and urged that he be sent—as had McCall—by water to unite with the Army of the Potomac. McClellan then added the following most significant observation: " An extension of my right wing to meet him may involve serious hazard to my flank and line of communications and may not suffice to rescue from any peril in which a strong movement of the enemy may involve him. . . . The junction of his force with the extension of my present position will not admit of delay. . . . The enemy are massing their troops near our front." [12] That this was an accurate assessment of the developing situation was soon to be attested.

[10] Thomas to McDowell, June 8, 1862, *C.C.W.*, I, 275–76; McDowell to McClellan, June 12, 1862, 15 *O.R.*, 97.

[11] Ropes, *Story of the Civil War*, II, 159; Cook, *Siege of Richmond*, 290–91; Stine, *Army of the Potomac*, 74; Stanton to McClellan, June 11, 1862, McClellan Papers.

[12] McClellan to Stanton, June 12, 1862, Lincoln Papers.

On June 12, the spectacular exploit of the dashing Confederate cavalryman, "Jeb" Stuart, got underway. With 1,200 troopers, the "beau sabreur" of the South swept around McClellan's right flank and rear, fighting small but successful skirmishes at Hawes's Shop and Old Church, making a few insignificant captures of men and supplies, crossing the Chickahominy at Forge Bridge, and riding completely around the Federal Army with the loss of but one man and one gun. Stuart had noticed the weak position of McClellan's great base of supplies at White House, but had been hurriedly chased away at Tunstall's Station by Reynolds' brigade. McClellan ordered his cavalry in immediate pursuit, but to no avail. Praises of the gray cavalry exploit rang from Southern newspapers. The enemy's action, however, served still further to convince McClellan of the vulnerability of his right wing and of his important base at White House.[13]

Despite the promises of friendship and all-out support from Stanton, the Federal administration was not satisfied with McClellan. Consequently, Burnside was brought to Washington from the North Carolina capes to confer with the civilian authorities. The inside story of the "Burnside incident" is related by the influential Quartermaster General, Meigs:

> The country was impatient. The President felt the pressure, and finally against [Burnside's] protest, he sent Burnside to relieve McClellan; but at Burnside's earnest request, left him with discretion, after acquainting McClellan with the contents of the order in his pocket, not to deliver it, if any assurance of progress could, under this pressure, be obtained from him.
>
> Burnside obtained such assurances as he thought justified him in not taking command of the army on the Peninsula, and returned to the President and reported leaving McClellan in command.[14]

---

[13] Stuart's report, 12 *O.R.*, 1036, 1039; Allan, *Army of Northern Virginia*, 62–64; W. T. Robins, "Stuart's Ride Around McClellan," *B. & L.*, II, 275.

[14] Meigs, "The Relations of President Lincoln and Secretary Stanton to the Military Commanders in the Civil War," *loc. cit.*, 291.

Meanwhile, McClellan was occupied with devising plans for the final movement against the Confederate capital. As always, he was extremely tight-lipped about his anticipated strategy and tactics. Writing to Ellen on June 15, however, he gave her in general terms his plan of campaign against Lee: " I shall make the first battle mainly an artillery combat. As soon as I gain possession of the ' Old Tavern ' I will push them in upon Richmond and behind their works; then I will bring up my heavy [siege] guns, shell the city, and carry it by assault." [15]

But the Union commander was uneasy following Stuart's raid. Therefore, on June 15 he ordered a limited reconnaissance by Casey to New Market, near the James River, probably with a view to a later change of base by the Army of the Potomac from the Pamunkey to the James. This sortie was made in small force, however, as McClellan did not wish too many blue soldiers to be seen south of White Oak Swamp for fear they might tip Lee off as to the Union commander's likely movements in the future. At the same time, McClellan wisely began sending transports laden with ammunition, food, and other supplies from his base at White House to Harrison's Landing on the James. He dispatched also his topographical engineers to examine the ground between the Richmond and York River Railroad and White Oak Swamp, while Averell's cavalry reconnoitered the known roads leading to the James. Although discovering a fairly accurate map of Henrico County, McClellan ordered additional maps to be made of the country between the Chickahominy and the James. Unfortunately, none of the available maps contained all the roads in this region.[16]

The Confederate strategists, however, were not idle. Lee in Richmond was evolving a bold plan of campaign aimed at

[15] McClellan to his wife, June 15, 1862, *M.O.S.*, 405.
[16] Stine, *Army of the Potomac*, 75; General A. L. Abbot to Ropes, February 17, 1895, Ropes, *Story of the Civil War*, II, 162, 163n; 12 *O.R.*, 64, 119, 153, 159, 169; 13 *O.R.*, 19, 193, 228; *M.O.S.*, 411; *B. & L.*, II, 379, 407, 408.

driving the Union Army from the doorstep of Richmond and destroying it in battle. Lee's original plan called for Jackson, after threatening still another northward movement in the Valley, to march swiftly and stealthily to Ashland. From there, Stonewall, perhaps with the assistance of part of Stuart's cavalry, was to move around McClellan's right flank and cut his communications with his large White House base, while Lee with the bulk of the Southern Army would assail the Federals on the southwest side of the Chickahominy. Consequently, Lee sent Whiting's division and a brigade to Jackson—and advertised this movement to the Federals—in order to keep McDowell, Banks, Shields, and Frémont from being allowed to join McClellan. Stonewall took these units, and with his own troops and Major General Richard S. Ewell's, began on June 17 his march from the Valley toward Richmond, his total force numbering now about 25,000 men. Lee's scheme was an audacious one, and posed a menacing threat to the exposed Union right wing. Had it been possible, this was the time for McClellan, if reinforced by McDowell, to have moved against Lee and beaten him to the offensive punch before Jackson could arrive on the Federal right flank.[17]

About this time, after a protracted period, the unusually heavy rains began to diminish and the ground began to harden. McClellan's troops had been engaged in entrenching their positions on and about the old Fair Oaks battlefield, and the Confederates were likewise busy with the spade and axe. One of McClellan's staff officers, the Count of Paris, was of the opinion that the National commander planned to advance carefully, by stages, taking full advantage of his superior heavy siege artillery. On June 18, the remainder of Franklin's Sixth Corps crossed to the southwest side of the Chickahominy and went into position on Sumner's right. Now, the Federal force on the right bank presented an entrenched front of almost four miles in length, running from White Oak Swamp through

[17] Lee to Jackson, June 16, 1862, 14 *O.R.*, 598, 602; Webb, *The Peninsula*, 122–24; Johnston's *Narrative*, 108; Upton, *Military Policy*, 274–75.

Golding's farm to the Chickahominy. Between the swamp and the James River were miles of uncharted, guerilla-infested country—a forbidding no-man's-land. On the northeast side of the Chickahominy, Porter's Fifth Corps stretched from Dr. Gaines's house about three miles to a point just northwest of Mechanicsville, where the Federal pickets were but four and a half miles from Richmond. On the nineteenth, McClellan moved McCall's division from Gaines's farm to Beaver Dam Creek. The weather had now become clear and extremely hot. The Union bridges across the Chickahominy were nearing completion. McClellan had on June 20 a little over 105,000 men present for duty, including, of course, many noncombatants.[18]

As the National commander was readying the final advance on the Confederate capital, Lee himself was perfecting plans to assume the initiative. With his command marching rapidly toward Richmond from the Valley, Jackson rode ahead to attend an important council of war. A new plan of attack, different from Lee's original one, was drawn up. Fear was now expressed for the safety of Stonewall were he to move alone against the Federals on the northeast side of the Chickahominy. By the new plan, Jackson, Longstreet, Major General A. P. Hill, and D. H. Hill were all to move against McClellan's White House communications and right wing, while Magruder, Huger, and Major General Theophilus Holmes were to stand on the defensive on the southwest side of the river against the bulk of McClellan's army. The date fixed upon to assail the Northern Army was June 26. Lee apparently did not believe that McClellan would dare to try to hold his position near Richmond by changing his base of operations to the James near Harrison's Landing. Instead, Lee thought that the Federal commander would withdraw back down the Peninsula toward West Point and Williamsburg. This is most likely why Lee placed the bulk of his army on the northeast side of the Chickahominy, in order to fall upon the head and flank of the Union

[18] Paris, *The Civil War*, II, 75; Cook, *Siege of Richmond*, 227–31; Stine, *Army of the Potomac*, 78–79; Barnard's report, 12 *O.R.*, 115; *B. & L.*, II, 315.

Army as it supposedly would endeavor, in retreat, to cross the river at Bottom's Bridge and the railroad bridge.[19]

On June 24, McClellan learned from a Confederate deserter that Jackson was moving in force from Gordonsville to Frederick Hall with the intention of falling upon the Federal right flank and rear. Consequently, McClellan ordered Porter to send a detachment toward Walnut Grove and Bethesda Church, informing him that he might soon have to withstand an assault by superior numbers. The bulk of the Federal Army, on the southwest side of the Chickahominy, was in an almost unassailable position behind the extensive fieldworks constructed between Golding's farm and White Oak Swamp. That evening, McClellan telegraphed Stanton, " I hope to open on enemy's batteries tomorrow morning." [20]

In the meantime, Lee had been strengthening the fortifications about Richmond. He had been reinforced, in recent days, by approximately 16,000 soldiers from North Carolina, by over 5,000 from South Carolina, and by six regiments from Georgia. He was also being joined by some 25,000 under Jackson. Allowing for the casualties at Fair Oaks and for the otherwise incapacitated men, Lee was to have, in the coming Seven Days Battle, the largest army he was ever to command in the war, probably some 90,000, as opposed to McClellan's 91,169 effectives.[21]

But McClellan believed he was actually fighting an enemy army twice as large as it was. " Reliable sources " placed the Confederate numbers facing him at nearly 200,000 men. On June 25, the General sent a perspicacious and strongly worded wire to Stanton. " I incline to think," McClellan stated, " that Jackson will attack my right and rear." He then declared that

---

[19] Daniel H. Hill, "Lee's Attacks North of the Chickahominy," *B. & L.*, II, 347; Longstreet, *Manassas to Appomattox*, 120–21; Lee's report, 13 *O.R.*, 493–94.

[20] Cook, *Siege of Richmond*, 304; *M.O.S.*, 408; McClellan's report, 12 *O.R.*, 49; McClellan to Stanton, June 24, 1862, McClellan Papers.

[21] Lee's report, 12 *O.R.*, 490; 14 *O.R.*, 589, 645; Johnston, " Manassas to Seven Pines," *loc. cit.*, 217–18; Livermore, *Numbers and Losses*, 86; Johnston's *Narrative*, 145–46.

he was in no way responsible for his lack of proper numbers, as he had " not failed to represent repeatedly the necessity of reinforcements; that this was the decisive point, and that all the available means of the Government should be concentrated here." The responsibility in case of disaster, McClellan averred, " must rest where it belongs." He concluded by asserting, " I feel that there is no use in again asking for reinforcements." In the words of an officer of the Fifth Corps, " Richmond could only be captured by regular [siege] approaches or by assault. Regular approaches required time and a well secured base of supplies. Assault required superior force and ample reserves." McClellan had neither.[22]

The great Seven Days Battle began on June 25 with the combat at Oak Grove. On that morning, McClellan ordered an advance of his lines on the Williamsburg road near Seven Pines preparatory to the general advance slated for the twenty-sixth. The movement " was directed toward the ultimate occupation of the plateau of Old Tavern." Heintzelman deployed Hooker's division perpendicular to the Williamsburg road, facing west. At 8:00 A. M., Hooker advanced across swampy ground, but encountered strong opposition from Huger's gray-clad division. After the Federals had gained some little ground, Heintzelman, for unknown reasons, ordered Hooker back to his starting point.[23]

McClellan arrived on the field at Oak Grove at 1:00 P. M., and assumed personal command of the battle. Riding out to the forward picket lines to get a closer view of the enemy, the Union commander whipped off his coat and climbed to the top of a tree. There, he calmly took notes of the Confederate

[22] Swinton, *Army of the Potomac*, 143; McClellan to Stanton, June 25, 1862, McClellan Papers; see Freeman, *R. E. Lee*, II, 116; Cook, *Siege of Richmond*, 302; McClellan's *Report*, 122; 12 *O.R.*, 269; Powell, *Fifth Corps*, 74.
[23] McClellan's report, 12 *O.R.*, 49–50; 13 *O.R.*, 95; *M.O.S.*, 410; Marks, *Peninsula Campaign*, 221; Francis W. Palfrey, " The Seven Days' Battles to Malvern Hill," Dwight (ed.), *Campaigns in Virginia*, 226; William B. Franklin, " Rear-Guard Fighting During the Change of Base," *B. & L.*, II, 366; Stine, *Army of the Potomac*, 75ff; Cook, *Siege of Richmond*, 294, 296–99; Allan, *Army of Northern Virginia*, 73–74.

MECHANICSVILLE TO
WHITE OAK SWAMP

R. H. Kramer

Old Church

Bethesda Church

Shady Grove Church

Mechanicsville

Walnut Grove Church

Ellerson's Mill

Beaver Dam Creek

New Bridge

Dr. Gaines

Gaines's Mill

New Cold Harbor

Old Cold Harbor

McGhee's

Barker's Mill

Watt's

Powhite Creek

Boatswain Creek

Grapevine Bridge

Alexander's Bridge

Sumner's Lower Bridge

Dr. Trent's

Woodbury's Br.

Courtney's Br.

Duane's Br.

Golding's

Garnett's

New Bridge

Old Tavern Road

Nine Mile Road

Fair Oaks Station

Savage's Station

Allen's

Dispatch Station

To White House

To Williamsburg

Bottom's Bridge

Chimney's

White Oak Bridge

To Glendale

Peake's

WHITE   OAK   SWAMP

Seven Pines

Redoubt

Twin Houses

Oak Grove

Barker's

White Oak Creek

Charles City Road

To Glendale

Williamsburg Turnpike

position, although narrowly averting death from a sudden fusilade of musketry from the graycoats. Learning of Hooker's earlier success and of his strange withdrawal by Heintzelman, McClellan immediately ordered " Fighting Joe," aided by a brigade of Keyes's Fourth Corps, to attack again and regain the ground previously won. Against tenacious resistance and a severe fire, this was accomplished by Hooker, the battle ending with the Union pickets but four miles from Richmond. Each side lost approximately five hundred casualties at Oak Grove. But while this combat was being fought, ominous gray forces were gathering near the Union right wing, northeast of the Chickahominy. Jackson's rapidly marching troops had reached Ashland, about nine miles north of Richmond on the R. F. & P. Railroad.[24]

The morning of June 26—the day of the battle of Mechanicsville—dawned clear and very still. At Union headquarters, McClellan was still suffering a bit from neuralgia, although the attacks of malaria had passed. The deployment of the various Federal corps, from right to left, were as follows: Porter's Fifth Corps was on the northeast side of the Chickahominy; then, on the southwest side of the river were Franklin's Sixth Corps, Sumner's Second Corps, Heintzelman's Third Corps, with Keyes's Fourth Corps in reserve. In order to comply with the administration's unrevoked order to keep his right wing thrown out toward Hanover Court House, and to cover the railway which supplied his army as far as White House, McClellan was obliged to leave Porter on the left bank of the Chickahominy. Porter's line had been facing the river—parallel to it—with McCall on the right at Mechanicsville, and Bridgadier General George Sykes and Brigadier General George W. Morell near Gaines's Mill. According to Porter, " the faulty location of the Union army, divided as it was by the Chickahominy, was from the first realized by General McClellan, and

[24] Cook, *Siege of Richmond*, 294, 296–99; Paris, *The Civil War*, II, 84–85; Thomas T. Ellis, *Leaves from the Diary of an Army Surgeon* . . . (New York, 1863) , 109; reports of Armistead, Wright, Ransom, 13 *O.R.*, 791, 804, 817.

141

became daily an increasing cause of care and anxiety to him."
However, the National commander still hoped, once the
promised divisions of McDowell joined him, to be able to
undertake his long-nurtured scheme of changing his base of
operations to the James River.[25]

It was Lee's plan, when Jackson neared Hanover Court
House, to shift most of the Confederate divisions from the
right bank of the Chickahominy to the left bank, and with
this overwhelming force to " sweep down the [northeast] side
of the Chickahominy, towards the York River, laying hold of
McClellan's communications with White House." Lee expected
Jackson, on June 26 at the latest, to move north of Beaver Dam
Creek and envelop Porter's right flank and rear; but on that
morning Stonewall was delayed by Union pickets, who destroyed
the bridge over the Tolopotomoy Creek in front of him. After
repairing the bridge, Jackson was further retarded by trees
which had been felled across the road, as well as by the fatigue
of his weary troops. Pressing on, however, Jackson reached
Hundley's Corner, only three miles north of Porter's right
flank, at 4:30 P.M. (just as the battle of Mechanicsville was
about to commence), and then went into bivouac for the rest
of the day![26]

Divining the Confederate attack on the Fifth Corps, McClellan himself, accompanied by Porter, placed McCall's division
in position early on the morning of the twenty-sixth on the
east bank of Beaver Dam Creek. The line extended from
the Chickahominy on the left to a point beyond the upper
Mechanicsville road on the right. The position was a very
strong one, with high banks along the creek, woods—with
slashings—on the right, and rifle pits in front. While enemy
infantry could cross the creek by way of the upper Mechanics-

[25] Porter, "Hanover Court House and Gaines's Mill," loc. cit., 324; James
Longstreet, "The Seven Days, Including Frayser's Farm," B. & L., II, 397;
Barnard's testimony, C.C.W., I, 403–404; Paris, The Civil War, II, 85–86.

[26] Swinton, Army of the Potomac, 144; Allan, Army of Northern Virginia,
79–80; see G. F. R. Henderson, Stonewall Jackson and the American Civil War
(New York, 1902), II, 16–25; Ropes, Story of the Civil War, II, 171–72.

ville road, artillery could only be gotten over readily by the road at Ellerson's Mill, at which point the Federals had constructed an epaulment. After having posted the troops, McClellan returned to his headquarters on the right bank of the Chickahominy. When the firing commenced in the afternoon of the twenty-sixth, however, he soon rode back to join Porter on the field, and remained there until midnight.[27]

On the Confederate side, the divisions of A. P. Hill, Longstreet, and D. H. Hill crossed to the northeast side of the Chickahominy on the morning of the twenty-sixth. Apparently awaiting the appearance of Jackson on the Union right-rear, Lee delayed the attack until mid-afternoon. When Stonewall failed to arrive, A. P. Hill sent his 14,000 men forward against McCall's 9,000. Apparently afraid to wait longer for fear of wrecking Lee's plan, A. P. Hill moved incautiously across the open ground to assail McCall frontally. At Mechanicsville, Hill's division split, part going down the turnpike toward the Union right, and the other part moving along the Ellerson's Mill road to strike McCall's left-center. The Federals allowed the grayclads to approach quite close to Beaver Dam Creek—part of the enemy column marching in broad view along a road parallel to the Union line—then, when the head of the Confederate column drew near, the entire blue line opened a murderous fire. Musketry volleys and artillery blasts caught Hill's men in front and flank, mowing them down like wheat before a reaper, and scattering them to the four winds. Jefferson Davis had ridden out from Richmond to join Lee on the battlefield, just in time to witness Hill's bloody repulse. Brisk firing by the picket lines continued until 9:00 P.M. The Southerners suffered a loss in the battle of Mechanicsville of 1,484 killed and wounded (no figures for the missing); Porter's

[27] Powell, *Fifth Corps*, 76, 78, 81; Cook, *Siege of Richmond*, 307; Webb, *The Peninsula*, 125–27; J. R. Sypher, *History of the Pennsylvania Reserve Corps . . .*, 198, 206; Porter, " Hanover Court House and Gaines's Mill," *loc. cit.*, 328, 331; Paris, *The Civil War*, II, 91; Ropes, *Story of the Civil War*, II, 172.

men lost but 49 killed, 207 wounded, and 105 missing, a total loss of 361.[28]

At dawn on June 27, Lee again tried to force Porter's line at Beaver Dam Creek. The attack was smaller than the one on the twenty-sixth, and was easily thrown back by the Federals. However, Jackson had by this time passed McCall's line on the northern (or right) flank and turned the position, forcing Porter to pull McCall back to a new line.[29]

In the brief lull after the battle of Mechanicsville, McClellan once again addressed himself to Stanton as regards the small, scattered, independent Federal armies in northern Virginia. " I will beg that you put some general," said McClellan, " in command of the Shenandoah and of all the troops in front of Washington for the sake of the country." Unknown to McClellan, this very policy was at last being adopted by Lincoln on the evening of June 26. A Presidential order united the armies of Banks, Frémont, and McDowell into the new Army of Virginia, to be commanded by Major General John Pope, the Western general and favorite of the Radicals on the Committee on the Conduct of the War. The new army, Lincoln stated, was to have a three-fold duty: to protect Washington, to safeguard West Virginia, and to aid in the attack expected to be made by McClellan on Richmond. Pope himself met with the Radicals on the floor of the Senate at this time, severely criticized McClellan, and spoke glibly of his own dash and prowess. Playing upon Lincoln's anxiety for the safety of Washington, Pope urged the immediate recall of McClellan's whole army from the Peninsula to the front of the Federal capital.[30]

On June 27, the bloody battle of Gaines's Mill—the third day

[28] Swinton, *Army of the Potomac*, 145; Goss, *Recollections*, 56; Powell, *Fifth Corps*, 76–81; Sypher, *Pennsylvania Reserves*, 206–16; Porter, " Hanover Court House and Gaines's Hill," *loc. cit.*, 330–31; Livermore, *Numbers and Losses*, 82; *B. & L.*, II, 331n.

[29] Stine, *Army of the Potomac*, 80–81; McClellan's *Report*, 122.

[30] McClellan to Stanton, June 27, 1862, McClellan Papers; Order of Lincoln, June 26, 1862, Stanton Papers; New York *Tribune*, June 26 and 27, 1862; Pope's testimony, *C.C.W.*, I, 279.

of combat of the Seven Days Battle—was fought. Anticipating Lee's strategy of turning his right and gaining Porter's rear, and seeing that the right flank of the Fifth Corps was too much in the air at Beaver Dam Creek, McClellan, about 3:00 A. M. on the twenty-seventh, withdrew Porter to a previously examined position of some strength behind Boatswain Creek, near Gaines's Mill. It was not feasible for McClellan to move the bulk of his army over to the northeast side of the Chickahominy to aid Porter, because his communications with his former base of supplies at White House had already been cut by Jackson's movement and by Stuart's cavalry. Nor could he immediately withdraw Porter directly from Beaver Dam Creek to the southwest bank of the Chickahominy, for this would expose the rear of the Union Army to Jackson, who, by using the lower bridges of the Chickahominy, as well as those near Dr. Trent's, might perhaps outrace or intercept the march of the Army of the Potomac to its new base on the James River. An intermediate position for Porter was, therefore, necessary—a position where the Fifth Corps could fight Stonewall and the other enemy divisions in order to gain time for the safe withdrawal of the long Union wagon trains and heavy siege ordnance to the haven on the James. During the previous night, the bulk of Porter's supply wagons and heavy guns had been removed to the southwest bank of the Chickahominy. Early on the morning of the twenty-seventh, Porter skillfully moved his men to the new position behind Boatswain Creek, the Confederates following closely. Porter had approximately 25,000 effectives with which to oppose about 57,000 grayclad soldiers. Remembering Pinkerton's recent reports that he was facing an enemy army of " over 180,000 " men, McClellan felt unable to reinforce Porter to any considerable extent, believing that the Southerners were in great strength southwest of the Chickahominy.[31]

[31] Swinton, *Army of the Potomac*, 146–49; McClellan's *Report*, 125; Webb, *The Peninsula*, 127, 129, 130, 135; Ropes, *Story of the Civil War*, II, 174–75; Powell, *Fifth Corps*, 83; 12 *O.R.*, 55, 57; Livermore, *Numbers and Losses*, 83.

The Union Fifth Corps occupied a convex line of battle—selected by McClellan—along a partially wooded ridge which followed the left bank of Boatswain Creek. It extended from near the Watts house on the Federal left northeastward to the vicinity of the McGhee house. Porter's position covered his line of retreat across the Chickahominy at Woodbury's, Duane's, Alexander's, and the Grapevine bridges. This naturally strong position was improved by felling trees and digging rifle pits. Porter's new line was, however, necessarily long for the number of troops at his disposal, and his right flank was somewhat in the air. At first the enemy thought that Porter's main line was behind Powhite Creek instead of Boatswain Creek. When the Federal position was finally uncovered, Lee ordered A. P. Hill to attack Porter frontally, with Longstreet in reserve and to the right, while D. H. Hill and Jackson were to assail the Federal right and rear. Porter's plight looked grim in view of the heavy odds and conspicuous talent arrayed against him.[32]

Before the enemy attack began, Porter informed McClellan —who was at army headquarters at Dr. Trent's on the southwest side of the Chickahominy—that he hoped to be able to hold his ground without aid, but that reinforcements should be readied in case he needed them. When he saw the large numbers deployed against him, Porter sent no one less than Chief Engineer Barnard himself to McClellan for the reinforcements. Entering McClellan's tent a little after 9:00 A.M., Barnard found the commanding general catching some sleep. Despite the vitally important nature of the information he carried, Barnard made no effort to awaken McClellan, but merely returned in silence to his own quarters! There has never been any adequate explanation of Barnard's fantastic conduct here. Not until 2:00 P.M. was McClellan " advised of General Porter's need of assistance." Barnard had failed also to send Porter the badly needed axes which he had promised him. Although he was just across the Chickahominy from the battlefield,

---

[32] Powell, *Fifth Corps*, 83–84; Allan, *Army of Northern Virginia*, 85, 86; Lee's report, 13 *O.R.*, 492, 757; *B. & L.*, II, 334; Webb, *The Peninsula*, 129.

McClellan was unable to hear the sounds of the battle because of the dense woods and the fact that the wind was blowing in the opposite direction.[33]

By noon of June 27, Porter had skillfully deployed his troops as follows: Sykes's division of Regulars was on the right, between the Old Cold Harbor and New Cold Harbor roads leading to Barker's Mill; Morell's division was on the left, south of the road to New Cold Harbor; McCall's division was in reserve behind Morell; and Brigadier General Philip St. George Cooke's cavalry division was on Porter's extreme left near the Chickahominy. On the Confederate side, A. P. Hill appeared about noon in the vicinity of New Cold Harbor. Longstreet was on Hill's right, extending toward the Chickahominy. Hill's attack was delayed until after 2:00 P. M. by the tardy arrival of Jackson on his left—Stonewall having been slowed by Union sharpshooters posted behind roadblocks—and by Longstreet's being held back on the Confederate right until Jackson's arrival caused an extension of Porter's line to the northeast to meet him.[34]

At approximately 2:30 P. M., A. P. Hill's division of some 13,000 men attacked the right portion of Morell's position. The graycoats ran into a storm of artillery and infantry fire which inflicted heavy casualties and drove Hill back to his starting point. Renewed attacks by A. P. Hill on Morell were again repulsed. Then Longstreet came up on Hill's right, and fiercely assailed Morell—now reinforced by McCall—only to be repelled in his initial onslaughts. A number of Franklin's heavy siege guns on the right bank of the Chickahominy were brought into effective service, shelling the Southerners across the river at a range of two and a half miles.[35]

[33] McClellan's report, 12 *O.R.*, 55; Powell, *Fifth Corps*, 85; Porter, "Hanover Court House and Gaines's Mill," *loc. cit.*, 335; McClellan, "The Peninsular Campaign," *loc. cit.*, 181; Sypher, *Pennsylvania Reserves*, 224; see John B. DeMotte, "The Causes of a Silent Battle," *B. & L.*, II, 365.

[34] Powell, *Fifth Corps*, 86–91, 107; *B. & L.*, II, 334; Allan, *Army of Northern Virginia*, 86–87, 90; Jackson's report, 13 *O.R.*, 553; Alexander, *Military Memoirs*, 124ff.

[35] Reports of Lee and A. P. Hill, 13 *O.R.*, 492, 836–37; Allan, *Army of Northern Virginia*, 87–88; Powell, *Fifth Corps*, 94–98; *B. & L.*, II, 359, 367.

At about 4:00 P.M., Brigadier General Henry W. Slocum's splendid division of about 8,000 men was sent by McClellan—who had finally been informed of Porter's need for assistance—across the Chickahominy to the assistance of the Fifth Corps. It arrived just in time to move forward with McCall to succor Morell in halting Longstreet's first blows. Thus far, Porter had beaten back all attacks. Lee, commanding in person, then saw Jackson's command finally come into position on the Confederate left. The usually aggressive Stonewall, however, delayed his attack, hoping that A. P. Hill and Longstreet would be able to drive the Federals across his front so that he could enfilade them. Seeing that they could not do this, Jackson threw his four powerful divisions against Sykes's lone division of Regulars on the Union right, but was everywhere checked in his initial thrusts.[36]

Although Porter now called for additional reinforcements, if possible, so well did Magruder demonstrate against the bulk of the National Army on the right bank of the Chickahominy, that McClellan's appeal to his other corps commanders for aid for Porter was turned down, except for two brigades from Sumner. Finally, outnumbering Porter fully two to one, the entire Confederate line, at about 6:30 P.M., launched an overwhelming, coordinated attack against the whole Fifth Corps line, Brigadier General John B. Hood's Texas brigade of Whiting's division breaking through the center of Morell's division. The deterioration on Porter's left was enhanced by the confusion resulting from the repulse of an attack by Cooke's Union cavalry against the enemy right. Porter was obliged to withdraw his lines from the ridge behind Boatswain Creek to the woods near the bridges over the Chickahominy—a withdrawal that was, on the whole, successfully carried out with heavy rear guard fighting. With the hard-pressing graycoats endangering the movement to the bridges, McClellan sent across two of Sumner's brigades to the relief of Porter. They

---

[36] Powell, *Fifth Corps*, 100; Walker, *Second Corps*, 61; Sypher, *Pennsylvania Reserves*, 224–33; Henderson, *Stonewall Jackson*, II, 31–34; 13 *O.R.*, 493.

arrived just in time to check the pursuing Confederates. By early morning of the twenty-eighth, the Fifth Corps—having destroyed the bridges behind it—was safely across the Chickahominy on the southwest bank, the enemy being unable to interfere with the passage.[37]

The bitterly contested battle of Gaines's Mill was over. The Federals had lost a total of 22 guns and the following casualties: 894 killed, 3,107 wounded, 2,836 missing—a total loss of 6,837. The Confederates lost approximately 8,751 killed and wounded. A noted Confederate general asserts that the intrepid Porter had " handled his . . . men with an ability unsurpassed on any field during the war " by a corps commander. Then, too, the Southerners believed, erroneously, that McClellan had, by his forced withdrawal from Gaines's Mill, been cut off from his supposed base at White House. With his supplies captured, they believed, he would soon be obliged to surrender his army en masse or see it annihilated. What the enemy did not know was that McClellan, forseeing Lee's strategy, had already taken decisive steps in moving the bulk of his enormous supplies from White House to the James River at Harrison's Bar.[38]

While the battle of Gaines's Mill was in progress, a simultaneous though lesser combat was taking place late in the evening of the twenty-seventh at Garnett's farm on the Nine Mile road. There, Hancock's brigade of " Baldy " Smith's division of Franklin's Sixth Corps, was fired upon by thirty Confederate artillery pieces. Hancock replied with a like number of guns, and, after a sharp bombardment, silenced the enemy fire. Then, near dusk, grayclad infantry assailed Hancock's lines, only to be hurled back in a bloody repulse.[39]

While Porter was fighting two to one odds on the left bank

[37] McClellan's report, 12 *O.R.*, 57–59; reports of Longstreet, Lee, Jackson, and D. H. Hill, 13 *O.R.*, 493, 556, 626, 757; Powell, *Fifth Corps*, 100–107; Stine, *Army of the Potomac*, 82–86; *B. & L.*, II, 340–42, 344–46; Webb, *The Peninsula*, 133–35.

[38] Livermore, *Numbers and Losses*, 82–83; *B. & L.*, II, 340–42, 359; Ropes, *Story of the Civil War*, II, 180, 211; Alexander, *Military Memoirs*, 130.

[39] Stine, *Army of the Potomac*, 86–87; *B. & L.*, II, 367; Walker, *Second Corps*, 63; *C.C.W.*, I, 622–23; Ellis' *Diary*, 137–38.

of the Chickahominy, the bulk of McClellan's army on the right bank—about 55,000 men—was being held in place by the masterful game of bluff being played by "Prince John" Magruder with about 30,000 Confederate soldiers. Magruder fired large quantities of shot and shell, marched troops around continuously, made small local attacks, and in general gave the impression that he had about twice as many men as he actually did have. McClellan has been sharply criticized for not having gone right into Richmond with his left wing—as if that could easily be done—while Lee was engaged at Gaines's Mill. However, if Porter could hold back twice his numbers for over eight hours in a hastily prepared position, it seems likely that Magruder could do even better behind extensive and leisurely prepared fieldworks in front of the Confederate capital. Such a "swing into Richmond" by McClellan would have had to have been made without any supply lines, and would have been endangered in the rear after Lee had pushed Porter back. While McClellan has been censured for not moving right into Richmond at that time, it might be noted that Grant, in 1864, with more men, was unable to do this following a severe battle (Cold Harbor) on the same ground near Gaines's Mill.[40]

On the night of June 27, just after the battle of Gaines's Mill, McClellan told his corps commanders, at his headquarters at Savage's Station, of his decision to go ahead with his long-contemplated change of base to the James River, the Army of the Potomac to proceed there as quickly as possible while covering the movement of its tremendous wagon trains and herd of beef cattle. The Federal Army had 25,000 tons of essential supplies to move by land to the James, along with 25,000 horses and mules, 5,000 wagons, 2,500 beeves, and some 85,000 soldiers. All were now crammed into the narrow space between the Chickahominy and White Oak Swamp, and all had to be gotten over that impassable barrier at the White Oak

[40] McClellan's *Report*, 130–31; Paris, *The Civil War*, II, 105–106.

Bridge bottleneck. But two things worked in favor of the Union effort: the major part of Lee's army had been drawn to the northeast side of the Chickahominy, and the Confederate chieftain had committed himself to the mistaken concept of what McClellan would do in his serious predicament. Lee, after Gaines's Mill, believed that the Federal commander would either renew the fight for his supposed base at White House, or else would retreat back down the Peninsula toward West Point and Williamsburg. The gray leader was completely baffled and unaware of McClellan's real intention. However, the change of base enterprise assumed somewhat the character of a retreat since it was undertaken immediately after tactical defeat at Gaines's Mill. Instead of a deliberate, voluntary march, it assumed the nature of a hasty withdrawal, with the right flank of the Union Army exposed to attack from the direction of Richmond, and with the rear menaced from the north.[41]

Having ordered the march to the James after Porter's withdrawal to the southwest side of the Chickahominy, and seeing the desperate nature of the movement confronting him in his efforts to extricate his army from its perilous position, McClellan let go a blast at Stanton concerning the reasons for the Union defeat at Gaines's Mill. This was the famous " Savage's Station Dispatch " of 12:20 A. M. on June 28. This insubordinate indictment was one of the most extraordinary messages ever sent by a military officer in the field to his civilian superior. Said McClellan to the Secretary of War:

> I now know the full history of the day. On this side of the river (the right bank) we repulsed several strong attacks. On the left bank our men did all that men could do, all that soldiers could accomplish, but they were overwhelmed by vastly superior numbers, even after I brought my last reserves into action. The loss on both sides is terrible. . . .

[41] McClellan's report, 12 *O.R.*, 60; *C.C.W.*, I, 355; *B. & L.*, II, 325; Henderson, *Stonewall Jackson*, II, 30; Webb, *The Peninsula*, 136–37; Swinton, *Army of the Potomac*, 154.

If we have lost the day we have yet preserved our honor, and no one need blush for the Army of the Potomac. I have lost this battle because my force was too small.

I again repeat that I am not responsible for this, and I say it with the earnestness of a general who feels in his heart the loss of every brave man who has been needlessly sacrificed to-day. . . . Please understand that in this battle we have lost nothing but men, and those the best we have.

In addition to what I have already said, I only wish to say to the President that I think he is wrong in regarding me as ungenerous when I said that my force was too weak. I merely intimated a truth which to-day has been too plainly proved. . . .

I feel too earnestly tonight. I have seen too many dead and wounded comrades to feel otherwise than that the government has not sustained this army. If you do not do so now the game is lost.

If I save this army now, I tell you plainly I owe no thanks to you or to any other persons in Washington.

You have done your best to sacrifice this army.[42]

Writing three weeks later to his wife about his Savage's Station dispatch, McClellan admitted that " it was pretty frank and quite true. Of course they will never forgive me for that. I knew it when I wrote it; but as I thought it possible that it might be the last I ever wrote, it seemed better to have it exactly true."[43] The last two sentences of the dispatch were grounds enough for McClellan's instant dismissal. But, for reasons of his own, Stanton remained silent on the grave charges against him.

When this telegram arrived at the War Department, two of the men in the telegraph office deleted the offensive paragraphs at the end of the message, and presented Stanton with the " censored " wire. Soon, however, the Secretary learned of the complete contents of McClellan's dispatch; but he remained silent. Certainly, McClellan was unable to prove his

[42] McClellan to Stanton, June 28, 1862, McClellan Papers; 12 *O.R.*, 61.
[43] McClellan to his wife, July 20, 1862, *M.O.S.*, 452.

serious charges of Stanton's deliberately trying to sacrifice the Army of the Potomac. It is well known, however, that the Secretary disliked the General intensely, despite his protestations of friendship and support. He had tried several times—partly successfully—to prevent a number of divisions from joining McClellan on the Peninsula. But the last two paragraphs of the Savage's Station dispatch would have been better left unsaid. McClellan's action here was disrespectful and insubordinate. Why Stanton did not reply to it and why he did not use it as a lever to relieve McClellan from command is not known. He certainly wanted him removed, as was seen in the offers of the command to Hitchcock and Burnside, as well as in Stanton's considering the Radical general, Joe Hooker, as a successor to McClellan.[44]

On June 28, the day after Gaines's Mill, McClellan, as he reports it, " went to Savage's Station, and remained there during the day and night, directing the withdrawal of the trains and supplies of the army." Early on that day, his telegraphic communications with Washington were severed. But Lee, believing erroneously that McClellan would strive to recapture White House or else retreat down the Peninsula toward Williamsburg, on the twenty-eighth, sent troops sweeping down the left bank of the Chickahominy to cut the imaginary Federal lines of communication with the Pamunkey and to intercept the supposed Union retreat at Bottom's Bridge and the railroad bridge. However, all the Confederates found at White House were the smoking piles of surplus stores destroyed by the Northerners before evacuating the place. Not until late in the evening of the twenty-eighth did Lee at last comprehend McClellan's movements and intentions.[45]

McClellan's conduct throughout the change of base expedition to the James River has been often misunderstood. The Federals had as yet received little information of the country

[44] Bates, *Lincoln in the Telegraph Office*, 109–11; *C.C.W.*, I, 339–40; *Browning's Diary*, I, 559; W. M. Tilghman to Stanton, May 22, 1862, Stanton Papers.
[45] McClellan's *Report*, 131; Cook, *Siege of Richmond*, 324, 327; Longstreet, *Manassas to Appomattox*, 130; Allan, *Army of Northern Virginia*, 97.

between White Oak Swamp and the James. The Union engineers sent out by McClellan to map that region had not returned before the Seven Days Battle began. In moving his various units toward the James, McClellan was conducting an operation, in part, of discovery and exploration. " He was therefore obliged," one of his staff officers writes, " throughout the whole of this dangerous expedition, to assure himself personally of the direction indicated to each of his corps, and was therefore prevented from commanding in person at all the battles that were fought on the route . . ." [46] How well McClellan selected the defensive positions and how skillfully he posted his troops in covering the withdrawal may be judged from the results of the remaining combats of the Seven Days.

There occurred only one action, of relatively minor proportions, on June 28. W. F. Smith's division of Franklin's Sixth Corps was attacked near Golding's early in the afternoon by Confederate forces under Colonel George T. Anderson. After stubborn fighting, the men in gray were hurled back with loss, including a number of prisoners seized by the Federals. During the course of the day—except at Golding's—the rival forces facing each other behind the entrenched lines around Seven Pines and Fair Oaks, namely, Huger's and Magruder's commands on the Confederate side, and Sumner's, Franklin's, and Heintzelman's on the Union side, remained stationary and inactive.[47]

The route of the movement to the James took the Federals to a great natural barrier—the White Oak Swamp—and it was a feat to get the army and its enormous wagon trains safely across. During the course of the morning of the twenty-eighth, the main span—called the White Oak Bridge—was rebuilt, while a new one was constructed at a secondary crossing at Brackett's Ford. Artillery pieces and the long trains could cross only at these two bridges, and only with ease at the White Oak Bridge.

[46] Paris, *The Civil War*, II, 109.
[47] *B. & L.*, II, 369; reports of G. T. Anderson and Magruder, 13 *O.R.*, 661, 706; Ellis' *Diary*, 138–39; *C.C.W.*, I, 623; Allan, *Army of Northern Virginia*, 98.

McClellan placed Keyes's Fourth Corps on the south side of the morass, covering the Federal crossings and watching the approaches on the Quaker, Charles City, Darbytown, and New Market roads from the direction of Richmond. During the day, Porter's battered Fifth Corps crossed the swamp and marched toward Malvern Hill on the James, soon to be followed by Keyes. So well were McClellan's movements masked that Magruder and Huger, behind the enemy works on the right bank of the Chickahominy, were unaware of their nature. Moving south of White Oak Swamp, Keyes accidentally discovered an old, uncharted, grass-covered road running parallel to the vital Quaker road and east of it, leading also toward Malvern Hill. He successfully opened it up for use by the struggling Union wagon trains.[48]

Finally, near nightfall on June 28, when Lee became aware of the true nature of McClellan's change of base plan, it was too late to attack that day. And in order to give the toiling Federal trains an extra day to make a safe start for the James, McClellan instructed Sumner, Heintzelman, and W. F. Smith to remain on the north side of White Oak Swamp during the whole of the twenty-ninth, covering Savage's Station and the roads from Richmond. Slocum's division of the Sixth Corps was, during the night of June 28, ordered across the swamp to relieve the Fourth Corps, which was then to follow Porter to Malvern Hill.[49]

The morning fog and rain on the twenty-ninth aided the Federals in the delicate operation of evacuating their works around Fair Oaks. By the afternoon of that day, McClellan's train of 5,000 wagons and his herd of 2,500 beeves had safely crossed treacherous White Oak Swamp, though necessarily moving at a snail's pace. Meanwhile, Stuart's Confederate cavalry was securing what little booty remained unburned at White House. Stuart was thus unable to rejoin Lee's main

[48] Swinton, *Army of the Potomac*, 154–55; 12 *O.R.*, 60–61, 118–19; 13 *O.R.*, 192; *B. & L.*, II, 370; Paris, *The Civil War*, II, 121.
[49] 13 *O.R.*, 494; Ropes, *Story of the Civil War*, II, 187; *B. & L.*, II, 370.

body in time to participate in any of the succeeding combats of the Seven Days Battle.[50]

Early on the morning of June 29, having finally grasped the nature of McClellan's movement, Lee drew up an excellent though ambitious plan of battle designed to intercept and destroy the vulnerable Federal divisions and trains on their tortuous route to the James. Longstreet and A. P. Hill were to cross to the southwest side of the Chickahominy at New Bridge, move by the Nine Mile and Darbytown roads to the New Market (or Long Bridge) road, and fall upon the right flank of the exposed Union column; Huger was to pursue on the Charles City road and Magruder on the Williamsburg pike, and were to strike also the Federal right flank; Jackson and D. H. Hill were to cross at the Grapevine Bridge, move on Savage's Station, and fall upon the rear of the southward-moving blue forces. Lee had at his disposal no less than five roads to pursue and cut off portions of the elongated National Army. Then, too, the pace of the Federal infantry was slowed by the cumbersome wagon trains preceding them, while the grayclad infantry was moving off in front of the Confederate wagons. Lee's plan and the dispositions of the two armies early on the twenty-ninth offered several inviting chances for the Southerners to turn McClellan's enterprise into a hopeless rout and debacle.[51]

McClellan's headquarters was moved across to the south side of White Oak Swamp on the morning of June 29. Early in the day, the Federal forces were withdrawn from their works about Fair Oaks, and were put in position at Allen's farm near Orchard Station, a point approximately two miles west of Savage's Station. Seeing that Magruder was pressing too closely, Sumner, in command of the Union forces north of the swamp, determined to make a stand at Allen's farm. The divisions of Richardson and Sedgwick were placed in line of battle on the north side of the railroad, while Heintzelman's

---

[50] Walker, Second Corps, 65; 12 O.R., 160; 13 O.R., 497, 515–17.
[51] Lee's report, 13 O.R., 494; Allan, Army of Northern Virginia, 101.

Third Corps continued the line on the south side. Magruder deployed his command on both sides of the railroad facing the Federals. At about 9:00 A. M., the Confederate officer opened the battle of Allen's Farm. The main enemy attack struck the blue line at the juncture of Richardson's and Sedgwick's divisions, where the Fifty-third Pennsylvania, especially, did valiant work in meeting the gray assaults. The three enemy attacks were stemmed and then completely thrown back by Sumner in fierce fighting.[52]

After having accomplished his immediate goal of keeping Magruder at arm's length, Sumner reluctantly fell back as ordered to Savage's Station. This was essential, since it was unknown by McClellan when Jackson would cross the Chickahominy and menace the Union rear near the station. McClellan personally indicated to Sumner the positions he wanted occupied in front of Savage's Station. Soon there was presented the impressive spectacle of 20,000 blueclad soldiers drawn up in line of battle in the clearing west and south of the station, with Franklin on the right and Sumner on the left, facing west, between the railroad and the Williamsburg pike. The ground rises gradually from the station toward the west and south, therefore the Federals would be firing slightly uphill; but they had a good open field of fire in front of them. Probably misunderstanding his orders to move the Third Corps back to the station and form on Sumner's left, Heintzelman instead marched it to safety across White Oak Swamp without informing Sumner of his action. Heintzelman stated later that he saw the ground about the station already filled with a sufficient number of blue troops.[53]

Magruder had expected the arrival momentarily of Jackson, but that usually energetic officer was delayed for a long time

[52] Webb, *The Peninsula*, 137; Stine, *Army of the Potomac*, 86–87; Walker, *Second Corps*, 65–66; McClellan's *Report*, 132–33; *B. & L.*, II, 371n; Ellis' *Diary*, 124–26.

[53] Walker, *Second Corps*, 66–69; Paris, *The Civil War*, II, 116; Marks, *Peninsula Campaign*, 249; *B. & L.*, II, 181, 372; Sumner's report, 13 *O.R.*, 50–51, 99; Swinton, *Army of the Potomac*, 156; McClellan's *Report*, 134.

in rebuilding the Grapevine Bridge, and never did appear on Sumner's right-rear as anticipated. Aided by a huge thirty-two-pounder rifled gun—called the "Land Merrimac"—Magruder, at about 5:00 P. M. on the twenty-ninth, heavily assailed Sumner's lines in repeated attacks lasting until 9:00 P. M. He was thrown back each time with severe losses by the unyielding blue defenders. At the height of the battle of Savage's Station, McClellan rode onto the field amidst frantic cheering, passed along the Federal lines, ordered several batteries to open with grape and canister on the advancing enemy, and departed when he saw that the graycoats could not breach Sumner's lines. After having repulsed Magruder, Sumner, after a protracted debate with Franklin, only reluctantly consented to follow McClellan's direction to fall back across White Oak Swamp.[54]

The casualties at Savage's Station are not exactly known. The Confederates acknowledged a loss of 4,000 men, and claimed a Union loss of 3,000. However, a usually reliable Federal source places the blue casualties at but 700 or 1,000. McClellan's victory at Savage's Station was invaluable in keeping open the road leading to the crossing at White Oak Bridge and in removing for a time the immediate threat by Jackson and Magruder to the Union rear. One sorry note was the fact that the Federal commander was obliged to abandon the general hospital at the station, including 2,500 sick and wounded soldiers, although he did leave behind surgeons and ample medical supplies.[55]

On the afternoon of the twenty-ninth—while Sumner was fighting at Allen's Farm and Savage's Station—McClellan ordered Keyes's Fourth Corps to proceed to Malvern Hill to protect Turkey Bridge, where the road to Harrison's Landing crossed Turkey Island Creek. Porter's Fifth Corps was to move into position on Keyes's right. By 6:30 P. M., the advance ele-

[54] Swinton, *Army of the Potomac*, 156; Walker, *Second Corps*, 68–69; Marks, *Peninsula Campaign*, 250, 257; *B. & L.*, II, 373–75; Ellis' *Diary*, 154–55.
[55] Webb, *The Peninsula*, 140–41; Marks, *Peninsula Campaign*, 230; Ellis' *Diary*, 124, 128.

ments of Heintzelman's Third Corps reached the Charles City road in the march down the Quaker road. McClellan reported of his own activities on the twenty-ninth that he " passed the day in examining the ground, directing the posting of troops, and securing the uninterrupted movement of the trains." A cavalry brush at Willis' Church, however, revealed to McClellan that the enemy had grasped the nature and direction of his movement, and were closing in on the right flank of his long column from the four roads to the west as well as on his rear from the north. The situation for McClellan was still extremely critical. Many Confederate officers felt that his position was hopeless. But Franklin states that, " as a result of the dispositions made by the commanding general of the [Union] troops a whole day was gained in getting a large part of the army to the James River without serious opposition, and into a proper defensive position." [56]

June 30 was a hot sunny day. Of the fateful seven days of battle, it was the crucial one for McClellan in his efforts to extricate the Army of the Potomac from its perilous position. As a Southern officer acknowledged, " every condition seemed favorable " to Lee at this time. By early morning, all the Union elements had safely crossed White Oak Swamp, and at 10:00 A. M. Franklin burned the White Oak Bridge. But the Federal Army was now strung out all the way from the swamp to the James. McClellan reported that he " then examined the whole line from the swamp to the left, giving final instructions for the posting of the troops and the obstructions on the roads toward Richmond." He personally placed his units in the following positions to cover the movement of his supply trains: the divisions of W. F. Smith and Richardson at White Oak Swamp, with orders to keep Jackson north of that barrier; the Third Corps and the divisions of Slocum, Sedgwick, and McCall covering the three roads which approached the vital Quaker road from the west. At the James River, the Fifth Corps, facing

[56] McClellan's report, 12 *O.R.*, 62; *M.O.S.*, 442; McClellan's *Report*, 132; Franklin, " Rear-Guard Fighting During the Change of Base," *loc. cit.*, 376.

west, was covering Malvern Hill, supported by the Fourth Corps.[57]

On the Confederate side, Magruder was ordered to move down the New Market road; Huger, down the Charles City Road; and Longstreet (including A. P. Hill), down the Darbytown road to the point where it intersects the New Market (or Long Bridge) road, then northeastward along the New Market road toward the Quaker road, which it joins at the important crossroads point of Glendale. Jackson was instructed to cross White Oak Swamp, on the Union rear, along the Quaker road, and unite with the other gray units at Glendale, or else to strike the Federals' right flank while they were confronting the three Confederate columns approaching from the west.[58]

On Sunday, June 29, most of Jackson's troops had done little but remain in camp. Now, on the crucial thirtieth, Stonewall's powerful force of some 30,000 men appeared a little before noon along the northern edge of White Oak Swamp. He was opposed by Franklin with about 18,000 Federals. Jackson's guns opened strongly against the Union position. After an initial advantage, however, the Confederate pieces were steadily outshot by the Federal guns in one of the famous artillery duels of the war. The firing lasted until sunset. Jackson's cavalry, under Colonel Thomas T. Munford, made a temporary lodgment on the south side of the morass at Brackett's Ford, but Stonewall failed to support them, and the Southern troopers were soon pushed back to the north side. With his soldiers suffering under the superior Union artillery fire, and from sharpshooters, Jackson made a few feeble, probing sorties with his infantry, all of which were easily contained. Despite the skill with which Franklin directed the Union defense at the battle of White Oak Swamp, it appears that Stonewall was

[57] Alexander, *Military Memoirs*, 138, 141; *B. & L.*, II, 375, 377; Paris, *The Civil War*, II, 123; McClellan's *Report*, 135; Ropes, *Story of the Civil War*, II, 193.

[58] See H. J. Eckenrode and Bryan Conrad, *James Longstreet: Lee's War Horse* (Chapel Hill, 1936), 77; Swinton, *Army of the Potomac*, 157.

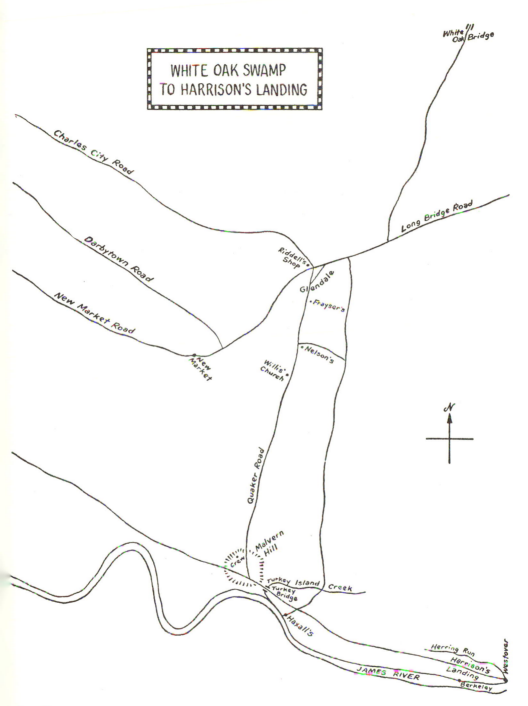

WHITE OAK SWAMP
TO HARRISON'S LANDING

White
Oak Bridge

Charles City Road

Long Bridge Road

Darbytown Road

Riddell's Shop

New Market Road

Glendale

Frayser's

New Market

Nelson's

Willis' Church

N

Quaker Road

Crew

Malvern Hill

Turkey Island Creek

Turkey Bridge

Haxall's

Herring Run

Harrison's Landing

Westover

JAMES RIVER

Berkeley

R. W. Kramer

unusually inert here, and far from the vigorous, resourceful soldier that the Federals in the Shenandoah Valley had learned to fear. His performance was a distinct disappointment to the Confederate side. If he could have crossed White Oak Swamp in force during the course of the day, it would probably have been disastrous for McClellan's forces then fighting at Glendale, for Stonewall would have been squarely on the right flank and rear of the then-hard-pressed Union soldiers in line of battle just west of the vital Quaker road artery.[59]

Meanwhile, on the morning of the thirtieth, while Franklin and Jackson were jousting at the swamp, powerful grayclad forces were approaching from the west toward the Federal troops around Glendale. Longstreet and A. P. Hill were moving via the New Market road toward its intersection with the Quaker Road at Glendale (or Riddell's Shop). About noon these Confederate divisions encountered elements of McClellan's Second, Third, and Fifth Corps, posted approximately one mile west of, and parallel to the Quaker road near the intersection. On Longstreet's left, Huger, advancing slowly along the Charles City road—which joins also the other roads at Glendale—was opposed by Slocum's division. Magruder, at first misunderstanding his orders, was out of reach on the New Market road, well behind Longstreet, while Holmes was advancing along the River road toward Malvern Hill. Since the road south from White Oak Bridge, too, comes out at the Glendale intersection, it was apparent that if Longstreet, A. P. Hill, and Huger could force their way through to this crossroads point, they would cut McClellan's army in two, with Franklin at the swamp being hopelessly caught between two overpowering forces. Longstreet's efforts to achieve this goal resulted in the confused and often misunderstood battle of Glendale.[60]

[59] Alexander, *Military Memoirs*, 135, 136, 142, 143–53; *B. & L.*, II, 378–81; Jackson's report, 13 *O.R.*, 556–57; H. B. McClellan, *The Life and Campaigns of Major-General J. E. B. Stuart* . . . (Boston, 1885), 82n; Henderson, *Stonewall Jackson*, II, 49–70; Walker, *Second Corps*, 72; Webb, *The Peninsula*, 142–43; Ellis' *Diary*, 131–32.

[60] Swinton, *Army of the Potomac*, 158; Ropes, *Story of the Civil War*, II, 194–96; Palfrey, "The Seven Days' Battles to Malvern Hill," *loc. cit.*, 249–51.

McClellan had deployed his forces to the west of the vital Glendale intersection in a level country of dense pine woods, which contained but an occasional cultivated clearing. On the right, perpendicular to the Charles City road, McClellan posted Slocum's division to oppose Huger's advance. On Slocum's left—but not connecting with him—was Kearny's division, nearly parallel to the Charles City road and perpendicular to the New Market road, his left resting on the latter highway. Connecting with Kearny's left, on the south side of the New Market road, was McCall's battered division, nearly at right angles to that road, and almost parallel to the Quaker road, which was close to half a mile in McCall's rear. Hooker's division was on McCall's left, and Sedgwick's division formed a second line in the rear of McCall. After posting the troops, McClellan rode to the James River near Harrison's Bar, where he went aboard Commander John Rodgers' flagship to confer with the naval officer about the support of his gunboats. They discussed also the position of defense which the Army of the Potomac would have to assume in order to make contact with the supplies already brought by ship from the former base at White House.[61]

On the Confederate side, both Davis and Lee were present on the field near Glendale. They expected much of Huger, then moving down the Charles City road, although Slocum's blueclad division was prepared to contest this advance about a mile west of the Glendale intersection. Huger had approximately 9,000 men to Slocum's 6,000. However, Slocum had more axes than did Huger, and sought to delay the gray advance down the road by blockading the route with fallen trees. In a log-chopping contest—the "battle" of the axemen—Huger tried unsuccessfully to cut *up* the felled trees as fast as the Federals cut them *down* in front of him! The ringing sounds of the axes drowned out the feeble artillery fire which Huger opened at 3:00 P. M.—a fire which was more than matched by

---

[61] Reports of Kemper and Strange, 13 *O.R.*, 762, 768; Swinton, *Army of the Potomac*, 158; McClellan's report, 12 *O.R.*, 64–67; *C.C.W.*, I, 586; *B. & L.*, II, 397; see Freeman, *R. E. Lee*, II, 189; Ropes, *Story of the Civil War*, II, 198.

that of Slocum's cannon. Huger had failed to get through to Glendale.[62]

Longstreet determined to wait no longer for Huger, Magruder, Jackson, or Holmes. At 3:00 P. M., he threw forward his own division against McCall's reduced brigades south of the New Market road, but was brought to a standstill by the Pennsylvania Reserves in his initial thrusts. Then, Longstreet committed A. P. Hill to the battle. A Confederate assault on Kearny's left was repelled in furious fighting. Renewing his attacks on the crippled McCall, Longstreet succeeded in pushing back his left and center and threatening the vital Quaker road. Several Federal batteries changed hands a number of times in the seesaw struggle. The hand-to-hand fighting here was as stubborn as any of the war. Clubbed muskets were swung and bayonets crossed. Penetrating a few hundred yards after McCall's sullenly retiring troops, Longstreet's men received an enfilading fire from Hooker which drove them across Sedgwick's front. Sedgwick poured murderous volleys into the graycoats, who recoiled toward their starting point. Although several Union batteries were lost, and although McCall lost a portion of his original ground, the National Army succeeded in containing Longstreet's serious threat to the Quaker road and to Franklin at White Oak Swamp. In essence, the Southern onslaughts at Glendale were repulsed with heavy losses to the Confederates. Sumner had drawn back two brigades from White Oak Swamp to assist in repelling the enemy blows at a critical moment. Darkness brought an end to the firing and to the carnage of June 30 at Glendale. Had Longstreet or Jackson broken through, the fate of the Army of the Potomac would probably have been sealed. The Southern general, D. H. Hill, speaking of McClellan's performance on the thirtieth, asserts, " Escape seemed impossible for him, but he *did* escape, at the same time inflicting heavy damage upon his pursuers." [63]

[62] Allan, *Army of Northern Virginia*, 112–13, 119; reports of Lee, Huger, Mahone, 13 *O.R.*, 495, 759–60, 789–90, 797; Alexander, *Military Memoirs*, 140, 143.
[63] Stine, *Army of the Potomac*, 89–92; reports of Kearny, McCall, Seymour,

While McClellan's forces at White Oak Swamp and Glendale were checking Lee's attacks on the afternoon of June 30, grayclad units under Holmes and Wise were moving down the River road along the left bank of the James in an attempt to seize Malvern Hill and Turkey Bridge, where the Quaker road joins the highway leading to the new Federal base at Harrison's Landing. McClellan himself went aboard the *Galena* in order to make a reconnaissance up the James to see if any enemy soldiers were moving down the River road. Seeing the approach of Holmes's force, Porter's command on Malvern Hill, although outnumbered four to one, opened fire on the enemy—a fire which was augmented by the huge one-hundred-pounder shells from the *Galena*. An enemy battery of six field pieces was destroyed and Holmes's infantry completely broken up into a rout. In this so-called battle of Malvern Cliff (or Turkey Bridge), two Confederate guns were seized by the Federals. Lee's final threat in his four-pronged attack on the thirtieth had failed, just as had the others. Before midnight, McClellan's cumbersome wagon trains and beef herds had reached Haxall's in safety.[64]

The first of July dawned hot and still. The Union Army, its morale and spirit still excellent, was now united at Malvern Hill. Not a single regiment had been lost in the recent difficult movement. The pursuing Confederate Army, then concentrated at Glendale, was pushed swiftly down the Quaker road toward Malvern Hill on the morning of the first. The key to the area, Malvern Hill, is an elevation about sixty feet above the level ground at its base. There was an open plain—surrounded by dense woods—of half a mile at the foot of the hill. The summit was a large open plateau, amphitheater-like in shape, and measuring about one and a half miles in length and

Lee, Longstreet, Wilcox, A. P. Hill, and Field, 13 *O.R.*, 163, 390–92, 403, 495, 759, 777, 838, 842; *C.C.W.*, I, 364, 587–88; Swinton, *Army of the Potomac*, 158–59; Webb, *The Peninsula*, 144–47; Powell, *Fifth Corps*, 138–39; see Freeman, *R. E. Lee*, II, 179–200.

[64] Paris, *The Civil War*, II, 129; McClellan's report, 12 *O.R.*, 67; Holmes's report, 13 *O.R.*, 107, 910–11; Webb, *The Peninsula*, 151–52; Ellis' *Diary*, 132–34.

three-quarters of a mile in width. The hill was bordered on the west, south, and east by marshes and creeks, the best approach to it being from the north, where the Quaker road ran past the Crew House.[65]

During the night of June 30, and in the early morning hours of July 1, McClellan himself—aided by Porter, Brigadier General Andrew A. Humphreys, and Barnard—selected the positions for the Federal artillery and infantry. McClellan personally placed many of his units in the exact dispositions he wanted, his keen eye for terrain being evidenced here above all battlefields. His lines were admirably selected for defense. Most of the battles on the Peninsula—in fact, most in the East—had been fought largely in wooded areas. But that of Malvern Hill was waged chiefly on open terrain, the ripe fields of corn and wheat, the seemingly endless lines of infantry and artillery, and the curving James River to the southwest making a magnificent setting for the spectacular grapple about to ensue between the two grim, united armies. After posting the troops in position on the hill, and after " having made arrangements for instant communication from Malvern by signals " in the event of any serious trouble, McClellan boarded Rodgers' flagship just off Haxall's in order " to select the final location for the army and its depots." [66]

The Union commander had posted his units as follows: Porter's corps, with sixty guns, was on the left of the Malvern Hill plateau near the James River, where McClellan had correctly estimated the main Confederate attack would be made; then, on Porter's right, from left to right, were the divisions of Couch, Kearny, Hooker, Sedgwick, Richardson, W. F. Smith, Slocum, and Brigadier General John J. Peck. McClellan's right, on lower ground, was strengthened by felling

[65] Paris, *The Civil War*, II, 146; Goss, *Recollections*, 66; Francis W. Palfrey, " The Battle of Malvern Hill," Dwight (ed.), *Campaigns in Virginia*, 255; *B. & L.*, II, 412; Ropes, *Story of the Civil War*, II, 201.

[66] Fitz John Porter, " The Battle of Malvern Hill," *B. & L.*, II, 414; McClellan's *Report*, 135, 138; Marks, *Peninsula Campaign*, 288–89; Webb, *The Peninsula*, 154.

trees, forming abatis, and blockading the roads. Five Union gunboats helped to protect his left flank. The General placed also a number of his heavy thirty-two-pounder siege guns near the Crew house to supplement his powerful field artillery. The great strength of the position selected by McClellan was readily acknowledged by the Confederate generals opposing him.[67]

Lee deployed his troops as well as the dense woods in front of the Federal-held plateau permitted. From left to right were Whiting's division, one of Ewell's brigades, D. H. Hill's division, two of Huger's brigades, Magruder's command, with Brigadier General Charles S. Winder's brigade and the rest of Ewell's division in reserve to the left, while the divisions of Longstreet and A. P. Hill were in reserve to the right. Jackson was in command on the Confederate left.[68]

At about 1:00 P. M., the Southern artillery belched forth shot and shell against the Federal positions. The fire was quickly silenced by McClellan's overpowering field artillery, by the heavy siege guns at the Crew house, and by the gunboats. The first in a series of heavy but piecemeal enemy attacks was made at 3:00 P. M. by D. H. Hill against Couch's front. The thrust was easily repulsed. This was followed by a succession of separate, disjointed assaults made before sunset, the seemingly endless waves of grayclad troops under D. H. Hill, Huger, Magruder, and A. P. Hill melting away under the fearful Union musketry and artillery fire. Although the Crew house was the key to the Federal position and the scene of the heaviest fighting, McClellan felt more concerned about his extreme right, posted on lower ground. However, no major attack developed there. Once again, the redoubtable Stonewall Jackson " took no initiative," although he had the best chance of making any progress against McClellan's weakest point, his right-rear.[69]

[67] Swinton, *Army of the Potomac*, 161; McClellan's *Report*, 138; Frothingham, " The Peninsular Campaign of 1862," *loc. cit.*, 116; 13 *O.R.*, 496, 557, 627.

[68] Porter, " The Battle of Malvern Hill," *loc. cit.*, 256.

[69] Stine, *Army of the Potomac*, 93, 97; McClellan's report, 12 *O.R.*, 68; Webb, *The Peninsula*, 159, 162–67; Confederate reports, 13 *O.R.*, 495–96, 612, 618–20;

The Union commander had spent part of the afternoon aboard a gunboat in conference with Rodgers of the navy. Then he received an appeal from his Third Corps commander, Heintzelman, that his presence on the field would further encourage the men. Answering the summons immediately, McClellan, a little after 4:30 P. M., rode along the positions under Confederate attack, inspecting the infantry and artillery dispositions, and reassuring the cheering soldiers with his calm bearing and confident air. He had a very close call at one point when an enemy solid shot struck the ground just in front of him. A private soldier noted that, with victory in the air, "the enthusiasm for him grew in intensity rather than decreased." [70]

Long after dark the firing continued, until approximately 9:00 P. M. "The field of battle," wrote an observer, "had become a scene of the most magnificent pyrotechnics," as flaming shells arched across the sky to burst with blinding flashes against the backdrop of the forest. Despite their gallant efforts, the Confederates could make no impression on the stanch Union line. When the grayclad legions withdrew, the light guns of Colonel Henry J. Hunt's Artillery Reserve pursued them, but the growing gloom of night halted any hope of a counterattack. Lee had probably attacked this almost-impregnable position on Malvern Hill because of his belief that the Federals had been demoralized in the previous six days of fighting by day and marching at night. He had paid a fearful price in blood for his daring. Fitz John Porter, walking later over the fields across which the Southerners had charged, stated that "few steps could be taken without trampling upon the body of a dead or wounded soldier. . . . In some places the bodies were in continuous lines and heaps." As D. H. Hill of Lee's army acknowledged, "The Battle of Malvern Hill was

628–29, 634–35, 643, 650–51, 697–98, 719, 722–24, 728, 794–95, 800, 813–15; see Freeman, *Lee's Lieutenants*, I, 588–604; Swinton, *Army of the Potomac*, 161–63.
    [70] Marks, *Peninsular Campaign*, 299; Ellis' *Diary*, 136; William W. Averell, "With the Cavalry on the Peninsula," *B. & L.*, II, 431; Goss, *Recollections*, 69.

a disaster to the Confederates." It ended all hope of destroying or even of defeating the Army of the Potomac.[71]

The casualties at Malvern Hill are not precisely known, as the fighting there culminated a week of continuous combat, with no time being available for daily roll calls. Jackson admitted a loss of 2,162 in his command alone at Malvern Hill, and he was one of the least engaged on the Southern side. The Confederate losses must have been at least 5,000, and probably were actually closer to 7,000. One Civil War authority estimates the Federal casualties as being " not above one-third " of the enemy loss.[72]

McClellan and his army could not remain on Malvern Hill, even though they had been completely victorious there, " for the army was under the imperious necessity of reaching its supplies." It had been separated from its old base at White House for days, and ammunition, food, and forage were running low. Commander Rodgers of the navy informed the General that he would have to base his army below City Point on the James River, as the Federal vessels could not operate safely above that place. Harrison's Landing—the home of two Presidents of the United States—seven miles southeast of Malvern Hill was the point selected as the new Union base on the James. During the night of July 1, McClellan successfully moved his infantry, artillery, and wagons trains through a heavy rainstorm to the new base. The Federal wagon trains and rear guard were skillfully handled by Keyes, who opened up several new roads and then obstructed them when all the Union troops and wagons had passed safely by. Having completed the operation successfully, the National Army was now encamped on the old estates of Berkeley and Westover, the site being on a peninsula

[71] Webb, *The Peninsula*, 165, 167; Walker, *Second Corps*, 83; *C.C.W.*, I, 574; Porter, " The Battle of Malvern Hill," *loc. cit.*, 425; D. H. Hill, " McClellan's Change of Base and Malvern Hill," *B. & L.*, II, 391, 394.

[72] Jackson's report, 13 *O.R.*, 559; Allan, *Army of Northern Virginia*, 135; Swinton, *Army of the Potomac*, 163; Livermore, *Numbers and Losses*, 84–85.

between the James River and Herring Run—one easily defended against any enemy attack.[73]

The spectacular Seven Days Battle was over. It was the greatest combat that had ever been fought on the shores of the New World. The largest Confederate army ever to be assembled during the war—some 90,000-odd men—had been opposed by McClellan in approximately equal strength. The Southerners, according to Livermore, suffered a loss of 3,478 killed, 16,261 wounded, 875 missing, a total loss of 20,614; while McClellan had lost 1,734 killed, 8,062 wounded, 6,053 missing, a total loss of 15,849. The fact that McClellan had inflicted heavier losses on the enemy than he himself had suffered, was due in part to the fact that the Southerners were doing the attacking in all of the combats of the Seven Days. Also, the graycoats, it will be noted, lost twice as many men killed and wounded—that is, shot down—as did the Federals. However, since he was withdrawing under pressure, McClellan lost many more men captured than did his opponent. It was one of the rare instances during the war that Lee, whether on the defensive or offensive, sustained heavier casualties than he inflicted.[74]

A few concluding comments on McClellan's change of base operation reveal the degree of success he had gained. " Under ordinary circumstances," Lee declared in his official report, " the Federal army should have been destroyed." Confederate D. H. Hill owns that, " throughout this campaign we attacked just when and where the enemy wished us to attack." However, the New York *Times* correspondent Swinton remarks, " the faults of Lee's offensive receive as little attention as the merits of McClellan's defensive. For, in an unsuccessful campaign [i. e., the whole Peninsula campaign of the Federals], the slightest fault is accounted mortal. Men regard only the ill

[73] Swinton, *Army of the Potomac*, 164; McClellan's *Report*, 135, 140–41; Walker, *Second Corps*, 78, 87; Webb, *The Peninsula*, 167; C.C.W., I, 409–10, 436.
[74] Pickett's statement, *Browning's Diary*, II, 32; Livermore, *Numbers and Losses*, 86; B. & L., II, 315, 317.

that has happened, and not the worse that might have happened had it not been prevented." Fitz John Porter holds that, in the Seven Days Battle, " each antagonist accomplished the result for which he aimed: one insuring the temporary relief of Richmond; the other gaining the security on the north bank of the James, where the Union army, if our civil and military authorities were disposed, could be promptly reenforced, and from whence only, as subsequent events proved, it could renew the contest successfully." However, when all this is said to McClellan's credit, the fact remains, as Ropes states, that " the moral and political effect of the whole series of movements and battles was entirely to the advantage of the Confederates. . . . The abrupt change of the part played by the Federal general from the role of the invader to that of the retreating and pursued enemy was too dramatic not to arrest general attention. . . . Lee was the hero of the hour." [75]

But, placed in a hopeless position, in part by the policies and orders of the administration in Washington, and in part by the fantastic overestimates of the enemy numbers by Pinkerton's men and others, McClellan had nonetheless, in his capable actions in the seven days' change of base operation, not only saved his army from destruction, but, by his own skill and the magnificent staying qualities of his soldiers, had preserved intact also the Union cause, just when its sands had seemed to be running out.

[75] Lee's report, 13 *O.R.*, 497; D. H. Hill, " McClellan's Change of Base and Malvern Hill," *loc. cit.*, 395; Swinton, *Army of the Potomac*, 164, 165; Porter, " The Battle of Malvern Hill," *loc. cit.*, 423; Ropes, *Story of the Civil War*, II, 208, 209.

Chapter Seven

"The True Defense of Washington"

> When you contrast the policy I urged in my
> letter to the President with that of Congress and
> of Mr. Pope, you can readily agree with me that
> there can be little natural confidence between
> the government and myself. We are the anti-
> podes of each other.
>
> —*George B. McClellan*

IN most ways, Abraham Lincoln was a talented and truly great
man. In areas which were outside of his range of special
knowledge, his fine common sense usually sufficed to show him
sounder in judgment than most of his better-informed lieutenants. But he was weakest in the field of military strategy and
tactics—especially in the first years of the war—and he was a
bit slow in learning from instructive experiences which had
just occurred. This was shown in the debate as to the course
to pursue after the Seven Days Battle.

For a time, it seemed that the President had grasped the
situation fully. "The evacuation of Corinth," he wrote on
June 28, the day after the battle of Gaines's Mill, "and our
delay by the flood in the Chickahominy, has enabled the enemy
to concentrate too much force in Richmond for McClellan to
successfully attack." Then, in answer to McClellan's famous
Savage's Station Dispatch to Stanton, Lincoln replied in a
moderately toned message that manfully ignored, in the crisis

of the moment, the General's insubordinate, disrespectful charges. " Save your army at all events," he beseeched McClellan. " Will send reinforcements as fast as we can. . . . If you have had a drawn battle or a repulse it is the price we pay for the enemy not being in Washington. We protected Washington and the enemy concentrated on you. Had we stripped Washington he would have been upon us before the troops sent could have got to you. . . . It is the nature of the case & neither you or the Govt. is to blame." This message showed that the President had not as yet perceived that no sizeable Confederate army would dare to march directly upon Washington from Richmond while McClellan's massive host was camped on the doorstep of the Southern capital. At no time during the whole Peninsula campaign was Washington menaced. No one—least of all McClellan—had ever suggested " stripping Washington " of defensive troops.[1]

Then, on June 28, Stanton sent a direct order to Halleck, at Corinth, Mississippi, to send 25,000 men " immediately " to McClellan on the Peninsula. However, despite this somewhat panicky telegram to Halleck, and despite the receipt of McClellan's scorching, gloomy Savage's Station dispatch of the twenty-eighth, the erratic Secretary, on the twenty-ninth, wired Seward in New York the following amazing message: " General McClellan will probably be in Richmond within two days." Stanton could not help but see that McClellan would be fortunate to extricate his army from its grave predicament, and that he needed sizeable reinforcements—the 25,000 ordered by Stanton from Halleck and then some. Lincoln, on the twenty-eighth, had implored McClellan to " save " his " army at all events." Perhaps Stanton—known to be in league with the Radicals— wanted to give the impression that McClellan was near to a striking victory, and then, when he failed to take Richmond, to castigate him as incompetent in order to get rid of him. At any rate, on July 2, the President sent the General another

[1] Lincoln to Seward, June 28, 1862, Lincoln Papers; Lincoln to McClellan, June 28, 1862, McClellan Papers.

reassuring telegram: " If you think you are not strong enough to take Richmond just now, I do not ask you to. Try just now to save the army, material, and personnel, and I will strengthen it for the offensive again as fast as I can." [2]

Down on the Peninsula, McClellan held a grand review of his troops at Harrison's Landing on the Fourth of July. This was good for soldier morale. The General, according to a war correspondent present, was " received everywhere with the most enthusiastic demonstrations." [3] McClellan then issued another of his typical proclamations, addressed to the " Soldiers of the Army of the Potomac ":

> Your achievements of the last ten days have illustrated the valor and endurance of the American soldier. Attacked by vastly superior forces, and without hope of reinforcements, you have succeeded in changing your base of operations by a flank movement, always regarded as the most hazardous of military expedients. . . . Upon your march you have been assailed day after day with desperate fury by men of the same race and nation skilfully massed and led; and under every disadvantage of numbers and necessarily of position also, you have in every conflict beaten back your foes with enormous slaughter.
>
> Your conduct ranks you among the celebrated armies of history. No one will now question that each of you may always say with pride, " I belonged to the Army of the Potomac."
>
> You have reached this new base complete in organization and unimpaired in spirit. . . . I have personally established your lines. . . . Your government is strengthening you with the resources of a great people. [4]

This message was not quite as bombastic as earlier ones composed by McClellan, and is illustrative of several façades of the General. It was complimentary to all: to his army, to the enemy, to himself—even, to a lesser degree, to his government. Although

[2] Stanton to Halleck, June 28, 1862, Stanton to Seward, June 29, 1862, 14 *O.R.*, 271, 275–77; Lincoln to McClellan, July 2, 1862, McClellan Papers.
[3] Cook, *Siege of Richmond*, 342.
[4] McClellan Papers, July 4, 1862.

174

in personal dispatches to Lincoln and Stanton he was often outspoken, highly critical, and even offensive on occasion, McClellan never addressed himself to his soldiers in other than lofty sentiments regarding his superiors in Washington. He was a true Union man through and through. Yet, he considered his Southern opponents as being also integral parts of that Union, who, if necessary, would have to be coerced by armed might to return to it.

Back in Washington, the Federal administration quickly did an about-face on the previous order to Halleck to send 25,000 men to McClellan, and allowed those troops to remain in the West. Then, on July 4, Lincoln gave McClellan the discretionary power of keeping his army on the James near Richmond or of bringing it back to the neighborhood of Washington. " To reinforce you," said the President, " so as to enable you to resume the offensive within a month, or even six weeks, is impossible." He indicated, however, that McClellan would soon receive 25,000 reinforcements from Burnside, from Hunter, and from forces in northern Virginia. " I will do the best I can," the General replied, " with such force as I have." [5] It might be noted here that very few of the indicated reinforcements were ever sent to the Army of the Potomac on the James.

McClellan received more encouraging word from Washington in the form of a communiqué from his Chief of Staff, Marcy. " I have seen the President and Secretary of War," Marcy reported. Ten thousand men from Hunter, ten thousand from Burnside, and eleven thousand from here have been ordered to reinforce you as soon as possible. . . . The President and Secretary speak very kindly of you and find no fault." This latest information upped the number of men McClellan could now expect from 25,000 to 31,000. And on July 5, Lincoln sent the General a grateful note. " A thousand thanks," said the President, " for the relief your two dispatches . . . gave me. Be assured the heroism and skill of yourself and

[5] Stanton to Halleck, June 30, 1862, 14 *O.R.*, 279–80; Lincoln to McClellan, July 4, 1862, 12 *O.R.*, 72; McClellan to Lincoln, July 4, 1862, Lincoln Papers.

175

officers and men is, and forever will be, appreciated. If you can hold your present position we shall hive the enemy yet." This seemed to indicate that Harrison's Bar would probably be used as the springboard for a renewed offensive as soon as the reinforcements which had been pledged to McClellan were sent.[6]

McClellan's outward relations with the Secretary of War appeared—at least to McClellan—to be improving. Following the death of one of his (Stanton's) children, Stanton wrote to McClellan on July 5: "Be assured that you shall have the support of this Department as cordially and faithfully as was ever rendered by man to man, and if we should ever live to see each other face to face you will be satisfied that you have never had from me anything but the most confiding integrity." At approximately the same time, the Secretary asserted to McClellan's Chief of Staff in Washington, "General Marcy, I have from the commencement of our acquaintance up to the present moment been General McClellan's warmest friend. I feel so kind toward him that I would get down on my knees to him if it would serve him. Yes sir, if it would do him any service I would be willing to lay down naked in the gutter and allow him to stand upon my body for hours." At the very moment, however, that Stanton was making these statements to the General, he and Chase were maneuvering to remove McClellan from command and replace him with the friend of the Radicals, John Pope.[7]

On the morning of July 7, Lincoln called Pope to the White House for a conference with himself and Senator Browning. It is not known precisely what was discussed at this conclave, but immediately afterward the President left by steamer for

[6] Marcy to McClellan, July 4, 1862, Lincoln to McClellan, July 5, 1862, McClellan Papers.

[7] Stanton to McClellan, July 5, 1862, Marcy to McClellan, sometime in July, 1862, *ibid.*; Chase's Diary, as quoted in Jacob W. Schuckers, *Life and Public Services of Salmon Portland Chase* (New York, 1874), 447; H. C. Fahnestock to Jay Cooke, July 7, 1862, quoting conversation with Chase, Ellis P. Oberholtzer, *Jay Cooke, Financier of the Civil War* (Philadelphia, 1907), I, 197–98.

the James River. Arriving that night at Harrison's Bar, Lincoln was so anxious to see the troops that, escorted by McClellan, he " reviewed the army by moonlight." The President was accompanied by Francis P. Blair and Peter Watson; Stanton remained behind in Washington. That evening, McClellan handed Lincoln a confidential paper—the famous " Harrison's Bar Letter." " I conceived it a duty," the General stated in his official report, " in the critical position we then occupied, not to withhold a candid expression of the more important of these views from the commander-in-chief." Previously, the President had stated that he would like to have McClellan's views on the general military situation throughout the country.[8]

In this paper, McClellan called for the " conservative " view in prosecuting the war, in contradistinction to the Radical concept of waging ruthless war. He felt that hostilities should not be waged against the civilian population of the South, but only against the enemy armed forces. He asserted that private property should not be seized, and that the " forcible abolition of slavery should [not] be contemplated for a moment." McClellan opposed extreme military arrests and military government in the conquered areas. Should slaves be freed in the course of the fighting, the slave-owners should receive compensation. He went on to say that " a declaration of radical views, especially upon slavery, will rapidly disintegrate our present armies." The armies of the Union, he declared, should be concentrated more, with fewer scattered, independent commands. He stated that a General-in-Chief should be named, though he did not ask that post for himself. McClellan concluded the paper by saying, " I may be on the brink of eternity; and as I hope forgiveness from my Maker, I have written this letter with sincerity towards you and from love of my country." The General relates that Lincoln read the paper at once, in his presence, and thanked him for it.[9]

[8] Nicolay and Hay, *Abraham Lincoln*, V, 453; Powell, *Fifth Corps*, 181; Heintzelman's Journal, entry of July 8, 1862; McClellan's *Report*, 144.
[9] McClellan to Lincoln, " Confidential," July 7, 1862, Lincoln Papers; *M.O.S.*, 487.

This famous Harrison's Bar Letter showed that McClellan believed the President to be essentially a conservative Republican, in whom he could confide. The Union commander felt, apparently, that military affairs could not be considered in a vacuum, and that political matters had to be discussed also—even by a soldier. Whether or not such a course was wise at that time, it was not an unusual practice in the Civil War for a general in the field to address such a communication to the Chief Executive. And apparently Lincoln was not troubled by McClellan's stepping out of his strict military sphere in this instance. The greatest misfortune of the letter to its writer, however, did stem from the anti-Radical tenor of its contents. Secretary of the Navy Welles states that the document —soon made known to cabinet members—helped " Stanton to get rid of McClellan at headquarters." [10]

On the following day—July 8—Lincoln closely questioned McClellan and his highest generals, " separately and alone," about the present situation of the Army of the Potomac. After answering perfunctory questions about numbers and the enemy, McClellan stated that the camp at Harrison's Landing was sufficiently healthy to be maintained. Then Lincoln asked a question that must have chilled the General: " If you desired, could you remove the army safely " from the James? McClellan limited his reply by saying only that " it would be a delicate & very difficult matter " in the presence of the enemy.[11]

The President continued the interrogation of the Federal generals on the next day. Sumner, Heintzelman, Porter, and Keyes were asked about the health of the army on the James, whether it could be removed safely if necessary, and whether it was safe at Harrison's. All but Keyes felt the camp site was healthy, and that the condition of the men was good. All agreed that the army was secure in its present position. With the exception of Keyes, each general believed that if the Army

[10] Welles, *Lincoln and Seward*, 191.
[11] Keyes's testimony, March 27, 1863, *C.C.W.*, I, 612–13; "July 8, 1862: Gen. McClellan," Lincoln Papers.

of the Potomac were removed from the Peninsula near Richmond, the Union cause would receive perhaps a mortal blow. Keyes urged the President to " take it back to Washington." [12]

Obviously, from the tenor of the questions, Lincoln was deeply concerned about the safety of the Federal Army, and whether it should even be allowed to remain on the Peninsula at all—even though he had just previously given McClellan the discretionary power of deciding the matter himself. The nature of the queries seems to indicate that perhaps the President had already made up his mind that the army would have to be withdrawn from the James to the neighborhood of Washington, and that he was hoping to get heavy support for such an enterprise from McClellan and his corps commanders. If so, Lincoln was sadly disappointed. It is not known why Franklin was not interrogated, as he was one of McClellan's favorite corps commanders. A later military analyst says of the Union Army's position then at Harrison's, " It is evident that operations from the James as a base would have pinned Lee's army and kept up a pressure upon him, only to be measured by the reinforcements sent to the Army of the Potomac." [13]

While Lincoln was sounding out the generals on the Peninsula, the Radicals of the Committee on the Conduct of the War brought their champion, Pope, before the group on July 8 for questioning of their own. Pope's statements were obviously aimed at pleasing the Radicals on the committee. He condemned the whole concept of the Peninsula campaign, and said that McClellan's army should be brought back to Washington at once. He contended that he was for attack and not delay, that he believed in fighting and not in strategy. Pope supported the political views expressed by the Radicals in their questions to him. He then made the somewhat astonishing statement that had he been McClellan back in March, he would

---

[12] Heintzelman's Journal, entry of July 9, 1862; " July 9, 1862: Gen. Sumner," " July 9, 1862: Gen. Heintzelman," " July 9, 1862: Gen. Porter," " July 9, 1862: Gen. Keyes," Lincoln Papers; Keyes, *Fifty Years' Observation*, 486–87.

[13] Frothingham, " The Peninsula Campaign of 1862," *loc. cit.*, 119.

have marched directly to Richmond and right on through the Confederacy to New Orleans! [14]

Back on the James River, the President had concluded his trip of inspection. McClellan was not too heartened by the conversations. " His excellency," the General wrote his wife Ellen, " was here yesterday and left this morning. He found the army anything but demoralized or dispirited; in excellent spirits. I do not know to what extent he had profited by his visit; not much I fear." On July 11, having returned to Washington, Lincoln reported to Stanton and Browning that McClellan's army was " still a large one, and in good condition, although much diminished, consisting when it was sent there of 160,000 men." The President was still laboring under the erroneous impression that the General had taken with him to the Peninsula such a great force; whereas, in reality, as McClellan had pointed out several times previously, the Federal Army there never numbered over two-thirds that size.[15]

A great decision was made in Washington on July 11. On that day, Stanton telegraphed Major General Henry W. Halleck that, by the President's order, he was to become General-in-Chief and was to repair at once to the Union capital. Perhaps Lincoln and Stanton realized that the strategy and tactics for which they had been responsible had proved, in their directing hands, to be wanting, and that Halleck, nominally responsible for the Federal successes in the West, could repeat his " triumphs " in the East as commanding general of the Union armies. According to Welles, however, it was chiefly the pressure which Stanton, Chase, and Pope had been placing on Lincoln that led him to appoint Halleck to the top military post, vacant for four months. Welles states that it was part of an intrigue on the part of Stanton and Chase " to get rid of McClellan." Although the choice of Halleck was, at the time, a natural one for Lincoln to make, it was soon to prove a most unfortunate one, for " Old Wooden Head "—as he was

---

[14] Pope's testimony, July 8, 1862, *C.C.W.*, I, 276–82.
[15] McClellan to his wife, July 9, 1862, *M.O.S.*, 446; *Browning's Diary*, I, 557.

known—was to prove most inept, irresolute, and cantankerous as General-in-Chief.[16]

Halleck in 1862 was forty-seven years old, but his thin gray hair and ring of chin whiskers made him appear older. His smallish, stoop-shouldered frame carried a large, bulbous head, which was ever tilted forward or to one side. An ample paunch, flabby cheeks, and a double chin increased his unmilitary appearance. However, it was his bulging, fishlike eyes and sallow yellow complexion that were first noticed by a visitor. Add to this his irritable and harsh address, his habit of ever chewing or smoking cigars while continually scratching his elbows, and his halting method of speaking, and one can perceive that " Old Brains " lacked the martial cast of many of the glittering generals in blue who adorned the Washington scene. His assets were of a scholarly nature, and some of them were considerable. He had written books on military science and tactics, on international law, and on bitumen. He had taught at Harvard, had drawn up the constitution of California, and had been head of a mining company and a railroad.[17]

Beyond this solid array of scholarly attainments, however, Halleck had little else to recommend him. The new General-in-Chief—who was to become so important a factor in McClellan's remaining months of service—soon evinced his incapacity for his important station. Lincoln termed him a moral coward, who struggled mightily to evade any responsibility; in short, " little more . . . than a first-rate clerk." Stanton, according to McClellan, said that " Halleck . . . was . . . probably the greatest scoundrel and most barefaced villain in America . . . that he

[16] Stanton to Halleck, July 11, 1862, 14 *O.R.*, 314, 371; see John Gibbon, *Personal Recollections of the Civil War* (New York, 1928) , 40; *Welles's Diary*, I, 108–109.

[17] William T. Lusk, *War Letters of William Thompson Lusk* (New York, 1911) , 170; New York *Tribune*, May 31, 1862; *Welles's Diary*, I, 373; Lew Wallace, *Lew Wallace, An Autobiography* (New York, 1906) , II, 570–71; *Bates's Diary*, 293; James Harrison Wilson, *Under the Old Flag* (New York, 1912) , I, 98–99; William E. Doster, *Lincoln and Episodes of the Civil War* (New York, 1915) , 178–79; E. Hannaford, *Story of a Regiment* (Cincinnati, 1868) , 346; George W. Cullum, *Biographical Register of the Officers and Graduates of the United States Military Academy . . .* (New York, 1868) , I, 573–74.

was totally destitute of principle." McClellan's own opinion of his new superior was as follows: " Of all men whom I have encountered in high position, Halleck was the most hopelessly stupid. It was more difficult to get an idea through his head than can be conceived by any one who never made the attempt. I do not think he ever had a correct military idea from beginning to end." It was for Welles, however—who saw a good deal of Halleck—to give the most accurate and penetrating picture of the new Union General-in-Chief. " He has," wrote Welles in his diary, " a scholarly intellect and . . . some military acquirements, but his mind is heavy and irresolute. It appears to me that he does not possess originality and that he has little real talent. What he has is educational." Continuing, the Navy Secretary declared, " Halleck originates nothing, anticipates nothing, to assist others; takes no responsibility, plans nothing, suggests nothing, is good for nothing." All he could do was " scold and smoke and scratch his elbows." Although most other observers agreed with this dim view of Halleck, Lincoln nonetheless retained him as General-in-Chief for well over a year and a half.[18]

Meanwhile, military operations on the Peninsula were not at a complete standstill, although both armies needed time before an all-out campaign could again be undertaken. On July 2, a Confederate detachment on the south bank of the James, at Coggin's Point, suddenly opened fire with forty-seven rifled guns on McClellan's camp across the river at Harrison's Landing. The Federals returned the fire vigorously. On the following day, McClellan sent over a force which cleared out the enemy and securely established itself on the south bank of the river. Perhaps his success here had something to do with a telegram to Lincoln, in which McClellan stated, " I am more and more convinced that this army ought not to be withdrawn from here, but promptly reinforced and thrown again upon Richmond. I dread the effects of any retreat upon the

[18] *Hay's Diary*, 167, 176; Gurowski's *Diary*, 297; *M.O.S.*, 137; *Browning's Diary*, I, 605; *Welles's Diary*, I, 107, 119, 121, 180, 216, 320, 329, 364, 373, 383, 384, 444.

morale of the men." As yet, the promised reinforcements had not been sent to McClellan.[19]

At the same time, the President was concerned about the number of troops needed for the task undertaken by the Army of the Potomac. " Sending men to that army," declared Lincoln to a friend, " is like shoveling fleas across a barnyard—not half of them get there." On July 13, he wired McClellan, bemoaning the number of men absent without leave from the ranks since the beginning of the Peninsula campaign. " If . . . you had these [22,500 to 30,000] men with you," asserted the President, " you could go into Richmond in the next three days." Of course, it was not quite that easy a job for the Federal Army. McClellan replied that he had, at Harrison's, 88,665 men " present for duty." He explained thoroughly to the President the final difference between the total number of men carried on the muster rolls of an army and the actual number of combat effectives—a distinction which Lincoln was long in understanding.[20]

Then, on July 14, Pope, commanding the newly formed Army of Virginia in front of Washington, issued a most remarkable and damaging manifesto to his troops, many of whom had fought gallanty against Stonewall Jackson: " I have come to you from the West, where we have always seen the backs of our enemies; from an army whose business it has been to seek the adversary and to beat him when he was found; whose policy has been attack and not defense. . . . I presume that I have been called here to pursue the same system and to lead you against the enemy. . . . Let us study the probable lines of retreat of our opponents, and leave our own to take care of themselves. Let us look before us, and not behind. Success and glory are in the advance, disaster and shame lurk in the

---

[19] Alexander, *Military Memoirs*, 171–72; Swinton, *Army of the Potomac*, 172; McClellan's *Report*, 147; McClellan to Lincoln, July 12, 1862, Lincoln Papers.

[20] See Carl Sandburg, *Abraham Lincoln, The War Years* (New York, 1939), I, 495; Lincoln to McClellan, July 13, 1862, McClellan Papers; *M.O.S.*, 447; 14 *O.R.*, 321; McClellan to Lincoln, July 15, 1862, Lincoln Papers.

rear." [21] Pope later admitted to Jacob D. Cox that the proclamation had been dictated to him by Stanton.[22] The wording and style are quite similar to the Secretary's manifesto in the New York *Tribune* on February 20, noted previously. Pope's proclamation was followed by a series of harsh "Radical" orders, aimed at crushing the spirit of the pro-Confederate citizenry in occupied areas of Virginia.[23]

It is not known whether Stanton was responsible for these orders, as he was for Pope's manifesto. On July 14, Lincoln told Browning "that all that Stanton had done in regard to the army had been authorized by him the President." And McClellan's opinion of the Secretary had come down even lower than before. The General undoubtedly had been informed of Stanton's actions in regards to Halleck, Pope, and the latter's strong orders against the Virginia noncombatants. Writing to his wife of the Secretary, McClellan did not bother to restrain himself: "I think that he is the most unmitigated scoundrel I ever knew, heard or read of; I think that (I do not wish to be irreverent) had he lived in the time of the Savior, Judas Iscariot would have remained a respected member of the fraternity of the Apostles, and that the magnificent treachery and rascality of E. M. Stanton would have caused Judas to have raised his arms in holy horror and unaffected wonder." It would be difficult to conceive of a situation where a general in the field and his civilian superior were more at odds with each other than in this Peninsula campaign.[24]

At this same time, the Radicals of the Committee on the Conduct of the War were moving to increase the tempo of their attacks on McClellan, in order to have him removed from command. On July 15, after having conveniently neglected to inform the only pro-McClellan committeeman of the meeting, that body suddenly decided to abolish the rule

[21] 18 *O.R.*, 473–74.
[22] Cox, *Military Reminiscences*, I, 222.
[23] 16 *O.R.*, 50–52.
[24] *Browning's Diary*, I, 559; McClellan to his wife, July 13, 1862, McClellan Papers.

which kept secret the testimony and hearings of the committee, and to allow the use of this information on the floor of Congress. The next day, referring to this material, Chandler spoke forth in frenzied style on the Senate floor. He labeled all of McClellan's decisions and operations inept and wasteful of human lives. He termed the General a liar, said he had refused to take Richmond when it was in his grasp, and insisted upon his removal. Chandler shouted that the General's Democratic supporters were nothing less than traitors. Finally, he implied that Lincoln himself was partly to blame himself because he had stood behind McClellan for so long.[25]

But at Harrison's Landing, McClellan refused to give up on his pleas to retain his army on the James. " It appears manifestly to be our policy," he stated in a dispatch to Lincoln on July 17, " to concentrate here everything we can possibly spare from less important points to make sure of crushing the enemy at Richmond. . . . Nothing should be left to chance here. I would recommend that General Burnside, with all his troops, be ordered to this army, to enable it to assume the offensive as soon as possible." On the next day, McClellan continued to press the administration for a decision concerning reinforcements. He wired the President, " Am anxious to have determination of government, that no time may be lost in preparing for it. Hours are very precious now, and perfect unity of action necessary." Obtaining no reply to his message, and, in fact, having received no communications at all from the administration for a number of days, McClellan complained to Ellen, " If our dear government will show some faint indication of brains or courage we can finish the work in a short time. . . . Their game seems to be to withhold reinforcements, and then to relieve me for not advancing, well knowing that I have not the means to do so." On the twentieth, the General once again unburdened himself to his wife: " I have tried to do my best, honestly and faithfully, for my country. That I have to a certain extent failed I do not believe to be my fault, though

[25] *C.C.W.*, I, 102; *Congressional Globe*, 37th Cong., 2nd Sess., 3386–92.

my self-conceit probably blinds me to many errors that others see." [26]

Back in Washington, a significant dinner took place on July 21, with Pope, Chase, Samuel L. Casey, and a Mr. Horton present. Pope voiced the opinion that his former commander in the West, and now General-in-Chief, Halleck, would help in the campaign to remove McClellan from command. According to Chase, Pope "regarded it as necessary for the safety and success of his operations that there should be a change in the command of the Army of the Potomac. He believed that Genl. McClellan's incompetency and indisposition to active movements were so great, that if, in his operations, he should need assistance, he could not expect it from him. He had urged upon the President the importance of superseding Genl. McClellan before the arrival of Halleck. . . . The President, however, had only promised that he (Genl. Pope) should be present at his interview with Genl. Halleck, when he would give the latter his opinion of McClellan." Apparently, Lincoln was not going to be stampeded into any hasty action on this important matter, for the following day brought forth this entry in Chase's diary: "This morning I called on the President. . . . I urged upon the President the importance of an immediate change in the command of the Army of the Potomac. . . . The President came to no conclusions, but said he would confer with Gen. Halleck on these matters." [27]

It had been intended by the Union administration to reinforce McClellan for the offensive with Burnside's 8,000 men from the coast of North Carolina under the command of Major General Jesse L. Reno, and with 5,000 from the South Carolina littoral under Major General Isaac I. Stevens. These troops were then temporarily at Newport News, Virginia. Now, however, this force was ordered not to join McClellan at Harrison's;

---

[26] McClellan to Lincoln, July 17, 1862, Lincoln Papers; McClellan to Lincoln, July 18, 1862, McClellan Papers; McClellan to his wife, July 18 and 20, 1862, *M.O.S.*, 450–51, 452–53.

[27] *Diary and Correspondence of Salmon P. Chase* (Washington, 1903), 46–47, 47–48.

instead, they were earmarked for use in front of Washington. This nettled McClellan. On the twenty-third, he exclaimed to his wife, " What good has been done to me or to the country by my ' popularity' in the North? It has not prevented my enemies from withholding all support from me; it did not hinder them from almost ruining my army; it brings me not a man." He believed that the Confederates facing him numbered 200,000 men, whereas in reality the enemy had but approximately one-third that many soldiers.[28]

Then McClellan ordered a reconnaissance in force from Harrison's toward Richmond, looking forward to resuming the offensive against the enmy as soon as his force was increased. " Fighting Joe " Hooker led this expedition by way of Glendale to Malvern Hill. There, the Federals came up against a grayclad force. In a stiff skirmish—sometimes called the " second battle of Malvern Hill "—Hooker succeeded in driving the enemy off the hill and capturing over 100 prisoners. McClellan appeared on the field near the end of the combat, apparently well pleased at the result. A short time later, following up his success in defeating the enemy's effort to shell him out of his camp at Harrison's, McClellan pushed out cavalry reconnaissances from Cole's house, near Coggin's Point, toward Petersburg. The Union commander was eager to resume the general offensive against Lee, interrupted by the Seven Days Battle.[29]

On July 24, J. N. Alsop of New York wrote to McClellan on the Peninsula. Alsop had traveled with Halleck on the train from Corinth to Washington. He informed the commander of the Army of the Potomac that Halleck " said that McClellan was the ablest military man in the world." If true, this augured well for the future relations of the two soldiers. Then, on the afternoon of the twenty-fifth, the new Union General-in-Chief arrived suddenly and unannounced at Harri-

---

[28] 9 *O.R.*, 404, 405, 409; 14 *O.R.*, 300, 305; 20 *O.R.*, 365, 367; McClellan to his wife, July 23, 1862, *M.O.S.*, 454; McClellan's report, 12 *O.R.*, 51.

[29] Ellis' *Diary*, 175–77; Sypher, *Pennsylvania Reserves*, 330; Swinton, *Army of the Potomac*, 170–71; Goss, *Recollections*, 74; McClellan to Halleck, August 3, 1862, McClellan's *Report*, 148.

son's Landing to see the army and to confer with its commander and his subordinates. Strangely, McClellan had not been informed by his government of the appointment of Halleck to that high post, learning of it only through the newspapers. " In all these things," McClellan wrote disgustedly to Ellen, " the President and those around him have acted so as to make the matter as offensive as possible." The inside story of the real reason for Halleck's visit was recorded by Browning in his diary on the twenty-fifth, after the Senator had just conversed with Lincoln: " The President told me that Genl Halleck had gone to the army at James River, and was to have supreme command of the entire army—that he was satisfied McClellan would not fight and that he had told Halleck so, and that he could keep him in command or not as he pleased." Browning noted that Lincoln said that if he could send McClellan 100,000 reinforcements, the General would claim that the Confederates had 400,000, and that to advance he would need still more men.[30]

At Harrison's Bar, Halleck took a quick look at the troops, and held a conversation with McClellan. Writing to his wife after his first conference with the General-in-Chief, McClellan declared, " I think that Halleck will support me and give me the means to take Richmond." Continuing the councils, Halleck learned that the Army of the Potomac now numbered nearly 90,000 men, and that its commander accepted the intelligence reports of Pinkerton and the others stating that Lee had 200,000. McClellan said, however, that with 30,000 reinforcements he would undertake a movement against the Confederate capital, in view of his superior artillery and with the aid of the Federal gunboats. Halleck then told him that only 20,000 reinforcements were available, and that if these would not suffice the Union Army would be withdrawn from the James to the vicinity of Washington. McClellan finally agreed to advance

[30] Alsop to McClellan, July 24, 1862, McClellan Papers; 14 *O.R.*, 337–38; *M.O.S.*, 455; McClellan to his wife, July 27, 1862, *M.O.S.*, 456; *Browning's Diary*, I, 563.

against Richmond with the 20,000 men promised. " There was a chance," he said to Halleck, and he was " willing to try it." He then showed Halleck on a map his plan to cross in force to the south side of the James and move on Petersburg, thereby severing a number of vital railroads from the deep South to Richmond. Lee himself acknowledged that so long as the National Army was astride the James near Richmond, he could not weaken the Southern Army defending the capital in order to move northward toward Washington. Petersburg was then practically undefended. Despite McClellan's arguments, Halleck termed his suggested operation south of the James—by which Grant was to win the war two years later—impracticable, and vetoed it.[31]

As soon as the General-in-Chief departed from the Peninsula for Washington, McClellan called a council of war of his corps commanders, and informed them of Halleck's proposition regarding the 20,000 pledged reinforcements. Present at this meeting were McClellan, Sumner, Heintzelman, Porter, Franklin, and Burnside. Rather than take the army back to Washington, where they had started the campaign, all the generals present voted to remain on the James and move against Richmond from there. Heintzelman describes the decision in these words: " We were all in favour of an immediate advance, so soon as Gen. Burnside's forces arrive." Communicating later with Halleck by wire, McClellan stated to the General-in-Chief, " I am sure that you will agree with me that the true defense of Washington consists in a rapid and heavy blow given by this army upon Richmond."[32]

Meanwhile, anti-McClellan forces were active on the Washington scene. After an inflammatory speech against the General on the floor of the Senate, another strong voice was heard from.

[31] McClellan to his wife, July 25, 1862, *M.O.S.*, 455; Halleck's " Memorandum for the Secretary of War," July 27, 1862, 14 *O.R.*, 337; *C.C.W.*, I, 437, 454–55; 5 *O.R.*, 42; Ropes, *Story of the Civil War*, II, 242, 243; Lee to Jackson, 18 *O.R.*, 917; 12 *O.R.*, 1018.

[32] Heintzelman's Journal, entries of July 26–28, 1862; McClellan to Halleck, July 26, 1862, 14 *O.R.*, 333–34.

Jay Cooke, powerful Philadelphia financier who managed the war loans for the Union government, urged Lincoln to remove McClellan from command and put a more dashing general at the helm. Pope was known then as a dashing general. Then, on July 26, Chase received a visit from Pope—now his new friend. According to the Secretary of the Treasury, Pope voiced fear that McClellan was about to move on Richmond and cheat him out of winning the final victory of the war, with its inevitable honors. " I replied," said Chase, " that no such advance would be made or, if made and successful, would only restore undeserved confidence and prepare future calamities." [33]

The struggle over the disposition of the Army of the Potomac continued. McClellan took up his cudgels again, determined, if at all possible, to persuade his superiors to retain the army on the James near the Confederate capital. " My opinion," he said to Halleck on July 28, " is more & more firm that here is the defense of Washington & that I should be at once reinforced by all available troops to enable me to advance. Retreat would be disastrous to the army & the cause, I am confident of that." Writing later that day to Mrs. McClellan, the General exclaimed, " I hear nothing as yet from Washington. . . . I am getting dreadfully tired of doing nothing. . . . Burnside is still kept from me. I am getting no reinforcements, and presume that Burnside will be ordered to Washington the first thing I know. Then I shall be in a pretty predicament— too strong to remain here and too weak to advance." On the twenty-ninth, the Federal administration directed Meigs " to send all steamers that can be obtained to James River." Although McClellan was not informed right away of what was about to take place, the collecting and dispatching of a large number of empty vessels to the James could only mean that the Army of the Potomac was going to be withdrawn from the Peninsula. And on the thirty-first, Halleck wired the follow-

[33] Cooke's manuscript account of this visit with Lincoln, in Oberholtzer, *Jay Cooke*, I, 199–201; *Chase's Diary*, 50; Robert B. Warden, *Account of the Private Life and Public Services of Salmon Portland Chase*, 441–42.

ing intelligence of dubious merit to McClellan: " General Pope again telegraphs that the enemy is reported to be evacuating Richmond and falling back on Danville and Lynchburg." [34]

Steps were being taken in the National capital that would let fall an avalanche of despair on McClellan and his army. On July 30, Halleck instructed McClellan to ship back to Washington all his sick and wounded men as quickly as possible. " Advise me of their removal," Halleck added. This was to be done, he said, " in order to enable you to move in any direction." One cannot help but get the impression that it had already been decided in Washington to withdraw McClellan's army from the Peninsula, and that this shipping off of his sick and wounded soldiers was a preliminary step in such a plan; for men who are sick and wounded but who will recuperate and soon be back in the ranks are not normally sent away unless it is desired to deploy the army in another area. McClellan reported that " the sending off our sick and supplies was pushed both day and night as rapidly as the means of transportation permitted." [35]

Then the fateful order was prepared in the Federal capital. Speaking of the idea of withdrawing McClellan's army from the Peninsula to the front of the capital, Meigs stated, " I . . . made up my mind that it would be necessary. Mr. Lincoln found out that this was the opinion at Washington and expressed great regret that such was the opinion." If this was true, the President nonetheless allowed the army to be withdrawn. At 7:45 on the evening of August 3, the recall order was drawn up in Washington and dispatched over Halleck's signature to McClellan. " It is determined," the directive stated, " to withdraw your army from the Peninsula to Aquia Creek. . . . Its real object and withdrawal should be concealed even

[34] McClellan to Halleck, July 28, 1862, McClellan Papers; McClellan to his wife, July 28, 1862, *M.O.S.*, 457; Meigs's Diary, entry of July 29, 1862; Halleck to McClellan, July 31, 1862, 14 *O.R.*, 344.

[35] Halleck to McClellan, July 30, 1862, *M.O.S.*, 491, 494.

from your own officers. . . . The entire execution of the movement is left to your discretion and judgment." The General-in-Chief followed this up with another message the next day, saying to McClellan, " The President expects that the instructions which were sent to you yesterday with his approval will be carried out with all possible dispatch and caution." [36]

The order was a staggering blow to McClellan. However, he made one last desperate appeal to Halleck—an argument so strong as to invite close attention:

> Your telegram of last evening is received. I must confess that it has caused me the greatest pain I ever experienced, for I am convinced that the order to withdraw this army to Aquia Creek will prove disastrous to our cause. . . .
>
> This army is now in excellent discipline and condition. We hold a debouche on both banks of the James River, so that we are free to act in any direction, and, with the assistance of the gunboats, I consider our communications as now secure. We are (25) twenty-five miles from Richmond, and are not likely to meet the enemy in force sufficient to fight a battle, until we have marched (15) fifteen to (18) eighteen miles, which brings us practically within (10) miles of Richmond. Our longest line of land transportation would be from this point (25) twenty-five miles; but with the aid of the gunboats we can supply the army by water during its advance, certainly to within (12) twelve miles of Richmond.
>
> At Aquia Creek we would be (75) seventy-five miles from Richmond, with land transportation all the way.
>
> From here to Fort Monroe is a march of about (70) seventy miles; for I regard it as impracticable to withdraw this army and its material except by land.
>
> The result of the movement would thus be a march of (145) one hundred and forty-five miles to reach a point now only (25) twenty-five miles distant, and to deprive ourselves

---

[36] Meigs, " The Relations of President Lincoln and Secretary Stanton to the Military Commanders in the Civil War," *loc. cit.*, 296; McClellan to his wife, August 4, 1862, *M.O.S.*, 462; Halleck to McClellan, August 3, 1862, McClellan's *Report*, 153; Halleck to McClellan, August 4, 1862, McClellan Papers.

entirely of the powerful aid of the gunboats and water transportation. Add to this the certain demoralization of this army, which would ensue, the terribly depressing effect upon the people of the North, and the strong probability that it would influence foreign powers to recognize our adversaries, and there appear to me sufficient reasons to make it my imperative duty to urge, in the strongest terms afforded by our language, that this order may be rescinded, and that, far from recalling this army, it be promptly reinforced to enable it to resume the offensive. . . .

Here, directly in front of this army, is the heart of the rebellion. . . . Here is the true defense of Washington; it is here, on the banks of the James, that the fate of the Union should be decided.[37]

There can be little doubt that the decision to withdraw the Army of the Potomac from the Peninsula played right into the hands of the enemy. Noting the great advantages to the Federals of being astride the James near Richmond, Confederate General E. P. Alexander remarks, " Fortunately for us, Lincoln and Halleck recalled McClellan and his army to Washington without ever realizing them; although McClellan had tried hard to impress them upon his superiors." Another prominent Southern general, Richard Taylor, asserts that, for the Federals, " the true line of attack was on the south of the James, where Grant was subsequently forced by the ability of Lee; but it should be observed that after he took the field, McClellan had not the liberty accorded to Grant." The Union was to pay a stern price in blood and treasure during the next two years before another blue-clad army again got as close to Richmond.[38]

What were the principal forces behind the removal of McClellan's army from the James? They have already been alluded to. Pope had been playing upon Lincoln's anxiety for the safety of Washington, and had even urged the removal of

[37] McClellan to Halleck, August 4, 1862, 16 *O.R.*, 8.
[38] Alexander, *Military Memoirs*, 61, 172; Richard Taylor, *Destruction and Reconstruction* . . . (New York, 1879), 94.

the Army of the Potomac from the Peninsula himself. Welles said that the recall order was quite probably issued " to get rid of McClellan." In his wartime diary, Welles relates that Stanton was at this time so anxious to oust the General that he neglected many important duties of his office. " The introduction of Pope here, followed by Halleck," wrote Welles, " is an intrigue of Stanton's and Chase's to get rid of McClellan. A part of this intrigue has been the withdrawal of McClellan and the Army of the Potomac from Richmond, and turning it into the Army of Washington [sic] under Pope. . . . McClellan and the Army of the Potomac, on Halleck's recommendation, first proposed by Chase, were recalled from in the vicinity of Richmond." In his own diary, Chase acknowledged that he and Stanton urged Lincoln to supersede McClellan with Pope. Welles—who was never a supporter of McClellan—said that " Pope himself had great influence in bringing Halleck here, and the two, with Stanton and Chase, got possession of McC's army and withdrew it from before Richmond." McClellan struck the accurate chord in a letter to Ellen at this time: " When you contrast the policy I urged in my [Harrison's Bar] letter to the President with that of Congress and of Mr. Pope, you can readily agree with me that there can be little natural confidence between the government and myself. We are the antipodes of each other; and it is more than probable that they will take the earliest opportunity to relieve me from command and get me out of sight." [39]

In answer to McClellan's lengthy appeal for revocation of the recall order, Halleck said, " You cannot regret the order of withdrawal more than I did the necessity of giving it. It will not be rescinded and you will be expected to execute it with all possible promptness." In a subsequent private letter to McClellan, the General-in-Chief indicated that he too was

[39] Pope's testimony, C.C.W., I, 279; Welles, *Lincoln and Seward*, 193; *Welles's Diary*, I, 83, 105, 108, 109; *Chase's Diary*, entries following September 2, 1862, quoted also in Schuckers, *Salmon P. Chase*, 447, and in *M.O.S.*, 479–80; McClellan to his wife, July 31, 1862, August 2, 1862, August 2, 1862, *M.O.S.*, 459–60.

conservative on political matters, and believed the President to be similarly inclined. " It is my intention," Halleck continued, " that you shall command all the troops in Virginia as soon as we can get them together." Speaking of Pope and Burnside, Halleck declared, " I wish them to be under your immediate command, for reasons which it is not necessary to specify." And despite his pledges of friendship to McClellan, and his statement that he wanted him to command the main Union army in Virginia, " Halleck," according to Chase, " had sent Burnside to James River to act as second in command or as adviser of McClellan—in reality to control him." Then, after his visit to Harrison's Landing, the General-in-Chief, in the presence of Chase, berated all of McClellan's military operations, especially his Seven Days effort. Pope then condemned McClellan in even stronger terms, and said that Halleck agreed with him as to McClellan's incompetence.[40]

Writing home on August 10, McClellan still could not get over the removal of his army from Harrison's, and saw evil days ahead for the Union cause. " They are committing a fatal error," he asserted, " in withdrawing me from here, and the future will show it. I think the result of their machination will be that Pope will be badly thrashed within ten days, and that they will be very glad to turn over the redemption of their affairs to me." Unfortunately for the Federals, this prognostication was to be proved all too true. On the eleventh, another letter showed that McClellan had lost little of his acute powers of observation. " I presume," he wrote, " Pope is having his hands quite full today; is probably being hard pressed by Jackson. I cannot help him in time, as I have not the means of transportation; but I foresee that the government will try to throw upon me the blame of their own delays and blunders. So be it." [41]

[40] Halleck to McClellan, August 5 and 7, 1862, McClellan Papers; Halleck to McClellan, August 6, 1862, 12 *O.R.*, 83; New York *Tribune*, July 26, 1862; Keyes to Stanton, May 13, 1862, Stanton Papers; *Chase's Diary*, entry of August 15, 1862, quoted also in Schuckers, *Salmon P. Chase*, 448, and in *M.O.S.*, 475n.
[41] McClellan to his wife, August 10 and 11, 1862, *M.O.S.*, 465–66.

Chapter Eight

"A Deliverer Had Come"

> [McClellan] has acted badly in this matter, but we must use what tools we have. . . . Unquestionably he has acted badly toward Pope! He wanted him to fail. That is unpardonable, but he is too useful just now to sacrifice.
>
> —*A. Lincoln*

THE verbal battle fought by McClellan to keep his army on the Peninsula near Richmond had been lost. The Army of the Potomac was now ordered back to Aquia Creek, near Washington, to reinforce Pope's Army of Virginia for the new overland movement toward the Confederate capital. McClellan said, a few weeks later, to Cox, "If Pope was the man they had faith in, then Pope should have been sent to Harrison's Landing to take command, and however bitter it would have been, I should have had no just reason to complain." He felt it would require considerable sacrifices before the army got back to a position as close to Richmond as he was then abandoning. "The worst that could be said of the Peninsula Campaign," writes Emory Upton, "was that thus far it had not been successful. To make it a failure was reserved for the agency of General Halleck." Referring to the withdrawal of McClellan's army, Welles declared, "I . . . have doubted if H[alleck], unprompted, would himself have done it. It was a specimen of Chase's and Stanton's tactics. They had impressed the President with their ideas that a change of base was necessary." [1]

[1] Cox, *Military Reminiscences*, I, 242; Upton, *Military Policy*, 324, 331; John

196

McClellan's official returns show that he had about 88,435 men present for duty equipped at Harrison's. To eventually embark this large force for the vicinity of Washington was no easy task. McClellan had been ordered to ship off his sick and wounded first. The army, therefore, would have to remain to cover this operation, as well as to protect the removal of the enormous supplies accumulated on the James. Seeing that it would not be a rapid enterprise, McClellan tried to assure Halleck that he was striving to carry out the recall orders. " I will obey the order as soon as circumstances permit. . . . I have only been able to send off some 1,200 sick. No transportation. There will be no delay that I can avoid." The operation, however, was a slow one. This was due in part to the wharf facilities at Harrison's Bar, which were quite limited, with only a few vessels at a time able to tie up there.[2]

On August 9, the General-in-Chief wired McClellan that he feared a Confederate sortie against Pope in the direction of the Potomac River. " You must send reinforcements instantly to Aquia Creek," Halleck insisted. " Considering the amount of transportation at your disposal, your delay is not satisfactory. You must move with all possible celerity." McClellan tried to reassure Halleck. " There has been," he declared, " no unnecessary delay, as you assert—not an hour's—but everything has been and is being pushed as rapidly as possible to carry out your orders." That McClellan was moving with the utmost speed is shown by a dispatch on August 10 from the Assistant Quartermaster of the Army of the Potomac, Captain C. G. Sawtelle, to Quartermaster General Meigs. Sawtelle reported that all vessels were in use, adding, " If you could cause a more speedy return of the steamers sent away from here it would facilitate matters."[3]

Codman Ropes, *The Army Under Pope* (New York, 1881) , 16, 31, 32; *Welles's Diary,* I, 120, 121.

[2] 14 *O.R.,* 312; *B. & L.,* II, 547; McClellan to Halleck, August 6, 1862, McClellan's *Report,* 151, 160; Ingalls to Marcy, August 7, 1862, 12 *O.R.,* 79, 84–85.

[3] Halleck to McClellan, August 9, 1862, Sawtelle to Meigs, August 10, 1862, 12 *O.R.,* 85; McClellan to Halleck, August 10, 1862, McClellan's *Report,* 159.

But the General-in-Chief was not satisfied. On the tenth, he brusquely informed McClellan that the Confederates were fighting Pope at Cedar Mountain, and that " there must be no further delay in your movements. That which has already occurred was entirely unexpected, and must be satisfactorily explained." McClellan had been working all day to embark his incapacitated men and his supplies in the 100-degree heat, and was a bit angered by Halleck's sharp note. He replied sharply in a message of his own: " You are probably laboring under some great mistake as to the amount of transportation available here." He asked for additional transports to expedite the withdrawal. " I fear," he went on, " you do not realize the difficulties of the operation proposed. . . . The present moment is probably not the proper one for me to refer to the unnecessarily harsh and unjust tone of your telegrams of late." " I repeat," said McClellan in a later wire that day, " that I have lost no time in carrying out your orders." That McClellan was pressing the embarkation to the limit of the existing facilities is shown by a statement from Rufus Ingalls to Meigs: " We have embarked troops from this point to the full extent of our ability. Colonel Falls and others will tell you so. . . . Up to this moment the thing could not have been done faster." [4]

There came, on August 12, a partial recantation from Halleck for his unfair accusations against McClellan. " Perhaps," said Old Brains, " we were misinformed as to the facts; if so, the delay could be explained. Nothing in my telegram was intentionally harsh or unjust, but the delay was so unexpected that an explanation was required. . . . Not a single moment must be lost in getting additional troops in front of Washington." A few hours later, the wires carried an answer from McClellan to the Commanding General. It was a long dispatch. McClellan mentioned the great weakening of the enemy force guarding the eastern approach to Richmond. A

[4] Halleck to McClellan, McClellan to Halleck, August 10, 1862, McClellan to Halleck, August 11, 1862, 12 *O.R.*, 86; *Welles's Diary*, I, 71; Ingalls to Meigs, August 15, 1862, 14 *O.R.*, 377.

number of Southern units had marched westward to reinforce Jackson at Gordonsville. McClellan stated that these Confederate forces could not regroup quickly. He therefore begged permission to assail the relatively small grayclad force stationed about three miles west of Malvern Hill. " This effort would, it seems to me, have the effect to draw back the forces now before General Pope, and thus relieve Washington from all danger." He insisted that as fast as the steamers were arriving at Harrison's, he was filling them and sending them back to Aquia Creek. Halleck, however, ignored the General's suggested attack against Richmond from the James, and by his silence required that the withdrawal from the Peninsula continue.[5]

McClellan was spending much of his time in trying to convince his superiors that he was not procrastinating in sending off his troops. In a later telegram to Halleck on August 13, he mentioned the lack of wharf facilities at Yorktown and at Fortress Monroe, and stated that two weeks ago he had ordered two wharves for the fort. " But," said McClellan, " you countermanded the order." He pointed out the same deficiency at Aquia, and urged Halleck's speed in remedying it. He referred also to the handicap of shallow water at the disembarkation point at Aquia. McClellan then described the huge operation involved in moving the Army of the Potomac to the Peninsula at the start of the campaign that spring—a movement which had taken six weeks to complete. " There shall be no unnecessary delay," he proclaimed again, " but I cannot manufacture vessels. I state these difficulties from experience. . . . It is not possible for anyone to place this army where you wish it, ready to move, in less than a month. If Washington is in danger now this army can scarcely arrive in time to save it. It is in much better position to do so from here than Aquia." [6]

On the morning of the thirteenth, McClellan rode seventy

[5] Halleck to McClellan, August 12, 1862, 12 *O.R.*, 87; McClellan to Halleck, August 12, 1862, 14 *O.R.*, 372–73.
[6] McClellan to Halleck, August 12, 1862, 12 *O.R.*, 87–88.

miles to the nearest direct telegraph office at Jamestown Island, but transmitter trouble there forced him to ride on to Fortress Monroe and then to cross the bay by ship to Cherrystone Inlet on the Eastern Shore. He arrived there late at night, after having traveled all day. Anxious to learn Halleck's views in detail, McClellan sent him a terse telegram: " Please come to office; wish to talk to you [by wire]. What news from Pope? " Receiving no reply after an hour, McClellan wired again, giving details of the situation in his front, and reporting a large Confederate movement northward from the enemy capital toward Pope. A little over an hour later, a brief reply came back from Halleck: " There is no change of plans. You will send up your troops as rapidly as possible. There is no difficulty in landing them. . . . Do so with all possible rapidity." Then, before McClellan could decipher and read Halleck's message, the General-in-Chief went to bed without waiting to hear what McClellan had traveled so far to communicate. Although it was 3:30 in the morning, McClellan was so incensed that he dashed off a telegram to his wife. " My communication with Halleck was unsatisfactory in the extreme," he declared. " He did not even behave with common politeness; he is a *bien mauvais sujet*—he is not a gentleman. . . . I fear that I am very mad, and think I have a perfect right to be so. Every day convinces me more and more that it is the intention of Halleck and the government to drive me off." [7]

After the bulk of the sick, wounded, artillery, cavalry, and supplies had been shipped off, two corps of McClellan's army began the long march back toward Fortress Monroe on August 14. Burnside—whose corps had sailed from the fort—retained the steamers which he had used in his movement to Aquia Creek. Only four steamers had been provided by the War Department up to that time for McClellan's infantry, and these were " too large to go to Harrison's Landing." This explains

---

[7] McClellan's report, McClellan to Halleck, August 13 and 14, 1862, Halleck to McClellan, August 14, 1862, 12 *O.R.*, 88–89; McClellan to his wife, August 14, 1862, *M.O.S.*, 467.

the reason for marching the soldiers down to Old Point Comfort. Late on the evening of the fourteenth, McClellan telegraphed Halleck a warning: " I don't like Jackson's movements. He will suddenly appear where least expected." But not until Lee saw that the withdrawal of McClellan's army from the James was really underway, could he safely move northward in force against Pope. As Lee acknowledged, the threatening position held up until then by McClellan at Harrison's had prevented him from shifting any more troops to succor Jackson, who was facing Pope's superior numbers in the vicinity of Culpeper Court House.[8]

It has been seen that back in Washington Stanton and Chase were striving to bring about McClellan's downfall. The Secretary of War was now trying to obtain statements from various persons which would show that McClellan's withdrawal from the Peninsula was being made in a dilatory fashion. This new scheme, however, backfired on Stanton. Major General John A. Dix at Fortress Monroe wired the War Department on August 16 that " from all accounts the movement is progressing rapidly and successfully." Captain Charles Wilkes of the navy informed his chief that " McClellan's army has moved rapidly and successfully." Adjutant General Thomas, sent by Stanton to Fortress Monroe to check up on McClellan's performance, sent back this dispatch to the Secretary: " I parted with General McClellan yesterday at 3 o'clock p. m. The movement was progressing finely and will be successful. The army is in . . . splendid fighting order. . . . No one could have made the movement more skillfully or in less time." Meanwhile, Welles was noting in his diary that it was " strange that this change of military operations should have been made without Cabinet consultation." " But," he added, " Stanton is so absorbed in his scheme to get rid of McClellan that other and more important matters are neglected." And up to the time of Wilkes's

<hr />

[8] McClellan's report, McClellan to Halleck, August 14, 1862, 12 *O.R.*, 89; Powell, *Fifth Corps*, 192–93; Swinton, *Army of the Potomac*, 174, 175n; Stine, *Army of the Potomac*, 119–20.

dispatch, the Secretary of the Navy had not even been informed of the movement of McClellan's army from the James to Aquia. " I have not been advised," said Welles, " of army movements by either the Secretary of War or General Halleck." [9]

While the foes of McClellan in Washington were endeavoring to undermine him, the removal of the Army of the Potomac from the Peninsula continued. The General stated in his official report that, by August 16, " all the troops and material were en route by land and water." With their cumbersome wagon trains to protect in the land withdrawal, the Federals had to be wary of any enemy attempt to embarrass the movement. Everything went smoothly, however. By the seventeenth, the whole army, except the rear guard, had crossed the Chickahominy River near its mouth by means of a 2,000-foot pontoon bridge thrown up by Captain James C. Duane of the Engineers. The rear guard crossed on the eighteenth. Porter's Fifth Corps, which had reached Williamsburg on August 16, arrived at Newport News on the eighteenth. By the twentieth, the whole corps was on the water bound for Aquia. McClellan, at Williamsburg, telegraphed Halleck on the eighteenth, "[I] will be sure to have the troops ready to embark as fast as transports are on hand. Please hurry horse transports and those for batteries." [10]

But the General-in-Chief continued to press McClellan on the necessity for swift movements. " It is of vital importance," he exclaimed on August 19, " that you send forward troops as rapidly as possible. . . . We want immediately all the men that can possibly be sent." McClellan replied patiently, " Porter is embarking as rapidly as possible. . . . No time shall be lost in pushing off the troops as rapidly as possible." As examples of McClellan's driving energy in fulfilling Halleck's instructions, two messages from the Army of the Potomac commander to

[9] Dix to Halleck, Wilkes to Welles, Thomas to Stanton, August 16, 1862, 18 *O.R.*, 578–80; *Welles's Diary*, I, 83.
[10] McClellan's report, 12 *O.R.*, 90–91; McClellan to Halleck, August 17 and 18, 1862, 18 *O.R.*, 590, 595.

two of his corps leaders might be noted. To Heintzelman McClellan said, " You will make use of every vessel that arrives at Yorktown, both during the night and day, to embark your troops. Not one moment must be lost in carrying out this order. You will please direct the officers commanding the troops in the different vessels to sail as soon as they are loaded." And to Porter: " Please push off your troops without one moment's delay. The necessity is very pressing—a matter of life and death." McClellan was obliged to spend almost as much time in trying to convince his government that he was not dawdling as he was in striving to carry out the orders given him.[11]

By the twentieth of August, the whole Army of the Potomac was in the process of embarking at Fortress Monroe, Yorktown, and Newport News. With Porter already on the water, Heintzelman's Third Corps sailed on the twenty-first from Yorktown. But the strain was beginning to show on Halleck, who now evidenced traces of anxiety and alarm. " The forces of Burnside and Pope are hard pressed," he said to McClellan, " and require aid as quickly as you can send it. Come yourself as soon as you can." McClellan replied that he hoped to be able to get away on the twenty-second, and asked whether he was to come to Aquia or Washington. He wrote that day to Ellen, " Now they are in trouble they seem to want the ' Quaker,' the ' procrastinator,' the ' coward,' and the ' traitor.' · *Bien* . . ." On the following day, the General vented his feelings in another letter home. " I think," he said, " they are pretty well scared in Washington, and probably with good reason. I am confident that the disposition to be made of me will depend entirely upon the state of their nerves in Washington. If they feel safe there I will, no doubt, be shelved. . . . I . . . am not fond of being a target for the abuse and slander of all the rascals in the country. Well, we will continue to trust in God and feel certain that all is for the best." Later on the evening of the twenty-first, McClellan wired again to Halleck, in regard to

[11] Halleck to McClellan, McClellan to Halleck, McClellan to Heintzelman, August 19, 1862, McClellan to Porter, August 20, 1862, 18 *O.R.*, 599, 605, 606.

203

ammunition, " I can supply any deficiency that may exist in
General Pope's army. . . . The forage is the only question for
you to attend to. Please have that ready for me at Aquia."
Nowhere is there an indication but that McClellan was endeavoring wholeheartedly to assist Pope and Halleck in uniting
the two armies in the best possible manner. In obedience to
an order from the General-in-Chief, McClellan set Keyes's
Fourth Corps to work to strengthen and hold the defenses of
Yorktown.[12]

Shortly after noon on August 23, McClellan, at Old Point
Comfort, telegraphed Halleck that " Franklin's corps has started.
I shall start for Aquia in about an hour. No transports yet for
Sumner's corps." Sailing up the bay that night, McClellan
wrote to his wife, " I take it for granted that my orders will
be as disagreeable as it is possible to make them, unless Pope is
beaten, in which case they will want me to save Washington
again. Nothing but their fears will induce them to give me
any command of importance or to treat me otherwise than with
discourtesy." The ensuing events were to prove the accuracy
of this statement.[13]

Arriving at Aquia Creek early on the morning of the twenty-
fourth, McClellan found things to be about as he had expected.
" This is a wretched place," he declared in a letter to Ellen,
" utterly unfit for the landing and supplying of a large body
of troops. They have at last found it out, though H[alleck]
insisted upon it that there were ample facilities for all purposes." McClellan spent the better part of the day in wiring
his superiors in Washington, asking them to tell him what his
exact status was and what he should be about. " Reynolds,
Reno, and Stevens are supposed to be with Pope," he informed
Halleck. " Please inform me immediately exactly where Pope
is and what doing; until I know that I cannot regulate Porter's

[12] McClellan's report, Halleck to McClellan, McClellan to Halleck, August 21,
1862, 12 O.R., 91, 92; 18 O.R., 606; McClellan to his wife, August 21 and 22,
1862, M.O.S., 469–70.
[13] McClellan to Halleck, August 23, 1862, 12 O.R., 93; McClellan to his wife,
August 23, 1862, M.O.S., 471.

movements." He asked if he was to command the united Army in Virginia, as the Commanding General had pledged. " Please define my position and duties," he beseeched his superior. Not until after 11:00 P. M. did Halleck reply. " I do not know," he confessed, " where General Pope is or where the enemy in force is." He carefully refrained from commenting on McClellan's status and duties at Aquia. In reply to still one more supplication from McClellan as to his position, Halleck, just before midnight, wired back, " There is nothing more to communicate tonight. . . . Good night." [14]

On August 25, McClellan went to Falmouth, near Fredericksburg, to confer with Burnside. His Sixth Corps commander, Franklin, was then at Alexandria. On the twenty-sixth, Franklin received the following instructions from Halleck: " You will march your corps by Centerville toward Warrenton, reporting to General Pope in the absence of General McClellan from the immediate field of operations." Halleck soon saw, however, that Franklin's artillery had not yet arrived from the Peninsula, and instructed him to postpone his march. [15]

Although in touch with the administration by telegraph, McClellan, at Fredericksburg, could still not obtain any orders defining his status or position. Apparently, Halleck did not want him to get too far away from Washington or too close to Pope, for on the morning of the twenty-sixth he wired McClellan, " Perhaps you had better leave General Burnside in charge at Aquia Creek and come to Alexandria, as very great irregularities are reported there. General Franklin's corps will march as soon as it receives transportation." Fredericksburg is twelve miles south of Aquia, and McClellan's units were to move by rail from Aquia to Fredericksburg, then up the line of the Rappahannock toward the area where Pope was supposed to be confronting Lee. As the historian of the Army of the

---

[14] McClellan to his wife, August 24, 1862, *M.O.S.*, 528; McClellan to Halleck, Halleck to McClellan, August 24, 1862, 12 *O.R.*, 93–94; 18 *O.R.*, 645.

[15] Halleck to Franklin, August 26, 1862, 18 *O.R.*, 676; Franklin to Ropes, as quoted in Ropes, *Story of the Civil War*, II, 315.

Potomac, J. H. Stine, says of this arrangement, it "was a dangerous move; the line was entirely too long, reaching from Fredericksburg to Sulphur Springs, opposite Warrenton; the line was weak and liable to be pierced at any point by either Longstreet or Jackson; but this was the plan decided upon by Halleck. . . . He was managing the battle from his office at Washington." Many high-ranking Federal officers felt at this time that Halleck should have taken command in person in the field of the Union forces then in northern Virginia—like Grant was to do in 1864—but this he shunned like the plague.[16]

August twenty-seventh was a trying day for the Union generals striving to reinforce Pope with troops from Aquia and Alexandria, and the telegraph wires were kept singing with messages coming from both McClellan's and Halleck's headquarters. McClellan arrived at Alexandria early that morning, and informed Halleck that Sumner's corps had begun to disembark at Aquia. The General-in-Chief then said that "Franklin's corps should move out by forced marches" from Alexandria toward the front, but cautioned McClellan that the railroad to Fredericksburg was not guarded properly. At 10:00 A. M., McClellan reported that he had directed Franklin "to prepare to march with his corps at once," and that he had given Burnside his personal cavalry escort to reconnoiter along the Rappahannock. A little later, Halleck sent a very important directive to McClellan: "Take entire direction of the sending out of the troops from Alexandria. Determine questions of priority in transportation, and the places they shall occupy." He said that Franklin should move out "as soon as possible." Halleck stated that he could learn nothing from Pope of the situation confronting him. The Union generals endeavoring to assist Pope were thus operating in a complete fog, due to the inability to get information from the front.[17]

[16] Halleck to McClellan, August 26, 1862, 12 *O.R.*, 94; Stine, *Army of the Potomac*, 123.

[17] McClellan to Halleck, Halleck to McClellan, August 27, 1862, 12 *O.R.*, 94, 95; McClellan's *Report*, 171.

Seeing that if Franklin and Sumner moved out separately they would be more liable to overwhelming defeat in detail, McClellan, at 11:20 on the morning of the twenty-seventh, asked of the General-in-Chief, " Would it not be advisable to throw the mass of Sumner's corps here to move out with Franklin to Centreville or vicinity? " With the paucity of intelligence from the front as to locations of Union and Confederate troops—due to the fact that Pope's communications had been cut—McClellan was determined to act prudently. Replying to McClellan's query about " bringing up " Sumner's command from Aquia to Alexandria, Halleck, in a significant and revealing dispatch, stated, " From your knowledge of the whole country about here you can best act. I have had no time to obtain such knowledge. . . . More than three-quarters of my time is taken up with the raising of new troops and matters in the West. I have no time for details. You will therefore, as ranking general in the field, direct as you deem best, but at present orders for Pope's army should go through me." [18]

A few minutes after noon on August 27, McClellan told Halleck that he had ordered Franklin's corps to be " in readiness to move at once." He reported, however, that heavy firing had been heard at Centerville, and that he had no cavalry to send out on reconnaissance along the roads toward the front. About an hour later, McClellan asserted to the Commanding General that " Franklin's artillery have no horses. . . . I can pick up no cavalry. I have no means of knowing the enemy's force between Pope and ourselves. Can Franklin, without his artillery or cavalry, effect any useful purpose in front? . . . I do not see that we have force enough in hand to form a connection with Pope, whose exact position we do not know." The country between Manassas and Alexandria was heavily wooded, with numerous roads crossing it in all directions. Being ignorant of the whereabouts of the enemy units, Franklin's 11,000 men, without artillery and especially without

[18] McClellan to Halleck, Halleck to McClellan, August 27, 1862, 18 *O.R.*, 689, 691; see Ropes, *Story of the Civil War*, II, 316.

cavalry vedettes, would be quite liable to ambush by superior forces. Earlier that day, Brigadier General George W. Taylor's brigade of Slocum's division of the Sixth Corps had been badly cut up by a superior Southern force at Bull Run Bridge.[19]

Anxious to come to the best possible solution of the thorny problem confronting them, McClellan, at 1:35 P. M. on the twenty-seventh, wired Halleck, " If you will give me even one squadron of good cavalry here, I will ascertain the state of the case." He felt that the corps of Franklin and Sumner should not advance " until they can have their artillery and cavalry." Not hearing from the General-in-Chief, McClellan informed him that he had ordered Sumner's corps to Alexandria, and that Couch's division of Keyes's Fourth Corps had been called up from Yorktown. With his exact position, status, and duties still undefined, McClellan exclaimed to Halleck, " I am not responsible for the past and cannot be for the future, unless I receive authority to dispose of the available troops according to my judgment. Please inform me at once what my position is. I do not wish to act in the dark." [20]

Then, late on the evening of the twenty-seventh, McClellan received word that a railroad train had been fired upon by the Confederates near Burke's Station, just fourteen miles from Alexandria. Consequently, he told Halleck, he had halted Cox's command—then under orders to entrain along the same rail line—together with Franklin's corps, until morning. Upton's considered opinion on this decision seems just: " Had General McClellan sent General Cox forward by train to be waylaid, possibly captured, knowing that the enemy was on the railroad, he would not have been accused of stupidity—he would have been justly charged with criminality." Writing briefly to Ellen that night, McClellan said, " I shall do all I can to help [Halleck] loyally and will trouble him as little as possible. . . .

[19] McClellan to Halleck, August 27, 1862, 12 *O.R.*, 96; McClellan's *Report*, 173; Upton, *Military Policy*, 348; R. L. Dabney, *Life and Campaigns of Lieut.- Gen. Thomas J. Jackson* . . . (New York, 1866) , 520.
[20] McClellan to Halleck, August 27, 1862, 12 *O.R.*, 96–97.

McClellan and his Wife

Our affairs here are much tangled up, and I opine that in a day or two your old husband will be called upon to unravel them. In the meantime, I shall be very patient, do to the best of my ability whatever I am called upon to do." [21]

Shortly after noon on August 28, the General-in-Chief instructed Franklin to march his Sixth Corps " toward Manassas Junction, to drive the enemy from the railroad." However, qualifying this order, Halleck added, " If you have not received [McClellan's] orders act on this." But McClellan, as noted before, had been given discretionary power to move these units out as he saw fit; in fact, he had been instructed by the Commanding General to " direct as you deem best." Halleck had also ordered him to " take entire direction of sending out of troops from Alexandria." Now, McClellan received word of another Federal fiasco—the defeat at Bull Run Bridge of Colonel E. Parker Scammon's brigade, which had advanced without cavalry or artillery. McClellan, therefore, wanted Franklin to march only if properly equipped with guns and mounted men. However, despite a number of sharply worded telegrams between McClellan and Halleck during the afternoon and evening of the twenty-eighth—in which McClellan exercised his proper authority in not sending Franklin out " naked "—the arrival later that night of the Sixth Corps artillery enabled Franklin to be moved out early the next morning anyway. [22]

At about this time, near Manassas, while contending with the main enemy army, Pope was not too busy to try to woo some of McClellan's generals away from Little Mac and toward his own camp. According to Porter, who was then conversing with Pope, the latter declared to him, " McClellan is to have nothing to do with this campaign. That is decided." The Radical general then continued: " I hope we will be successful in this campaign and I think we will in the next fight—and if

[21] McClellan to Halleck, August 27, 1862, *C.C.W.*, I, 459; Upton, *Military Policy*, 350; McClellan to his wife, August 27, 1862, *M.O.S.*, 529.
[22] Halleck to Franklin, August 28, 1862, 18 *O.R.*, 707–709; *B. & L.*, II, 499; 16 *O.R.*, 406; 12 *O.R.*, 97; *C.C.W.*, I, 459, 460.

successful as I hope and expect, I will be at the highest round of the ladder, and will take care of such of McClellan's friends as stick to me." [23]

And on the twenty-eighth, Secretary of War Stanton re-entered the drama. He addressed the following memorandum to Halleck, consisting of a series of questions whose tenor seems to indicate that he was desirous of getting answers which would reflect unfavorably upon McClellan's performance in the movement from the Peninsula to the vicinity of Washington:

> I desire you to furnish me information upon the following points:
>
> 1st. At what date you first ordered the general commanding the Army of the Potomac to move from James River.
>
> 2d. Whether that order was or was not obeyed according to its purport with the promptness which, in your judgment, the national safety required, and at what date the movement commenced.
>
> 3d. What order has been given recently for the movement of Franklin's Corps, and whether it was obeyed as promptly as the national safety required.
>
> 4th. You will furnish me copies of the orders referred to in the foregoing inquiries. [24]

Two days later, Halleck replied as follows to the second question: "The order was not obeyed with the promptness I expected and the national safety, in my opinion, required." The General-in-Chief then made the erroneous statement that McClellan did not begin the withdrawal movement from Harrison's Landing until July 14. "When General McClellan's movement was begun it was rapidly carried out; but there was an unexpected delay in commencing it. General McClellan reports the delay as unavoidable." Halleck dodged completely answering the question as to McClellan's degree of obedience

[23] Fitz John Porter, "The Campaign of Northern Virginia under Major-General John Pope," F. J. Porter Papers.
[24] Stanton to Halleck, August 28, 1862, 18 *O.R.*, 706.

to any orders moving Franklin out.[25] The use to which Stanton was to put this information will soon be seen.

Returning to the efforts to reinforce Pope, McClellan informed Halleck on the morning of August 29 that Franklin's corps was in motion, but that he could give him only two squadrons of cavalry. " Franklin has but 40 rounds of ammunition," McClellan continued, " and no wagons to move more. I do not think Franklin is in condition to accomplish much if he meets with serious resistance." Cox, who was present, heard McClellan say to Franklin in parting, " Go, and whatever may happen, don't allow it to be said that the Army of the Potomac failed to do its utmost for the country." However, while McClellan was striving to get the troops organized to move out to aid Pope, his chief detractors and opponents in the cabinet, Stanton and Chase, were doing their best to discredit him and have him removed from command. On the twenty-ninth, Chase recorded in his diary, " The Secretary of War called on me in reference to Genl. McClellan. He has long believed and so have I, that Genl. McClellan ought not to be trusted with the command of any army of the Union. . . . Called on Genl. Halleck, and remonstrated against Gen. McClellan commanding." [26]

So concerned was McClellan with the critical military situation of Pope as well as that near the National capital, that, on the afternoon of the twenty-ninth, he sent the following message to the President (dispatching a copy to Halleck) : " I am clear that one of two courses should be adopted: First, to concentrate all our available forces to open communications with Pope; Second, to leave Pope to get out of his scrape, and at once use all our means to make the capital perfectly safe. No middle ground will now answer. Tell me what you wish me to do, and I will do all in my power to accomplish it. I wish to know what my orders and authority are. I ask for nothing,

[25] Halleck to Stanton, August 30, 1862, *ibid.*, 739–41.
[26] McClellan to Halleck, August 29, 1862, 12 *O.R.*, 98; Cox, *Military Reminiscences*, I, 236; *Chase's Diary*, 62.

but will obey whatever orders you give. I only ask a prompt decision, that I may at once give the necessary orders. It will not do to delay longer." [27] Much has been written into the words, " leave Pope to get out of his scrape," by hostile critics of McClellan. Many readers of the message get an ugly connotation from this phrase. However, as Ropes says, " We take it as clear enough to any reasonable man that this was simply a short mode of stating the idea." The words were, " in the hurry of the moment couched by General McClellan in the ungracious terms " noted. " The words were certainly unfelicitous, but time pressed. They certainly conveyed the idea." [28] Emory Upton's comment on this phrase is incisive: " Wise and soldierly as was this appeal, its language was unfortunate. . . . It was construed to mean that he wished the destruction of [Pope] and his army, and was regarded as a key not only to his orders relating to Franklin, but to all his movements and actions from the time he was directed to withdraw from the Peninsula. The candid reader will bear in mind that the despatch was written in haste and without weighing of words." [29]

A short time later, the President replied to McClellan. " Yours of today just received," he said. " I think your first alternative, to wit, ' to concentrate all our available forces to open communication with Pope,' is the right one, but I wish not to control. That I now leave to General Halleck, aided by your counsels." [30] Lincoln did not answer McClellan's oft-repeated request for specific orders defining his position and authority.

At noon on August 29, the debate over the disposal of Franklin and Sumner resumed. " Do you wish the movement of Franklin's corps to continue? " McClellan asked the General-in-Chief. " He is without reserve ammunition, and without transportation." A little later, receiving no reply from Halleck,

[27] McClellan to Lincoln, August 29, 1862, 12 *O.R.*, 98.
[28] Ropes, *The Army Under Pope*, 161.
[29] Upton, *Military Policy*, 354.
[30] Lincoln to McClellan, August 29, 1862, 12 *O.R.*, 98.

McClellan asked him how far he wanted Franklin to proceed. Then, hearing reports from various sources—including Halleck's office—of a large Confederate force near Vienna moving toward Chain Bridge, McClellan exercised the discretion and authority given him previously by the Commanding General, and halted Franklin's column of approximately 11,000 men near Annandale. To have pushed it forward in its present condition, McClellan felt, would have been rash and dangerous in the extreme. Still receiving no word from Washington, McClellan asked Halleck where he wished Sumner's corps posted for the defense of the capital, and repeated his query about Franklin. Another hour passed without a reply from his superior. McClellan wired once again: " I anxiously await reply to my last dispatch in regard to Sumner. Wish to give the order at once." He said that he did not think Franklin should be pushed beyond Annandale. Halleck finally answered in a brusque message, asking McClellan why he had halted Franklin at Annandale.[31]

The General-in-Chief soon communicated a little more fully and explicitly. " I want Franklin's corps," he declared, " to go far enough to find out something about the enemy. Perhaps he may get such information at Annandale as to prevent his going further. Otherwise he will push on toward Fairfax. Try to get something from direction of Manassas, either by telegram, or through Franklin's scouts. Our people must move more actively, and find out where the enemy is. I am tired of guesses." Here it can be seen that Halleck sent Franklin out chiefly to get information, not to join Pope as Heintzelman and Reno had previously done. Halleck apparently intended to use Franklin (and possibly Sumner) for the defense of the capital, although this was just the opposite of the President's view on the matter. Arriving at Annandale, Franklin did obtain information about the situation in the direction of Pope's army near Manassas, and relayed it back to headquarters.[32]

[31] McClellan to Halleck, Halleck to McClellan, August 29, 1862, *C.C.W.*, I, 462, 463; 12 *O.R.*, 98–99.

[32] Halleck to McClellan, August 29, 1862, *C.C.W.*, I, 463; Ropes, *The Army Under Pope*, 159–60; 18 *O.R.*, 722.

But the Union Commanding General was not satisfied with what McClellan had done. In the evening of August 29, he issued a blast at McClellan. " I have just been told," said he, " that Franklin's corps stopped at Annandale. . . . This is all contrary to my orders. Investigate and report the fact of this disobedience. That corps must push forward, as I directed, to protect the railroad and open our communications with Manassas." Of course, this was not true, as shown by Halleck's directive to McClellan earlier that afternoon. Although not directly accused himself of disobeying orders, a bristling McClellan was determined that Franklin should not be falsely accused either. Replying to Halleck's barb, McClellan said that, as he had mentioned in his three previous messages, and as Halleck himself had noted in one of his own, the size of the enemy force reported to be near Vienna was unknown to the Federals. He asserted that it was dangerous to push Franklin further than Annandale, where he had obtained the information already sent back. Franklin himself, said McClellan, was at Alexandria, trying to get the quartermaster to relinquish to him the much-needed supplies and transportation for his corps. " Please give distinct orders," he continued, " in reference to Franklin's movements of tomorrow. . . . It is not agreeable to me to be accused of disobeying orders when I have simply exercised the discretion you committed to me." This emphatic pronouncement silenced Old Brains. He could not or did not reply. Therefore, at 10:00 P. M., McClellan wired him as follows: "Not hearing from you, I have sent orders to General Franklin to place himself in communication with General Pope as soon as possible." He said that he had instructed Franklin to move at 6:00 A. M. the next morning.[33]

Writing briefly to his wife at this time, McClellan appeared disgusted at the confusion existing about the Federal capital and in northern Virginia. " I have a terrible task on my hands

---

[33] Halleck to McClellan, McClellan to Halleck, August 29, 1862, *C.C.W.*, I, 465; 12 *O.R.*, 99–100; Ropes, *The Army Under Pope*, 162; Ropes, *Story of the Civil War*, II, 320.

now," he declared, " perfect imbecility to correct. No means to act with, no authority, yet determined, if possible, to save the country and the capital. . . . I am not permitted to go to the post of danger! . . . . I do not know whether I shall be permitted to save the capital or not. . . . I am heartsick with the folly and ignorance I see around me. God grant that I may never pass through such a scene again." [34]

On August 30, a series of telegrams was exchanged between McClellan and Halleck having to do with the lack of wagons to transport the ammunition and supplies of Franklin's and Sumner's corps. The General-in-Chief was apparently ignorant of the inability of the quartermasters to provide the necessary transportation, and he was critical of Franklin's delay in marching beyond Annandale. McClellan did his best to augment the meager number of wagons by relinquishing his own headquarters wagon train as well as unloading some of Banks's supply train and using the vehicles to help supply Franklin. Then, on his own authority, McClellan instructed Sumner's corps to follow Franklin's in the direction of Fairfax Court House. He had even sent out all his cavalry escort, leaving him with only a tiny camp guard. " You now have," he stated to Halleck on the thirtieth, " every man of the Army of the Potomac who is within my reach." Writing his usual letter to Ellen later that day, McClellan said that he had " sent up every man I have, pushed everything, and am here on the flat of my back without any command whatever." Trying to correspond with her again that night, the General was at a low ebb: " I feel too blue and disgusted to write any more now, so I will smoke a cigar and try to get into a better humor. They have taken all my troops from me! I have even sent off my personal escort and camp-guard, and am here with a few orderlies and the aides. I have been listening to the sound of a great battle in the distance. My men engaged in it and I away. I never felt worse in my life." [35]

[34] McClellan to his wife, August 29, 1862, *M.O.S.*, 530.
[35] McClellan to Halleck, Halleck to McClellan, August 30, 1862, 12 *O.R.*, 100–

While these events were transpiring on August 30 near Alexandria, Pope, outnumbering the Confederates by about 76,000 to 49,000, was being thoroughly outgeneraled by Lee, Jackson, and Longstreet at the Second Battle of Bull Run. The outcome of the combat was as disastrous to the Union arms as was the first epic struggle on that bloody battleground thirteen months before. Franklin's corps reached Centerville at about 6:00 P. M., too late to participate in the great battle. Before the eventful day was over, the Fifth Corps commander, Porter, from Centerville, reported Pope's defeat to McClellan. Porter stated that Pope, at a council of war of the corps commanders, told them that, as regards an order just received from Halleck not to fall back to Alexandria where McClellan was stationed, " there are political considerations which control, not the safety of the army." And Pope had been playing the political game to the hilt with the anti-McClellan Radicals in the cabinet and on the Committee on the Conduct of the War, with the obvious desire to win a decisive victory himself.[36]

And then the intriguers perpetrated on the thirtieth an event of signficant importance to McClellan, Lincoln, and the Union, and they did it behind the President's back. Stanton drew up a paper, with Chase's assistance, which warned the Chief Executive not to continue McClellan in command of any Federal army, and demanded that he dismiss him immediately. It charged that McClellan was an out-and-out traitor. Stanton, Chase, Bates, and Caleb B. Smith signed it, and called upon Welles to do likewise. Welles said that while he agreed that McClellan should be removed from command, he felt that the paper was disrespectful in form toward Lincoln, and refused to endorse it. Montgomery Blair, of course—a McClellan supporter—could not even be approached on the matter. Seward was out of town. Stanton and Chase would not present

101; 18 *O.R.*, 744–45, 747–48; George B. McClellan, "From the Peninsula to Antietam," *B. & L.*, II, 548–49; Paris, *The Civil War*, II, 304.

[36] Livermore, *Numbers and Losses*, 88–89; Ropes, *The Army Under Pope*, 162–64; Porter to McClellan, August 30, 1862, 18 *O.R.*, 568–69.

216

the document to the President, however, without Welles's signature, and the old Secretary of the Navy remained adamant in his refusal. Later in the day, Stanton denounced McClellan in violent terms. Welles recorded that, " Stanton, intriguing against [McClellan], wanted to exclude him from command. Chase seconded the scheme." [37]

McClellan finally received on August 30 the long-sought-after order defining his status and command. He repeated it to Halleck the following day to ascertain if he had understood it correctly, declaring that " under the War Department order of yesterday I have no control over anything except my staff, some 100 men in my camp here, and the few remaining near Fort Monroe." The order to which McClellan referred stated slyly that " General McClellan commands that portion of the Army of the Potomac that has not been sent forward to General Pope's command. By order of the Secretary of War." This left McClellan in command of practically nothing. Writing on the morning of the thirty-first to his wife, McClellan declared, " I feel like a fool here, sucking my thumbs and doing nothing but what ought to be done by junior officers. I leave it all in the hands of the Almighty. I will try to do my best in the position that may be assigned to me." And a little later: " I am left in command of *nothing*—a command I feel fully competent to exercise, and to which I can do full justice." During the course of the day, he was occupied in readying the fortifications on both the south and north banks of the Potomac to withstand an assault on Washington by the victorious enemy should it come. Cox, while going about with McClellan to inspect the various forts, noted that the General " was, at this time, a little depressed in manner, feeling keenly his loss of power and command, but maintaining a quiet dignity that became him better than any show of carelessness would have done. He used no bitter or harsh language in criticising others. Pope and McDowell he plainly disliked, and rated them low

[37] *Welles's Diary*, I, 93–99; *Chase's Diary*, 62.

as to capacity for command; but he spoke of them without discourtesy or vilification." [38]

With the extent of Pope's defeat finally becoming clear to him, the Union General-in-Chief was on the spot. As information of an alarming nature continued to pour in, Halleck began to show signs of disintegration. Late at night on the thirty-first, he turned to McClellan. " I beg of you," he pleaded, " to assist me in this crisis with your ability and experience. I am utterly tired out." This was the most courteous message that McClellan had received from his superior in weeks. He replied promptly: " I am ready to afford you any assistance in my power, but you will readily perceive how difficult an undefined position, such as I now hold, must be. At what hour in the morning can I see you alone, either at your house or the office? " The Commanding General's aide responded, " General Halleck has gone to bed. . . . He will see you at any time to-morrow morning that will suit your convenience." In spite of Halleck's retirement to bed, McClellan telegraphed again an hour later, giving what intelligence he had of Pope's serious defeat at Manassas, and asserting, " To speak frankly— and the occasion requires it—there appears to be a total absence of brains, and I fear the total destruction of the army. . . . The occasion is grave and demands grave measures. The question is the salvation of the country." After recommending a number of specific measures for the safeguarding of the capital, McClellan stated, " Please answer at once. I shall be up all night, and ready to obey any orders you give me." Determined not to let McClellan outlast him in the all-night vigil, Halleck climbed out of bed and wired McClellan at 1:30 A. M. on September 1, " I shall be up all night and ready to act as circumstances may require. I am fully aware of the gravity of the crisis, and have been for weeks." [39]

[38] McClellan to Halleck, August 31, 1862, 12 *O.R.*, 102; McClellan to his wife, August 31, 1862, *M.O.S.*, 532; Cox, *Military Reminiscences*, I, 241.

[39] *Welles's Diary*, I, 99; Halleck to McClellan, McClellan to Halleck, August 31, 1862, Halleck to McClellan, September 1, 1862, 12 *O.R.*, 103, 104; McClellan to Halleck, Major John J. Key to McClellan, August 31, 1862, 18 *O.R.*, 773, 774.

While McClellan was endeavoring to safeguard the capital of the Union, the cabinet intriguers arrayed against him drew up another round-robin paper on September 1, hoping that Welles would sign this one. It called upon Lincoln to remove McClellan from command, on grounds that an army was not safe in his hands. Blair would, of course, not sign it. Neither would Welles, who still felt the whole procedure to be disrespectful to the President. Seward was again out of town. "This movement," wrote Welles in his diary, "originates with Stanton, who is mad . . . and determined to destroy McClellan." Further on, Welles noted that "Chase . . . said it was designed to tell the President that the Administration must be broken up, or McC dismissed. . . . It was evident there was a fixed determination to remove, and if possible to disgrace McClellan. Chase frankly stated that he desired it, that he deliberately believed McClellan ought to be shot." Without Welles's signature, however, the conspirators felt unwilling to submit the ultimatum to Lincoln.[40]

Back in the arena of military operations, the Confederates continued to press the retreating, disorganized army of Pope. On September 1, Stonewall Jackson was partially successful in a sharp attack at Ox Hill (Chantilly), near Germantown and Fairfax Court House. The combat resulted in the death of two excellent Union soldiers—Generals I. I. Stevens and Phil Kearny. Following this new Federal reverse, Halleck wired McClellan that "General Pope was ordered this morning to fall back to [the] line of fortifications [about Washington]." [41]

On the morning of the first, McClellan's services were in demand at the Federal capital. Halleck wired him, asking, "Is the general coming up to Washington, and if so at what hour will he be here? I am very anxious to see him." McClellan mounted his horse and rode toward the capital to try to settle matters about his anomalous position. Arriving at the General-

---

[40] *Welles's Diary*, I, 100–104; *Chase's Diary*, 63.
[41] Swinton, *Army of the Potomac*, 192; Halleck to McClellan, September 1, 1862, 18 *O.R.*, 787.

in-Chief's headquarters, McClellan was unaware that Burnside had again just been offered the command of the united Union army, but that he had again refused it, saying that McClellan was the best man for the position. It was still expected by many that Halleck himself would assume command in the field, but this idea seemed extremely repugnant to him. According to McClellan, the Commanding General then *verbally* instructed him " to take command of [Washington's] defenses, expressly limiting my jurisdiction to the works and their garrisons, and prohibiting me from exercising any control over the troops actively engaged in front under General Pope." Halleck rejected McClellan's suggestion that the General-in-Chief go in person to the field to ascertain the true state of affairs with Pope.[42]

At about the time McClellan was riding into Washington to confer with Halleck, Pope sent a dispatch to the Commanding General complaining bitterly of the alleged poor spirit and bad conduct of high-ranking officers of McClellan's Army of the Potomac then serving with him. " The constant talk," Pope contended " is that the Army of the Potomac will not fight; that they are demoralized by withdrawal from the peninsula. . . . These men are mere tools and parasites." He held that the officers disliked serving under him, that they preferred McClellan. Terming such true soldiers as Heintzelman, Kearny, Hooker, Porter, Reno, Reynolds, and Stevens " tools and parasites " who " will not fight," was an unfair indictment. The heavy casualties of the Army of the Potomac units fighting under Pope at Second Bull Run explode this contention completely. But as a result of it, Halleck asked McClellan to confer that afternoon with the President at the house of the General-in-Chief. As McClellan described the interview in his official report, the President said that he had " always been a friend "

[42] Halleck to McClellan, September 1, 1862, McClellan Papers; Burnside's testimony, December 19, 1862, *C.C.W.*, I, 650; Cox, *Military Reminiscences*, I, 254; McClellan's *Report*, 182–83; McClellan, " From the Peninsula to Antietam," *loc. cit.*, 549.

of the General, and asked, as a personal favor to him, that McClellan use his influence to induce the Army of the Potomac to cooperate with Pope, the Chief Executive claiming that it had not been doing so. McClellan stoutly denied this charge of negligence of duty on the part of his men. Lincoln, however, insisted that he telegraph Porter immediately, calling upon him to aid Pope wholeheartedly. McClellan replied that he would do so cheerfully. The President then warmly thanked him and said he would never forget McClellan's cordial assistance in this crisis.[43]

However, in reality, Lincoln was far from pleased with McClellan. His private secretary, Hay, recorded in his diary that " the President was very outspoken in regard to McClellan's present conduct. He said it really seemed to him that McC. wanted Pope defeated. . . . The President seemed to think him a little crazy. Envy, jealousy, and spite are probably a better explanation for his present conduct. . . . He acts as chief alarmist and marplot of the Army." Hay continued by saying that " Stanton was loud about the McC. business. He was unqualifiedly severe upon McClellan. He said that after these battles there should be one Court Martial if never any more. He said that nothing but foul play could lose us this battle & that it rested with McC. and his friends. Stanton seemed to believe very strongly in Pope. So did the President for that matter." In relying upon Pope, however, the administration was leaning on a broken reed. Due to the misleading stories circulated by Pope and his Radical supporters, it was widely believed in Washington and elsewhere that McClellan and his associates were directly responsible for Pope's defeat at Manassas. Count Gurowski, for example, noted this belief in his diary: " The intrigues, the insubordination of McClellan's pets, have almost exclusively brought about the disasters at . . . Bull Run, and brought the country to the verge of the grave." [44]

[43] Pope to Halleck, September 1, 1862, Powell, *Fifth Corps*, 251–52; *B. & L.*, II, 498–99; McClellan's report, 12 *O.R.*, 104.
[44] *Hay's Diary*, 45–46; Gurowski's *Diary*, 258.

McClellan hastened to send off the dispatch to Porter at Lincoln's request, after insisting to the President that such a course was unnecessary, that the units of his Army of the Potomac serving with Pope had done their full share in the fighting against Lee. The dispatch to Porter read: " I ask of you, for my sake, that of the country, and the old Army of the Potomac, that you and all my friends will lend the fullest and most cordial co-operation to General Pope in all the operations now going on. The destinies of our country, the honor of our arms, are at stake, and all depends now upon the cheerful co-operation of all in the field. This week is the crisis of our fate. Say the same thing to my friends in the Army of the Potomac, and that the last request I have to make of them is, that for their country's sake they will extend to General Pope the same support they ever have to me." [45] As expected by McClellan, Porter replied in this vein: " You may rest assured that all your friends, as well as every lover of his country, will ever give, as they have given to General Pope their cordial co-operation and constant support in the execution of all orders and plans. Our killed, wounded, and enfeebled troops attest our devoted duty." [46]

Early on the morning of September 2, there came to Halleck a most notable confession of failure by an army commander. Said Pope from Fairfax Court House, " Unless something can be done to restore tone to this army it will melt away before you know it. . . . You had best at once decide what is to be done. The enemy is in very heavy force and must be stopped in some way. These forces under my command are not able to do so in the open field, and if again checked I fear the force will be useless afterwards." [47] This remarkable admission offered no suggestions to remedy the rout. The noted military scientist, G. F. R. Henderson, states that Pope's " errors had been flagrant. . . . His want of prudence had thwarted his

---

[45] McClellan to Porter, September 1, 1862, 12 *O.R.*, 104.
[46] Porter to McClellan, September 2, 1862, *ibid.*
[47] Pope to Halleck, September 2, 1862, 18 *O.R.*, 796–97.

best endeavours." He had ruined the cavalry of the army. " As a tactician," declares Henderson, " Pope was incapable. As a strategist he lacked imagination, except in his dispatches." [48] It is the opinion of the Second Corps historian, Brigadier General Francis A. Walker, in speaking of Pope, that " The braggart who had begun his campaign with insolent reflections . . . upon the Army of the Potomac and its commander . . . had been kicked, cuffed, hustled about, knocked down, run over, and trodden upon as rarely happens in the history of war. His communications had been cut; his headquarters pillaged; a corps had marched into his rear, and had encamped at its ease upon the railroad by which he received his supplies; he had been beaten or foiled in every attempt he had made to ' bag ' those defiant intruders; and, in the end, he was glad to find a refuge in the entrenchments of Washington, whence he had sallied forth, six weeks before, breathing out threatenings and slaughter." [49] On the second of September, Halleck telegraphed this order to Pope: " You will bring your forces as best you can within or near the line of fortification. General McClellan has charge of all the defenses, and you will consider any direction, as to disposition of the troops as they arrive, given by him as coming from me. . . . It is impossible for me to leave Washington." [50]

The Federal administration was now so concerned for its safety that a steam warship was anchored in the Potomac, ready to carry the President, cabinet members, and other high government officials to safety should the capital fall. Lincoln directed that all government clerks and employees should be armed with muskets and formed into emergency companies to assist in the defense of Washington. In one of his frequent panics, Stanton ordered that everything be shipped right away from the Washington arsenals to New York. McClellan immediately protested, and, through Halleck's mediation, finally convinced

[48] Henderson, *Stonewall Jackson*, II, 186.
[49] Walker, *Second Corps*, 91–92.
[50] Halleck to Pope, September 2, 1862, 18 *O.R.*, 797.

the Secretary that there was a chance the capital could be saved, and that the muskets and guns should remain in Washington, where they could be destroyed at the eleventh hour should capture seem inevitable. With the dome of the Union caving in about them, the administration leaders did not know where to turn. At the height of the crisis, President Lincoln took the only reasonable step remaining, and it was one of the most able and courageous decisions he ever made.[51]

At approximately 7:30 on the morning of September 2, while eating breakfast at his house in Washington, McClellan was interrupted by two worried visitors. They were none other than the President and the General-in-Chief. Lincoln stated that he had just received information that there were 30,000 stragglers of Pope's army choking the roads leading to Washington. He now realized that Pope had been terribly beaten and routed. Lincoln and Halleck both considered the capital lost. According to McClellan, the Chief Executive then asked him, verbally, " as a favor to him," to " take steps at once to stop and collect the stragglers, to place the works in a proper state of defense, and to go out to meet and take command of the army when it approached the vicinity of the works; then to place the troops in the best position—committing everything to my hands." But no orders were given by the President, Secretary of War, or General-in-Chief to McClellan to do more than undertake this defensive task. McClellan instantly agreed to do his best to carry out the President's request, without conditions, saying that he would pledge his life that he could save the capital. Lincoln and Halleck repeated that it was too late, but that they would be glad to have McClellan try.[52]

This verbal directive was the only one given McClellan, except the following one, issued on September 2, right after Lincoln's visit to McClellan's house: " Major-General McClel-

---

[51] *M.O.S.*, 536; 18 *O.R.*, 807; McClellan to Halleck, Halleck to McClellan, September 2, 1862, 18 *O.R.*, 802, 805.

[52] McClellan's report, 12 *O.R.*, 105; *M.O.S.*, 535; McClellan, " From the Peninsula to Antietam," *loc. cit.*, 549–50; McClellan to his wife, September 2, 1862, *M.O.S.*, 566; McClellan Papers, Vol. 109.

lan will have command of the fortifications of Washington and
of all the troops for the defense of the capital." This order—
the only one McClellan could obtain from his superiors—re-
stricted him to the command of the troops falling back upon
Washington, but *only* for the defense of the capital. Nothing
was issued to grant him authority to command the army in the
field away from Washington. After a conversation with Lincoln,
Senator Browning wrote of the reappointment of McClellan to
command: " When the rebels crossed into Maryland [Lincoln]
sent for Burnsides [*sic*] and told him he must take command of
our army, march against the enemy and give him battle. Burnsides declined—said the responsibility was too great—the consequences of defeat too momentous—he was willing to command
a Corps under McClellan, but not willing to take the chief
command of the army—hence McClellan was reinstated." [53]

Lincoln, on September 2, had to defend in cabinet session
his courageous act of placing McClellan once again in command.
It was one of his finest moments of the war. All were present
but Seward. The President entered the room, immediately
announced McClellan's reappointment, and said he would be
responsible to the country for it. A buzz of disbelief followed.
" There was," wrote Welles, " a more disturbed and desponding
feeling than I have ever witnessed in council; the President
was greatly distressed." Chase related that, in reaction to the
almost unanimous opposition of the cabinet members, " the
President said . . . he would gladly resign his plan; but he could
not see who could do the work wanted as well as McClellan."
Chase suggested Burnside, Hooker, or Sumner. Welles asserted
that Chase felt that giving the army to McClellan " would prove
a national calamity." Of those present, only Blair did not
denounce McClellan. He stated that Stanton and Chase
" actually declared that they would prefer the loss of the capital
to the restoration of McClellan to command." A number of
years after the war, Blair wrote of this heated cabinet session,

[53] Francis W. Palfrey, *The Antietam and Fredericksburg* (New York, 1882),
5; *B. & L.*, II, 551; *Browning's Diary*, I, 589–90.

"The bitterness of Stanton on the reinstatement of McClellan you can scarcely conceive. He preferred to see the capital fall. McClellan was bound to go when the emergency was past, and Halleck and Stanton furnished a pretense." Despite the loud outcry from the cabinet, Lincoln was firm in his decision, and McClellan remained in command—for the time being at least.[54]

Despite Pope's previous untrue and vicious personal insults against him, McClellan, on the second, in a cordial telegram to that general, suggested the positions about Washington which Pope's retreating units were to occupy. Next day, however, Pope blatantly asserted, in a dispatch to Halleck's headquarters, the false charge that "everybody in this army considers [McClellan] responsible for the failure to send forward Sumner and Franklin and Cox or anybody else, and for the inefficient condition in which they did arrive, without artillery and with only 40 rounds of ammunition. There is, and can be no good feeling here under these circumstances. Beg the general [Halleck], if nothing else can be done, to command himself." In order to save himself from being openly removed from his position, Pope requested on the second that he be relieved of his command. Effective the following day, after he and his scattered troops reached the environs of Washington, Pope's command of the ill-starred Army of Virginia terminated, and that army become a part of the old Army of the Potomac. Pope was then shipped out to Minnesota to watch the Indians.[55]

In the late afternoon of September 2, McClellan determined to ride south from the Potomac to meet the retreating troops— still nominally commanded by Pope until they reached the vicinity of Washington—and get them into position to meet any possible Confederate onslaught upon the National capital. Riding south and west from Alexandria along the road to

[54] *Welles's Diary*, I, 104–106; *Chase's Diary*, 64–65; Blair to Porter, April 3, 1879 and April 22, 1870, McClellan Papers; *M.O.S.*, 545.

[55] McClellan to Pope, September 2, 1862, McClellan's *Report*, 184; 18 *O.R.*, 808; Stine, *Army of the Potomac*, 156; Cullum, *Biographical Register*, II, 50.

Fairfax Court House, McClellan began to come upon the debris of Pope's retreating army. Many units were intermingled, a large number of the men being unable to find their own organizations. Some of these troops, numb with fatigue, stopped along the roadside to light fires, boil coffee, and await their regiments. Wildly careening wagons and stampeded artillery batteries dashed down the road, heedless of any human impedimenta in the way. Convoys of reserve horses and mules, tethered together by ropes, charged madly across the countryside, unattended. Orderlies were galloping back and forth, searching for particular officers or commands. The most faint-hearted fugitives were in an utter panic, spreading stories of abject catastrophe and annihilation. Yet there were some regiments in good enough order to form lines of resistance to any close enemy pursuit. It was through this backwash of war that McClellan and his several aides made their way.[56]

Finally, McClellan came upon the commander of this routed soldiery. He describes the scene as follows: " A regiment of cavalry appeared, marching by twos, and sandwiched in the midst were Pope and McDowell with their staff officers. I never saw a more helpless-looking headquarters." Formal salutes and bows were exchanged between the three generals. McClellan instructed Pope where to station his various units in the works of Washington. Before Pope could ride on, a brigade commander in General Rufus King's division, John Hatch, hearing from the brief conversation that McClellan was again in command, rode a few paces to the rear of the group and shouted down the column—loud enough for Pope to hear—that their beloved leader of the Peninsula was again at their head. Like a chain reaction the word went down the endless line of weary dust-clad men. Boisterous cheers for Little Mac rent the clear evening air. Pope remained outwardly calm. He and McDowell requested permission to proceed back toward Washington.

[56] McClellan's report, 12 *O.R.*, 105; Cox, *Military Reminiscences*, I, 243; De Trobriand, *Army of the Potomac*, 301ff; Paris, *The Civil War*, II, 300; Swinton, *Army of the Potomac*, 195.

227

Hearing some gunfire—probably from the rear guard on the Vienna-Chantilly road—McClellan granted it, exchanged salutes with them, and rode toward the front.[57]

In the gathering gloom of approaching nightfall, McClellan made his way along the road, still choked with disorganized troops. Men rubbed their eyes in wonderment. Could it be possible? It looked like McClellan—" our George "—but that was inconceivable! Yet there he was, once more at their head. He had no insults for them, as Pope had had; he had only praise and a word or two of encouragement. An eyewitness writes, " The scene that followed can be more easily imagined than described. From extreme sadness we passed in a twinkling to a delirium of delight. A Deliverer had come." Seeing the almost hopelessly entangled units on the road, McClellan ordered the men to return at once to their old positions in the fortifications of Washington, held for so many months during the previous fall and winter, and familiar to the men. They were to remain there until McClellan could determine Lee's intentions. The morale of the men was instantly raised. When the troops reached their old camps and works around the capital, McClellan immediately inspected every position. According to an army surgeon, his " reception by the officers and soldiers was marked by the most unbounded enthusiasm. In every camp his arrival was greeted by hearty and prolonged cheering, and manifestations of the wildest delight. Many of the soldiers . . . wept with joy at having again for their commander one upon whom they could place implicit reliance. Already his hurried visit to our camps has wrought a remarkable change in the soldiers." Placing the men in position in the works and supplying them with some of their more urgent needs, McClellan now felt confident that the capital could be saved.[58]

[57] *M.O.S.*, 537; Cox, *Military Reminiscences*, I, 245; McClellan, " From the Peninsula to Antietam," *loc. cit.*, 550.
[58] George Kimball to R. U. Johnson and C. C. Buel, November, 1887, *B. & L.*, II, 550n; see Bruce Catton, *Mr. Lincoln's Army*, 47–54; Paris, *The Civil War*, II, 306; Ellis' *Diary*, 214; McClellan's report, 12 *O.R.*, 105.

Reasoning correctly that Lee would cross the upper Potomac into Maryland rather than menace Washington frontally, McClellan posted the Second and Twelfth Corps at Tenallytown, and the Ninth Corps on the Seventh Street road. This would guard against a *coup de main* by the graycoats upon the capital from the left bank of the Potomac. He reported his actions to Halleck, who then said, according to McClellan, that his " command included only the defenses of Washington and did not extend to any active column that might be moved out beyond the line of works; that no decision had yet been made as to the commander of the active army." The Presidential order removing Pope did not mention McClellan's precise status and sphere of action, although it seems to have been generally considered that he was again in overall command of Pope's former forces.[59]

While General Meade might write the almost unanimous opinion of the army that " everything is now changed; McClellan's star is again in the ascendent, and Pope's has faded away," the Radical politicians in Washington were seeking scapegoats for the utter failure of their favorite general. On Stepember 3, Pope's friend and supporter, Chase, recorded in his diary that " Pope came over and talked with the President, who assured him of his entire satisfaction with his conduct; assured him that McClellan's command was only temporary." Welles noted that " the defeat of Pope and placing McC in command of the retreating and disorganized forces after the second disaster at Bull Run interrupted the intrigue which had been planned for the dismissal of McClellan, and was not only a triumph for him but a severe mortification and disappointment for both Stanton and Chase." [60]

Seeing that the Federals were being quickly rallied in the extensive fortifications of Washington, Lee, on September 3, set his victorious army in motion toward Leesburg, the Potomac

[59] McClellan, " From the Peninsula to Antietam," *loc. cit.*, 551; *M.O.S.*, 549.
[60] Meade to his wife, George Gordon Meade (ed.), *The Life and Letters of George Gordon Meade . . .* (New York, 1913), I, 307; *Chase's Diary*, 65–66; *Welles's Diary*, I, 109.

River, and Maryland and Pennsylvania. McClellan did what little reorganizing he could, from the second to the fifth, while the Army of the Potomac was within the works of the capital. Then, on the fifth, still largely unorganized and improperly supplied in many respects, he headed the Union Army westward out of Washington to cross swords again with the triumphant invaders of Lee.[61]

But the President was feeling ill toward McClellan in several respects, especially toward the General's conduct in the recent campaign. " McClellan is working like a beaver," said Lincoln to John Hay. " He seems to be aroused to doing something, by the sort of snubbing he got last week. I am of the opinion that this public feeling against him will make it expedient to take important command from him. . . . He has acted badly in this matter, but we must use what tools we have. . . . Unquestionably he has acted badly toward Pope! He wanted him to fail. That is unpardonable, but he is too useful just now to sacrifice." [62] Lacking full and authentic information, and hearing only the charges from the Radical side, the President had been deceived. McClellan had done his utmost to aid Pope while at the same time safeguarding the capital, and nothing he ever did, said, or wrote, indicated otherwise.

Meanwhile, across the Atlantic in Great Britain, a diplomatic situation was developing which was considerably influenced at this time by the fortunes of the struggling blue and gray armies on the North American continent. The diplomatic historian, Thomas A. Bailey, feels that the period immediately after Pope's defeat was the most critical one for the North. At this time, interventionist feeling was at its highest in England. Recognition of Confederate independence—and with it the forceful lifting of the Federal blockade—was a topic of conversation at British cabinet meetings, and was favored by the Prime Minister, Lord Palmerston, and by Earl Russell, the Foreign

[61] Paris, *The Civil War*, II, 309; Goss, *Recollections*, 95–96.
[62] *Hay's Diary*, 47.

Minister. On August 2, 1862 (remember that it took several weeks for word to reach Europe by ship from America), the British cabinet determined to defer intervention until military events in America became more decided in favor of one side or the other. Palmerston felt that October would probably be a ripe time to make such a move. With Lincoln and Seward determined to risk war, even, with England to prevent foreign meddling in the American conflict, Pope's defeat and Lee's invasion of Maryland brought the recognition and intervention question to a head. After hearing of the Union defeat at Second Bull Run, Palmerston declared to Russell, " The Federals . . . got a very complete smashing . . . even Washington or Baltimore may fall into the hands of the Confederates. If this should happen, would it not be time for us to consider whether in such a state of things England and France might not address the contending parties and recommend an arrangement upon the basis of separation? " In reply, Russell said, " I agree with you that the time is come for offering mediation to the United States Government, with a view to recognition of the independence of the Confederates. I agree further that, in case of failure, we ought ourselves to recognize the Southern States as an independent State." A few days later, Palmerston wrote again to Russell: " It is evident that a great conflict is taking place to the northwest of Washington, and its issue must have a great effect on the state of affairs. If the Federals sustain a grave defeat, they may be at once ready for mediation, and the iron should be struck while it is hot. If, on the other hand, they should have the best of it, we may wait awhile and see what may follow." The British cabinet was, apparently, almost unanimous in supporting Palmerston and Russell on intervention. On September 26, Russell asserted to W. E. Gladstone, " The views which Palmerston and I entertain . . . had the offer of mediation to both parties in the first place, and in the case of refusal by the North, to recognition of the South." Only a solid victory by Lee north of the Potomac was needed by Palmerston to begin his actual steps for intervention. It is the opinion of Bailey that the Confederates were closer to final victory on the eve of the Antietam campaign than at any other time during the war.[63]

Against a backdrop of bitter opposition from his own government, could McClellan, with an army still disordered, unevenly supplied, and recently routed and humiliated, reorganize that agglomeration of soldiers and employ it to bring to bay Lee's triumphant gray host in the hills of western Maryland? Considering the diplomatic crisis, it was absolutely essential for the Union that the great Confederate soldier should not be permitted to win another decisive victory, especially on Federal soil. He had to be checked and forced to give up the invasion of the North at all hazards. The fate of the republic rested on McClellan and his Army of the Potomac now more than ever. Neither he nor the Union could afford to lose this campaign.

[63] See Thomas A. Bailey, *A Diplomatic History of the American People* (New York, 1946) , 363, 364; Ephraim Douglass Adams, *Great Britain and the American Civil War* (London, 1925) , II, 31–43; Samuel Flagg Bemis, *A Diplomatic History of the United States* (New York, 1942) , 373; John Holladay Latané, *A History of American Foreign Policy* (New York, 1934) , 382, 383; Donaldson Jordan and Edwin J. Pratt, *Europe and the American Civil War* (Boston, 1931) , 114.

Chapter Nine

Through the Mountain

> I thought I knew McClellan, but this move-
> ment of his puzzles me.
>
> —*Stonewall Jackson*

GENERAL Lee and I knew each other well in the days before
the war," wrote McClellan after Appomattox. " We had
served together in Mexico and commanded against each other
in the Peninsula. I had the highest respect for his ability as a
commander, and knew that he was not a general to be trifled
with or carelessly afforded an opportunity of striking a fatal
blow." At Second Bull Run the great Confederate soldier had
proved that statement to be only too true. On September 3,
1862, after having driven the defeated army of Pope back
into the forts of Washington, Lee wrote to Jefferson Davis that
" the two grand armies of the United States that have been
operating in Virginia, though now united, are much weakened
and demoralized." On the following day, the Southern commander told his President that he intended to cross the Potomac
with his victorious army and invade Pennsylvania. Before dark
on the fourth, he began crossing the river at White's Ford
near Leesburg, some thirty miles upstream from Washington.
The last of Lee's men had crossed to the Maryland side by the
seventh.[1]

The Confederate general's plan was not to strike directly
at the fortified cities of Washington or Baltimore, but " so to

---

[1] *M.O.S.*, 553–54; Lee to Davis, September 3 and 4, 1862, 28 *O.R.*, 590, 592,
604–605; 27 *O.R.*, 145.

233

manoeuvre as to cause McClellan to uncover them." His first project was to establish communications with his Richmond base by marching into western Maryland and opening up the Shenandoah Valley. Then, moving up the Cumberland Valley, he would menace the cities of Pennsylvania. He hoped to draw McClellan far enough toward the Susquehanna River so as " to afford him either an opportunity of seizing Baltimore or Washington, or of dealing a damaging blow to the [Union] army far from its base of supplies." Lee's route would be through Frederick, Maryland, then on to the western side of the South Mountain range, using that lofty barrier as a screen for his right flank in the march into the Keystone State. However, McClellan, at Washington, was on the chord of the arc which Lee would be obliged to describe if the gray general decided to move on Baltimore or Washington.[2]

On the day that Lee began crossing the Potomac—September 4—McClellan's field units were disposed in the following manner: Reno's Ninth Corps was on the Seventh Street road; Hooker's First Corps was at Upton's Hill; Brigadier General Alpheus Williams' Twelfth Corps, Sumner's Second Corps, and Couch's division were at Tenallytown; and Franklin's Sixth Corps was at the Alexandria Seminary. For the stationary garrison to man the formidable works of Washington, McClellan assigned Heintzelman's Third Corps, Major General Franz Sigel's Eleventh Corps, and Porter's Fifth Corps—a total force of 72,500 men under the command of Banks. This large force would certainly be enough, it was thought, to reassure the administration and the General-in-Chief. But as will be seen, Halleck was, throughout the entire campaign, overalarmed for the safety of the capital—a fear not acquiesced in this time by the President.[3]

McClellan's field army was composed, in large part, of the debris which had drifted back in utter defeat from Manassas.

[2] Alexander, *Military Memoirs*, 223, 225; Longstreet, *Manassas to Appomattox*, 279; Ropes, *Story of the Civil War*, II, 337; Paris, *The Civil War*, II, 310.
[3] McClellan's *Report*, 186; Palfrey, *The Antietam*, 5–6; 28 *O.R.*, 202, 214.

It was in a sad state of disorganization, lacking many essentials such as clothing, shoes, ammunition, and other supplies. The cavalry was in a wretched condition after Pope's inept handling of it in the recent campaign. McClellan stated that he would have held the army near Washington until the major needs were attended to, but Lee's march into Northern territory forced the Union commander to meet him at any cost, regardless of the condition of the blueclad troops. The reorganization, so far as it could be effected, would have to be done on the march. Into this discouraging situation McClellan threw himself with such zeal and determination that even his implacable enemies, Nicolay and Hay, were forced to admit that, in this crisis, "[McClellan's] conduct was exemplary." [4]

The National commander now divided his army into wings. The Right Wing was placed under Burnside, and included Hooker's First Corps and Reno's Ninth Corps. The Center was commanded by Sumner, and contained his own Second Corps and Williams' Twelfth Corps. The Left Wing was commanded by Franklin, and comprised his own Sixth Corps and Couch's division of Keyes's Fourth Corps (the remainder of the latter corps having been left on the lower Peninsula). Porter's Fifth Corps was detained for the defense of the capital until September 12, when two divisions of it were ordered to join McClellan's army in western Maryland, the remaining division being dispatched from Washington on the sixteenth. Before Porter joined him in force after the battle of South Mountain, McClellan had about 67,000 men. [5]

On September 5, learning of Lee's crossing of the Potomac, McClellan determined to begin moving his army northwestward from Washington toward Frederick. He would advance along several parallel roads, so that his army would be in a line, rather than in a column fifty miles in length on one road and

[4] *M.O.S.*, 551–52; 28 *O.R.*, 184; *Letters of General Meade*, I, 309; *Chase's Diary*, 82; Nicolay and Hay, *Abraham Lincoln*, VI, 28.

[5] Swinton, *Army of the Potomac*, 197; Palfrey, *The Antietam*, 6–7; 27 *O.R.*, 40; Ropes, *Story of the Civil War*, II, 336.

therefore liable to be crushed in front before the rear could get up. The Federal cavalry had been sent on the third to the Poolesville fords to observe the enemy movement. With the main Union movement getting underway on the fifth, McClellan instructed Burnside's Right Wing to advance along the Brookeville-Urbanna-New Market road, the Center under Sumner to march on the Rockville-Frederick road, and Franklin's Left Wing to use the road through Offutt's Crossroads near the mouth of the Seneca River, which empties into the Potomac. By the evening of the fifth, Burnside's command had reached Leesborough. From that point, Hooker was to move directly toward Frederick, while Reno was to march toward the same place by way of Damascus. On the sixth, McClellan moved Sumner to Rockville, the Sixth Corps and Sykes's division to Tenallytown, and Couch's division to Offutt's Crossroads.[6]

Lee's movements and intentions were still unknown to McClellan. The poor condition of the blue cavalry prevented it from rapidly developing the unfolding situation. It was not clear whether Lee intended to move against Washington from along the left bank of the Potomac, whether he would march on Baltimore, or whether he resolved to invade Pennsylvania. In any case, McClellan determined to be prepared for any exigency, and to move with circumspection. On the fifth, he received a telegram from Halleck, who said, " I think there can now be no doubt that the enemy are crossing the Potomac in force, and that you had better dispatch General Sumner and additional forces to follow. If you agree with me, let our troops move immediately." However, two days later, McClellan got a somewhat contradictory message from his superior: " I think we must be very cautious about stripping too much the forts on the Virginia side. It may be the enemy's object to draw off the mass of our forces, and then attempt to attack from the Virginia side of the Potomac." In reply, McClellan declared, " I think [the Confederates] are beyond the Monocacy." On

[6] Swinton, *Army of the Potomac*, 197; McClellan's *Report*, 186, 188; *M.O.S.*, 553; Powell, *Fifth Corps*, 259.

the seventh, McClellan himself left Washington, setting up his headquarters at Rockville. But the confidence of the President in the General was not too enthusiastic at this time. He confided to Welles that McClellan's ability ended with organizational duties. " He can't go ahead," said Lincoln; " he can't strike a blow." [7]

With Lee's army at Frederick, the Federal garrison of some 13,000 men stationed at Harper's Ferry demanded attention. Although Harper's Ferry was important as a defense against an enemy movement down the Shenandoah Valley toward the Potomac, it was useless now that the enemy forces were actually north of the river in Maryland, and was liable to be seized by the enterprising Lee. In a message on September 7 to the Union commander at the ferry, Colonel Dixon S. Miles, Halleck, however, revealed that he failed to appreciate the situation on the military chessboard. " Our army is in motion," he said to Miles. " It is important that Harper's Ferry be held to the latest moment. The Government has the utmost confidence in you, and is ready to give you full credit for the defense it expects you to make." Before leaving Washington, McClellan had advised the General-in-Chief that if it was insisted upon that Miles not be permitted to join his army, at least he be instructed to take a fortified position atop Maryland Heights, the key position about Harper's Ferry. Halleck, however, ignored this sound advice. Consequently, on September 11, McClellan wired Halleck again, saying, " Colonel Miles . . . can do nothing where he is, but could be of great service if ordered to join me. I suggest that he be ordered at once to join me by the most practicable route." Halleck replied in a typical fashion. " There is no way," he asserted, " for Col. Miles to join you at present. The only chance is to defend his works until you can open a communication with him." Halleck was in error, however, as to the impossibility then of the 13,000 blue soldiers getting

[7] See Henderson, *Stonewall Jackson*, II, 210–11; McClellan's *Report*, 185; Halleck to McClellan, September 5, 1862, 28 *O.R.*, 182; Halleck to McClellan, September 7, 1862, *C.C.W.*, I, 471; McClellan to Halleck, September 8, 1862, *C.C.W.*, I, 471; *Welles's Diary*, I, 124.

out of Harper's Ferry. Miles could have marched them north-westward along the Potomac, crossed at Williamsport, marched toward Pennsylvania, and soon have joined up with McClellan's right. Or, he could have crossed the Shenandoah River, moved southeastward along the right bank of the Potomac for a short distance, crossed over, and connected with McClellan's left.[8]

Halleck's bungle, however, helped unwittingly to place Lee at a disadvantage which went far toward causing the failure of his campaign. Astounded to learn that the Federal garrison had been retained at the ferry, Lee felt obliged to dislodge Miles before concentrating west of the South Mountain range.[9] Apparently seeing at a glance the hopeless position in which Halleck had left Miles, Lee could not pass up the opportunity of snuffing out a force of 13,000 blueclad soldiers and capturing the large amount of military supplies at Harper's Ferry. But such a move would divide the Confederate Army in two, at least for a time.

By the late evening of September 8, McClellan had received sufficient intelligence to convince him that Lee's main intentions were in western Maryland, and he told Halleck that he had "determined to advance the whole [Union] force to-morrow." The Commanding General seemed to agree with McClellan, saying to him that "it seems to me that a sufficient number of your forces to meet the enemy should move rapidly forward, leaving a reserve in reach of you and Washington at the same time." But on the ninth, he was cautioned by Stanton's assistant, Tom Scott, that there were "over 100,000" enemy troops near Frederick. McClellan's cavalry leader, Alfred Pleasonton, reported the foe at 110,000 strong. Governor Andrew Curtin of Pennsylvania wired that the Confederates in Maryland numbered over 200,000. And shortly thereafter, the well-meaning Governor placed the figure at 190,000 gray-

<hr />

[8] Swinton, *Army of the Potomac*, 200; Halleck to Miles, September 7, 1862, Julius White, "The Surrender of Harper's Ferry," *B. & L.*, II, 612; McClellan to Halleck, September 11, 1862, 28 *O.R.*, 254; *C.C.W.*, I, 478; McClellan's *Report*, 190; Ropes, *Story of the Civil War*, II, 331, 333.

[9] Lee's report, 27 *O.R.*, 145.

coats in Maryland, supported by 250,000 on the southern bank of the Potomac—a total of 440,000 hostile soldiers facing McClellan! [10]

Seeing with almost unbelieving eyes that Halleck had left the Harper's Ferry garrison to be plucked, Lee at Frederick determined on September 9 to send half of his army under Jackson to do just that. So deliberate and cautious had been McClellan's advance thus far from Washington, that Lee felt Harper's Ferry could be reduced, its garrison captured, and the two wings of his army reunited west of South Mountain before being confronted by the Army of the Potomac. Jackson was to divide his force into three groups, one to seize Loudon Heights, another to occupy Bolivar Heights, and the third to capture Maryland Heights. This would ring the ferry with Confederate guns, and render Miles's force in the town helpless. Lee with Longstreet's command was to march along the National Turnpike to either Boonsboro or Hagerstown. These fateful directions of September 9 comprised what was designated as Special Orders No. 191, and which subsequently became known as the famous " Lost Dispatch." Lee issued three copies of this important order: one to Jackson, one to Longstreet, and one to D. H. Hill who was at that time *not* under Jackson's orders. Stonewall, however, laboring under the impression that Hill *was* in his command, also issued him a copy of Special Orders No. 191. Thus, two copies of the same directive were on their way to D. H. Hill. Unfortunately for the Confederates, the copy to Hill from Lee's headquarters was lost by a careless staff officer outside of Frederick.[11]

By this time, Lee's plans had crystalized. He informed Major General John G. Walker that after capturing Harper's

[10] McClellan to Halleck, Halleck to McClellan, September 8, 1862, *C.C.W.,* I, 471–73; Scott to McClellan, September 9, 1862, 28 *O.R.,* 230; *M.O.S.,* 568–69; Curtin to McClellan, Lincoln to McClellan, McClellan to Lincoln, Halleck to McClellan, September 10, 1862, 28 *O.R.,* 232, 233, 248, 477; *C.C.W.,* I, 477–78; Curtin to Lincoln, September 11, 1862, 28 *O.R.,* 256, 257, 258, 263.

[11] 27 *O.R.,* 42, 145; 28 *O.R.,* 603–604; Alexander, *Military Memoirs,* 228–29; Longstreet, *Manassas to Appomattox,* 212; see Freeman, *Lee's Lieutenants,* II, 715–22.

Ferry, he would concentrate his army at Hagerstown, and destroy the B. & O. Railroad tracks. Then, he planned to march northward, seize Harrisburg, and tear up the tracks of the Pennsylvania Railroad, after which he would move against Baltimore, Washington, or Philadelphia. When Walker gaped at Lee's audacity in dividing his forces when McClellan was in pursuit, Lee asked him if he were "acquainted with General McClellan." When Walker replied in the negative, Lee stated of the Union commander, "He is an able general but a very cautious one. His enemies among his own people think him too much so. His army is in a very demoralized and chaotic condition and will not be prepared for offensive operations—or he will not think it so—for three or four weeks. Before that time I hope to be on the Susquehanna." Then on the tenth, Jackson's three columns left Frederick for their stations about Harper's Ferry, while Lee and Longstreet moved toward Boonsboro.[12]

On September 11, McClellan dispatched an important communiqué to Washington. He informed Halleck that reports indicated the enemy forces numbered 120,000 at Frederick and stated that Washington was therefore free from the threat of a direct Confederate attack from across the Potomac. "The momentous consequences involved in the struggle of the next few days," he continued, "impel me, at the risk of being considered slow and overcautious, to most earnestly recommend that every available man at once be added to this army." He asked for one or two of the three corps then stationed at the Federal capital. He declared also that Miles's force at Harper's Ferry was in a dangerous position, "liable to be cut off by the enemy," and urged again that it be added to his field army at once. He predicted that Lee would try to knock Miles off. "If we should be so unfortunate," he concluded, "as to meet with defeat, our country is at their mercy." The General might have saved his energy in regard to the garrison at Harper's

[12] John G. Walker, "Jackson's Capture of Harper's Ferry," *B. & L.*, II, 605–606.

General Robert E. Lee

Ferry, however, for Halleck—like Stanton and Lincoln before him—was adamant in insisting upon leaving small isolated forces scattered about to be gobbled up by the omnipresent enemy. In reply to McClellan's message, the President himself stated that if Porter, Heintzelman, and Sigel were all sent to the field, there would be a dearth of Federal troops on the south side of the Potomac at Washington. He told McClellan that Porter alone would be sent to join him. "I am for sending you all that can be spared," said Lincoln, "and I hope others can follow very soon." But to get at the Federal capital, Lee would first have to overcome McClellan's army in battle in the field. It seems logical, therefore, that the Federal authorities would have done well to have concentrated the great mass of the Union corps with McClellan, rather than split them up into two fairly large bodies, one in the field and one at Washington. It would be easier for Lee to overcome both of these bodies separately than to defeat them in united form. Even after the dispatching of Porter to the field, over 50,000 men remained stationary at Washington.[13]

Near midnight on the eleventh, in accordance with Lincoln's instructions, Morell's division of Porter's Fifth Corps was ordered to march from the capital to join McClellan's army in the field. It moved out at 6:00 A. M. on the twelfth. By the evening of the eleventh, McClellan's units were disposed in the following manner: Reno's Ninth Corps at New Market, Hooker's First Corps at Brookeville, Williams' Twelfth Corps at Damascus, Sumner's Second Corps at Clarksburg, Franklin's Sixth Corps at Barnesville, Couch's division at Poolesville, Sykes's division at Middleburg, and Pleasonton's cavalry scouting toward Point of Rocks and Westminster. On the morning of September 12—a full day before the discovery of Lee's Special Orders No. 191—McClellan judged correctly the Confederate intentions. "I feel perfectly confident," he telegraphed Halleck,

[13] McClellan to Halleck, Lincoln to McClellan, September 11, 1862, *C.C.W.*, I, 479–81; *M.O.S.*, 555.

" that the enemy has abandoned Frederick, moving in two directions, viz: On the Hagerstown and Harper's Ferry roads." [14]

Then, a chance to speed the pursuit of Lee revealed itself to McClellan. He telegraphed the General-in-Chief at midnight on the eleventh that President Garrett of the B. & O. Railroad had offered enough railroad cars to move 28,000 men from Washington to Frederick. McClellan therefore asked Halleck to send Porter's Fifth Corps—which had just been ordered to join him—by rail, instead of compelling it to make a long and fatiguing march over dusty roads, especially since this march would take two days longer than by train. On the afternoon of the twelfth, Halleck replied, insisting—without giving any reasons—on moving Porter by footpower toward Frederick. The Commanding General then asked McClellan if it were possible for him to " open communication with Harper's Ferry." McClellan, then near Urbanna, said that he had already ordered cavalry to try to get through to Miles at the ferry. A return wire from Halleck finally placed Miles's garrison under McClellan's command. " You will endeavor," said the General-in-Chief, " to open communication with him, and unite your forces with his at the earliest possible moment." The order came too late, however, to save the 13,000 Federals there from capture or annihilation.[15]

McClellan's advance on September 13 saw Pleasonton's cavalry move to a point near the eastern foot of the South Mountain range; Couch's division reach Licksville; Franklin arrive at Buckeystown; Sykes's division move into Frederick, accompanied by the First, Second, and Twelfth corps; and the bulk of the Ninth Corps pass through Frederick to Middletown. The same evening saw Jackson's three columns of Lee's army nearing the heights overlooking Harper's Ferry, Longstreet in the vicinity of Hagerstown, D. H. Hill on the National Road

[14] Powell, *Fifth Corps*, 261–62; Palfrey, *The Antietam*, 6, 7; McClellan's *Report*, 186; McClellan to Halleck, September 12, 1862, *C.C.W.*, I, 482.
[15] McClellan to Halleck, Halleck to McClellan, September 11 and 12, 1862, *C.C.W.*, I, 482–83; see Swinton, *Army of the Potomac*, 201.

between Turner's Gap in the South Mountain and Boonsboro to the west, and Stuart's cavalry holding the passes of the mountain.[16]

Even before finding Lee's " Lost Dispatch," McClellan had been pretty reliably informed of the enemy movements by his cavalry. As a result, the Union Army was now in rapid motion westward. Yet, on September 13, McClellan received a dispatch from Halleck, which, just the opposite from one Lincoln sent calling for speedy pursuit of Lee, warned the Union commander that he was advancing too far from Washington. " Until you know more certainly the enemy's forces south of the Potomac," said Old Brains, " you are wrong in thus uncovering the capital. I am of opinion that the enemy will send a small column toward Pennsylvania so as to draw your forces in that direction, then suddenly move on Washington." But McClellan and Lincoln had much the better grasp of the strategic picture than did the Union General-in-Chief.[17]

When the Army of the Potomac entered Frederick, the loyal townsfolk, cheering and waving flags, vied with each other in lavishing gifts of fresh water, fruit, and other edibles upon the dusty blueclad soldiers—a marked contrast with the cool reception given the Johnny Rebs in that town. McClellan wrote to Ellen of the scene in Frederick when he rode through: " I can't describe to you for want of time the enthusiastic reception we met with yesterday at Frederick. I was nearly overwhelmed and pulled to pieces. I enclose with this a little flag that some enthusiastic lady thrust into or upon Dan's bridle. As to flowers—they came in crowds! In truth, I was seldom more affected than by the scenes I saw yesterday and the recep-

[16] McClellan's *Report*, 186, 195; Palfrey, *The Antietam*, 13–14; see Matthew Forney Steele, *American Campaigns* (Washington, 1922), I, 265.

[17] See Longstreet, *Manassas to Appomattox*, 212; Lincoln to McClellan, September 12, 1862, Halleck to McClellan, September 13, 1862, McClellan's testimony, March 2, 1862, *C.C.W.*, I, 439, 484; Lincoln to McClellan, September 12, 1862, 28 *O.R.*, 270, 277.

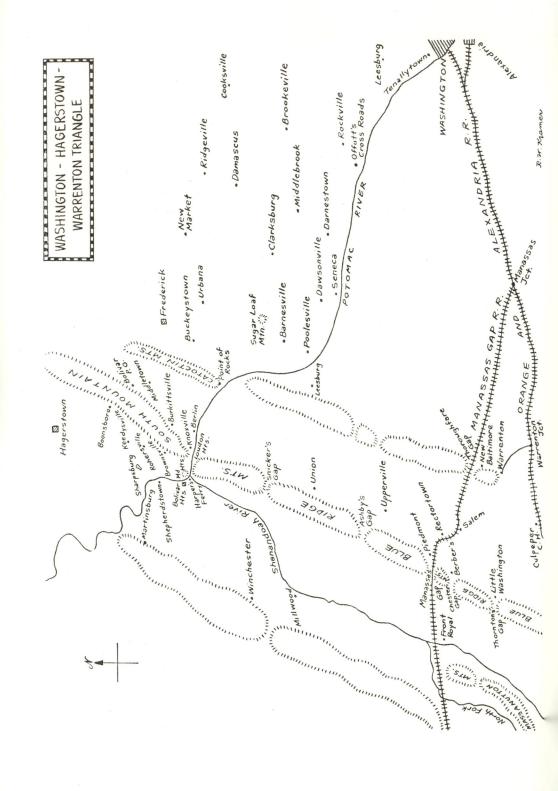

WASHINGTON - HAGERSTOWN -
WARRENTON TRIANGLE

tion I met with. . . . Men, women, and children crowded around us, weeping, shouting, and praying." [18]

Then it happened. The Union Twelfth Corps was encamped outside of Frederick on ground previously occupied by D. H. Hill's Confederate division. On September 13, two Federal soldiers of the Twenty-seventh Indiana regiment, lolling on the grass, noticed a singular brown package near them. Upon examination, they found that it contained three cigars, about which was wrapped a piece of paper containing writing. About to enjoy the smokes, the two soldiers glanced casually at the writing on the paper. It contained names and positions of enemy divisions. The paper was rushed through channels to McClellan's headquarters tent, reaching him sometime before 6:20 P. M. This document turned out to be the lost copy of Lee's important Special Orders No. 191, drawn up by the Southern commander on the ninth. Thinking possibly that it was a *ruse de guerre*, McClellan had the handwriting verified by a Union officer, who recognized it as belonging to a former army associate of his before the war—a man who was now one of Lee's aides. McClellan did not, of course, know of any changes which might possibly have been made in the Confederate plans during the four days of the order's existence. While aware of its problematical limitations, the National commander realized the possibilities opened to him to destroy Lee's army in detail while it was separated. He was reported as asserting to a brigadier shortly after receiving the lost dispatch, " Here is a paper with which if I cannot whip ' Bobbie Lee ' I will be willing to go home." [19]

But the lost order badly misled McClellan on one vital point. It placed Longstreet at Boonsboro at the western foot of South Mountain, when in reality his position had already been changed by Lee to Hagerstown, thirteen miles further

[18] Walker, *Second Corps*, 93–94; McClellan to his wife, September 14, 1862, *M.O.S.*, 571–72.

[19] Silas Colgrove, " The Finding of Lee's Lost Order," *B. & L.*, II, 603; 27 *O.R.*, 42; Stine, *Army of the Potomac*, 159; Palfrey, *The Antietam*, 20–22; Allan, *Army of Northern Virginia*, 343; Gibbon, *Personal Recollections*, 73.

west. Consequently, McClellan thought that D. H. Hill *and* Longstreet were both in or very near the passes of the South Mountain range on the thirteenth and fourteenth. He therefore moved with heavier force, and slower, against this supposed enemy force of some 30,000 than he would probably have done if he thought only D. H. Hill was at South Mountain. "The losing of the dispatch," writes Hill of this situation, "was the saving of Lee's army. . . . In the battle of South Mountain the imaginary foes of the Lost Dispatch were worth more to [the Confederates] than ten thousand men." McClellan noted also that Lee intended to concentrate his army (including Jackson's force then investing Harper's Ferry) at Boonsboro, not at South Mountain, and that it was at Boonsboro, probably —as shown by his subsequent orders—that McClellan expected to fight the battle, not at the mountain.[20]

McClellan's reaction to this fine opportunity was energetic. While he would perhaps have done better to have pushed his weary legions further onward that night, he did nonetheless act with unusual speed for a cautious man. He saw that Franklin's Left Wing, when once through Crampton's Gap to the south, would be in the rear of Major General Lafayette McLaws' enemy force investing Harper's Ferry from Maryland Heights. And when the Federal Right Wing and Center under Burnside and Sumner got through Turner's Gap or Fox's Gap, they would be between Longstreet and D. H. Hill, and Jackson. However, McClellan's pressing duty at the moment, according to his instructions from Halleck, was to try to relieve the besieged Miles at the ferry, if Miles still held out.[21]

Accordingly, McClellan, at 6:20 on the evening of September 13, inaugurated a movement which was to upset Lee's calculations to a considerable degree. Franklin, then at Buckeystown, was ordered to move at daybreak on the fourteenth by

[20] D. H. Hill, "The Battle of South Mountain, or Boonsboro," *B. & L.*, II, 570, 573; Jacob D. Cox, "Forcing Fox's Gap and Turner's Gap," *ibid.*, 585.

[21] Lee's report, 27 *O.R.*, 146; Henry Kyd Douglas, "Stonewall Jackson in Maryland," *B. & L.*, II, 624; Palfrey, *The Antietam*, 27-28; Swinton, *Army of the Potomac*, 201.

way of Jefferson, Burkittsville, and Crampton's Gap toward Rohersville. From that point, he was to capture or defeat McLaws and relieve Miles at Harper's Ferry, and to interpose his Left Wing between the forces of Jackson and Longstreet. "My general idea," said McClellan to him, "is to cut the enemy in two and beat him in detail." The Union commander concluded this urgent directive to Franklin with this appeal: "I ask of you, at this important moment, all your intellect and the utmost activity that a general can exercise." The game on the Federal left was now in Franklin's hands. The other blue units on the right and center were ordered to march at daylight on the fourteenth toward Turner's Gap on the National Pike. McClellan informed Halleck that while he would move rapidly, he feared that it would be too late to rescue Miles unless that soldier "makes a stout resistance." [22]

While Fortune was favoring McClellan that morning, she did an about face in the evening, and cast her favor back upon Lee. A pro-Confederate citizen of Fredrick, accidentally present at the headquarters of McClellan, heard of the receipt of Lee's lost dispatch by the Federals, and saw the Union commander send couriers flying with orders to speed up the movement of his various units to take advantage of the opportunity just offered. This man made his way through the lines to the enemy, and related that McClellan now knew of Lee's plans and was marching on South Mountain from the east. This information enabled Lee to order four brigades of D. H. Hill's division back from Boonsboro to Turner's Gap, where the National Road penetrates South Mountain. Perhaps this turn of fate would save the Confederates from disaster. Lee was compelled to fight at the South Mountain passes in order to gain time for Jackson's forces to capture Harper's Ferry and then reunite with Longstreet west of the mountain range. Although he could earlier have held the gaps in force, Lee apparently felt that McClellan

[22] McClellan to Franklin, September 13, 1862, Palfrey, *The Antietam*, 28–30; McClellan to Halleck, McClellan to Lincoln, September 13, 1862, *C.C.W.*, I, 485–86.

would not move swiftly enough to embarrass his reconcentration.[23]

Early on the morning of the fourteenth, a personal messenger from Miles arrived at McClellan's headquarters. He bore a dispatch from Miles which said that the Harper's Ferry garrison could certainly hold out two days longer—that is, until September 16. A little after noon on the fourteenth, McClellan, then at Middletown, dispatched three couriers with three copies of a direct order to Miles. This order stated that the Federals were then assailing the South Mountain passes. "You may count on our making every effort to relieve you," the directive continued. "Hold out to the last extremity. If it is possible, reoccupy the Maryland heights with your whole force. If you can do that, I will certainly be able to relieve you. . . . Hold out to the last." Unfortunately, before this garrison had been placed under McClellan's orders, Miles had obeyed literally Halleck's earlier order to hold Harper's Ferry by actually determining to hold the town itself—which is at the bottom of a pocket surrounded by mountains—with his entire force, instead of placing his men upon one or more of the dominant heights.[24]

The fourteenth of September dawned clear and hot. Marching from daybreak, the vanguard of McClellan's army quickly crossed Middletown Valley and began ascending the foothills of South Mountain. The whole Army of the Potomac was now in motion westward. Franklin was approaching Crampton's Gap to the south, which was defended by detachments from McLaws' command. Burnside, at the same time, was marching toward Turner's Gap (six miles north of Crampton's), held by D. H. Hill and later by Longstreet. Burnside's battle at Turner's and Fox's Gaps will be discussed first, although it

---

[23] Alexander, *Military Memoirs*, 230; Allan, *Army of Northern Virginia*, 345; Swinton, *Army of the Potomac*, 201; Longstreet, *Manassas to Appomattox*, 220.
[24] McClellan's *Report*, 191; Palfrey, *The Antietam*, 25; *Chase's Diary*, 81; Ezra D. Simons, *A Regimental History: The One Hundred and Twenty-Fifth New York State Volunteers* (New York, 1888), 32; McClellan to Halleck, September 14, 1862, *C.C.W.*, I, 486; McClellan to Miles, September 14, 1862, McClellan's *Report*, 191.

must be remembered that Franklin's battle at Crampton's Gap was taking place simultaneously.[25]

South Mountain was, for the Confederates, a splendid defensive position. Troops placed on its summit and slopes, if properly handled, could hold back several times their own number for considerable time. The National Turnpike penetrates the 1,300-foot mountain wall at Turner's Gap—a pass 400 feet below the summit. The only other practicable pass in the range north of Crampton's Gap is Fox's Gap, one mile south of Turner's. At Bolivar Post Office on the National Road, near the eastern foot of the range, a road branches off to the left (or south)—the Old Sharpsburg Road—curves around, and crosses the mountain at Fox's Gap. Also at Bolivar Post Office, a road turns off to the right (or north)—the Old Hagerstown Road—and runs through Mt. Tabor Church. Then ascending the mountain, it reaches the summit one mile north of Turner's Gap, and runs southward along the crest until it again intersects the pike at Turner's Gap at the so-called Mountain House. A mountaintop road runs along the crest from Fox's Gap to the Mountain House. If assaulted frontally, even in superior numbers, the frowning heights promised bloody, perhaps prohibitive losses.[26]

McClellan's Right Wing reached Bolivar Post Office in mid-morning of September 14. There, Burnside turned Reno's Ninth Corps to the left on the Old Sharpsburg Road to attack Fox's Gap, while Hooker's First Corps was shunted off to the right on the Old Hagerstown Road to outflank Turner's Gap on the north. Brigadier General John Gibbon's Iron Brigade was to move forward on the pike to assail Turner's Gap frontally at the Mountain House. While the mass of Reno's and Hooker's troops were moving up, Pleasonton's cavalry and advance ele-

---

[25] J. L. Smith, *History of the 118th Pennsylvania Volunteers* . . . (Philadelphia, 1905), 32; Cox, *Military Reminiscences*, I, 278; David L. Thompson, " In the Ranks to the Antietam," *B. & L.*, II, 557; Sypher, *Pennsylvania Reserves*, 362.

[26] The best maps of the area are: *O.R. Atlas*, Plate XXVII, Map 3; *B. & L.*, II, 568; George A. Hussey and William Todd, *History of the Ninth Regiment, N.Y.S.M.* . . . (New York, 1889), 188; McClellan's *Report*, 194–95.

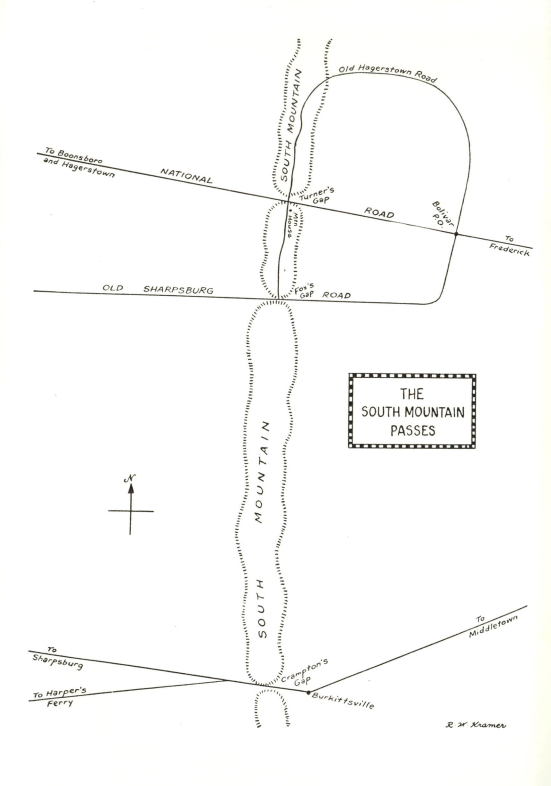

ments of Cox's Kanawha Division made probing attacks at Fox's and Turner's, feeling for a soft spot in the Confederate's defensive line.[27]

Marching to support Pleasonton and Cox—now in action— a Union soldier in the ranks took a look to the eastward " upon the beautiful, impressive picture " before entering the combat. Glancing backwards, he beheld a stirring scene: " Each column [was] a monstrous, crawling, blue-black snake, miles long, quilled with the silver slant of muskets at a ' shoulder,' its sluggish tail writhing slowly up over the distant eastern ridge; its bruised head weltering in the roar and smoke upon the crest above, where was being fought the battle of South Mountain." The Confederate commander on the summit of South Mountain, D. H. Hill, viewing the martial pageant below—one of the most sublime of the war—describes the advancing blue legions in the valley below in the following manner: " The marching columns extended back as far as the eye could see in the distance. . . . It was a grand and glorious spectacle, and it was impossible to look at it without admiration." [28]

At approximately 7:00 A. M., at Fox's Gap, Cox's two Union brigades moved forward in force on the south side of the Old Sharpsburg Road against Brigadier General Samuel Garland's brigade of D. H. Hill's division. Because of their advantage in position, the Confederate artillery fire was more effective than that of the Federals. Lieutenant Colonel Rutherford B. Hayes's Twenty-third Ohio regiment rapidly outflanked Garland on the enemy right. By 10:00 A. M., Garland was dead, and his brigade, assisted by another, was routed. Southern reinforcements arrived, but Cox repulsed them and held his position near the summit. A lull now occurred in the battle, during which time both sides brought up additional troops at both Fox's and Turner's Gaps.[29]

---

[27] Stine, *Army of the Potomac*, 161; Palfrey, *The Antietam*, 33–34.

[28] Thompson, " In the Ranks to the Antietam," *loc. cit.*, 581; D. H. Hill, " The Battle of South Mountain, or Boonsboro," *loc. cit.*, 564.

[29] Cox, " Forcing Fox's Gap and Turner's Gap," *loc. cit.*, 586–87; D. H. Hill, " The Battle of South Mountain, or Boonsboro," *loc. cit.*, 562–67; McClellan's *Report*, 195–96.

There had been practically no fighting in the morning at Turner's, although Burnside could have attacked to advantage there with Hooker's First Corps. McClellan now arrived in person at Burnside's command post on the National Pike at the foot of the range, and took over the personal direction of the battle. As at Fox's Gap, so too at Turner's, the position of the Confederates enabled them to use their artillery more effectively than the Federals. While Hooker's corps was moving via the Old Hagerstown Road to assail Hill's left flank north of Turner's Gap, Hill was being reinforced by four brigades of Longstreet's command, which had countermarched from Boonsboro. Having reached the slope of the mountain, Hooker ordered his divisions directly against the Confederates north of Turner's Gap. The Union soldiers had to climb the steep side of the mountain and dig the graycoats out with the bayonet from behind trees, rocks, and bushes. The attack was made with great dash and skill. Meade's division succeeded in enveloping Hill's left flank and advancing southward down the crest of the range toward the Mountain House. At the same time, late in the afternoon, Reno, at Fox's Gap, successfully stormed the enemy on the summit. The whole line of Hill and Longstreet was hurled back over the crest, Reno falling at the head of his corps at dusk. The Southerners had been pushed beyond the summit to a position untenable for further fighting by the grayclads the next morning. In this fierce battle, the flank attacks of McClellan had tipped the scales in his favor. The fighting finally died down near 9:00 P. M. The casualties at Turner's and Fox's Gaps, according to Livermore, were, for the Federals, 325 killed, 1,403 wounded, and 85 missing—a total loss of 1,813; and for the Confederates, at least 325 killed, 1,560 wounded, and 800 missing—a total loss of 2,685.[30]

Meanwhile, Franklin was pushing toward Crampton's Gap in an endeavor to execute the latest order he received from McClellan, which stated: " Send back to hurry up Couch.

[30] Swinton, *Army of the Potomac*, 203–204; Stine, *Army of the Potomac*, 166–74; Cox, *Military Reminiscences*, I, 287–91; Sypher, *Pennsylvania Reserves*, 365–73; Palfrey, *The Antietam*, 35–40; Livermore, *Numbers and Losses*, 90–91.

Mass your troops and carry Burkittsville at any cost. . . . You must follow the enemy as rapidly as possible." Franklin's object was to force his way through Crampton's Gap into Pleasant Valley, and from there move to the relief of Miles, who had been ordered by McClellan to hold out to the last at Harper's Ferry. The Confederate general McLaws, besieging the ferry from Maryland Heights, was responsible also for the defense of Crampton's Gap, a pass located six miles south of Turner's. Hearing of Franklin's approach, he sent some reinforcements to assist Munford's cavalry at Crampton's.[31]

Swinging down the road from Burkittsville to the gap, Franklin deployed W. F. Smith's division to the left (or south) and Slocum's to the right of the road. The enemy was posted behind a stone wall at the base of the mountain, with supporting troops on the slope and crest. Once again Confederate artillery had the advantage of position. At about noon, Franklin sent his two divisions forward in an impetuous charge. The enemy right was flanked by Smith's brigades, setting the stage for Slocum to administer the *coup de grace*. In the decisive action, Slocum moved two of his brigades frontally against the pass, while with the third he completely enveloped the left flank and rear of the gray line, and hurled the entire enemy force from the gap and crest. The bitter combat had lasted three hours. The Confederates lost, reportedly, in the battle of Crampton's Gap, 62 killed, 208 wounded, and 479 missing—a total loss of 749—in addition to an artillery piece, 700 muskets, and 3 battle flags. The Union loss was 113 killed, 418 wounded, and 2 missing—a total loss of 533 men. The aggregate loss of the day at the various gaps at South Mountain was 2,346 for the Federals and at least 3,434 for the Southerners. And in all of these actions, McClellan's troops did the attacking against somewhat outnumbered Confederates who were in excellent defensive positions of great natural strength on the mountain.[32]

[31] Palfrey, *The Antietam*, 31–32; *O.R. Atlas*, Plate XXVII, Map 3; *B. & L.*, II, 593; McClellan to Franklin, September 14, 1862, McClellan's *Report*, 192.
[32] Franklin's testimony, March 30, 1863, *C.C.W.*, I, 626; William B. Franklin,

But what of McClellan himself during the day's fighting? He had stationed himself with Burnside on the National Road near the eastern foot of South Mountain. From there he had directed the fighting of the afternoon. A Union soldier describes the dramatic scene surrounding his army commander in this way:

> Here, upon our arrival, we found General McClellan sitting upon his horse in the road. . . . As each organization passed the general, the men became apparently forgetful of everything but their love for him. They cheered and cheered again, until they became so hoarse they could cheer no longer. It seemed as if an intermission had been declared in order that a reception might be tendered to the general. . . . A great crowd continually surrounded him, and the most extravagant demonstrations were indulged in. Hundreds even hugged the horse's legs and caressed his head and mane. While the troops were thus surging by, the general continually pointed with his finger to the gap in the mountain through which our path lay. It was like a great scene in a play, with the roar of the guns for an accompaniment.[33]

That night, McClellan set up his personal headquarters in a little house along the pike. A corporal of Gibbon's famed Iron Brigade, searching for the provost marshal's quarters in order to turn over some prisoners, was directed by mistake to the army commander's chamber. Thrusting open the door and bursting into the room, the dumfounded corporal beheld McClellan seated at a table, poring over some maps and papers. Annoyed at the sudden and unannounced entrance, Little Mac demanded somewhat abruptly, "What do you want?" The stammering noncom explained that he had some prisoners to turn over but had been directed to the wrong door. Melting a bit, McClellan asked the boy's name and unit. When told

"Notes on Crampton's Gap and Antietam," *B. & L.*, II, 592–96; *M.O.S.*, 562–63; Palfrey, *The Antietam*, 32; Allan, *Army of Northern Virginia*, 348–50; 27 *O.R.*, 183, 861.

[33] George Kimball to R. U. Johnson and C. C. Buel, November, 1887, *B. & L.*, II, 551n.

it was the Iron Brigade, the General exclaimed, "Oh, you belong to Gibbon's brigade. You had some heavy fighting up there tonight." "Yes, sir," the lad replied, "but I think we gave them as good as they sent." "Indeed you did," declared McClellan; "you made a splendid fight." After a pause, the soldier grew bolder, saying, "Well, General, that's the way we boys calculate to fight under a general like you." Pleased by the compliment, McClellan got up, circled the table, and clasped the corporal's arm in a warm embrace. "If I can get that kind of feeling amongst the men of this army," he said, "I can whip Lee without any trouble at all." [34]

The battle of South Mountain doomed Lee's invasion of Maryland and his threatened incursion into Pennsylvania. McClellan had moved with far greater rapidity than Lee had anticipated, and had penetrated the difficult South Mountain barrier at a time when the Southern Army was divided into two isolated halves. He had outmaneuvered the Confederates and had driven them from the three key gaps in the mountain. He had demonstrated also that his army was not as dispirited or disorganized as Lee believed. More important, he had wrested the initiative from the enemy. When learning of the Federal commander's swift penetration of Crampton's Gap, Stonewall Jackson had this to say of his former West Point classmate: "I thought I knew McClellan, but this movement of his puzzles me." [35]

Lee realized the setback he had suffered. "The day has gone against us," he declared in a message to McLaws. "This army will go to Sharpsburg and cross the Potomac River." The Confederate invasion of the North had come to an end. Thus was the decisiveness of McClellan's triumph of September 14 at South Mountain revealed. But perhaps even more important to the fiber of the Army of the Potomac than the victory just won was that of which a Union officer wrote. He stated that the battle's "influence on the morale of our troops was of far

[34] Gibbon, *Personal Recollections*, 78–79.
[35] Walker, "Jackson's Capture of Harper's Ferry," *loc. cit.*, 611.

greater advantage than the loss of men and material of war sustained by the enemy. It was a success when, of everything else, success was needed to restore the waning confidence of the rank and file." McClellan promptly informed Lincoln of his victory. The anxious President replied, " God bless you, and all with you. Destroy the rebel army if possible." [36]

After his defeats at the gaps, Lee at first felt that he would have to retreat immediately across the Potomac into Virginia. But when Stonewall Jackson wrote that he could march from Harper's Ferry and join Lee and Longstreet at Sharpsburg, the Confederate commander determined to remain north of the Potomac and risk battle again. Perhaps Lee felt that he could not get over the Potomac before the closely pursuing Federals would be upon his rear. Therefore, to enable Jackson to send to safety the enormous amount of supplies he would capture at Harper's Ferry, and to give him a day or two to join Longstreet and D. H. Hill, Lee decided to make a stand along the Antietam Creek east of Sharpsburg. This was ground, Cox says, " which offered an excellent field for a defensive battle, leaving [Lee] free to resume his aggressive campaign or to retreat into Virginia according to the result." Ropes terms it " one of the boldest and most hazardous decisions in [Lee's] whole military career." [37]

Shortly after the firing had ceased at South Mountain, McClellan ordered a rapid pursuit of the Confederates at daybreak on the fifteenth. He states that " the orders given to [Burnside's] troops on the right were that if they found the enemy on the march to attack him at once; if they found him in a strong position, then to put our troops in position and make all the arrangements for an attack, but not to attack until I came up." At 1:00 A. M. on the fifteenth, McClellan issued an important order to his Left Wing commander. Franklin

[36] Lee to McLaws, September 14, 1862, 110 *O.R.*, 618–19; William Henry Locke, *The Story of the Regiment* (New York, 1872), 122; Lincoln to McClellan, September 15, 1862, *C.C.W.*, I, 489.

[37] 108 *O.R.*, 618; Cox, *Military Reminiscences*, I, 296–97; Ropes, *Story of the Civil War*, II, 348, 349, 351.

was directed to take Rohersville and to hold it against any Confederate attack from Boonsboro; also to hold the road from Rohersville to Harper's Ferry. He was then ordered to the relief of Miles at the ferry, " attacking and destroying such of the enemy as you may find in Pleasant Valley." If Miles could be relieved, Franklin was then instructed to move to Boonsboro, at which place McClellan intended attacking Lee if the enemy determined to make a stand there. However, if the graycoats fell back from Boonsboro to Sharpsburg, Franklin was directed to " fall upon him and cut off his retreat." McClellan's orders to Franklin were clear, precise, and vigorous. The usually-reliable Left Wing commander, however, was for once not quite up to the full measure of his instructions.[38]

Meanwhile, Lee had withdrawn Longstreet and D. H. Hill from Boonsboro across Pleasant Valley and Elk River into the valley of the Antietam. McClellan, as soon as ammunition wagons could be brought to the top of South Mountain and cartridge boxes refilled, moved his units in pursuit. Pleasonton's cavalry so harassed the gray horsemen of Brigadier General Fitzhugh Lee that the able enemy cavalryman lost two guns and was delayed in joining the main Confederate body along the Antietam at Sharpsburg. Nor was the Southern retreat effected in the best of order. The grayclads had left their dead and wounded in McClellan's hands, and the wake of their withdrawal was strewn with abandoned arms and equipment. However, if Jackson captured the large Federal stores at Harper's Ferry, that would more than make up for the losses suffered at South Mountain and during the retreat.[39]

Moving to the relief of the ferry, McClellan sent out numerous couriers with messages to Miles that help was on the way and that he was to hold out to the last. At frequent intervals along the advance, Franklin fired signal guns—which were heard

---

[38] McClellan's testimony, March 2, 1863, *C.C.W.*, I, 440, 487; McClellan to Franklin, September 15, 1862, McClellan's *Report*, 193, 200.

[39] Meade's report, Stine, *Army of the Potomac*, 171; Swinton, *Army of the Potomac*, 204–205; Longstreet, *Manassas to Appomattox*, 228; Henderson, *Stonewall Jackson*, II, 227.

by the besieged Federals—showing the progress of his march toward the relief of Miles.[40]

Early on the morning of September 15, Jackson's three detachments had reached the tops of Maryland, Bolivar, and Loudon Heights. The bombardment of the town and Federal garrison began at once. After two hours' resistance—which resulted in only a relatively few Union casualties—Miles, with the very reluctant agreement of all of his brigade commanders, at about 9:00 A. M. hoisted the white flag signalling ignominious capitulation. Having fearlessly exposed himself during the bombardment, Miles was killed a few moments after having raised the white flag, when several Confederate batteries continued firing, apparently not having seen the flag or Jackson's signal to cease fire. For the Federals, it was, as Stine terms it, a " disgraceful surrender." Miles had failed to obey McClellan's direct order to " hold out to the last." [41]

One bright episode for the Federals in the dismal affair at Harper's Ferry was the exploit of Colonel B. F. (" Grimes ") Davis. After considerable opposition, Davis finally wrung from Miles permission to attempt to escape with his cavalry brigade from the besieged town. Moving out silently to the northwest during the night of September 14, along the Chesapeake and Ohio Canal towpath near the Potomac River, Davis encountered only a few grayclad skirmishers, and made good his escape without loss. He had the good fortune also to capture Longstreet's reserve amunition wagon train of forty-five vehicles before joining up with McClellan's army. The Confederate general, J. G. Walker, who invested Harper's Ferry from Loudon Heights, is of the opinion that Miles could have escaped with his whole infantry force during the night of the

[40] McClellan's testimony, March 2, 1863, *C.C.W.*, I, 440; Swinton, *Army of the Potomac*, 205; Paris, *The Civil War*, II, 329.

[41] Bradley T. Johnson and Henry Kyd Douglas, " Stonewall's Intentions at Harper's Ferry," *B. & L.*, II, 615–18; Walker, " Jackson's Capture of Harper's Ferry," *loc. cit.*, 609–11; White, " The Surrender of Harper's Ferry," *loc. cit.*, 613–14; Simons, *Twenty-Fifth New York*, 31–34; Stine, *Army of the Potomac*, 181; Freeman, *Lee's Lieutenants*, II, 193–200.

fourteenth along the same route taken by Davis; but Miles did not even make the attempt.[42]

Jackson captured 12,520 Federal soldiers at Harper's Ferry on September 15—the largest surrender of American forces in war up to that time in our history. Stonewall seized also 73 artillery pieces, 13,000 muskets, and a very large quantity of other valuable military stores. He designated A. P. Hill and part of his command to conclude the details of the surrender and to parole the prisoners, while he and Walker hastened to join Lee at Sharpsburg. Jackson and Walker united with the main Confederate Army on the Antietam early on the sixteenth; but A. P. Hill's command did not arrive on the field of battle until the afternoon of the seventeenth, at the crisis of the combat.[43]

Early on the fifteenth, Franklin—now through Crampton's Gap and into Pleasant Valley—began showing signs of hesitation. He stated to McClellan that he had encountered McLaws' enemy battle line two miles in front of him to the left. " As soon as I am sure that Rohersville is occupied," he continued, " I shall move forward to attack the enemy. . . . If Harper's Ferry has fallen—and the cessation of firing makes me fear that it has—it is my opinion that I should be strongly reinforced." About two hours later, Franklin sent another dispatch to McClellan, reporting that the enemy was in two lines of battle extending east and west across Pleasant Valley. " They outnumber me two to one," he claimed. " It will of course not answer to pursue the enemy under these circumstances. I shall communicate with Burnside as soon as possible. In the meantime I shall wait here until I learn what is the prospect of reinforcement. I have not the force to justify an attack on the force I see in front. I have had a very close view of it, and its position is very strong." Writing after the war, Franklin contended that he and " Baldy " Smith examined the Confederate

[42] 28 *O.R.*, 305; Alexander, *Military Memoirs*, 232, 236; Walker, " Jackson's Capture of Harper's Ferry," *loc. cit.*, 611; *Chase's Diary*, 85.
[43] Jackson's report, Alexander, *Military Memoirs*, 237; *B. & L.*, II, 618; Swinton, *Army of the Potomac*, 207; Palfrey, *The Antietam*, 27.

position, and " concluded that it would be suicidal to attack it."
Franklin says further that " it is evident therefore that a fight
between General McLaws' force and mine could have no effect
upon the surrender of Harper's Ferry. Success on my part
would have drawn me further away from the [Union] army and
would have brought me in dangerous nearness to Jackson's
force, already set free by the surrender. McLaws' supports were
three and a half miles from him, while my force was seven
miles from the main army." [44]

Receiving Franklin's communiqué saying that he was outnumbered two to one, McClellan ordered him to cover the
left of the advancing Army of the Potomac by watching the
Confederate force before him until the night of the sixteenth.
Then he was to join the main body at Keedysville, after dispatching Couch's division to occupy Maryland Heights. Mc-
Laws, therefore, not being attacked, gradually and skillfully
withdrew from Franklin's front and joined Lee at Sharpsburg
on the morning of the seventeenth, in time to participate in
the Battle of Antietam.[45]

McClellan had ordered Burnside early on the morning of
September 15 to march immediately with the Ninth Corps on
the Old Sharpsburg road. At 8:00 A. M., Burnside assured the
commanding general that his troops were in motion on the
road. Four hours later, however, riding along this road, McClellan discovered to his astonishment that the Ninth Corps " had
not stirred from its bivouacs, and still blocked the road for
[Sykes's] regular division." Burnside could not be found with
his soldiers to explain this divergence from McClellan's orders.
Somewhat nettled at his old friend's procrastination, McClellan,
to speed things along, sent the following message to Burnside
at 12:30 P. M.: " General McClellan desires you to let Gen.
Porter's go on past you, if necessary. You will then push your
own command on as rapidly as possible. The general also

[44] Franklin to McClellan, September 15, 1862, McClellan's *Report*, 194; Franklin, " Notes on Crampton's Gap and Antietam," *loc. cit.*, 596.
[45] McClellan's *Report*, 194; Palfrey, *The Antietam*, 44–45.

desires to know the reason for your delay in getting started this morning." [46] This episode marks the beginning of Burnside's strange mental paralysis which was to impair seriously McClellan's battle plans at Antietam and to limit his success.

On the morning of September 15, Longstreet and D. H. Hill reached Sharpsburg, and Lee placed them in position on a line running north and south "along the range of hills between the town and the Antietam" Creek. At Sharpsburg, Lee would be on the right flank and rear of any movement by McClellan against McLaws. On the afternoon of the fifteenth, on the Federal side, only Sykes's division of Porter's Fifth Corps and Richardson's division of Sumner's Second Corps had arrived on the field at Antietam; Burnside did not reach there until about sundown. It was, therefore, too late in the day for McClellan to have launched an attack, even if he had wanted to. [47]

Riding on from Boonsboro ahead of his marching troops, McClellan, late in the afternoon of the fifteenth, came to the hills bordering the east bank of the Antietam. He discovered sizeable numbers of grayclad soldiers, as well as enemy artillery batteries, on the heights across the river. As McClellan and his staff dismounted, several Confederate rifled guns opened fire on the Union commander's party. McClellan was walking slowly to the right, examining the enemy position carefully with his field glasses. The Southern gunners soon got the range, and shells began bursting quite close to the group. McClellan sent his staff officers behind the ridge to take cover from the flying missiles, while he himself continued to peer through the glasses. The projectiles whined by just over his head. "I noted with satisfaction," writes Cox, who was standing nearby, "the cool and business-like air with which he made his examination under fire." [48]

---

[46] *M.O.S.*, 586.

[47] Palfrey, *The Antietam*, 42; Paris, *The Civil War*, II, 333; McClellan's *Report*, 200; Powell, *Fifth Corps*, 266; *C.C.W.*, I, 440; *M.O.S.*, 587.

[48] McClellan's *Report*, 200; *M.O.S.*, 586, 587; Jacob D. Cox, "The Battle of Antietam," *B. & L.*, II, 631; Cox, *Military Reminiscences*, I, 300.

As late as the afternoon of September 16, with the bulk of Lee's army confronting him across the Antietam, McClellan received a dispatch from General-in-Chief Halleck which revealed that Old Brains had still not sized up the strategic picture on the military chessboard: "I think you will find the whole force of the enemy in your front has crossed the [Potomac] river. I fear now more than ever that they will recross at Harper's Ferry, or below, and turn your left, thus cutting you off from Washington. This has appeared to me to be a part of their plan, and hence my anxiety on the subject." [49] McClellan, however, had placed Franklin in position to guard against any such movement by the enemy. Halleck was, apparently, adhering with grim tenacity to his preconceived views of the course he believed Lee would take, regardless of contrary reports from McClellan and others reaching him from the field for the past two weeks. But McClellan, and Lincoln, had grasped the true nature of the situation, and saw that the great battle of the campaign would be fought in western Maryland, not close to the National capital. McClellan and Lee had, inevitably, reached the meeting of the ways.

---

[49] Halleck to McClellan, September 16, 1862, McClellan's *Report*, 187; *M.O.S.*, 556.

Chapter Ten

The War's Bloodiest Day

> The razing of the walls of Jericho by encircling marches of priests and soldiers, at the signal of long-drawn blasts of sacred horns and shouts of the multitude, was scarcely a greater miracle than the transformation of the conquering army of the South into a horde of disordered fugitives before an army that two weeks earlier was flying to cover under its homeward ramparts.
>
> —*James Longstreet*

WRITING many years after the Civil War, General George B. Davis, Judge Advocate General, said of the Army of the Potomac, " In none of the hard fought battles that adorn its glorious history did it meet with such desperate, determined, hand to hand resistance as it encountered on this memorable September morning, in the woods and cornfields and lanes that fill the landscape from river to river in the smiling valley of the Antietam." [1] Just how did this terrible pageantry of war unfold that fall day in the hills of western Maryland, and what was McClellan's role in it? The story of this great combat forms one of the epic pages in American military history.

By the afternoon of September 15, 1862, both McClellan and Lee had arrived on the field near Sharpsburg. The Union commander established his headquarters at the Pry house, located on the north side of the Boonsboro road atop a hill over-

---

[1] George B. Davis, " The Antietam Campaign," Military Historical Society of Massachusetts, *Campaigns in Virginia, Maryland and Pennsylvania, 1862–1863* (Boston, 1903), 27.

looking the Antietam Creek to the west. His staff had strapped telescopes to stakes which had been driven into the ground on the Pry lawn. These, with field glasses which had been propped on fences, enabled McClellan to scan the countryside in various directions. On the Confederate side, Lee's headquarters was set up in tents just west of the village along the northern side of the road to Sharpsburg.[2]

Looking through his glasses, McClellan noticed, late on the afternoon of the fifteenth, that the Confederate infantry was " ostentatiously displayed " on the ridge west of the Antietam. Nor was there just grayclad infantry in front of him; numerous artillery pieces frowned grimly over the hill-crests south and north of the town. McClellan noted with satisfaction, however, that most of his units were arriving on the field before dark. Only Franklin's Sixth Corps was any distance away, being encamped in the neighborhood of Maryland Heights. As was his nature, however, McClellan was not going to be rash in hastily assailing an enemy he believed to number approximately 120,000 men.[3]

Situated near a great bend of the Potomac River, the village of Sharpsburg was surrounded by a picturesque landscape of cultivated fields, occasional copses of trees, and steep out-croppings of limestone. The rolling farmlands were clothed in the brilliant raiment of autumn.

Sharpsburg Heights was the name given to the ridge which runs north and south and passes just outside of the eastern suburbs of the town. Striking out to the north from Sharpsburg was the Hagerstown pike; south of the village, this highway continued on to Harper's Ferry. The road west of town led to Shepherdstown, where the only ford of the Potomac in the vicinity was located. The Boonsboro road entered Sharpsburg

---

[2] See the excellent Maps of the Battle of Antietam, prepared by the Antietam Battlefield Board; also that in *B. & L.*, II, 636. Charles Carleton Coffin, " Antietam Scenes," *B. & L.*, II, 682; Palfrey, *The Antietam*, 119; Stine, *Army of the Potomac*, 219.

[3] Swinton, *Army of the Potomac*, 208; Cox, *Military Reminiscences*, I, 302; Longstreet, *Manassas to Appomattox*, 234.

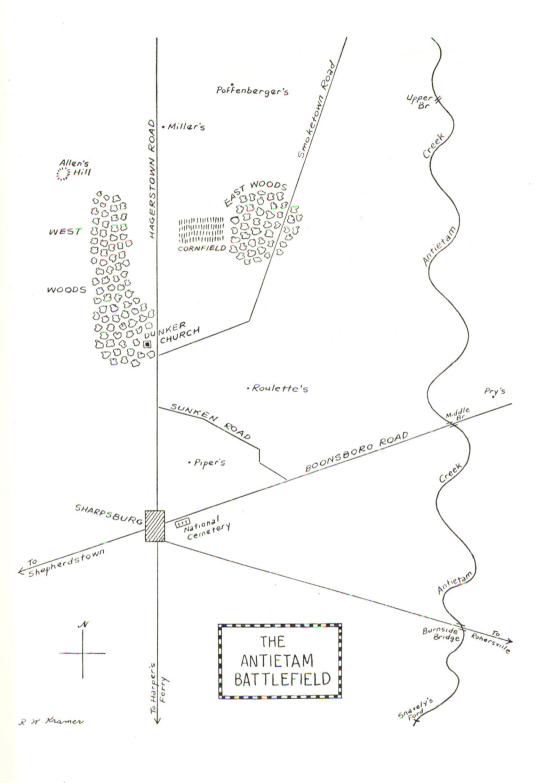

THE
ANTIETAM
BATTLEFIELD

R W Kramer

from the east. About a mile east of the town, the Antietam Creek flowed in a southerly direction. It was crossed by four stone bridges in the vicinity of the battlefield: the most northern was the bridge over which passed the road to Keedysville; the next one downstream was the one which carried the Boonsboro road eastward; then came the famous span by which the road to Rohersville crossed the Antietam, known afterwards as the Burnside Bridge; finally, the bridge near the confluence of the Antietam and the Potomac carried the pike leading to Harper's Ferry over the sluggish stream.

Approximately a mile north of town, on the west side of the Hagerstown pike, stood the white Dunker Church. Extending northward from the church for over a half mile was the West Woods. Opposite this forest, across the pike, was the Cornfield, bordered on its Antietam side by the East Woods. The Smoketown road ran north-northwestward through this grove. About two-thirds of the way from the town to the Dunker Church, an old sunken road—now famous as Bloody Lane—zigzagged to the east and southeast from the Hagerstown pike. The country was largely open and rolling, far different from the level, heavily forested terrain of Virginia.[4]

Lee posted his grayclad forces on the Sharpsburg Heights, his line running north and south and lying to the east of the Hagerstown–Harper's Ferry pike. Longstreet's command was stationed along the ridge to the south of the Boonsboro road; D. H. Hill's was to the north of that road; Jackson's was on Hill's left; the bulk of the Confederate artillery was on the high ground to the east of Sharpsburg (where the National Cemetery is now situated); and Stuart's cavalry and horse artillery were in position on a knoll to the left and rear of Jackson. The enemy line north of the town ran approximately midway between the Hagerstown Pike and Antietam Creek.[5]

[4] Allan, *Army of Northern Virginia*, 372; Powell, *Fifth Corps*, 210, 267, 268–69; Henderson, *Stonewall Jackson*, II, 239–41; Swinton, *Army of the Potomac*, 208–209; Palfrey, *The Antietam*, 48–49, 50–52.
[5] Longstreet, *Manassas to Appomattox*, 235; Swinton, *Army of the Potomac*, 209; Allan, *Army of Northern Virginia*, 377.

266

McClellan's dispositions by nightfall on the fifteenth were as follows: Sykes's division of Regulars was posted on the high ground on the eastern bank of the Antietam to the left (south) of the Boonsboro road; Richardson's division was on Sykes's right on the north side of that road, the remainder of Sumner's Second Corps being placed behind Richardson; Hooker's First Corps was on the right of Richardson, with Pleasonton's cavalry posted temporarily on the extreme right flank; the Twelfth Corps, now commanded by Major General J. K. F. Mansfield, was behind Hooker; and Burnside's Ninth Corps—soon to arrive on the field—would be stationed on the Federal left, to the east of the Burnside Bridge.[6]

The Antietam battlefield was well chosen by Lee to fight his defensive battle. Although enjoying somewhat a numerical superiority over Lee, McClellan's army faced a hazardous task in attacking the grayclad host. The two flanks of Lee's Army of Northern Virginia rested almost on the Potomac River, the battlefield thus being too cramped for sweeping maneuver. To assail the Confederate lines, McClellan would have to cross the Antietam—believed to be fordable only at the four bridges —and advance to the attack chiefly across open fields. The Southerners were posted on elevated ground, and would thus be firing down the throats of the Federals as they came surging up the ridge. The great difficulty of making successful attacks across open ground swept by artillery fire—as seen before at Malvern Hill—was soon to be demonstrated again at Fredericksburg and Gettysburg. At Antietam, Lee had a definite advantage in position, and McClellan's modest superiority in numbers was hardly enough to promise a decisive victory. To Lee's disadvantage, however, was the fact that, if hurled back in rout, he would be pinned against the Potomac River in his rear.

The sixteenth of September dawned foggy and damp. Although the mists lifted by late morning with a rise in temperature, the haze delayed McClellan's reconnaissances of the ground

[6] Stine, *Army of the Potomac*, 187–88; Palfrey, *The Antietam*, 48.

and his deployment of troops. During the forenoon, most of the Confederates engaged in the capture of Harper's Ferry arrived at Sharpsburg; but part of A. P. Hill's division was left at the ferry until it could dispose of the Federals captured there. Early that morning, McClellan wired Halleck in Washington, "Will attack as soon as situation of enemy is developed." [7]

When the fog lifted, McClellan noted that the Confederate infantry forces "were still concealed behind the opposite heights." But now he saw that the positions of a number of enemy artillery batteries had been changed since his previous inspection. McClellan took several hours to make careful personal examinations of the ground and to direct reconnaissances of the gray lines. Under a brisk artillery exchange, he posted his troops in the most advantageous positions from which to attack, stationed guns and reserve batteries, brought up ammunition and supplies, and saw to it that his hungry soldiers received their long-overdue food rations. In order to draw the Confederate fire, and thereby reveal their partially concealed positions, McClellan and his staff rode along the whole Union battle line in front of his advanced pickets. Wildly cheered by his own men, McClellan's canter evoked a wrathful fire from the enemy lines. The Federal guns responded. Speaking of the artillery duel which ensued, the combative D. H. Hill admitted that the Confederate pieces "could not cope with the . . . Yankee guns," adding that the contest here "was one of the most melancholy farces in the war." [8]

About noon on the sixteenth, McClellan rode to the left of his line. He saw that Burnside was not in a proper position to cross the Antietam, and issued orders to him to rectify his dispositions. McClellan then instructed the Ninth Corps commander "to reconnoitre the approaches to the bridge carefully."

[7] Stine, *Army of the Potomac*, 188; Palfrey, *The Antietam*, 56, 57; Paris, *The Civil War*, II, 339; Swinton, *Army of the Potomac*, 208; McClellan to Halleck, September 16, 1862—7:00 A. M., 28 *O.R.*, 307–308.

[8] McClellan's *Report*, 200, 201; Palfrey, *The Antietam*, 61; 28 *O.R.*, 307; *M.O.S.*, 588; Gibbon, *Personal Recollections*, 80; D. H. Hill's report, 27 *O.R.*, 1026.

"I . . . informed [Burnside]," said McClellan, "that he would probably be required to attack the enemy's right on the following morning." The orders were given to Burnside about noon; but at sunset McClellan discovered that his instructions had not as yet been carried out properly. He immediately drew up the following message to be delivered to Burnside, issuing it over the signature of his Acting Assistant Adjutant General, Lieutenant Colonel James A. Hardie: "The general commanding has learned that although your corps was ordered to be in a designated position at 12 m. to-day, at or near sunset only one division and four batteries had reached the ground intended for your troops. The general had also been advised that there was a delay of some four hours in the movement of your command yesterday. I am instructed to call upon you for explanations of these failures on your part to comply with the orders given you, and to add, in view of the important military operations now at hand, the commanding general cannot lightly regard such marked departure from the tenor of his instructions." This was the beginning of Burnside's procrastination at Antietam which was to embarrass McClellan to a great extent on the following day.[9]

Shortly after noon on the sixteenth, McClellan evolved his plan of battle. He would throw heavy forces against Lee's left flank in the vicinity of the East Woods. When that attack was well underway, Burnside was to attack the enemy right in force in the area around the Burnside Bridge. If these assaults proved successful, McClellan would strike the Confederate center with whatever force he had available. He determined to leave the actual fighting of the battle, as was his custom— and Lee's—to his corps commanders. General Palfrey states that McClellan's "plan seems to have been well suited to the position of affairs. . . . It was extremely simple, and ought to have been successful." However, the Union commander's efforts

[9] McClellan's *Report*, 201, 208; *M.O.S.*, 588–89; Palfrey, *The Antietam*, 59; 28 *O.R.*, 308; Stine, *Army of the Potomac*, 188. Cf. Cox, "The Battle of Antietam," *loc. cit.*, 632; Cox, *Military Reminiscences*, I, 384.

were to be weakened seriously by a series of blunders on the part of several of his corps commanders—notably Burnside— and by his own reluctance to exercise a large degree of tactical control of the battle.[10]

At approximately 2:00 P. M. on the sixteenth, McClellan ordered Hooker to cross the Antietam at the upper bridge with his First Corps and attack the Confederate left flank near the East Woods. Sumner was directed to move Mansfield's Twelfth Corps across the creek during the night to the support of Hooker, and to ready his own Second Corps for crossing early on the morning of the seventeenth. If the Confederates changed front to the north to protect their left flank, their lines would then be enfiladed by a flank fire from McClellan's powerful rifled ordnance on the east bank of the Antietam.[11]

Hooker commenced his movement at about 3:00 P. M. on the sixteenth. He crossed the upper bridge—accompanied for a time by McClellan himself—and swung around to the north and west toward the enemy left flank. His movement, easily observed by the Southerners, was beyond the range of Lee's guns. Hood's division was then faced to the north to meet Hooker's advance near the Miller farmhouse. The Federal march, however, had taken considerable time. It was dusk before the First Corps, facing south, come up against Hood's gray division. In a lively combat which lasted until dark, Meade's division succeeded in pressing the enemy back to the vicinity of the Miller house, Hood being reinforced by two brigades during the action. After dark, firing along the skirmish lines erupted intermittently, threatening to bring on a night action. Hooker, therefore, had succeeded in placing his corps on the left of the main Confederate line, but the enemy had

[10] McClellan's *Report*, 201–202, 208; Stine, *Army of the Potomac*, 188; Swinton, *Army of the Potomac*, 209; Allan, *Army of Northern Virginia*, 440; DeTrobriand, *Army of the Potomac*, 326; Palfrey, *The Antietam*, 59–60; William Allan, "Strategy of the Campaign of Sharpsburg or Antietam, September, 1862," *Campaigns in Maryland*, 94.

[11] Sypher, *Pennsylvania Reserves*, 378; Stine, *Army of the Potomac*, 188–89; S. D. Lee's report, Palfrey, *The Antietam*, 61, 73.

quickly changed front to the north to present a parallel line to the Federals and to meet head-on the heavy attack which all knew would come at daybreak.[12]

During the night, the Confederate divisions of McLaws and Major General R. H. Anderson arrived on the field to reinforce Lee. On the Union side, McClellan, before midnight, had pushed Mansfield's Twelfth Corps across the Antietam at the upper bridge. It went into position about one mile behind Hooker's corps, in the vicinity of the Poffenberger Woods. Unlike Lee—most of whose major attacks during the war were made too late in the day to follow up an initial success— McClellan apparently determined on the sixteenth to attack all-out at sunrise on the seventeenth, so that he would have more hours of daylight to improve any early victory.[13]

On the eve of battle, how did the two opposing armies compare numerically? Although McClellan asserted in his report that he had a total of 87,164 men available for duty, this was a careless and misleading estimate. It was based on the morning reports of his subordinates, and showed the total number of men in uniform—noncombatants as well as combatants—present for duty. There was a great difference, however, between the number of men present for duty and the number of combat effectives. Four-fifths of the present for duty is a liberal estimate for the effectives available to McClellan at Antietam, or about 69,732 men. The National commander later testified under oath before the Committee on the Conduct of the War that he had about 70,000 to 75,000 effectives at Antietam.[14]

On the Confederate side, a number of officers in gray, including Lee, contend that there were less than 40,000 Southern soldiers in action; but this seems to be a considerable

[12] Swinton, *Army of the Potomac*, 210; *M.O.S.*, 588ff.; John B. Hood, *Advance and Retreat* . . . (New Orleans, 1880), 42; Meade's report, Sypher, *Pennsylvania Reserves*, 388; Powell, *Fifth Corps*, 274; Stine, *Army of the Potomac*, 189–91.

[13] Palfrey, *The Antietam*, 57, 63.

[14] McClellan's *Report*, 214; Palfrey, *The Antietam*, 69–72; McClellan's testimony, March 2, 1863, *C.C.W.*, I, 441.

underestimate. Then too, there was a great difference between the number of men the Federals thought Lee had and the actual number of graycoats present. The Union military authorities in Washington, under Banks, made a separate and elaborate investigation of probable Confederate numbers—mostly from prisoners and pro-Northern Southerners—just before Antietam, and calculated that Lee had 97,445 effectives. In his testimony, McClellan stated his belief that the Confederates had " pretty close upon 100,000 men." Cox writes that " the rooted belief in Lee's preponderance of numbers had been chronic in the [Union] army during the whole year." Sumner testified that, in his opinion, Lee had 80,000 effectives at Sharpsburg. Longstreet states that his chief had, a week before Antietam, 61,000 men. According to the Richmond *Enquirer*, about 60,000 Southern soldiers were engaged in the battle. Ropes believes that Lee had 58,000 men on the field. On September 22, five days after the battle, official Confederate returns for infantry effectives alone showed 36,418 present for duty then. Adding to this the number of men in the cavalry and reserve artillery—about 8,000 men—would increase the figure to 44,418. Deducting 1,000 men of Colonel Edward L. Thomas' brigade of A. P. Hill's division, absent at Harper's Ferry, would leave 43,418 effectives present on September 22. By Lee's own admission to his President, scarcely any stragglers had rejoined his army by the twenty-first. Adding to the figure of 43,418 the probable Confederate casualties at Antietam—13,142—a total of 57,152 is obtained. Livermore thinks that 51,844 Southern effectives were engaged against McClellan at Antietam, but adds that the figure might well be 58,844. In speaking of the fighting at Sharpsburg, Palfrey asserts, " It is highly probable that all the wrestling that was done was done by nearly equal forces." It seems likely, however, that the Federals did outnumber the Confederates by at least 12,000 men. As will be seen, McClellan, believing that he was fighting a largely superior enemy, felt obliged to keep some of his troops in reserve, rather than putting all his men in the front lines.

Lincoln and McClellan on the Antietam Battlefield

Being on exterior lines and attacking largely across open fields, McClellan might well have had need of a superiority in his favor, as the later battles of Fredericksburg and Gettysburg were to demonstrate.[15]

The fateful seventeenth of September dawned gray and misty, but a warm sun was soon to clear away the clouds and bring on a perfect Indian Summer day. At the first signs of light—about 5:30 A. M.—Fighting Joe Hooker opened the Battle of Antietam. His goal was the high ground around the Dunker Church in the lower West Woods. Stonewall Jackson's gray line had been refused back in order to face northward against Hooker, and ran from the East Woods through the Cornfield into the West Woods. Fighting Joe, facing south, deployed Brigadier General Abner Doubleday's division on his right, Meade's in the center, and Brigadier General James B. Ricketts' on the left. A few hundred yards to the Union right was a height known as Allen's Hill. Unfortunately for the Federals, Hooker committed the grave error of neglecting to occupy this elevation with his artillery, from where he could have taken the Confederate line in flank and rear. This key knoll was occupied later in the morning by Jeb Stuart's horse artillery, from where the enemy guns embarrassed the Union right.[16]

Seeing by the glint of the sun on their muskets a large mass of grayclad infantry concealed amid the high stalks of the Cornfield, Hooker's brass guns near the Miller house opened a frontal artillery fire of grape and canister, while McClellan's powerful twenty-pounder-Parrott rifled ordnance enfiladed Jack-

[15] McClellan's *Report*, 213–14; see Freeman, *R. E. Lee*, II, 402n; McClellan's testimony, March 2, 1863, *C.C.W.*, I, 441; Cox, "The Battle of Antietam," *loc. cit.*, 658; Sumner's testimony, February 18, 1863, *C.C.W.*, I, 369; Longstreet, *Manassas to Appomattox*, 266; Richmond *Enquirer*, September 23, 1862; Ropes, *Story of the Civil War*, II, 282–83; 28 *O.R.*, 621; Allan, *Army of Northern Virginia*, 380; Lee to Davis, September 21, 1862, 27 *O.R.*, 143; Livermore, *Numbers and Losses*, 92–94; Palfrey, *The Antietam*, 66, 67–68; Stine, *Army of the Potomac*, 222; Davis, "The Antietam Campaign," *loc. cit.*, 68–69.

[16] Smith, *118th Pennsylvania*, 140–41; Palfrey, *The Antietam*, 72, 74; Meade's report, Sypher, *Pennsylvania Reserves*, 388; Walker, *Second Corps*, 99; Swinton, *Army of the Potomac*, 211–12; Antietam Battlefield Board Maps; Stine, *Army of the Potomac*, 207.

son's lines in the Cornfield from the Union positions east of the Antietam. It was one of the most destructive, murderous artillery fires of the war. " In the time I am writing," declared Hooker in his official report, " every stalk of corn in the northern and greater part of the field was cut as closely as could have been done by a knife, and the slain lay in rows, precisely as they had stood in their ranks a few moments before. It was never my fortune to witness a more bloody, dismal battlefield." A Confederate officer said, " Pray that you may never see another Sharpsburg. Sharpsburg was Artillery Hell." The effectiveness of McClellan's artillery was admitted by D. H. Hill, who stated, with some exaggeration, " The long range artillery of the Yankees, on the other side of the Antietam . . . concentrated their fire upon every [Confederate] gun that opened and soon disabled it." Throughout the battle, McClellan's guns were superb, Antietam being one of the finest examples of Union artillery superiority in the war.[17]

The infantry clash was swift and desperate following the artillery preparation. Spearheaded by Ricketts' division, Hooker forced Jackson's men out of the East Woods and the Cornfield after an hour's furious fighting. The graybacks fled in disorder into the West Woods. However, Meade's division on Ricketts' right, attempting to seize the West Woods, was hurled back. This put a crimp in the Federal assault. Ricketts, on Hooker's left, was advancing more rapidly than the right of the Union line, and was soon facing more to the west than to the south. Against stiffening opposition, Ricketts managed to reach the eastern edge of the West Woods just north of the Dunker Church; but he could go no further. The losses on both sides were staggering. Ricketts lost a third of his men; a Union brigade suffered forty-four per cent casualties; in two Confederate brigades, more than one half of the men were killed or

[17] Powell, *Fifth Corps*, 275; Sypher, *Pennsylvania Reserves*, 381; Palfrey, *The Antietam*, 61, 73–74; Hooker's report, 27 *O.R.*, 218; S. D. Lee to Alexander, D. H. Hill's report, Alexander, *Military Memoirs*, 247; Davis, " The Antietam Campaign," *loc. cit.*, 67.

wounded; a Southern division and a brigade commander were killed, and two other enemy generals were wounded. On Hooker's extreme right, Doubleday's division was held in check by the Confederate guns under Stuart, which had occupied the dominant Allen's Hill on the Federal right flank. Jackson was then reinforced by the arrival of four brigades under McLaws. Other troops were shifted also to bolster the Confederate left. As Colonel Allan states, " Lee had already stripped his centre and right to the utmost in ordering G. T. Anderson and J. G. Walker to the extreme left." [18]

In order to coordinate better the attack on the Federal right, McClellan had placed Hooker in temporary command of Mansfield's Twelfth Corps. Fighting Joe acknowledged that he did not throw Mansfield into the fight until, as he says, " all my reserves were engaged." However, he had waited too long. By the time Hooker called upon the Twelfth Corps for assistance, his own divisions had been pretty well shattered. He himself had been wounded in the foot and carried from the field, the command of his First Corps devolving upon Meade. With the exception of a small force of Ricketts' men which had gained a foothold along the eastern edge of the West Woods, Hooker's corps fell back " to the heights on the Poffenberger farm," near its starting point.[19]

A little before 7:30 A. M., Mansfield's Twelfth Corps was ordered forward " to support and relieve Hooker's troops." It had taken the wrong direction during the night after crossing the Antietam, and, at daybreak, was one mile behind Hooker's corps instead of being on its left. The deployment of the Twelfth Corps was also carried out in a slow manner. In the initial stages of the deployment, the aggressive old commander

[18] Palfrey, *The Antietam*, 74, 75, 77; Swinton, *Army of the Potomac*, 212–13; Sypher, *Pennsylvania Reserves*, 381–83; Hood, *Advance and Retreat*, 43–44; Stine, *Army of the Potomac*, 191–204; Allan, *Army of Northern Virginia*, 390.

[19] Hooker's testimony, March 11, 1863, *C.C.W.*, I, 581; Hooker's report, A. S. Williams' report, 27 *O.R.*, 217, 475–76; Cox, " The Battle of Antietam," *loc. cit.*, 635; Walker, *Second Corps*, 99; Paris, *The Civil War*, II, 343; Sypher, *Pennsylvania Reserves*, 384; Stine, *Army of the Potomac*, 384.

of the corps, Mansfield, was mortally wounded, Brigadier General Alpheus S. Williams succeeding him at the head of the Twelfth. Whereas Hooker had attacked largely in a southerly direction, the Twelfth Corps, in making its assault, was to move generally in a more southwesterly line.[20]

Williams formed the division of Brigadier General Samuel W. Crawford on the right and that of Brigadier General George S. Greene on the left of his line. Crawford, moving first, pressed back Hood's division and reached a point in the eastern edge of the West Woods to the north of the Dunker Church, where some of Ricketts' men were still holding on. Greene's well-handled division soon moved forward down the Smoketown road on the left of Crawford, and in a more westerly direction of advance. Crossing the Hagerstown pike against stubborn opposition from D. H. Hill, Greene succeeded in effecting a lodgment in the lower end of the West Woods, and captured the Dunker Church. During its sharp fight, the Twelfth Corps lost approximately 1,700 men out of about 7,000 engaged. It lost also the services of division commander Crawford, who was wounded, as well as those of three brigade commanders. It was now about 9:00 A. M., and the Twelfth Corps could advance no further. Not only that, but its hard-won, precarious position in the West Woods about the Dunker Church was under increasingly heavy pressure and looked as if it might have to be abandoned. Both sides were pretty well exhausted by the heavy fighting, which had been continuous since dawn. Had Hooker not committed the folly of attacking piecemeal with the First and Twelfth corps—but instead have thrown them in together in one line—it is difficult to see how Jackson could have fended off the blows and retained his position on the field.[21]

[20] Swinton, *Army of the Potomac*, 213; Palfrey, *The Antietam*, 77; see Steele, *American Campaigns*, I, 269; Cox, "The Battle of Antietam," *loc. cit.*, 639.

[21] Powell, *Fifth Corps*, 276; Swinton, *Army of the Potomac*, 213–14; Palfrey, *The Antietam*, 78–81; Stine, *Army of the Potomac*, 209–10; Allan, *Army of Northern Virginia*, 394, 396; 27 *O.R.*, 199; *B. & L.*, II, 600; Walker, *Second Corps*, 99.

Federal reinforcements were at hand, however. Sumner received the order at 7:30 A. M. to cross the Antietam with his Second Corps and move to the assistance of Hooker and Mansfield. He moved Sedgwick's division forward, closely followed by that of Brigadier General William H. French. Sumner's third division—Richardson's—advanced almost an hour later, probably because Morell's division of the Sixth Corps did not get up when expected to relieve it. By about 9:00 A. M., the bulk of the Second Corps had reached the area near the East Woods.[22]

So anxious was old Sumner to assail the foe, that he neglected to make even the most cursory reconnaissance of what was in front of him. He determined to throw Sedgwick's division westward at once across the Cornfield and into the West Woods to the north of the Dunker Church, where fragments of the Union First and Twelfth corps were still clinging. The combative Second Corps commander decided to accompany the troops of Sedgwick himself. Thus, he neglected to stay behind long enough to direct French to move forward immediately and simultaneously in line of battle on Sedgwick's left. As it was, without orders from Sumner, French diverged to the southwest (and away from Sedgwick's left), aiming to strike the area just to the south of Greene, who was holding on near the Dunker Church. Nor did Sumner wait even a short time for the delayed division of Richardson. Longstreet states that if Sumner had " formed the corps into lines of divisions, in close echelon, and moved as a corps, he would have . . . forced the battle back to to the [Potomac] river bank." McClellan would have done better, however, to have started Sumner across the Antietam earlier in the morning than 7:30.[23]

Deploying Sedgwick's division in a dense column with brigade front, Sumner moved westward through the park-like East Woods and into the Cornfield. Although he saw Craw-

[22] Palfrey, *The Antietam*, 82.

[23] Walker, *Second Corps*, 101; Ropes, *Story of the Civil War*, II, 365–66; Cox, " The Battle of Antietam," *loc. cit.*, 643; Longstreet, *Manassas to Appomattox*, 247.

ford's division now retiring from the West Woods across the Hagerstown pike, he saw no enemy soldiers in force in any direction. To the consternation of his subordinate generals, Sumner kept the division formed in the dangerous column of three tight brigade lines, hardly twenty yards separating the units. Also, he had neglected to throw out even a single regiment as flankers on the right or left. The hard-charging division rapidly penetrated the West Woods just north of the Dunker Church, the first brigade emerging from the western edge of the wood. Only Hood's relatively small force of men and guns appeared to be opposing Sumner in front. So dense was the Union column of brigades, however, that the Confederate artillery fire, weak as it was, could scarcely miss hitting home with each shot. Just as Sumner seemed to have won a decisive victory, Lee threw reinforcements against Sedgwick's uncovered left flank and rear. These were the divisions of McLaws and Walker, drawn from the Confederate right opposite Burnside. Under cover of limestone ledges, the graycoats now poured a terrific fire upon Sedgwick's helpless men. So closely had the headstrong Sumner formed the brigade lines that they were unable to wheel to the left (south) to confront their assailants. Surrounded on three sides by a curtain of fire, Sedgwick lost 2,200 of his 5,000 men in fifteen minutes. The able Sedgwick, though wounded three times, managed to keep his saddle while striving to extricate his remnants from the death-trap. Those Federals managing to escape to the north out of the West Woods ambush were with difficulty rallied into a defensive line to the west of the Cornfield, facing south.[24]

Seeing Sumner's initial attack with Sedgwick's division routed, the gallant elements of Greene's division holding on grimly to the ground they had wrested from the Southerners about the Dunker Church, were obliged, shortly after Sedg-

[24] Palfrey, *The Antietam*, 82–84, 86–87, 89–90; Walker, *Second Corps*, 102–108; Swinton, *Army of the Potomac*, 214–15; 27 *O.R.*, 193; Jubal A. Early, *Autobiographical Sketch and Narrative of the War Between the States . . .* (Philadelphia, 1912), 145; Ropes, *Story of the Civil War*, II, 364–66.

wick's repulse, to yield grudgingly their hard-earned gains. As Hooker had committed a fatal blunder in attacking without the Twelfth Corps, so too did Sumner err seriously in massing Sedgwick's division in a column of close brigades. He had done even worse in not moving simultaneously with all three of his divisions. Had he attacked otherwise than piecemeal, it is difficult to reject the belief that Sumner would have decisively won the day for McClellan.[25]

With Sedgwick's wrecked division falling back in disorder, and with the First and Twelfth corps barely able to hold a part of their gains, McClellan's right was in danger as thousands of yelping grayclad soldiers began moving forward into the breach left by Sedgwick's withdrawal. However, as Henderson states, "Smith's division of the Sixth Corps had been sent forward by McClellan to sustain the battle," and its arrival in the gap saved the Union Army from serious trouble. Trying to rush the blue lines immediately in the wake of Sedgwick's retiring brigades, McLaws pushed his counterattack too far, and McClellan's artillery opened on him and decimated his ranks. McLaws lost 1,103 men out of 2,893 engaged. The Confederates then retired to their position about the Dunker Church, leaving the East Woods, the Cornfield, and the Hagerstown pike in Federal hands. South of the church, meanwhile, several enemy batteries had been annihilated by the Union artillery fire.[26]

After the failure of his initial sortie, Sumner now threw French's division into the struggle. Richardson's division was expected momentarily to come into line of battle on French's left. "The combat which followed," declares Ropes, "was beyond a question one of the most sanguinary and desperate in the whole war." Starting from a point just to the east of the East Woods, French's three brigades—one of which was fighting its maiden battle—moved forward in a southwesterly direction

[25] Ropes, *Story of the Civil War*, II, 367; Palfrey, *The Antietam*, 88; Allan, *Army of Northern Virginia*, 403n; Stine, *Army of the Potomac*, 209, 210

[26] Henderson, *Stonewall Jackson*, II, 253; *M.O.S.*, 600; Alexander, *Military Memoirs*, 259; Swinton, *Army of the Potomac*, 215; Palfrey, *The Antietam*, 88, 90; Hood, *Advance and Retreat*, 44.

toward the Roulette house. Encountering three of D. H. Hill's veteran brigades, French drove the enemy from the Roulette buildings into the Sunken Road, which formed a natural trench for the Southerners. Here the remainder of Hill's division joined the three repulsed brigades, the Confederate position in the Sunken Road being strengthened by rails which were thrown up as a breastwork. Suffering from an enfilading fire from the West Woods, French was soon augmented on his left by Richardson's division.[27]

Hill's position in the Sunken Road—known afterwards as Bloody Lane—was a strong one against a frontal attack. However, any Federal force which could gain the flank of the Confederate position would trap the grayclads in the trench-like lane in an enfilading fire. Consequently, Hill attempted to forestall such attacks on his flanks by himself turning first Richardson's left and then French's right. Failing in this, he found himself in turn outflanked on both sides by the Federals. The fighting was furious and unrelenting—no quarter was asked and none given. Especially noteworthy was the action of Colonel Francis C. Barlow, who gained a dominant position on the Confederate flank and poured an irresistible enfilading fire down Hill's lines. Three hundred Southerners were compelled to surrender to Barlow, who was himself severely wounded. Confederate General Alexander says that " the whole lane was enfiladed, and the slaughter which took place in it strewed it with dead and wounded, probably as thickly as has ever been seen in this country." Hill, though reinforced by R. H. Anderson's division—drawn from Lee's right opposite Burnside—could not stem the blue tide. Richardson and French successfully stormed the Sunken Road, scattering the enemy soldiers over the hill toward the Piper farmhouse to the southwest. A Confederate brigadier was slain and two others wounded in the vicious melee. Trying in vain to regroup his routed troops, Hill was next driven in disorder from the Piper house

[27] Ropes, *Story of the Civil War*, II, 368; D. H. Hill's report, Swinton, *Army of the Potomac*, 216n; Walker, *Second Corps*, 110-11.

across the Hagerstown pike toward the high ground near the town of Sharpsburg, where a few Confederate batteries were posted. The situation was critical at the center of Lee's army.[28]

It was now about noon. Longstreet and D. H. Hill had but a few hundred men and some guns in hand to meet the formidable lines of French and Richardson. Longstreet himself and his personal staff helped to work the artillery pieces of a Confederate battery which had lost most of its men. While French's division was jaded and greatly reduced by its severe struggle, Richardson's was still in efficient fighting trim. At that time, any forward Union movement against Lee's center must have been successful, and the resulting penetration would likely have proved fatal to the Confederate Army. Unfortunately for McClellan, however, Richardson decided for some unknown reason that he had done enough, and determined merely to hold most of his gains. He pulled his line back about halfway from the Piper house to the Sunken Road, posting it along a ridge. Just as the firing here was tapering off, Richardson fell mortally wounded. McClellan replaced him with one of the ablest Union generals of the war, Winfield S. Hancock of the Sixth Corps. Hancock, unfamiliar with his new command, came up quickly and took over Richardson's division. He felt, however, that his line was too long and too thinly held to renew the attack. It was already being enfiladed by Confederate artillery fire coming over the West Woods from Allen's Hill. Thus, like Hooker, Sumner had attacked piecemeal with his divisions. But he had succeeded in forcing Lee to denude, practically, the Confederate right wing opposite Burnside in order to hold the center and left. Why Burnside had not attacked Lee's right many hours before was unknown to the Union officers below the Sunken Road.[29]

[28] Alexander, *Military Memoirs*, 262; Ropes, *Story of the Civil War*, II, 368–69; Lee's report, 27 *O.R.*, 150; Walker, *Second Corps*, 112–15; Stine, *Army of the Potomac*, 211–13; Palfrey, *The Antietam*, 97–100.

[29] D. H. Hill's report, Swinton, *Army of the Potomac*, 217; Longstreet to W. S. Rosecrans, Stine, *Army of the Potomac*, 213–14; Steele, *American Campaigns*, I, 272; Palfrey, *The Antietam*, 100–101; *M.O.S.*, 606; McClellan's *Report*, 206.

Porter held McClellan's center with his small reserve Fifth Corps. He was supporting Pleasonton's dismounted cavalrymen and horse artillery batteries which were making a series of small demonstrations along the Boonsboro road toward the town. Seeing the shattered condition of his right, however, McClellan, during the morning, sent two of Porter's brigades to that wing. Six battalions of Sykes's division of Regulars of the Fifth Corps were still supporting Pleasonton's guns. Warren's brigade had been ordered to support Burnside, and took position on the right-rear of the Ninth Corps. Thus, Porter was left with but one small brigade of Morell's division and a portion of Sykes's division—a little over 3,000 men in all—to hold the Union center. The Fifth Corps was, therefore, split, and McClellan could not use it for an attack then upon the Confederate center. Soon, the remainder of Morell's division relieved Richardson in support of artillery to the right of the Boonsboro road. One of Sykes's battalion commanders, Thomas M. Anderson, claimed many years after the war that he had witnessed a conversation about noon between Sykes, Porter, and McClellan on the field at Antietam. He said that Sykes informed him immediately after the conference that McClellan seemed inclined to throw forward the Fifth Corps (before it was split up) in an attack on the enemy's center. Porter, however, was reported as saying to the Federal commander, " Remember, General! I command the last reserve of the last army of the Republic." McClellan, according to this account, then deferred the attack.[30]

Shortly prior to this—a little before noon—McClellan himself made a dramatic appearance on the battle line, helping to rally Sedgwick's broken division in the edge of the West Woods. An eyewitness describes the scene in the following language typical of the 1860's: " General McClellan, with his large and imposing staff, rode upon the ground. . . . The deep and abiding enthusiasm that habitually followed him promptly greeted him.

[30] Swinton, *Army of the Potomac*, 218; McClellan's *Report*, 207–208; Powell, *Fifth Corps*, 283; *B. & L.*, II, 656.

Shouts, yells, and cheers of appreciation rent the air. This unusual noise, so loud that it was borne above the din of battle to the enemy's lines, brought on a vigorous and persistent shelling. Regardless of the flying, bursting missiles, there he sat astride his splendid charger, glass in hand, calmly reviewing the mighty hosts." [31]

Meanwhile, it was expected at McClellan's headquarters that Burnside would cross the Antietam in force by mid-morning and heavily assail the Confederate right. Up until noon, however, things remained relatively quiet on the Union left, despite the fact that Burnside's Ninth Corps (augmented by a Fifth Corps brigade), numbering approximately 13,000 men, was opposed only by Brigadier General D. R. Jones's small division of some 2,500 effectives. [32]

Near 1:00 P.M., McClellan received a valuable reinforcement: Franklin's Sixth Corps—comprising the divisions of Slocum and W. F. Smith—arrived on the field. The Union commander had intended holding Franklin's corps east of the Antietam, to use en masse against either the Confederate right or left as opportunity offered. However, at 1:00 P. M., McClellan saw that Franklin was needed in a defensive role to plug the gap between Sumner's center and right, where the Confederates, as seen, were threatening to attack Sedgwick's shattered division again. Part of Smith's division was used to fill this gap in Sumner's line. The remaining brigade—Colonel William H. Irwin's—made a heroic attack on the enemy lines around the Dunker Church, where small fragments of Greene's and Ricketts' men had earlier been holding on tenaciously. Receiving a galling fire on his left and right, however, Irwin could not holds his gains, and the entire Federal contingent about the church fell back a short distance. A small-scale Union attack cleared some grayclad sharpshooters from the Piper house, but

---

[31] Upton, *Military Policy*, 381; Ellis' *Diary*, 269, 275, 296; *M.O.S.*, 606; Smith, *118th Pennsylvania*, 42.

[32] James Harrison Wilson, *Under the Old Flag . . .* (New York, 1912), I, 110; Swinton, *Army of the Potomac*, 218; McClellan's *Report*, 214; Long, *Memoirs of Lee*, 218; Jones's report, 27 *O.R.*, 886.

could not hold that point. However, the threatened enemy attack had been thrown off balance and thwarted for the remainder of the day on that portion of the field.[33]

Franklin saw, shortly after he arrived, that one more heavy push would cave in the Confederate center, and quickly massed the bulk of his two divisions to strike the enemy about the Dunker Church. Such an attack as that prepared and urged by Franklin could hardly have been checked by the shattered Southern brigades available. But Franklin had been placed under Sumner's orders, the Second Corps commander being senior major general on that portion of the field. And Sumner, for once, had had enough fighting for one day. Always the dashing, courageous soldier, he lacked at times the moral courage of a general. Shaken by the terrible defeat and losses that his rashness had caused Sedgwick to suffer, Sumner rejected Franklin's request to attack, and ordered him to remain stationary and merely hold his lines. Overestimating his own losses, Sumner could not see the riddled condition of the relatively few men and guns holding Lee's center.[34]

At this very time, McClellan had instructed one of his aides, Assistant Engineer James H. Wilson, to take the following message to Sumner: " Tell the General to crowd every man and gun into ranks, and, if he thinks practicable, he may advance Franklin to carry the woods in front, holding the rest of the line with his own command, assisted by those of [Mansfield] and Hooker." Wilson states that, after reaching Sumner and conferring briefly with him, he found the general to be in " a demoralized state of mind." The old soldier declared to Wilson that the First, Second, and Twelfth corps were " all cut up and demoralized," and said that he would not attack

[33] McClellan's *Report*, 206–207; Stine, *Army of the Potomac*, 214–16; Palfrey, *The Antietam*, 95, 96, 101–102; Swinton, *Army of the Potomac*, 218–19.

[34] Franklin's testimony, March 30, 1863, *C.C.W.*, I, 626; Franklin's report, 27 *O.R.*, 61, 62, 277, 377; DeTrobriand, *Army of the Potomac*, 324; McClellan's *Report*, 207, 208; Palfrey, *The Antietam*, 54, 95–96, 121–22; Walker, *Second Corps*, 117–19; Ropes, *Story of the Civil War*, II, 370; Upton, *Military Policy*, 381.

because Franklin's corps was " the only organized command on this part of the field." McClellan soon rode forward to talk with Franklin and Sumner at the front lines. Before the Union commander came up, however, Confederate troops had arrived from left and right, and had filled the woods about the Dunker Church. Seeing his senior corps commander—the usually aggressive Sumner—positively opposed to renewing the attack, McClellan reluctantly agreed to allow him to have his way. While the Confederate center was practically unmanned, however—before McClellan came up—Sumner had missed another splendid opportunity to knock Lee's army to pieces. It was but another in the series of fatal errors committed by the Federal corps commanders that day. It resulted in part from McClellan's concept of allowing his corps leaders to control the actual fighting of a battle, and was similar to the misfortune which befell the Confederate corps commanders at Gettysburg in July of 1863 while Lee stood idly by. In letting Sumner have his way here, and not insisting upon his own idea of permitting Franklin to attack, McClellan apparently determined not to risk everything for the sake of gaining everything—it was not going to be make or break so far as he was concerned. Although they had gained some ground and had inflicted staggering losses upon the enemy, McClellan's right corps had themselves been roughly handled.[35]

But, as a Southern colonel writes of the Union fortunes, " the great mistake . . . of the day was the delay of Burnside's attack until the afternoon," not the fighting on the Federal right and center. Had Burnside attacked promptly on the left early in the morning as McClellan had ordered, while the heavy blue attacks were in progress on the right, Palfrey thinks that " Lee's army must have been shattered, if not destroyed." The vital nature of the assault by the Federal left is emphasized by Swinton: " The part assigned to General Burnside was of the

[35] Wilson, *Under the Old Flag*, I, 113–14; Franklin's report, 27 *O.R.*, 377; E. W. Sheppard, *The Campaign in Virginia and Maryland* . . . (London, 1911), 265.

highest importance, for a successful attack by him upon the Confederate right would, by carrying the Sharpsburg crest, force Lee from his line of retreat by way of Shepherdstown." But the behavior of the commander of the Union left was inexplicable. Cox, who knew Burnside well, states of his superior, " He shrank from responsibility with sincere modesty." [36]

As seen before, McClellan, on the night of September 15, had ordered Burnside to reconnoiter the approaches to the Antietam Creek in the vicinity of the Burnside Bridge. During the day of the sixteenth, after much delay on Burnside's part, his corps was moved into position on the high ground above the eastern approaches to the span. McClellan had informed him that he would most likely be ordered to attack early on the morning of the seventeenth. Shortly after dawn on the seventeenth—before 7:00 A. M.—McClellan directed Burnside " to form his troops and hold them in readiness to assault the bridge in his front and to await further orders." Burnside passed on the order to Cox, and had his command in position to attack before 8:00 A. M.[37]

Then, at 8:00 A. M., McClellan issued the order to Burnside to move in force across the creek, seize the heights near Sharpsburg, and advance northward against Lee's right flank. The attack was to coincide with the heavy blows that McClellan was lauching on the enemy left. Opposed to Burnside's 13,000 men was D. R. Jones's small division of about 2,430 men. In the immediate area across the bridge, which Burnside had been instructed to carry, there were but approximately 500 soldiers in gray under Brigadier General Robert Toombs. But Burnside did not obey McClellan's order. Instead of mounting a large-scale attack, as McClellan expected, Burnside experimented with feeble demonstrations at the bridge, despite the army commander's repeated, urgent orders to move in force

---

[36] Allan, *Army of Northern Virginia*, 439; Palfrey, *The Antietam*, 107; Swinton, *Army of the Potomac*, 219; Cox, *Military Reminiscences*, I, 390.

[37] Powell, *Fifth Corps*, 271; McClellan's *Report*, 201, 208, 209; *M.O.S.*, 588–89; Palfrey, *The Antietam*, 59, 110–11; Toombs's report, 27 *O.R.*, 424, 890; 28 *O.R.*, 308.

against Lee's right. As the precious morning hours slipped away without an attack by the Ninth Corps, Lee removed two-thirds of the force confronting Burnside to the Confederate left to hold that portion of the field against Hooker, Mansfield, and Sumner. Yet, as the number of enemy troops facing him steadily diminished during the morning, Burnside failed to increase the tempo of his weak efforts at the bridge. Had he attacked only half-heartedly, Lee would have been unable to shift troops from his right to his left, with the strong likelihood that McClellan's assaults north of Sharpsburg would have been overwhelmingly successful and decisive.[38]

Apparently it never occurred to Burnside or Cox to test the depth of the water of the Antietam Creek. Had they done so, they would have found that it could have been waded easily at almost any place. Speaking of the enemy, one of Burnside's soldiers states, " He flouted us all the morning with hardly more than a meager skirmish line, while his coming troops, as fast as they arrived on the ground, were sent off to the Dunker Church." Brigadier General Isaac P. Rodman's division of the Ninth Corps was sent down the creek about a mile below the bridge to look for a ford, and spent several valuable hours wandering aimlessly about when it could have crossed at almost any point. Colonel George Crook's brigade—ordered to force its way across the bridge—could not find the span, although it had been on the ground for almost two days, and stopped when it reached the edge of the water about half a mile above the bridge. Burnside then contented himself with throwing just two regiments against the bridge. These weak sorties were easily repulsed by Toombs.[39]

At army headquarters, McClellan, after issuing at 8:00 A. M. his positive order for Burnside to cross the creek and seize the

[38] McClellan's *Report*, 209; Ropes, *Story of the Civil War*, II, 366, 372; reports of D. R. Jones, Lee, and Toombs, 27 *O.R.*, 149, 886, 889; Alexander, *Military Memoirs*, 265; Davis, " The Antietam Campaign," *loc. cit.*, 65, 66.
[39] Henry Kyd Douglas, *I Rode with Stonewall* . . . (Chapel Hill, 1940), 159–60, 172, 173; Davis, " The Antietam Campaign," *loc. cit.*, 65; David L. Thompson, " With Burnside at Antietam," *B. & L.*, II, 661; Palfrey, *The Antietam*, 111–12.

heights beyond, waited impatiently for word of the results of that movement in force. Not hearing from Burnside, McClellan sent an aide to him with instructions to press the attack " at all hazards." Learning that Burnside had failed to mount an effective assault, McClellan, at 9:00 A. M., dispatched his Inspector General, Colonel D. B. Sackett, with imperative orders to carry the bridge " at the point of bayonet " if necessary. Sackett was to remain with Burnside to see that the affair was pushed. *Three hours later*, at 12 Noon, finding that Burnside had still not moved in force to carry out his orders to cross the creek, McClellan sent Colonel T. M. Key to him with a very strong order, insisting that he overrun the bridge regardless of loss of life, since the day depended on it.[40]

But Burnside persisted in using only small forces to attack Toombs's tiny command of some five hundred men behind the bridge. Finally, at *1:00* P. M., the bridge was carried with but two Union regiments—the Fifty-first Pennsylvania and the Fifty-first New York—Toombs's men being scattered up the hill to the west of the span. Then, despite the fact that he had the foe on the run, Burnside halted until *3:00* P. M. The two Federal regiments were easily followed across the bridge by Brigadier General Samuel Sturgis' division and Crook's brigade, while Rodman's division finally crossed the creek near Snavely's Ford on the left. However, Burnside and Cox allowed Sturgis' division to retire upon the plea of that division commander that his men were exhausted, although they had not been heavily engaged thus far. Brigadier General Orlando B. Willcox's division replaced that of Sturgis. McClellan, learning that Burnside had sat down for two hours when once across the creek, with the enemy retreating in front of him, dispatched Captain William F. Biddle with a final order for Burnside to move forward. If this directive was not obeyed promptly, Biddle was to use

[40] McClellan's *Report*, 209; William F. Biddle, in *United Service Magazine*, May, 1894, as quoted in Powell, *Fifth Corps*, 280–81; D. B. Sackett to McClellan, February 20 and March 9, 1876, *M.O.S.*, 609–11; Upton, *Military Policy*, 381n; Cox, " The Battle of Antietam," *loc. cit.*, 651, 653; Paris, *The Civil War*, II, 346.

an order in McClellan's own handwriting which would remove Burnside from command of the Ninth Corps and replace him with Morell. Burnside began making preparations a little after 3:00 P. M., and finally, at about 4:00 o'clock, surged forward again, easily capturing the high ground to the west of the bridge and driving the few Confederates facing him back to the edge of town. The delay, however, was fatal for Burnside. It enabled A. P. Hill to arrive on the field from Harper's Ferry just in time to succor the hard pressed graycoats.[41]

Burnside's divisions of Willcox on the right and Rodman on the left were driving D. R. Jones's broken division before them when A. P. Hill's Light Division came up on Rodman's left flank, just as the Northerners seemed to have won a decisive success. A raw Federal regiment allowed Hill's men—who were wearing blue uniforms captured at Harper's Ferry—to approach too close before being challenged. Suddenly, there was a crash of musketry at short range from the advancing " bluecoats." The Unionists were in a position somewhat similar to that in which Sedgwick's unfortunate division had been earlier in the day. However, had Rodman's units been properly handled, they still might have withstood Hill's attack and thrown him back. But the left of Rodman's division was crushed, its commander falling mortally wounded while endeavoring to rally his retiring troops. In heavy fighting, lasting until dark, the outmaneuvered Burnside was pressed back to the heights overlooking the bridge, where he held at least a part of his gains. His inexcusable procrastination, despite McClellan's specific and repeated orders, cost the National commander a crushing victory over Lee. The repulse of his tardy attack on McClellan's left ended the Battle of Antietam.[42]

[41] Stine, *Army of the Potomac*, 218, 219; Palfrey, *The Antietam*, 112, 113; Biddle, *loc. cit.*, Powell, *Fifth Corps*, 281n; Lee's report, 27 *O.R.*, 141, 150; McClellan's *Report*, 209ff; Toombs's report, Swinton, *Army of the Potomac*, 220–21; Burnside's testimony, March 19, 1863, *C.C.W.*, I, 640; Alexander, *Military Memoirs*, 266.

[42] A. P. Hill's report, 27 *O.R.*, 423, 886, 890, 980ff; Palfrey, *The Antietam*, 113–14; Cox, " The Battle of Antietam," *B. & L.*, II, 655; Rhodes, *History of the United States*, IV, 152; Stine, *Army of the Potomac*, 219.

The war's bloodiest day—indeed, the day of the greatest carnage that has ever been seen on the American continents—was over. How ferocious the fighting was may be seen from the accounts of two eyewitnesses. Touring the battlefield the day after the combat, the veteran New York *Tribune* war correspondent, Albert D. Richardson, wrote as follows of what he saw:

> Between the fences of a road immediately beyond the cornfield, in a space one hundred yards long, I counted more than two hundred Rebel dead, lying where they fell. Elsewhere, over many acres, they were strewn singly, in groups, and occasionally in masses, piled up almost like cordwood. They were lying—some with the human form undistinguishable, others with no outward indication of wounds—in all the strange positions of violent death. All had blackened faces. There were forms with every rigid muscle strained in fierce agony, and those with hands folded peacefully upon the bosom; some still clutching their guns, others with arms upraised, and one with a single open finger pointing to heaven. Several remained hanging over a fence which they were climbing when the fatal shot struck them.[43]

The Fifth Corps historian, Lieutenant Colonel William H. Powell, a hardened Regular Army officer and seasoned campaigner, describes the Antietam battlefield immediately after the great struggle in this way:

> The historian of this work rode over it . . . particularly that part where Generals Hooker and Sumner fought. He passed where now blighted stalks only indicated the field of waving corn when the battle commenced, and saw the dead lying all through its aisles; then cut into the barren field beyond where bodies attired mainly in Confederate uniforms were lying in ranks so regular that they must have been mowed down in swaths. Burying parties were already busily engaged, and had put away to rest many Union men. Still, here, as everywhere, they were scattered over the fields. The ground was strewn

[43] Albert D. Richardson, *The Secret Service* . . . (Hartford, 1865), 288–89.

290

with muskets, knapsacks, cartridge boxes, and articles of clothing, with the carcasses of horses, and with thousands of shot
and shell. Glancing at each corpse, he passed on to the road
by the Dunkard Church. Could it be that those were the faces
of his late antagonists? They were so absolutely black that
they looked almost as if they might be negroes. Their eyes
in many instances were protruding from their sockets; their
heads, hands, and limbs were swollen to twice their natural
size. Their marred and bloated remains, emptied of all that
made them manlike—human—were simply repulsive.

And thus it was, with an almost sickening sensation he
rode over this graveyard of unburied dead. No matter in what
direction he turned, it was all the same shocking picture,
awakening awe rather than pity, benumbing the senses rather
than touching the heart, glazing the eye with horror rather
than filling it with tears. And this was war in all its hideous-
ness.[44]

At 8:00 A. M. on September 18—the day after the battle—
McClellan telegraphed Halleck, " The battle of yesterday continued for fourteen hours, and until after dark. We held all we
gained, except a portion on the extreme left; that was obliged
to abandon a part of what it had gained. Our losses very heavy,
especially in general officers. The battle will probably be renewed
today. Send all the troops you can by the most expeditious
route." However, on the morning of the eighteenth, Burnside
was so demoralized that he felt he could not trust his own troops
to hold even his modest gains of the day before. Consequently,
McClellan sent him Morell's division as a reinforcement. This
example of Burnside's lack of mental stability was to be repeated
a number of times throughout the war, especially at Fredericksburg and Petersburg. Writing to his wife twelve days after
Antietam, as he was about to compile his official report of the
battle, McClellan stated, " I ought to treat Burnside *very*
severely, and probably will; yet I hate to do it. He is very slow;
is not fit to command more than a regiment. If I treat him

[44] Powell, *Fifth Corps*, 302–303.

as he deserves he will be my mortal enemy hereafter. If I do not praise him as thinks he deserves, and I know he does not, he will be at least a very lukewarm friend." [45]

After careful consideration, McClellan determined to attack on the nineteenth, rather than risk what he had gained by an attack with jaded soldiers on the eighteenth. He was aware, of course, that his troops had done the attacking at both South Mountain and Antietam. McClellan wrote in his official report of the campaign, " At this critical juncture I should have had a narrow view of the condition of the country had I been willing to hazard another battle with less than an absolute assurance of success. At that moment—Virginia lost, Washington menaced, Maryland invaded—the national cause could afford no risks of defeat. One battle lost, and almost all would have been lost. Lee's army might have then marched as it pleased on Washington, Baltimore, Philadelphia, or New York. It could have levied its supplies from a fertile and undevastated country; extorted tribute from wealthy and populous cities; and nowhere east of the Alleghanies was there another organized force able to arrest its march." [46]

The Army of the Potomac was really only in a semi-organized condition when it had been obliged to enter immediately upon an active campaign right on the heels of Pope's debacle at Second Bull Run. Now, the day after Antietam, many of McClellan's units were suffering from hunger; supplies had not yet arrived; forage was lacking. All of his corps commanders but one were opposed to a renewal of the battle on the eighteenth. His senior corps commander since the army was formed—Sumner—was quite vehement in his opposition to continuing the attacks. Testifying under oath, Sumner asserted, " It had been a very severe action—uncommonly severe. . . . Troops are not exactly prepared to make a rapid pursuit the next day after such a battle as that. . . . Knowing that . . .

---

[45] McClellan to Halleck, September 18, 1862, 28 *O.R.*, 322; McClellan to his wife, September 29, 1862, *M.O.S.*, 607, 616.

[46] McClellan's *Report*, 211.

reinforcements were on the march from Washington, I thought it was prudent for the general to halt a little after that severe action until his reinforcements came up." The reinforcements of which Sumner spoke were the excellent divisions of Couch and Humphreys, which arrived at Antietam about noon on the eighteenth. Had not Humphreys' division been detained for a day at Frederick by orders from Washington, it is unknown to what valuable use it may have been put by McClellan during the battle on the seventeenth. The fact of the matter was that, on the eighteenth, both armies were utterly exhausted after one of the longest sustained combats of a single day of the war. Neither force could march on the eighteenth, let alone fight effectively. Most of the men were practically out on their feet. As an example, eight Union regiments suffered over fifty-five per cent casualties of their numbers engaged.[47]

During the night of September 18, Lee abandoned the field of battle—including many of his dead and wounded soldiers—and, at Shepherdstown, retreated across the Potomac into Virginia. According to Livermore, out of approximately 69,000 available effectives at Antietam, McClellan absorbed the following losses: 2,108 killed, 9,549 wounded, 753 missing—an aggregate loss of 12,410. Lee suffered the following casualties out of probably 57,000 engaged: 2,700 killed, 9,024 wounded, 2,000 missing—a total loss of 13,724.[48]

McClellan's impressions of the battle were contained in a letter which he wrote to Ellen early on the morning of the eighteenth: " We fought yesterday a terrible battle against the entire rebel army. The battle continued fourteen hours; the fighting on both sides was superb. The general result was in our favor; that is to say, we gained a great deal of ground and

[47] Goss, *Recollections*, 112; Swinton, *Army of the Potomac*, 222; Wilson, *Under the Old Flag*, I, 117–18; Sumner's testimony, February 18, 1863, *C.C.W.*, I, 369; Hood, *Advance and Retreat*, 45; Lee's report, 27 *O.R.*, 152; Fox, *Regimental Losses*, 136–37.

[48] Swinton, *Army of the Potomac*, 222; Palfrey, *The Antietam*, 49; Livermore, *Numbers and Losses*, 92–94; McClellan's *Report*, 213; see also Joseph K. Barnes (ed.), *The Medical and Surgical History of the War of the Rebellion (1861–65)* . . . (Washington, 1875–88), Part I, lviii; Palfrey, *The Antietam*, 127.

held it. It was a success, but whether a decided victory depends on what occurs today." In his official report, McClellan continued to be reluctant to claim an overwhelming victory: " We had attacked the enemy in a position selected by the experienced engineer then in person directing their operations. We had driven them from their line on one flank, and secured a footing within it on the other. The army of the Potomac, notwithstanding the moral effect incident to previous reverses, had achieved a victory over an adversary invested with the prestige of recent success. Our soldiers slept that night on a field won by their valor and covered with the dead and wounded of the enemy." [49]

The importance of McClellan's success at Antietam is undisputed. James Ford Rhodes—never enthusiastic in ascribing any great military genius to McClellan—states with acumen, " To one who is biassed by the feeling that Lee had by this time shown himself almost invincible, it will be natural to speak well of the general who overcame him in any way on any terms. . . . Let us note the change of feeling at the North from depression before South Mountain to buoyancy after Antietam; let us reflect that a signal Confederate victory in Maryland might have caused the Northern voters at the approaching fall elections to declare for the peace that Jefferson Davis would offer from the head of Lee's victorious army, and that without McClellan's victory the Emancipation Proclamation would have been postponed and might never have been issued! " Frank L. Owsley, student of Confederate diplomatic history, asserts that only Lee's repulse in Maryland kept the British government from intervening in the war and probably recognizing Southern independence. Samuel Flagg Bemis states that the news of Antietam discouraged Palmerston and Russell from recognition of the Confederacy, and led to the English cabinet's decision against mediation and intervention. Diplomatically speaking, Bailey terms Antietam one of the world's most decisive battles.

[49] McClellan t~ his wife, September 18, 1862, *M.O.S.*, 612–13; McClellan's *Report*, 211.

Longstreet acknowledged the Confederate failure in Maryland against McClellan and the Union Army in this way: " The razing of the walls of Jericho by encircling marches of priests and soldiers, at the signal of long-drawn blasts of sacred horns and shouts of the multitude, was scarcely a greater miracle than the transformation of the conquering army of the South into a horde of disordered fugitives before an army that two weeks earlier was flying to cover under its homeward ramparts." [50]

Handicapped by the continual overestimates of Confederate numbers and by poor execution on the part of several of his corps commanders, and perhaps expected to accomplish more than was probable with an army which had recently been vanquished, disorganized, and humiliated, McClellan had none-theless at Antietam won a strategic success of inestimable consequence in the bloodiest single day's battle ever fought on the shores of the New World—a combat which claimed more casualties in one turn of the earth than have ever been suffered before or since by the American people in arms.

---

[50] Rhodes, *History of the United States*, IV, 154, 156; Frank Lawrence Owsley, *King Cotton Diplomacy* . . . (Chicago, 1931) , 360; Bemis, *Diplomatic History of the United States*, 373; Bailey, *Diplomatic History of the American People*, 364; Longstreet, *Manassas to Appomattox*, 239, 283.

Chapter Eleven

"He was not a Caesar"

Hard is the fate of those who serve republics.
—*William H. (Bull Run) Russell*

COULD the retreating Confederate Army be attacked in its retrograde movement across the Potomac and into the Old Dominion? McClellan, determining to test the enemy rear guard, got a sharp answer to this question. After an initial success on September 19, elements of Porter's Fifth Corps were sharply repulsed on the twentieth at the Shepherdstown crossing by Jackson's covering forces. Although a small affair, it showed the Federal commander that a hasty pursuit would not be an easy matter. It is the opinion of Confederate General Alexander that, " after the battle of Sharpsburg, rest, reorganization, and supplies were badly needed by both armies," and Lee voiced the same view. The Maryland campaign had been defensive in purpose on the part of the Federals, and McClellan had been forced to improvise on many things because of the poor condition of his army. Before resuming the grand offensive into Virginia, with the winter season approaching, he was first obliged to organize his army on an adequate scale for sustained operations.[1]

Surveying the plight of his army after Antietam, the Federal commander saw that there was a considerable lack of clothing and camp equipment, as well as a deficiency in cavalry horses. The Army of the Potomac had suffered a loss of ten general

[1] Jackson's report, 27 *O.R.*, 957; Powell, *Fifth Corps*, 293–301; Smith, *118th Pennsylvania*, 54–94; Fox, *Regimental Losses*, 293.

296

officers, and several corps had been badly shattered in the action of September 17. All this required time and attention to rectify. Then, too, McClellan did not have transportation at his disposal for even a single day's supply of food and forage were he to contemplate an immediate advance into Virginia. " Under these circumstances," declared the General in his official report, " I did not feel authorized to cross the river with the main army over a deep and difficult ford in pursuit of the retreating enemy, known to be in strong force on the south bank, and thereby place that stream, which was liable at any time to rise above a fording stage, between my army and its base of supply." In the pause after Antietam, the Southern Army went into bivouac first in the vicinity of Martinsburg, then at Winchester, while the National Army assumed a position near Harper's Ferry.[2]

There ensued then, for a period of about five weeks, a struggle between McClellan on the one hand, trying to get the needed supplies for his army, and the War Department on the other, which seemed unable to put them into his hands. On September 20, Welles recorded in his diary that Stanton and Chase were sneering at McClellan's " permitting " Lee to cross the Potomac into Virginia. " There is no abatement of hostility to McClellan," wrote Welles of the cabinet. Chase, visiting the wounded Hooker at a Washington hospital, told him that as early as the Union victory at Malvern Hill he had advised the administration to remove McClellan from command. Chase hinted, too, that the Army of the Potomac had been recalled from the Peninsula in order to get rid of McClellan. On the twenty-fifth of September, Welles said that " Stanton is dissatisfied, and he and those under his influence do not sustain and encourage McClellan." If it was the duty of the Secretary of War to support and assist his commanders in the field, then, as regards McClellan, Stanton does not seem to have made much effort to do so. On the same day, Hay noted in his diary that

[2] McClellan's *Report*, 216; Palfrey, *The Antietam*, 129–30; Goss, *Recollections*, 118; Paris, *The Civil War*, II, 538–39; Ropes, *Story of the Civil War*, II, 436.

Lincoln " said that McC was doing nothing to make himself respected or feared." [3]

The Radicals in Congress now resumed their smear campaign against McClellan, in spite of his recent victories. They termed him the same old coward, procrastinator, and traitor as before. Stories were circulated by the Radicals of McClellan's alleged treason at Antietam, where he was charged with sneaking into Lee's tent on the night of the sixteenth to receive his " instructions " from the Confederate commander as to how Lee wanted him to fight the battle the next day, as well as receiving and obeying later orders from Lee not to pursue the retreating Southern Army until it could escape across the Potomac.[4]

The twenty-second of September was a momentous date. On that day, Lincoln issued the Emancipation Proclamation. He said to the cabinet at that time, " The action of the army against the rebels has not been quite what I should have liked. But they have been driven out of Maryland, and Pennsylvania is no longer in danger of invasion. When the rebel army was at Frederick, I determined, as soon as it should be driven out of Maryland, to issue a Proclamation of Emancipation such as I thought most likely to be useful. . . . The rebel army is now driven out." [5] Thus, while McClellan had won enough of a victory to enable the President to issue the famous manifesto, apparently, according to Lincoln, he had not quite achieved the complete victory wanted.

No sooner had things quieted down on the upper Potomac, than a sharp exchange began again between McClellan and Halleck. The General-in-Chief wired his field commander on the twentieth, " We are still left entirely in the dark in regard to your own movements and those of the enemy. This should

---

[3] Richard B. Irwin, " The Removal of McClellan," *B. & L.*, III, 102–103; *Welles's Diary*, I, 142, 148; *Hay's Diary*, 51.

[4] Sydney H. Gay to A. S. Hill, September 25, 1862, Rhodes, *History of the United States*, IV, 184–85; Edgar Conckling to Joseph Holt, November 8, 1864, Joseph Holt Papers, Division of Manuscripts, Library of Congress.

[5] *Chase's Diary*, 87–88.

not be so. You should keep me advised of both, so far as you know them." McClellan replied to this barb with a brusque telegram of his own: " I telegraphed you yesterday all I knew, and had nothing more to inform you of until this evening. . . . I regret that you find it necessary to couch every dispatch I have the honor to receive from you in a spirit of fault-finding, and that you have not found leisure to say one word in commendation of the recent achievements of this army, or even to allude to them." McClellan revealed his future plans in a letter home at this time, declaring, " My present intention is to . . . go to work and reorganize the army. . . . It may be that, now that the government is pretty well over their scare, they will begin again with their persecutions and throw me overboard again. . . . My own judgment is to watch the line of the Potomac until the water rises, then to . . . reorganize the army as promptly as possible, and then if secesh remains near Winchester to attack him. If he retires, to follow him up and attack him near Richmond." [6]

On the first of October, Lincoln left Washington for a three-day visit to the Army of the Potomac near Harper's Ferry. He had told Assistant Secretary of the Interior J. P. Usher that he had expected McClellan to follow up his victory at Antietam by immediately crossing the Potomac and pressing hard after Lee. " After the battle of Antietam," the President said later to Hay, " I went up to the field to try to get [McClellan] to move." [7]

Arriving by rail in western Maryland, the President was escorted by McClellan and his top generals on a tour of the battlefields of South Mountain and Antietam. He also reviewed the troops. A Federal officer noted that Lincoln " looked pale and worn." " The President has . . . been well received " by the soldiers, wrote a Union surgeon, " but by no means so

---

[6] Halleck to McClellan, McClellan to Halleck, September 20, 1862, *C.C.W.*, I, 493; McClellan to his wife, September 22, 23, and 25, 1862, *M.O.S.*, 614–15.

[7] *Welles's Diary*, I, 157, 161; J. P. Usher, in Allen Thorndike Rice (ed.), *Reminiscences of Abraham Lincoln by Distinguished Men of his Time* (New York, 1888), 99; *Hay's Diary*, 218.

enthusiastically as General McClellan." The General told Lincoln that he was as anxious to move forward as was the President, and that he would do so as soon as possible. McClellan's reasons for not moving at once were satisfactory, said the Chief Executive, who then asserted that the needed supplies would be sent forthwith from the capital.[8]

The Union commander's account of his interview with the President was as follows:

> I urged him to follow a conservative course [as to slavery and emancipation], and supposed from the tenor of his conversation that he would do so. He more than once assured me that he was fully satisfied with my whole course from the beginning; that the only fault he could possibly find was that I was perhaps too prone to be sure that everything was ready before acting, but that my actions were all right when I started. I said to him that I thought a few experiments with those who acted before they were ready would probably convince him that in the end I consumed less time than they did. He told me that he regarded me as the only general in the service capable of organizing and commanding a large army, and that he would stand by me. . . . He told me . . . that he would stand by me against " all comers"; that he wished me to continue my preparations for a new campaign, not to stir an inch until fully ready, and when ready to do what I thought best. He repeated that he was entirely satisfied with me; that I should be let alone; that he would stand by me. I have no doubt that he meant exactly what he said. He parted from me with the utmost cordiality.[9]

The President's visit to the army and his conference with its commander was described by McClellan to Allen Thorndike Rice after the war. The General said that he believed the President had really intended to grant him all the time needed

[8] Richard Eddy, *History of the Sixtieth New York* . . . (Philadelphia, 1864), 185; Ellis' *Diary*, 306; William H. Hurlbert, *General McClellan* . . . (New York, 1864), 297–98; Cox, *Military Reminiscences*, I, 365–67, 376; Powell, *Fifth Corps*, 309.

[9] McClellan to his wife, October 2 and 5, 1862, *M.O.S.*, 627–28, 654, 655.

for reorganization. According to McClellan, Lincoln said to him on the battlefield, " General, you have saved the country. You must remain in command and carry us through to the end." " That will be impossible," replied Little Mac. " We need time. The influences at Washington will be too strong for you, Mr. President. I will not be allowed the required time for preparation." Lincoln answered by stating, " General, I pledge myself to stand between you and harm." " I honestly believe," said McClellan, " that the President meant every word he said, but that the influences at Washington, as I predicted, were too strong for him or any living man." On the Confederate side, while Lincoln was visiting the Union Army, Lee was astute enough soldier to comprehend the probable condition of his adversary. He wrote to Jefferson Davis on October 2, " I think [McClellan] is yet unable to move, and finds difficulty in procuring provisions more than sufficient from day to day." [10]

Then, an inexplicable thing happened. Just two days after Lincoln left the Army of the Potomac, McClellan was astonished to receive the following dispatch from Halleck: " The President directs that you cross the Potomac and give battle to the enemy, or drive him south. Your army must move now, while the roads are good." Halleck stated that if McClellan advanced east of the Blue Ridge he would be given 30,000 reinforcements, while if he moved up the Shenandoah Valley west of that range —as he had originally intended—he would receive but 12,000 to 15,000 additional troops. The General-in-Chief said that the President advised, but did not order the route east of the Blue Ridge, preferring it because it would place the Union Army closer to Washington. The order was then qualified with Halleck's stating that Lincoln was " very desirous " that McClellan " move as soon as possible." He declared that he had been instructed to say that both he and Stanton concurred in this Presidential directive. In reply to Halleck, McClellan said that, after a conference with several of his corps commanders, he still

---

[10] Rice (ed.), *Reminiscences of Abraham Lincoln,* xxxix–xl; Lee to Davis, October 2, 1862, 28 *O.R.,* 644.

determined to advance up the Shenandoah Valley so as to prevent Lee from again invading Maryland by that route. However, if the enemy retreated southward from Winchester, the line of Federal advance up the Shenandoah would then be unsatisfactory, due to the long line of communications by wagon road. He asserted that his First, Fifth, and Sixth corps were in need of shoes, clothing, and tents. However, he pledged that he would not lose an hour in striving to carry out the wishes of his superiors to advance " as soon as possible." [11]

Meanwhile, the role of the army in politics was a point of serious discussion among the men in uniform after the President had issued his Emancipation Proclamation on September 22. There was considerable opposition to the edict among some soldiers and officers in the Army of the Potomac, which even extended so far as talk of revolutionary intrigues against the government. As a result, McClellan called a number of his generals into conference. He stated that he agreed with them that the army must remain aloof from politics and take no part in the discussions over the proclamation.[12] As a result of this conference and of his determination to concern himself strictly with military matters, McClellan, on October 7, issued the important General Orders No. 163, a copy of which was transmitted to President Lincoln. This manifesto contained McClellan's views on civil-military relations, and should be noted in some detail. It stated:

> The Constitution confides to the civil authorities—legislative, judicial, and executive—the power and duty of making, expounding, and executing the Federal laws. Armed forces are raised and supported simply to sustain the civil authorities, and are to be held in strict subordination thereto in all respects. This fundamental rule of our political system is essential to the security of our republican institutions, and should be thoroughly understood and observed by every

---

[11] Halleck to McClellan, October 6, 1862, McClellan to Halleck, October 7, 1862, *C.C.W.*, I, 507–508, 514–15, 516–17, 517–18.
[12] Cox, *Military Reminiscences*, I, 359–62.

soldier. The principle upon which, and the object for which, armies shall be employed in suppressing rebellion must be determined and declared by the civil authorities, and the Chief Executive, who is charged with the administration of the national affairs, is the proper and only source through which the needs and orders of the Government can be made known to the armies of the nation.

Discussions by officers and soldiers concerning public measures determined upon and declared by the government, when carried at once beyond temperate and respectful expressions of opinion, tend greatly to impair and destroy the discipline and efficiency of troops by substituting the spirit of political faction for that firm, steady, and earnest support of the authority of the Government which is the highest duty of the American soldier. The remedy for political errors, if any are committed, is to be found only in the action of the people at the polls.

In thus calling the attention of this army to the true relation between the soldier and the Government, the general commanding merely adverts to an evil against which it has been thought advisable, during our whole history, to guard the armies of the Republic, and in so doing he will not be considered by any right-minded person as casting any reflection upon that loyalty and good conduct which has been so fully illustrated upon so many battle-fields.[13]

Although not personally agreeing with the wisdom of the President's sweeping decree, McClellan's admirable order apparently stifled for the time any revolutionary mutterings then prevalent in his army against the administration.

The extremely low water existing in the Potomac at this time rendered it impossible for McClellan to cover thoroughly the entire length of the river. On October 10, the enterprising Confederate cavalry leader, Jeb Stuart, accompanied by 1,800 troopers and several relays of fresh horses, commenced his second ride around the Federal Army. Crossing the Potomac above Williamsport, Stuart moved to Chambersburg, Pennsyl-

[13] 28 *O.R.*, 395.

vania, seized some horses, burnt some supplies, and recrossed the river on the twelfth at White's Ford near Poolesville. Pursued by 800 Union cavalrymen under Pleasonton and Averell, Stuart, with his fresh relays of horses, managed to elude his pursuers, who had no fresh mounts available. Pleasonton covered seventy-eight miles in twenty-four hours, and Averell rode two hundred miles in forty-eight hours, but all to no avail. At one point, Stuart's troopers—some of whom were wearing blue uniforms—were mistaken for Federals and remained unchallenged. McClellan had done everything humanly possible to cut Jeb off; but, aided by extraordinary good fortune, Stuart was able at this season of the year to recross the Potomac at almost any place he chose. The daring enemy exploit caused faces to redden in the North. Although the raid had actually done little damage, and had not endangered McClellan's army in the slightest, Lincoln was furious. McClellan's stock fell even lower in official Washington.[14]

A serious lack of essential supplies for his men—such as clothing, shoes, and tents—and the failure to forward adequate numbers of replacements of cavalry horses were the chief factors which prevented McClellan from rapidly getting the army in condition to renew the offensive campaign against Lee in Virginia. In a message to Halleck on October 11, McClellan mentioned these deficiencies. He felt that perhaps it was due to bad management on the part of the railroads. It is not known precisely where the fault lay. Colonel Powell states that, later, " upon investigation, train loads of supplies for the army were found on the tracks at Washington, where some of the cars had been for weeks." [15]

Realizing the vital importance of an adequate cavalry force, especially for an army about to invade hostile territory, McClellan became more concerned over the poor condition of that

[14] McClellan's *Report*, 219–21; Stine, *Army of the Potomac*, 225–29; Freeman, *Lee's Lieutenants*, II, 284–309; John G. Nicolay to Therena Bates, October 13, 1862, Nicolay Papers, Division of Manuscripts, Library of Congress.

[15] McClellan to Halleck, October 11, 1862, *C.C.W.*, I, 521; Ingalls' report, 27 *O.R.*, 78; Powell, *Fifth Corps*, 310–11.

McClellan in the years after Appomattox

arm. " It is absolutely necessary," he asserted to the General-in-Chief on October 12, " that some energetic means be taken to supply the cavalry of this army with remount horses. The present rate of supply is 1,050 per week for the entire army here and in front of Washington. From this number the artillery draw for their batteries." Cavalry commander Pleasonton wrote to Marcy that, " in consequence of the weakness of the battery horses, they having marched seventy-eight miles in the last twenty-four hours, they could not move the [artillery pieces]. . . . The horses could not pull up the hill, and I was obliged to use men." In still another communiqué to Halleck, McClellan said that he could collect no more than 1,000 mounted men to pursue Stuart. " Our cavalry," he continued, " has been constantly occupied in scouting and reconnoissances, and this severe labor has worked down the horses and rendered many of them unserviceable, so that at this time no more than one-half of our cavalry are fit for active service in the field."[16]

Then, on October 13, the President entered the scene again. In a long dispatch to McClellan, he chided the General on his alleged overcaution, saying that the fine autumn days must be used to advance against the enemy. He had much to say about lines of supply and communication. Claiming that McClellan was on the chord while Lee was on the arc of a circle, Lincoln argued that the Federals could outrace the enemy to Richmond. He did not seem to see that Lee would, in such an event, most likely allow McClellan to move a respectable ways toward Richmond and then move to cut the Union supply lines, as he had done to Pope in August, or else he would reinvade Maryland. The President told McClellan that, in his opinion, the line of advance east of the Blue Ridge would be better than the one up the Shenandoah Valley, because the former route would cover Washington more directly. He concluded by saying, " It is all easy if our troops march as well as the enemy; and it is unmanly to say that they cannot do it. This letter

[16] McClellan to Halleck, October 12, 1862, 27 *O.R.*, 77; Pleasonton to Marcy, October 12, 1862, *C.C.W.*, I, 522–23.

is in no sense an order." Nonetheless, it was true that the Federals were not then quite such good marchers, on the whole, as the Confederates—a fact which Halleck himself admitted.[17]

There ensued then the famous verbal exchange between McClellan and Lincoln over the condition and services of the Union cavalry. It began on October 25 with a wire from Mc-Clellan to Halleck, in which he quoted from the official report of Colonel Robert Williams—a former regular army cavalry officer, then commanding the First Massachusetts Cavalry—who pointed out some of the reasons for the run-down condition of the cavalry mounts, including sore tongue, lameness, fatigue, etc. Reading this dispatch, Lincoln lost his temper and dashed off the following barbed message to McClellan: " I have just read your dispatch about sore tongue and fatigued horses. Will you pardon me for asking what the horses of your army have done since the battle of Antietam that fatigues anything? " McClel-lan, not appreciating the President's sarcasm, nevertheless replied calmly in a lengthy communiqué. He gave the details of the severe work of his cavalry since he had left Washington on the seventh of September, including its picketing and scout-ing duties along 150 miles of the Potomac River, as well as reconnaissances and skirmishes during the pursuit of Stuart. " Indeed," said the General to Lincoln, " it has performed harder service since the battle [of Antietam] than before." He pointed out that the Federal cavalry arm was " in low con-dition " at the start of the Maryland campaign, following its ill-usage by Pope in the Second Bull Run venture. He con-cluded by stoutly averring, " If any instance can be found where overworked cavalry has performed more labor than mine since the battle of Antietam, I am not conscious of it." [18]

The following morning, the President resumed the argu-ment. He acknowledged to McClellan, " Yours in reply to

---

[17] Lincoln to McClellan, October 13, 1862, *C.C.W.*, I, 524–25; see Henderson, *Stonewall Jackson*, II, 295–96.

[18] McClellan to Halleck, Lincoln to McClellan, McClellan to Lincoln, October 25, 1862, *C.C.W.*, I, 546, 547.

mine about horses received. Of course you know the facts better
than I." Then, however, Lincoln claimed that the Confederate
cavalry " outmarched ours, having certainly done more marked
service on the peninsula and everywhere since." McClellan,
however, would not let this slur on his cavalry go unanswered.
That very day he replied to the President, giving a statement
as to the relative service of the two rival mounted arms. He
stated that the Chief Executive had been misinformed, and gave
a detailed day-by-day account of his cavalry's operations and
combats, showing its large scope of activity. McClellan declared
that, except for Stuart's two rides around the Union Army,
the blueclad cavalry had bettered the gray knights in most of
the horse jousts which had been fought. He asserted that Stuart
had naturally "outmarched" Pleasonton because the enemy
had fresh relays of horses in their latest ride, and had stolen
others in Pennsylvania; but he added that the Confederate
cavalryman had been obliged to leave behind him many broken
down mounts. "I know," said McClellan, "you would not
intentionally do injustice to the excellent officers and men"
of this branch. On the following day, Lincoln capitulated. In
a wire to McClellan on the twenty-seventh, the President
declared, " Most certainly I intend no injustice to any, and,
if I have done any, I deeply regret it." He admitted McClellan's
facts, as related by the General, to be unchallengeable. The
cheerless news received recently, he said, " may have forced
something of impatience into my despatches." [19]

With the rising of the water in the Potomac, and with the
eventual arrival of the bulk of his needed supplies, McClellan
set the large army in motion across the river on October 26.[20]
In order to obtain 20,000 reinforcements from Washington, he
decided to advance east of the Blue Ridge, as Lincoln had
urged. The bulk of Lee's army was at Winchester, in the
Shenandoah Valley, west of the Blue Ridge. A secondary Con-

---

[19] Lincoln to McClellan, McClellan to Lincoln, October 26, 1862, Lincoln to
McClellan, October 28, 1862, *ibid.*, 547, 548–49.

[20] Swinton, *Army of the Potomac*, 226; 27 *O.R.*, 11; 28 *O.R.*, 464, 626.

federate base of supplies had been established at Staunton, which provided safer lines of communication for Lee than did Richmond.[21] McClellan's plan of operations was set forth in his official report:

> The plan of campaign I adopted during this advance was to move the army, well in hand, parallel to the Blue Ridge, taking Warrenton as the point of direction for the main army; seizing each pass in the Blue Ridge by detachments, as we approached it, and guarding them after we had passed as long as they would enable the enemy to trouble our communications with the Potomac. It was expected that we would unite with the eleventh corps and Sickles' division near Thoroughfare Gap. We depended upon Harper's Ferry and Berlin for supplies until the Manassas Gap railway was reached; when that occurred the passes in our rear were to be abandoned, and the army massed ready for action or movement in any direction.
>
> It was my intention if, upon reaching Ashby's or any other pass, I found that the enemy were in force between it and the Potomac in the valley of the Shenandoah, to move into the valley and gain their rear.
>
> I hardly hoped to accomplish this, but did expect that by striking in between Culpeper Court House and Little Washington I could either separate their army and beat them in detail, or else force them to concentrate as far back as Gordonsville, and thus place the army of the Potomac in position either to adopt the Fredericksburg line of advance upon Richmond, or to be removed to the Peninsula, if, as I apprehended, it were found impossible to supply it by the Orange and Alexandria railroad beyond Culpeper.[22]

If the Union commander could move rapidly enough when once across the Potomac, there was the likelihood that Lee would be able to move only one of his two corps up the Valley in time to interpose between McClellan and the Confederate base,

[21] Allan, *Army of Northern Virginia*, 451–52; Alexander, *Military Memoirs*, 279.
[22] McClellan's *Report*, 235–36.

thus leaving the Southern Army divided into two isolated wings.[23] That McClellan's strategy was sound is shown by the fact that Lee fervently hoped the National Army would advance up the Valley rather than east of the Blue Ridge.[24]

The Ninth Corps led the Union advance across the Potomac on October 26, the fording being made by pontoon bridge at Berlin, five miles below Harper's Ferry. By November 2, the whole army had crossed, except Slocum's Twelfth Corps, which was left to garrison Harper's Ferry. Although good progress was made on the whole, Palfrey states that " heavy rains and the distribution of supplies that arrived late, delayed the movement somewhat." Then, shortly after noon on the twenty-sixth, Halleck dispatched a most important message to McClellan: " Since you left Washington . . . I have given you no orders. I do not give you any now. The government has instructed you with defeating and driving back the rebel army in your front. I shall not attempt to control you in the measures you may adopt for that purpose. . . . The President has left you at liberty to adopt them, or not, as you may deem best." However, while visiting the army in the first days of October, Lincoln had told Cox that he had left " definite direction " of military operations to the General-in-Chief. But, in the message quoted above, Halleck deferred to McClellan's judgment the control of the operations then underway. In other words, McClellan had been given practically a free hand in his movements by the President and the Commanding General. But, at the same time, Nicolay wrote Hay that Lincoln was becoming more and more irritated with McClellan and intended to prod him to move faster.[25]

Meanwhile, the Army of the Potomac was advancing steadily. Moving southward toward Warrenton, McClellan masked his movement by holding the gaps of the Blue Ridge as long as

[23] See Powell, *Fifth Corps*, 311.

[24] Lee to W. W. Loring, September 25, 1862, 28 *O.R.*, 82ff, 626; see Freeman, *R. E. Lee*, II, 424.

[25] Swinton, *Army of the Potomac*, 226; Palfrey, *The Antietam*, 131; McClellan's *Report*, 235; Halleck to McClellan, October 26, 1862, *C.C.W.*, I, 550; Cox, *Military Reminiscences*, I, 366; Nicolay to Hay, October 26, 1862, Nicolay Papers.

they could be used by the enemy to menace his communications. By threatening to push through one or more of them and fall upon a segment of Lee's army on its parallel march up the Valley, he forced the Confederate leader to keep Jackson's corps in the Valley near Winchester and Millwood. Writing briefly to Ellen at the commencement of his active operations, McClellan said, " I move a respectable number of troops across the Potomac today, the beginning of the general movement, which will, however, require several days to accomplish, for the cavalry is still terribly off. Yesterday a telegram received from the President asking what my ' cavalry had done since the battle of Antietam to fatigue anything.' It was one of those little flings that I can't get used to when they are not merited." [26]

With the Federal Army now advancing into Virginia, Secretary of War Stanton repeated a procedure which he had used before against McClellan at the termination of the Peninsula campaign. On October 27, he asked a series of loaded questions of Halleck, apparently designed and worded so as to obtain answers which would place the blame for the delay in the army's movement on McClellan, thereby absolving from censure the bureaus (especially the Quartermaster Department) of his own War Department as well as the General-in-Chief's office. McClellan was uninformed of this action, and was therefore not given an opportunity to answer the charges raised against him in the questions by Stanton. Unlike McClellan, Hitchcock, and Welles, Halleck had not the backbone to stand up for the men in the field against the Secretary. In his reply to Stanton's interrogations, Old Wooden Head gave him the answers he wanted to use against McClellan. " In my opinion," said Halleck—who had not had the inclination even to inspect the army in the field—" there has been no such want of supplies in the army under General McClellan as to prevent his compliance with the orders to advance against the enemy." The fact that Halleck, just a few days before, had stated to McClellan that

[26] Palfrey, *The Antietam*, 131; Stine, *Army of the Potomac*, 234–35; McClellan to his wife, October 26, 1862, *M.O.S.*, 656.

he had given him no orders whatsoever, was not mentioned by him in his reply to Stanton. Also, as seen, the President had stated that he had placed the control of active military operations in the hands of the General-in-Chief. It will be remembered that the directive of October 6 to McClellan to move had been qualified by the phrase, " as soon as possible." The army commander in the field was the best judge as to what was needed by his forces. He was better able to appraise this situation than Halleck, seated immovable at his desk in Washington. However, Halleck contradicted himself on October 28 by telling Heintzelman that " Mr. Lincoln has controlled military operations the past four weeks." [27]

To add to the confusion, a cabinet meeting took place on these matters. According to Welles's account of it in his diary on November 4, the conclave went as follows:

> Stanton, whose dislike of McC increases, says that Halleck does not consider himself responsible for army movements or deficiencies this side of the mountains. . . .
>
> The President did not assent to the last remarks of Stanton . . . but said Halleck should be, and would be, considered responsible, for he (the President) had told him (Halleck) that he would at anytime remove McC when H. required it, and that he (the President) would take the entire responsibility of the removal.
>
> Mr. Bates quietly suggested that Halleck should take command of the army in person. But the President said, and all the Cabinet concurred in the opinion, that H. would be an indifferent general in the field, that he shirked responsibility in his present position, that he, in fact, is a moral coward, worth but little as a critic and director of operations, though intelligent and educated.[28]

With his army steadily crossing the Potomac and advancing southward on the east side of the Blue Ridge, McClellan wired

---

[27] Stanton to Halleck, October 27, 1862, Halleck to Stanton, October 28, 1862, *C.C.W.*, I, 553–55; Heintzelman's Journal, entry of September 28, 1862.

[28] *Welles's Diary*, I, 179–80.

Lincoln on October 28, "Everything is moving as rapidly as circumstances will permit. . . . We need more carbines and muskets. I shall not wait for them, but ought to be supplied at once." Then, on the twenty-ninth, McClellan received a most encouraging telegram from the President: "*I am much pleased with the movement of the army.* When you get entirely across the river let me know." [29]

On the last day of October, McClellan dutifully reported his progress to Lincoln. He said that the blue army was steadily pushing toward Warrenton, but that he was "still very deficient" in cavalry and artillery horses. On the first of November, he told the President that all but one of his corps were now in the Old Dominion. "I . . . shall go forward from day to day as rapidly as possible," he declared. His advance, meanwhile, was causing Lee some concern. Seeing that McClellan was threatening his rear and line of communications, the Southern commander was obliged on the first to move half of the gray army under Longstreet, and almost all of his artillery and supplies through Front Royal and Chester Gap to Culpeper Court House, Jackson's corps being left in the Shenandoah Valley near Millwood. McClellan had thus succeeded in compelling Lee to divide his army into two widely separated halves, with the Blue Ridge Mountains between them.[30]

Upon reaching the Manassas Gap Railroad at Thoroughfare Gap in the Bull Run Mountains, the Army of the Potomac was joined, in a beautifully timed movement, by Heintzelman's Third Corps, Sigel's Eleventh Corps, and Brigadier General George D. Bayard's cavalry division, which had all marched from Washington on McClellan's orders. On November 6, the Federal Army was disposed as follows: the First Corps was at Warrenton; the Second Corps was at Rectortown; the Eleventh Corps was at New Baltimore; Brigadier General

[29] McClellan to Lincoln, October 28, 1862, 28 *O.R.*, 501; Lincoln to McClellan, October 29, 1862, *ibid.*, 504; *C.C.W.*, I, 556. Italics mine.
[30] McClellan to Lincoln, October 31, November 1, 1862, *C.C.W.*, I, 559–60; see Stine, *Army of the Potomac*, 237.

Daniel E. Sickles' division was at Warrenton Junction; the Fifth Corps was at Snicker's Gap; and the Sixth Corps was at Upperville. Since the receipt of Lincoln's message stating that he was quite pleased with the progress of the Union advance, it is important to note that McClellan had speeded up the tempo of his movements. " The enemy," wrote Lee to Davis on the sixteenth, " are advancing steadily from the Potomac. . . . They occupy the gaps in the mountains as they progress, and have already reached Manassas Gap. . . . [McClellan] is also moving more rapidly than usual, and it looks like a real advance." On the same day, in a dispatch to G. W. Smith in Richmond, Lee declared, " In my letter to the President of to-day, I endeavored to report . . . that McClellan's whole army is moving toward the Rappahannock with more activity than usual." Speaking of McClellan's advance since receipt of Lincoln's congratulatory order of October 29, Alexander says of the Union commander, " Indeed, the Confederates noted, during the . . . week, the unwonted vigor of his advance." Seldom one to vouchsafe the ability of McClellan, Ingalls nonetheless asserted in his official report that " the march from the Potomac at Berlin to Warrenton . . . was a magnificent spectacle of celerity and skill." [31]

By the seventh of November, McClellan's movements were so successful that his army was well concentrated about Warrenton. Lee, on the other hand, had been obliged to move Longstreet's corps to Culpeper Court House, while keeping Jackson's corps in the Valley near Millwood. The Confederate commander's two wings were over fifty miles apart—a good two days' march. By a short advance to the southwest, McClellan proposed to interpose his army between Lee's two widely separated segments. His chances were good of falling upon one of the halves of the Southern Army. To prevent this, Lee would have had to fall back precipitately, if possible, with Jackson's corps,

[31] Irwin, " The Removal of McClellan," *loc. cit.*, 102–103; Stine, *Army of the Potomac*, 238; Lee to Davis, Lee to G. W. Smith, November 6, 1862, 28 *O.R.*, 697; Alexander, *Military Memoirs*, 281; Ingalls' report, 27 *O.R.*, 96.

313

toward Gordonsville. McClellan had approximately 142,000 men as against some 85,000 grayclad soldiers.[32]

But now, despite the auspicious progress of the Union advance, a sudden and dramatic change of events took place. On November 5, in Washington, the axe fell, for the last time, on McClellan's head. On that day, Lincoln issued the following order:

> Executive Mansion,
> Washington,   , 186 .

> By direction of the President it is ordered that Major-General McClellan be relieved from the command of the Army of the Potomac, and that Major-General Burnside take command of that army. Also that Major-General Hunter take command of the corps in said army now commanded by General Burnside.

> That Major-General Fitz John Porter be relieved from the command of the corps he now commands in said army, and that Major-General Hooker take command of said corps.

> The general-in-chief is authorized, in [his] discretion, to issue an order substantially as the above, forthwith or as soon as he may deem proper.

> November 5th, 1862   A. Lincoln [33]

It is probable that McClellan never saw this order—written in the President's own handwriting—in its undated form. Scarcely had the ink on it dried, than Halleck took advantage of the discretion in time given by Lincoln to issue this directive:

> Major-General McClellan, Commanding, etc.–

> General: On receipt of the order of the President, sent herewith, you will immediately turn over your command to Major-General Burnside, and repair to Trenton, N. J. [the McClellans' new home], reporting on your arrival at that place, by telegraph for further orders.

> Very respectfully, your obedient servant,

> H. W. Halleck,
> General-in-Chief [34]

---

[32] 28 *O.R.*, 695, 696, 697, 698, 701–702, 703, 704, 705, 710; Swinton, *Army of the Potomac*, 226–27; Steele, *American Campaigns*, I, 288–89; see Irwin, "The Removal of McClellan," *loc. cit.*, 103n.   [33] *B. & L.*, III, 103.   [34] *Ibid.*

A dated copy of the first sentence of Lincoln's original undated order to Halleck was enclosed.

The removal orders had been drawn up in Washington on November 5. Brigadier General Charles P. Buckingham, on special duty in the War Department, had an office next to that of the Secretary of War. At 10:00 P. M. on the sixth, he was called into Stanton's office. Present besides the Secretary was General-in-Chief Halleck. Stanton gave Buckingham the change-of-command orders to deliver in person to McClellan and Burnside. Before leaving Washington, Stanton summoned Buckingham to his house early on the morning of the seventh, and explained to him why he was sending an officer of such high rank with the orders. According to Buckingham, Stanton said that he not only had no confidence in McClellan's military ability, but that he doubted very much his patriotism and loyalty. The Secretary feared that McClellan might not give up the command of the army, despite the specific orders.[35]

Stepping off his special train later that day near army head-quarters at Rectortown, Buckingham rode first to Burnside's headquarters at Salem. Arriving in the midst of a heavy snow-storm, he showed the orders to Burnside. At first, Burnside would not accept the command of the Army of the Potomac, saying that the responsibility of handling such a large army was too great, and that he had no confidence in himself. After considerable argument, however, Burnside finally consented to obey the order. Then, he and Buckingham rode immediately to McClellan's headquarters at Rectortown, five miles distant. They found him alone in his tent, examining some maps and papers. He received them in his usual cordial manner, and exchanged a few pleasantries before Buckingham handed him the dismissal orders. In complete control of himself, McClellan read them with a smile, looked up, and said pleasantly to Burnside, " I turn the command over to you." He had learned previously that a special train from Washington carrying Buck-

---

[35] Buckingham's statement, Stine, *Army of the Potomac*, 241; Paris, *The Civil War*, II, 555n–57n.

ingham had arrived in the vicinity, and that the principal occupant of it had gone directly to Burnside's headquarters without first stopping to report his presence to the commanding general. "I at once suspected," said McClellan, "that he brought the order relieving me from command, but kept my own counsel." Also, as noted previously, McClellan had had forebodings that he would be dismissed soon after the President's visit to the army.[36]

Now that the final blow had fallen, what were McClellan's feelings after Buckingham and Burnside had left his tent? He turned at once to his pen and wrote to his wife: "Another interruption—this time more important. It was in the shape of Burnside, accompanied by Gen. Buckingham. . . . They brought with them the order relieving me from the command of the Army of the Potomac. . . . No cause is given. . . . They [the administration] have made a great mistake. Alas for my poor country! I know in my inmost heart she never had a truer servant. . . . Do not be at all worried—I am not. I have done the best I could for my country; to the last I have done my duty as I understand it. That I must have made many mistakes I cannot deny. I do not see any great blunders; but no one can judge of himself. Our consolation must be that we have tried to do what was right." [37]

Officers and men in the National Army were greatly affected and profoundly moved by the government's sudden and unheralded dismissal of their beloved commander. "At first we could hardly believe it," said General DeTrobriand. The administration's action came "like a thunderbolt from an unclouded sky," exclaimed the historian of the Fifth Corps. An eyewitness describes the reaction to the removal in these words: "The publication of this announcement had a startling effect. . . . Sweeping denunciation, violent invective, were heaped with-

---

[36] Buckingham's statement, Stine, *Army of the Potomac*, 241–42; Burnside's statement, Sypher, *Pennsylvania Reserves*, 408; *M.O.S.*, 651–52; Paris, *The Civil War*, I, 555n–57n.

[37] McClellan to his wife, November 7, 1862, *M.O.S.*, 660.

316

out stint upon the Government. Subdued threats of vengeance, mutterings of insurrection slumbered in their incipiency. . . . The mails teemed with correspondence to friends and relatives at home denouncing the action of the War Department, raging at the authorities, and predicting the direst results." Meade reported to his wife on November 8, " The army is filled with gloom and greatly depressed. Burnside, it is said, wept like a child, and is the most distressed man in the army, openly says he is not fit for the position, and that McClellan is the only man we have who can handle the large army collected together." A Federal surgeon noted in his diary that " the excitement in camp is intense, there is nothing else talked of, and many, very many of the best officers express a desire to quit the service." [38]

In Washington, however, the feeling about the removal of McClellan was different from that existing with the army in the field. Wrote Count Gurowski in his diary, " Great and holy day! McClellan gone overboard! Better late than never." He then spoke of " all the deadly disasters " which had been supposedly caused by " this horrible vampire." A few days later, the Count was fearful of McClellan's using the army to overthrow the government and set up a dictatorship. Welles declared that " Stanton is gratified " by the General's deposition. But, Welles added, " I hope the War Department will sustain [Burnside] more earnestly than it did McClellan." Then the Secretary of the Navy, who was never an admirer of McClellan, said, " After he commenced to move, I was less prepared to see him displaced and the announcement came with a shock." [39]

" No one knows to this day, positively, why [McClellan] was relieved," writes the historian of the Army of the Potomac, and the statement remains true. No convincing, specific cause or reason, of an official nature, has ever been made public. The

[38] DeTrobriand, *Army of the Potomac*, 348; Powell, *Fifth Corps*, 316; Smith, *118th Pennsylvania*, 107–108; Meade to his wife, November 8 and 9, 1862, Meade (ed.), *Letters of General Meade*, I, 325, 326; Ellis' *Diary*, 310.
[39] Gurowski's *Diary*, 313–14, 315; *Welles's Diary*, I, 182, 183.

dispute over the delay in army supplies had ended two weeks before he was dismissed; he had adopted the administration's line of advance into Virginia; and the debate over when he would move had ended with his being congratulated by the President on the progress of his advance. The moment selected to dismiss him certainly seemed inopportune.[40]

The origins of McClellan's removal go back almost to the earliest months of his command in the East. The friction had begun between the General and the administration during the winter of 1861-1862, when he had not commenced active operations as quickly as the politicians would have liked. It mushroomed during the great debate over the route to be taken by the Federal Army in its movement against Richmond. It grew in intensity during the course of the Peninsula campaign, when bad weather and other difficulties slowed the Union advance. And it blazed forth irremediably during the ill-fated campaign of Pope in August of 1862. When Lincoln courageously turned again to McClellan as the only man who could salvage the army and retrieve the situation after the terrible defeat at Second Bull Run, his cabinet members were vociferous in their denunciations of the General's ability and even of his loyalty. Stanton and Chase had declared openly that they would prefer to see the capital fall to the enemy than to have McClellan reinstated. Montgomery Blair stated at the time, " McClellan was bound to go when the emergency was past." Chase relates that, when Pope took leave of the President, Lincoln had said to Pope that " McClellan's command was only temporary." And at approximately the same period, as noted previously, the Chief Executive had said to John Hay that feeling against McClellan " will make it expedient to take important command from him. . . . But he is too useful just now to sacrifice." [41]

[40] Stine, *Army of the Potomac*, 239; Irwin, " The Removal of McClellan," *loc. cit.*, 104; see, e. g., J. G. Randall, *The Civil War and Reconstruction* (Boston, 1937) , 312; Paris, *The Civil War*, II, 557, 558.

[41] *M.O.S.*, 545; *Chase's Diary*, 65–66; Lincoln to Hay, *Hay's Diary*, entry of September 5, 1862.

After the issuance of the Emancipation Proclamation—which McClellan had made possible—it was almost too much to expect the administration to retain in high command such conservative Democrats as McClellan and Buell. Following the battles of South Mountain and Antietam, when McClellan was striving desperately to supply the army and organize it for a sustained winter campaign in Virginia, the bitter hostility toward him broke out anew. Stanton, armed with reports—wrung from the weak-willed Halleck—claimed that the Army of the Potomac was well supplied with everything and could have advanced long before, and beseeched Lincoln to remove McClellan. General Haupt, after having just spoken with Assistant Secretary of War Peter Watson, stated that Stanton's and then Lincoln's patience " because completely exhausted " when McClellan refrained from advancing and called loudly for horses, shoes, and clothing. Consequently, on November 5—the day after the last of the fall elections, which had gone against the administration—Lincoln issued his order dismissing the General. Chase had told Hiram Barney on October 26 that it was inexpedient to remove McClellan before the elections, lest the motives be misconstrued as a sop to the Radicals. Soon after his action, the President told Frank Blair, Sr., that he was tired of trying to " bore with an auger too dull to take hold." Then Lincoln said of McClellan, " I said I would remove him if he let Lee's army get away from him, and I must do so. He has got the ' slows,' Mr. Blair." [42]

This story is told in substantially the same manner by Albert D. Richardson, war correspondent of the New York *Tribune.* Lincoln said to Richardson that when it took McClellan so long to cross the Potomac, and when he " allowed " Longstreet's

---

[42] Flower, *Edwin M. Stanton*, 192–94; Halleck to Stanton, October 28, 1862, Stanton Papers; Herman Haupt, *Reminiscences of General Herman Haupt* (Milwaukee, 1901), 157; Noah Brooks, *Washington in Lincoln's Time* (New York, 1895), 16; Chase to Barney, October 26, 1862, Chase Papers, Historical Society of Pennsylvania, Microfilm from Univ. of Florida; Frank Blair, Sr., to Montgomery Blair, November 7, 1862, William E. Smith, *The Francis Preston Blair Family in Politics* (New York, 1933), II, 144–45.

corps to move between the Union Army and Richmond, then he determined to remove him from command. "That," declared Lincoln, "was the last grain of sand which broke the camel's back. I relieved McClellan at once." Nicolay and Hay assert that the President felt, "before the end of October, that McClellan had no real desire to beat the enemy." According to the private secretaries, Lincoln said that if McClellan "should permit Lee to cross the Blue Ridge and place himself between Richmond and the Army of the Potomac he would remove him from command." They said that when the President learned that Longstreet's corps had reached Culpeper Court House, he had had enough—even though Jackson's corps was still in the Valley—and immediately issued the dismissal order.[43]

So intense and unrelenting had been the Radical attacks on McClellan's loyalty, that Lincoln had begun to believe these charges. Forgetting the General's recent victories at South Mountain and the Antietam, he said to Hay, "I began to fear [McClellan] was playing false—that he did not want to hurt the enemy. I saw how he could intercept the enemy on the way to Richmond. I determined to make that the test. If he let them get away I would remove him. He did so & I relieved him." It might be noted here that no Union general, including Grant, ever succeeded in getting around Lee's right flank and interposing between him and Richmond. The President repeated approximately the same language to a visitor at the White House, adding, "[McClellan] was lost in admiration of General Lee, and filled with that feeling, forebore to conquer him." Of course, it is doubtful if any general could have "conquered" Lee as easily as the President implied. As for Lincoln's unmerited charge that McClellan "was playing false"—was disloyal, in other words—it was one of the great Civil War President's most grievous errors and acts of injustice.[44]

[43] Richardson, *The Secret Service*, 324; Nicolay and Hay, *Abraham Lincoln*, VI, 188.
[44] Lincoln to Hay, *Hay's Diary*, 218–19; Francis B. Carpenter, *Six Months at the White House* (New York, 1867), 227.

At the time of the deposing of McClellan, Brigadier General James A. Garfield was a house guest of his close friend, Secretary Chase, who confided many official views to him. Garfield, writing to his wife at the time of the debate over the movement of McClellan's army after Antietam, said that Lincoln, finally realizing that he would alienate too many Radicals by retaining Little Mac in command, determined to remove him after the fall elections, for to do so earlier would give the Democrats an exploitable campaign issue before the people went to the polls. Apparently, Garfield meant that it would have been bad politics to fire a Democratic general immediately after he had won a crucial victory and defeated the enemy invasion of the North. It is significant that Garfield knew of the President's order to relieve McClellan on November 5, as it was not promulgated until the seventh. And at about the same time that McClellan was dismissed, another prominent Democratic general, Buell, commanding the Department of the Ohio and the largest Union army in the West, was relieved of his command. This came after Buell had stopped Bragg's invasion of Kentucky at the battle of Perryville on October 8. Yet, Lincoln apparently felt no qualms when he wrote on the same day that he removed McClellan that, " in considering military merit, it seems to me the world has abundant evidence that I disregard politics." [45]

A few days after the October elections in Pennsylvania— which had gone against the Republicans—the President was visited by William D. Kelley and Edward McPherson of Congress. They told him that many people with whom they had talked in the Keystone State believed that the election defeats were due to " the President's retention of McClellan." They urged Lincoln to replace him with a " fighting general." When Lincoln asked who should replace McClellan, Kelley mentioned " Fighting Joe " Hooker. But, Lincoln inquired, " would not

[45] Garfield to his wife, October 12, 1862, and November 5, 1862, Theodore C. Smith, *Life and Letters of James A. Garfield* (New Haven, 1925), I, 250–51, 253–54; Nicolay and Hay, *Abraham Lincoln*, VI, 281; Basler (ed.), *Collected Works of Lincoln*, V, 486.

Burnside do better? " Then the President closed the interview by saying, " We shall see what we shall see." [46]

That there was a considerable degree of Radical pressure evident in the President's removal of McClellan is indicated by the fact that, in the same order which ousted him, Fitz John Porter was dismissed also. This stemmed from the false accusations of the Radicals and of their favorite general, Pope, who sought to make Porter and McClellan the scapegoats for the embarrassing defeat at Second Manassas. The generals who took over the command of the corps of Burnside and Porter were Hunter and Hooker, both well known as Radicals. " In the autumn of 1862," comments Ropes on this matter, " there was a very bitter feeling in influential quarters in Washington against both McClellan and Porter, and this order of November 5th, removing them both from command, was the result of the hostility to them." [47]

The substitution of Burnside for McClellan has drawn considerable fire from soldiers and historians. It might be noted at the outset that Burnside *delayed five weeks* in confronting Lee with the National Army and attacking him. And when Burnside did assail the enemy at Fredericksburg in mid-December, he did so in the most inept and rash manner possible, hurling brigade after brigade in seventeen frontal, piecemeal assaults against an impregnable Confederate defensive position at Marye's Heights. The result was the most one-sided, humiliating defeat suffered by the Federals during the war. Knowing Burnside's glaring limitations, well might McClellan have exclaimed, " Alas for my poor country! " Few informed writers on the Civil War will disagree with the statement that, had McClellan remained in command of the Army of the Potomac, it would never have suffered such an inglorious vanquishment as that administered to the Union cause by Lee at Fredericksburg. The same might be said also of the unfortunate Federal

[46] William D. Kelley, in Rice (ed.), *Reminiscences of Abraham Lincoln*, 271–79.
[47] Ropes, *Story of the Civil War*, II, 441.

defeat at Chancellorsville in May of 1863, with Hooker in command. It is possible that Lincoln's removal of McClellan unwittingly extended the duration of the war for a year longer than it should reasonably have been expected to last. McClellan had learned much in the fifteen months in which he had been at the head of the Union Army, and Lincoln threw away that valuable combat schooling when he dismissed him.[48]

Lincoln had had many complimentary things to say to McClellan when he had visited the army after Antietam. But back in Washington, the Chief Executive held, as seen, somewhat different views of the General. At the time of his removal, the President said of him to a group of people, " He is an admirable engineer, but he seems to have a special talent for a stationary engine." And to Senator Browning: " For organizing, disciplining and preparing an army for the field and handling it in the field [McClellan] was superior to any of our Genls "; that " the battles of South Mountain and Antietam were fought with ability—as well as any Genl could have fought them, but McLellan [*sic*] was too slow in his movements." The President told Browning that he felt McClellan could have relieved Harper's Ferry, that he could have and should have annihilated Lee after Antietam, that he would not cross the Potomac immediately after the battle, and that his greatest defect was overcaution. Yet, just nineteen days after having relieved the General, Lincoln indicated that he had made a mistake. Writing on November 24 to Carl Schurz, the President stated, " I certainly have been dissatisfied with the slowness of Buell and McClellan; but before I relieved them I had great fears I should not find successors to them who would do better; and I am sorry to add that I have seen little since to relieve those fears." [49]

Although Lincoln had some pretty harsh things to say of McClellan out of earshot of the General—even questioning

[48] See *ibid.*, 442–43.
[49] John G. Nicolay to Therena Bates, November 9, 1862, Nicolay Papers; Isaac N. Arnold, *The Life of Abraham Lincoln* (Chicago, 1885), 300; Carpenter, *Six Months at the White House*, 255; *Browning's Diary*, I, 589–90; Lincoln to Schurz, November 24, 1862, Basler (ed.), *Collected Works of Lincoln*, V, 509–10.

his loyalty and patriotism—Little Mac apparently bore little malice toward the President. Writing in his official report, after having been summarily dismissed, he said of the Chief Executive: " I cannot omit the expression of my thanks to the President for the constant evidence given me of his sincere personal regard, and his desire to sustain the military plans which my judgment led me to urge for adoption and execution. I cannot attribute his failure to adopt some of these plans, and to give that support to others which was necessary to their success, to any want of confidence in me; and it only remains for me to regret that other counsels came between the constitutional commander-in-chief and the general whom he had placed at the head of his armies—counsels which resulted in the failure of great campaigns." [50]

Turning from the President to general military policy, McClellan had this to say near the end of his report: " In the arrangement and conduct of campaigns the direction should be left to professional soldiers. A statesman may, perhaps, be more competent than a soldier to determine the political objects and direction of a campaign; but those once decided upon, everything should be left to the responsible military head, without interference from civilians. In no other manner is success probable. The meddling of individual members of committees of Congress with subjects which, from lack of experience, they are of course incapable of comprehending, and which they are apt to view through the distorted medium of partisan or personal prejudice, can do no good, and is certain to produce incalculable mischief." [51]

In analyzing the rise and fall of the Young Napoleon, the perspicacious Swinton states, " To General McClellan personally it was a misfortune that he became so prominent a figure at the commencement of the contest; for it was inevitable that the first leaders should be sacrificed to the nation's ignorance of war." [52] On this important point, General U. S. Grant com-

---

[50] McClellan's *Report*, 239.
[51] *Ibid.*, 238–39.   [52] Swinton, *Army of the Potomac*, 228.

324

mented as follows on McClellan: " All my impressions are in his favor. . . . The test which was applied to him would be terrible to any man, being made a major-general at the beginning of the war. It has always seemed to me that the critics of McClellan do not consider this vast and cruel responsibility —the war, a new thing to all of us, the army new, everything to do from the outset, with a restless people and Congress. McClellan was a young man when this devolved upon him. . . . If [he] had gone into the war as Sherman, Thomas, or Meade, had fought his way along and up, I have no reason to suppose that he would not have won as high distinction as any of us." [53]

General Palfrey, whose writings are filled with instances of McClellan's alleged mistakes and shortcomings, nevertheless acknowledges at the end of his Antietam narrative that " there are strong grounds for believing that he was the best commander the Army of the Potomac ever had. . . . While the Confederacy was young and fresh and rich, and its armies were numerous, McClellan fought a good, wary, damaging, respectable fight against it. . . . With longer possession of command, greater things might fairly have been expected of him. . . . In such a war . . . it would probably have been impossible to retain in command of the Army of the Potomac a man who was not only a Democrat, but the probable Democratic candidate for the Presidency at the next election, and that his removal was therefore only a question of time. A growing familiarity with his history as a soldier increases the disposition to regard him with respect and gratitude." [54]

The historian of the Union Second Corps, General Walker, writes of McClellan, " Let military critics or political enemies say what they will, he who could so move upon the hearts of a great army, as the wind sways long rows of standing corn, was no ordinary man; nor was he who took such heavy toll of Joseph E. Johnston and Robert E. Lee an ordinary soldier." [55]

[53] John Russell Young, *Around the World with General Grant . . .* (New York, 1879), II, 216–17.
[54] Palfrey, *The Antietam*, 134–35.   [55] Walker, *Second Corps*, 138.

Perhaps the man best able to judge with authority the relative merits of each of the commanders of the Army of the Potomac was the great soldier in gray who had met them all on the field of battle—General Lee. A daughter of the Confederate chieftain was reported as saying that " Genl. McClellan was the only Genl. Father dreaded." After the war, Lee wrote to a friend, " As regards General McClellan, I have always entertained a high opinion of his capacity, and have no reason to think that he omitted to do anything that was in his power." When asked shortly after Appomattox who was the best Federal general he had faced during the war, Lee, without a moment's hesitation, pounding his fist on the desk, declared emphatically, " McClellan by all odds! " [56]

Upon receiving the orders relieving him from command, McClellan, at Burnside's request, remained with the army for several days to help him take over the reins, and to carry out several movements then underway. At the parting of McClellan and his generals, a scene ensued not unlike the farewell of George Washington and his lieutenants. As Meade describes it, " McClellan was very much affected, almost to tears, and said that separation from this army was the severest blow that could be inflicted upon him." When McClellan and Burnside rode up to Couch's headquarters, Couch voiced his regrets to McClellan about the loss of command, and then offered Burnside his congratulations on his promotion. Almost unable to speak, Burnside said in great earnestness, " Couch, don't say a word about it." He later told Couch that he did not want the command, but took it to keep it from going to Hooker. In a note that evening to Ellen, McClellan said, " I expect to start tomorrow morning. . . . I shall not stop in Washington longer than for the next train, and will not go to see anybody. I shall go on just as quietly as I can and make as little fuss as possible. The officers and men feel terribly about the change. I learn

[56] Quoted in letter to McClellan from " A Friend," Washington, D. C., March 28, 1863, McClellan Papers; see Lee to B. H. Wright, January 8, 1869, Freeman, *R. E. Lee*, IV, 477; Robert E. Lee, [Jr.], *Recollections and Letters of General Robert E. Lee* (New York, 1905), 415–16.

today that the men are very sullen and have lost their good spirits entirely." [57]

On November 10, a part of the Army of the Potomac was drawn up in long lines of review along the Warrenton–Alexandria road. The parting scene made a lasting impression on many men in blue. A Pennsylvanian wrote as follows of the moving farewell: " As [McClellan] rode between the lines, formed almost of their own accord to do honor for the last time to their beloved commander, grief and disappointment were on every face, and manly tears stood in many an eye that had learned to look on war without a tremor." [58] General Walker describes the scene in this manner: " Every heart of the thirty thousand was filled with love and grief; every voice was raised in shouts of devotion and indignation; and when the chief had passed out of sight, the romance of war was over for the Army of the Potomac." [59] An officer in blue wrote home one of the best accounts of the dramatic moment, mentioning the distinct threat of an uprising by the army against the government:

> As General McClellan passed along its front, whole regiments broke and flocked around him, and with tears and entreaties besought him not to leave them, but to say the word and they would settle matters in Washington. Indeed, it was thought at one time there would be a mutiny, but by a word he calmed the tumult and ordered the men back to their colors and their duty. As he passed our regiment he was thronged by men of other commands, making a tumultous scene beyond description. He was obliged to halt in front of us. . . . General ————, who was riding near McClellan, was forced by the crowd towards our line and I heard him say to another mounted officer close by that he wished to God McClellan would put himself at

---

[57] Burnside's statement, Sypher, *Pennsylvania Reserves*, 408; Powell, *Fifth Corps*, 318; Meade to his wife, November 9, 1862, Meade (ed.) , *Letters of General Meade*, I, 326; Darius N. Couch, " Sumner's Right Grand Division," *B. & L.*, III, 106; McClellan to his wife, November 9, 1862, *M.O.S.*, 652, 660–61.
[58] Irwin, " The Removal of McClellan," *loc. cit.*, 104.
[59] Walker, *Second Corps*, 137–38.

the head of the army and throw the infernal scoundrels at
Washington into the Potomac. This is *history*, and I give it
here to show the wild excitement pervading all branches of the
service, from the rank and file to the general officers. . . .
[McClellan] urged upon us all to return to our respective
commands. . . .

What do you think of such a man? He had it in his power
to be dictator—anything he chose to name—if he would but
say the word, but he preferred retirement rather than ambition.
He was not a Caesar.[60]

This little-known account gives an indication of the very real
danger of a military revolt against the government in Washington. The army was beside itself with anger at the administration. It was perhaps the greatest such danger the republic
has ever faced. A few days after Antietam, at McClellan's
headquarters, during a council of war of the top generals, no
less prominent a civilian official than John W. Garrett, President of the Baltimore and Ohio Railroad, had suggested using
the Army of the Potomac to coerce the administration by force
into adopting whatever policies the generals desired.[61] Another
article describes how McClellan snuffed out the threat of a
mushrooming rebellion:

Amid the impassioned cries and demonstrations of the men
[McClellan] took a last look of the troops who had followed
him with such unfaltering devotion. On the 11th, at Warrenton Junction, he entered with his staff a railroad train that
was about to start toward Washington. Here was stationed a
detachment of 2,000 troops. They were drawn up in a line,
and a salute was fired. The men then broke their ranks,
surrounded the car in which he was seated, uncoupled it from
the train and ran it back, insisting wildly that he should not
leave them, and uttering the bitterest imprecations against
those who had deprived them of their beloved commander.
The scene . . . was . . . one of fearful excitement. The moment

[60] Smith, *118th Pennsylvania*, 107n–108n.
[61] Cox, *Military Reminiscences*, I, 358–59.

was critical. One word, one look of encouragement, the lifting of a finger, would have been a signal for a revolt against lawful authority, the consequences of which no man can measure. McClellan stepped upon the front platform of the car, and there was instant silence. His address was short. It ended in the memorable words, " Stand by General Burnside as you have stood by me, and all will be well." The soldiers were calmed. They rolled the car onward, recoupled it to the train, and with one long and mournful huzza bade farewell to their late commander, whom many of them were destined never to behold again.[62]

McClellan himself describes the threatening situation in a moderate way: " The order depriving me of the command created an immense deal of deep feeling in the army—so much so that many were in favor of my refusing to obey the order, and of marching upon Washington to take possession of the government. My chief purpose in remaining with the army as long as I did after being relieved was to calm this feeling, in which I succeeded." [63]

Writing to his wife on the afternoon of the tenth, McClellan said, " I am very well and taking leave of the men. I did not know before how much they loved me nor how dear they were to me. Gray-haired men came to me with tears streaming down their cheeks. I never before had to exercise so much self-control. The scenes of today repay me for all that I have endured." [64]

For McClellan, however, only the preservation of the Union and the welfare of his troops mattered. His love for his men exceeded even his concern with his own reputation. His official report closes with the following passage: " I have not accomplished my purpose if, by this report, the army of the Potomac is not placed high on the roll of the historic armies of the world. Its deeds enoble the nation to which it belongs. Always ready for battle, always firm, steadfast, and trustworthy, I never

[62] George T. Curtis, " McClellan's Last Service to the Republic," 81–83, quoted in *B. & L.*, III, 104n.
[63] *M.O.S.*, 85, 652.
[64] McClellan to his wife, November 10, 1862, *ibid.*, 661.

called on it in vain; nor will the nation ever have cause to attribute its want of success, under myself, or under other commanders, to any failure of patriotism or bravery in that noble body of American soldiers." [65]

George B. McClellan had issued a number of flamboyant, Napoleonic manifestoes—largely for his own benefit—since he had put on the two stars of a major general. But they had been gradually becoming less rhetorical in form and content. Despite shortcomings, which all men have, he had grown immeasurably in stature since the early days of the war. His achievements had been substantial—some masterful. Now, the farewell address to the Army of the Potomac at his departure from the service was the finest effort of the so-called Young Napoleon of the West. It read:

> OFFICERS AND SOLDIERS OF THE ARMY OF THE POTOMAC:
>
> An order from the President devolves upon Major-General Burnside the command of this army.
>
> In parting from you, I cannot express the love and gratitude I bear to you. As an army, you have grown up under my care. In you, I have never found doubt or coldness. The battles you fought under my command will proudly live in our nation's history. The glory you have achieved, our mutual peril and fatigues, the graves of our comrades, fallen in battle and by disease, the broken forms of those whom wounds and sickness have disabled—the strongest associations which can exist among men—unite us still by an indissoluble tie. We shall ever be comrades in supporting the Constitution of our country and the nationality of its people.
>
> GEO. B. McCLELLAN
> *Major-General, U.S. Army* [66]

[65] McClellan's *Report*, 242.
[66] 28 *O.R.*, 551; *M.O.S.*, 653.

Critical Essay on Authorities [*]

Not the least valuable asset to the historian of the Civil War
are the battlefields over which the fighting raged in that conflict. Most of the fields which were the scenes of McClellan's
operations are in a good state of preservation. The easiest to
examine—because of the tablets and markers maintained by the
National Park Service—are Antietam, South Mountain (including Crampton's Gap), Fair Oaks, and the Seven Days' fields.
The battlefields of Rich Mountain, Carrick's Ford, Williamsburg, Yorktown, West Point, and Hanover Court House exist,
at least in part, but are not generally well marked.

For the student who wishes to see and examine Civil War
uniforms, weapons, and other accouterments, there are such
exhibits as the Smithsonian, the privately owned National
Museum at Gettysburg, and the National Park Service museums
at Fredericksburg, Antietam, Gettysburg, and Fort Harrison
near Richmond. Illustrations of battles, fields, generals, and
other Civil War scenes may be found in profusion in Francis
Trevelyan Miller's ten-volume *Photographic History of the
Civil War* (New York, 1911).

Manuscript Collections

Essential in any serious study of McClellan is the George B.
McClellan collection of the General's papers in the Division
of Manuscripts, Library of Congress. Bound in 154 large
volumes, these manuscripts include letters received by McClellan as well as copies of those written by him. It is surprising

[*] Only sources and works of especial assistance in this study are listed in
the bibliography. For others used on occasion, consult those cited in the
footnotes of the text.

how little use has been made of this collection by writers in the Civil War area. Other important papers in the Library of Congress, as regards McClellan's activities, are the Edwin M. Stanton Papers, the recently opened Robert T. Lincoln collection of the Civil War President's papers, and the personal papers of Ethan Allen Hitchcock, Montgomery C. Meigs, John G. Nicolay, Samuel P. Heintzelman, Salmon P. Chase, William B. Franklin, Fitz John Porter, Montgomery Blair, Gideon Welles, Benjamin F. Wade, Zachariah Chandler, Lyman Trumbull, William P. Fessenden, and Joseph Holt.

GOVERNMENT PUBLICATIONS

All scholars working in the military and civil affairs of the Civil War are indebted to the 128-volume War Department publication, *War of the Rebellion: A Compilation of the Official Records of the Union and Confederate Armies* (Washington, 1880-1901). This source is well indexed, and includes official reports of campaigns and battles, correspondence between officers and various civilian authorities, casualty tables, returns, and other statistical information. The work is divided into four series, each of which is further broken down into volumes, parts, and even supplements, all indicated by Roman numerals. After the thirty-fifth book appeared, the following ones were given Arabic serial numbers on their covers. Since references to this source in the present study are indicated by Arabic serial numbers only—instead of employing the cumbersome Roman numeral designations for series, volumes, parts, and supplements—the first thirty-five books must be *given* serial numbers in Arabic. The following table harmonizes the applied Arabic serial numbers to the official Roman numeral designations for the first thirty-five books of Series I:

Roman	Serial Numbers	Roman	Serial Numbers
Vol. I	1	Vol. XIII	19
" II	2	" XIV	20
" III	3	" XV	21
" IV	4	" XVI, Pt. I	22
" V	5	" XVI, Pt. II	23
" VI	6	" XVII, Pt. I	24
" VII	7	" XVII, Pt. II	25
" VIII	8	" XVIII	26
" IX	9	" XIX, Pt. I	27
" X, Pt. I	10	" XIX, Pt. II	28
" X, Pt. II	11	" XX, Pt. I	29
" XI, Pt. I	12	" XX, Pt. II	30
" XI, Pt. II	13	" XXI	31
' XI, Pt. III	14	" XXII, Pt. I	32
" XII, Pt. I	15	" XXII, Pt. II	33
" XII, Pt. II	16	" XXIII, Pt. I	34
" XII, Pt. II, Suppl.	17	" XXIII, Pt. II	35
" XII, Pt. III	18	" XXIV, Pt. I	36

The *Report of the Committee on the Conduct of the War* (Washington, 1863), is a verbatim record of important testimony, under oath, of principal soldiers and a few government civilian officials. It is a good corrective to some of the extravagant statements made in reports in the *Official Records*. For the Congressional debates of the Civil War period, see the *Congressional Globe*. The United States government also published a valuable study of the shortcomings of the policies of the civilian administrations: Emory Upton, *The Military Policy of the United States* (Washington, 1912). A recent and useful work is C. Joseph Bernardo and Eugene H. Bacon, *American Military Policy, Its Development Since 1775* (Harrisburg, 1955).

NEWSPAPERS

The newspapers of 1861–1862 furnish much less valuable information on military and political events than might be imagined. The accounts of campaigns and battles by most of the war correspondents are often inaccurate and distorted, often colored by the political preference of the editor. Probably the best military reporting was done by Horace Greeley's New York *Tribune*, an organ of the war party of the North. More hostile to the Lincoln administration were the New York *Herald* and the New York *Evening Post*. Perhaps the best Washington paper covering the early political scene was the *National Intelligencer*.

MAPS

Incomparably the best collection of Civil War military maps is the *Atlas to Accompany the Official Records of the Union and Confederate Armies*. These are maps, usually drawn to scale in color by military topographical engineers, which show plans of fortifications and fieldworks, troop dispositions, contours, localities, roads and railroads, and vegetation. Just about every combat of any proportions is included. However, the best maps of the battles of Antietam and South Mountain are those drawn by the Antietam Battlefield Board. The Department of Military Art and Engineering at the United States Military Academy has produced a convenient and graphic series of maps on Civil War campaigns and battles, *Civil War Atlas to Accompany Steele's "American Campaigns"* (West Point, 1950).

STATISTICAL AND REFERENCE WORKS

Valuable and authoritative compendiums of military men, events, and information are the following works: George W. Cullum, *Biographical Register of the Officers and Graduates of the United States Military Academy . . .* (New York, 1868); Francis B. Heitman, *Historical Register and Dictionary of the United States Army . . .* (Washington, 1903); Thomas H. S. Hamersly, *Complete Regular Army Register of the United States . . .* (Washington, 1880); and Frederick K. Phisterer, *Statistical Record of the Armies of the United States* (New York, 1883). The two standard works on Civil War casualties and numbers are: Thomas L. Livermore, *Numbers and Losses in the Civil War in America, 1861–1865* (Boston, 1900); and

William F. Fox, *Regimental Losses in the American Civil War, 1861–1865* . . . (Albany, 1889), which is a work of much greater scope than its title indicates. For important orders and addresses of Lincoln, the usual work cited is James D. Richardson, *A Compilation of the Messages and Papers of the Presidents* (Washington, 1896–99). Along with a lot of trivia, some valuable source material exists in the twelve volume set edited by Frank Moore, *The Rebellion Record: A Diary of American Events, with Documents* . . . (New York, 1862–68).

AUTOBIOGRAPHIES, MEMOIRS, AND PUBLISHED CORRESPONDENCE

The number of personal memoirs and recollections by prominent as well as minor actors in the Civil War drama is staggering. Of foremost importance, of course, in the present study is the memoir written by George B. McClellan, published after his death by William C. Prime, *McClellan's Own Story: The War for the Union* . . . (New York, 1887). Although painfully defensive in tone, this large volume is well written and lucid. It contains many valuable documents not found elsewhere, as well as many of the letters written by the General to his wife.

For Lincoln's writings, the standard authority now is Roy P. Basler (ed.), *The Collected Works of Abraham Lincoln* (New Brunswick, 1953), in nine volumes. It supersedes the older, less accurate, less complete work compiled by Nicolay and Hay. The *Collected Works of Lincoln* is a fine piece of workmanship, extremely accurate, with excellent annotations. It contains practically all of the known pieces of writing by Lincoln, but does not include the letters received by Lincoln from other correspondents. For a sampling of the latter, see the two-volume work by David C. Mearns, *The Lincoln Papers* (Garden City, 1948).

The correspondence of Stanton appears, in part, in the two old works on the Secretary, George C. Gorham, *Life and Public Services of Edwin M. Stanton* (Boston, 1899), and Frank Abial

Flower, *Edwin McMasters Stanton* . . . (Akron, 1905). The American Historical Association published the *Diary and Correspondence of Salmon P. Chase* (Washington, 1903). Other Chase correspondence appears in the two older works on the Secretary of the Treasury, Jacob W. Schuckers, *Life and Public Services of Salmon Portland Chase* (New York, 1874), and Robert B. Warden, *Account of the Private Life and Public Services of Salmon Portland Chase* (Cincinnati, 1874). Howard K. Beale has done a splendid job of editing *The Diary of Edward Bates, 1859–1866* (Washington, 1933). The famous *Diary of Gideon Welles* . . . (Boston, 1911), edited by John T. Morse, Jr., in three volumes, is of considerable value, even though portions of the entries were added at a somewhat later date by Welles. The published diary should be compared with the manuscript diary in the Library of Congress. Other diaries of value containing information pertinent to McClellan are the following: W. A. Croffut (ed.), *Fifty Years in Camp and Field: The Diary of Major-General Ethan Allen Hitchcock, U. S. A.* (New York, 1909); Theodore Calvin Pease and James G. Randall (eds.), *The Diary of Orville Hickman Browning, 1850–1864* (Springfield, 1925); and Allan Nevins and Milton Halsey Thomas (eds.), *The Diary of George Templeton Strong* . . . (New York, 1952).

Prominent soldiers who were associated with McClellan wrote their own recollections of the period. One of the best of these works, checked against the *Official Records*, is Jacob D. Cox, *Military Reminiscences of the Civil War* (New York, 1900). The noted railroad engineer and quartermaster officer, Herman Haupt, contributed a well-documented book, *Reminiscences of General Herman Haupt* (Milwaukee, 1901). Erasmus D. Keyes, *Fifty Years' Observation of Men and Events* (New York, 1884), is by McClellan's Fourth Corps commander on the Peninsula. The French brigadier, Regis DeTrobriand, severely criticizes McClellan in his *Four Years with the Army of the Potomac* (Boston, 1889). McClellan's Secret Service chief, Allan Pinkerton, wrote *The Spy of the Rebellion* . . .

(New York, 1883), which defends the high estimates made of Confederate numbers. A good personal narrative is that by a division commander under McClellan, John Gibbon, *Personal Recollections of the Civil War* (New York, 1928). The valuable letters to his wife by General Meade are included in George Meade (ed.), *The Life and Letters of George Gordon Meade* . . . (New York, 1913). John G. Barnard, *The Peninsular Campaign and Its Antecedents* . . . (New York, 1864), is an attack on McClellan's operations by his chief engineer, who was sympathetic to them in 1862. William R. Thayer, *Life and Letters of John Hay* (New York, 1915), contains correspondence of Lincoln's private secretary. A French nobleman serving on McClellan's staff on the Peninsula, the Prince de Joinville, wrote *The Army of the Potomac* (New York, 1862). Oliver O. Howard, a division commander under McClellan, is the author of *Autobiography of Oliver Otis Howard* (New York, 1907). One of McClellan's ablest subordinates is the subject of *Reminiscences of Winfield Scott Hancock* (New York, 1887). One of the finest accounts of actual campaigning and fighting is Colonel Thomas L. Livermore's *Days and Events, 1860–1866* (Boston, 1920). A good sketch of McClellan appears in James Harrison Wilson's *Under the Old Flag* (New York, 1912). The manager of the War Department telegraph office, David Homer Bates, contributes valuable pictures of Lincoln, Stanton, and McClellan in his *Lincoln in the Telegraph Office* (New York, 1907).

Opinions of prominent Confederate soldiers who fought against McClellan are of value. On the whole, the officers in gray spoke quite highly of him. Some of the more important Confederate memoirs are: Jefferson Davis, *The Rise and Fall of the Confederate Government* (New York, 1881); James Longstreet, *From Manassas to Appomattox* . . . (Philadelphia, 1908); Joseph E. Johnston, *Narrative of Military Operations* . . . (New York, 1874); John B. Hood, *Advance and Retreat* . . . (New Orleans, 1880); John B. Gordon, *Reminiscences of the Civil War* (New York, 1904); Richard Taylor, *Destruction*

337

and Reconstruction . . . (New York, 1879) ; E. P. Alexander, *Military Memoirs of a Confederate* . . . (New York, 1907) .

Among the almost infinite number of personal recollections about Lincoln, there are some which contain information of value concerning McClellan. Among these and other useful personal memoirs, are the following: Alexander K. McClure, *Abraham Lincoln and Men of War-Times* . . . (Philadelphia, 1892) ; Charles A. Dana, *Recollections of the Civil War* (New York, 1898) ; Hugh McCulloch, *Men and Measures of Half a Century* . . . (New York, 1889) ; James G. Blaine, *Twenty Years of Congress, 1860–1880* (Norwich, 1884) ; Horace Greeley, *Recollections of a Busy Life* (New York, 1869) ; George W. Julian, *Political Recollections* . . . (Chicago, 1884) ; Carl Schurz, *The Reminiscences of Carl Schurz* (New York, 1908) ; Lafayette C. Baker, *Spies, Traitors and Conspirators of the Late Civil War* (Philadelphia, 1894) ; Charles A. Dana, *Lincoln and His Cabinet* (Cleveland, 1896) ; and Noah Brooks, *Washington in Lincoln's Time* (New York, 1895) .

BIOGRAPHIES

Of the five major biographies of McClellan, perhaps the most successful for the military operations, though much too over-critical in denouncing the General's alleged ineptness, is Peter S. Michie, *General McClellan* (New York, 1901) , in the Great Commanders series. The best study of McClellan the man is William Starr Myers, *A Study in Personality: General George Brinton McClellan* (New York, 1934) ; but it neglects the military side. The three other books on McClellan—all undocumented—are popular accounts, rather thin in parts, and with a number of grave defects. They are: James Havelock Campbell, *McClellan: A Vindication of the Military Career of General George B. McClellan* (New York, 1916) ; H. J. Eckenrode and Bryan Conrad, *George B. McClellan, The Man Who Saved the Union* (Chapel Hill, 1941) ; and Clarence Edward Macartney, *Little Mac: The Life of General George B. McClellan* (Philadelphia, 1940) .

Biographies dealing with Lincoln usually include McClellan as a major figure, and the interpretations of the General by many of these writers are of value. There are four good one-volume books on Lincoln: Benjamin P. Thomas, *Abraham Lincoln: A Biography* (New York, 1952); Nathaniel Wright Stephenson, *Lincoln . . .* (Indianapolis, 1922); Lord Charnwood, *Abraham Lincoln* (London, 1916); and John G. Nicolay, *A Short Life of Lincoln . . .* (New York, 1902). The only authors who had use of the Lincoln Papers up to 1947, John G. Nicolay and John Hay, wrote a ten-volume life of Lincoln which is harsh toward McClellan, but which includes firsthand details not found elsewhere: *Abraham Lincoln, A History* (New York, 1890). The interpretation of Carl Sandburg in his four-volume classic, *Abraham Lincoln, The War Years* (New York, 1939), should not be missed. One of the most favorable treatments of McClellan *vis-à-vis* Lincoln is in the scholarly, fully documented four-volume work by J. G. Randall, *Lincoln the President . . .* (New York, 1945 and 1953). For the machinations of the Radical Republicans in Congress to have McClellan removed and disgraced, see T. Harry Williams, *Lincoln and the Radicals* (Madison, 1941), a thorough, well-written account.

Biographies on other prominent soldiers and politicians often have much to say of McClellan's relations with individuals written on. There is no adequate biography of Stanton, although one now underway by Benjamin P. Thomas promises to supply the need. To the earlier ones written by Gorham and Flower, mentioned before, might be added another of little value: Fletcher Pratt, *Stanton, Lincoln's Secretary of War* (New York, 1953). Charles W. Elliott's *Winfield Scott: The Soldier and the Man* (New York, 1937), is an excellent study of one of our greatest soldiers. Joseph M. Hughes, *General Johnston* (New York, 1892); D. B. Sanger, *James Longstreet . . .* (Baton Rouge, 1952); Richard Meade Bache, *Life of General George Gordon Meade* (Philadelphia, 1897); Walter H. Hebert, *Fighting Joe Hooker* (Indianapolis, 1944); Ben Perley Poore, *The Life and Public Services of Ambrose E. Burnside*

339

(Providence, 1882) ; Otto Eisenschiml, *The Celebrated Case of Fitz John Porter* . . . (Indianapolis, 1950), are biographies which leave a lot to be desired. Better are Francis A. Walker, *General Hancock* (New York, 1897) ; and Allan Nevins, *Frémont* . . . (New York, 1928). On Lee and his principal subordinates, the multi-volume works by Douglas Southall Freeman, *R. E. Lee, A Biography* (New York, 1934–35), and *Lee's Lieutenants, A Study in Command* (New York, 1942–44), are magnificent. Of principal Union political figures, the following are of value: Richard S. West, Jr., *Gideon Welles* . . . (Indianapolis, 1943) ; A. B. Hart, *Salmon Portland Chase* (Boston, 1899), besides the books on Chase by Schuckers and Warden, previously mentioned; and William E. Smith, *The Francis Preston Blair Family in Politics* (New York, 1933).

General Works and Monographs

There are a number of competent single-volume histories of the Civil War, each with a somewhat different treatment of McClellan's contribution: J. G. Randall, *The Civil War and Reconstruction* (New York, 1937) ; James Ford Rhodes, *History of the. Civil War, 1861–1865* (New York, 1917) ; George Fort Milton, *Conflict: The American Civil War* (New York, 1941) ; William Wood, *Captains of the Civil War* . . . (New Haven, 1921) ; and Volume Six of Edward Channing's *History of the United States* (New York, 1925). A valuable collection of articles by principal participants in the military campaigns is the four-volume work, edited by Robert Underwood Johnson and Clarence Clough Buel, *Battles and Leaders of the Civil War* (New York, 1884), although, like all similar accounts by actors in the drama, it must be used with caution. The following multi-volume general histories of the war are of use in considering McClellan's merits as a commander: Comte de Paris, *History of the Civil War in America* (Philadelphia, 1875), in four volumes; James Kendall Hosmer, *The American Civil War* (New York, 1913), in two volumes; John Codman Ropes, *The Story of the Civil War* (New York, 1899), in two volumes; Matthew Forney Steele, *American Campaigns* (Washington, 1922), in two volumes; and James Ford Rhodes, *History of the United States from the Compromise of 1850* (New York, 1896–1904), Vols. III–V.

Alexander Howard Meneely, *The War Department, 1861* (New York, 1928), depicts the mismanagement of that department under Simon Cameron. The standard work on the building of the Federal Army is the excellent two-volume effort of Fred Albert Shannon, *The Organization and Administration of the Union Army* (Cleveland, 1928). Burton J. Hendrick, *Lincoln's War Cabinet* (Boston, 1946), shows the hostility to McClellan in Lincoln's official family. The following specialized works bear examination: George E. Turner, *Victory Rode the Rails* ... (Indianapolis, 1953); F. Stansbury Haydon, *Aeronautics in the Union and Confederates Armies* ... (Baltimore 1941); William R. Plum, *The Military Telegraph During the Civil War* (Chicago, 1882); Joseph K. Barnes, *The Medical and Surgical History of the War of the Rebellion* ... (Washington, 1875–88); and George T. Ness, Jr., "Engineers of the Civil War," *The Military Engineer*, Vol. XLIV, No. 299 (May-June, 1952).

The standard diplomatic works on the Civil War are: Ephraim Douglass Adams, *Great Britain and the American Civil War* (New York, 1925), in two volumes; Donaldson Jordan and Edwin J. Pratt, *Europe and the American Civil War* ... (Boston, 1931); and Frank Lawrence Owsley, *King Cotton Diplomacy* ... (Chicago, 1931).

The two most useful books on the role of the Navy in McClellan's Peninsula campaign are Daniel Ammen, *The Atlantic Coast* (New York, 1883), and Charles B. Boynton, *The History of the Navy During the Rebellion* (New York, 1867–68). Wartime Washington is colorfully described by Margaret Leech in her *Reveille in Washington, 1860–1865* (New York, 1941). The three best books on the Regular Army are: Theo. F. Rodenbough, *The Army of the United States* ... (New York, 1896); William Addleman Ganoe, *The History of the United States Army* (New York, 1942); and Oliver Lyman

Spaulding, *The United States Army in War and Peace* (New York, 1937). A useful work is Morris Schaff, *The Spirit of Old West Point, 1858–1862* (Boston, 1907). The poor condition of the military establishment in 1861 is set forth in Frederic Louis Huidekoper, *The Military Unpreparedness of the United States* ... (New York, 1915).

There are a number of useful studies of several of McClellan's campaigns. For the 1861 campaign in western Virginia, see the valuable George B. McClellan, *Report on the Organization and Campaigns of the Army of the Potomac: To Which is Added an Account of the Campaign in Western Virginia* (New York, 1864). Alexander S. Webb, *The Peninsula: McClellan's Campaign of 1862* (New York, 1881), is a concise account of operations from Yorktown to Malvern Hill. For McClellan's role in the Second Bull Run campaign, see John C. Ropes, *The Army Under Pope* (New York, 1881). An adequate story of the battles of South Mountain, Harper's Ferry, and Antietam is given in Francis W. Palfrey, *The Antietam and Fredericksburg* (New York, 1882).

Two standard works on McClellan's Army of the Potomac are: William Swinton, *Campaigns of the Army of the Potomac* ... (New York, 1866), which, though old, is still one of the most brilliant, incisive analyses of the campaigns and their origins in existence, showing remarkable perspective for a book written one year after Appomattox; and J. H. Stine, *History of the Army of the Potomac* (Washington, 1893), which is good as to details of particular combats, but which is based on the assumption of considerable previous knowledge by the reader. For a study in the high command, from the viewpoint of the administration in Washington, see the interesting book by T. Harry Williams, *Lincoln and His Generals* (New York 1952).

Two of the best works on army life and the reaction of soldiers to the stress of battle are the excellent studies: Bruce Catton, *Mr. Lincoln's Army* (Garden City, 1951), and Bell Irvin Wiley, *The Life of Billy Yank* (New York, 1952).

342

Index